MW01630328

PICTURES
FOR
CHARIS

Kelli Connell

After an impression of the night before, I wake up softened by a happy thought: "X was adorable last night." This is the memory of… what? Of what the Greeks called charis: "*the sparkle of the eyes, the body's luminous beauty, the radiance of the desirable being*"; *and I may even add, just as in the ancient* charis, *the notion—the hope—that the loved object will bestow itself upon my desire.*

—*Roland Barthes, from* A Lover's Discourse

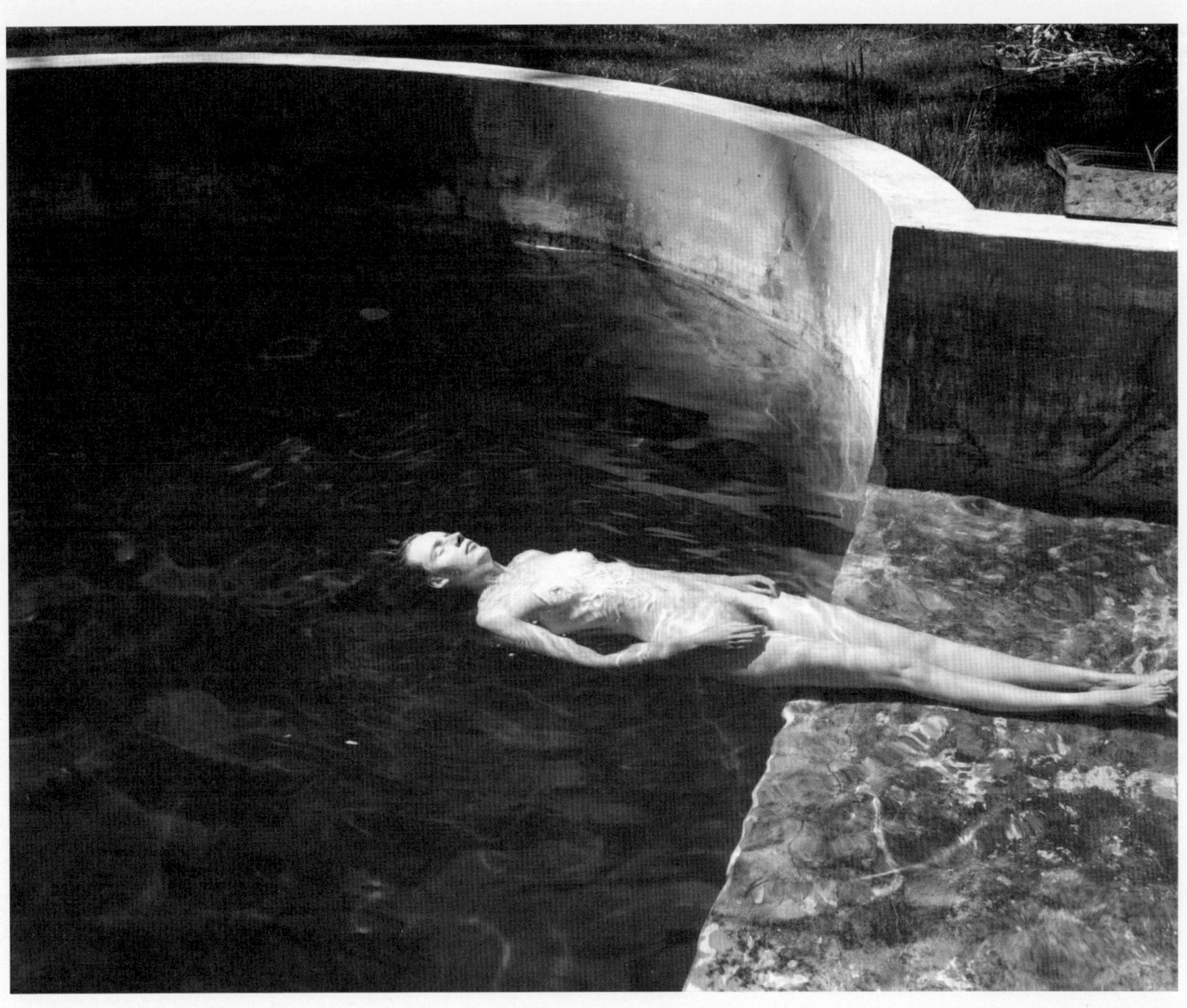

Edward Weston
Floating Nude, 1939

To Betsy—
for taking this journey

To Charis—
for sharing her story

And to all women—
with journeys yet to be taken and stories yet to be heard

PICTURES
FOR
CHARIS

Kelli Connell

aperture **ccp** Center for Creative Photography

CONTENTS

PROLOGUE

Evidence of the flood is everywhere. The air smells of dead fish from the waterlogged crawfish farms. A thick, slow-moving sludge of mud and debris fills the ditches on both sides of the road. Pale and bloated armadillos, frogs, opossums, and nutrias lie where the receding water left them. A Cajun café sits in an empty sea of parking lot. Up the road, a police officer and a pair of truck drivers talk next to a jackknifed semi in a trough of high water as a few people watch the scene from their porches. I pass a gas station where a man looks at a map spread out on the hood of his car. The GPS directions on his phone are of no help here.

A few miles from St. Martinville, a bridge is out and traffic loops past a stranded FedEx truck. I drive by a building close to the road where the straight-as-a-board bottom half of a baby alligator is sticking out of an air conditioning unit as two men ponder the situation. In the near distance, I watch as a couple in a kayak paddle through the front door of their home.

As I park my car on New Market Street, I feel out of place and useless—a person possessed of frivolous intentions. I have driven to St. Martinville on a pilgrimage to photograph a tree. I had dreamed about this tree, how I would photograph it, how I would feel standing before it. I thought I would arrive on one of those thick, lazy, Louisiana summer days when heat slows down daily routines, and people and animals alike are most active at dawn and dusk. Here, everyone and everything is in motion. Water rushes by in ditches and swells Bayou Teche. People are busy helping their families or their neighbors, sweeping water out of houses, rolling up soggy carpets, and pulling things into their yards. They drive around town to see how far the waters of Bayou Teche have reached; they take pictures and talk on their cellphones.

I am the only person in town standing still.

I look up at the Evangeline Oak. I can't get near enough with the small lake now formed at its base. Beads of sweat drip down my back. I stand there for a long time. Louis Daguerre's 1838 *Boulevard du Temple* comes to mind. His exposure was anywhere from four to ten minutes long—long enough for everything in motion to go missing, to be erased. Only the man shining shoes and his customer remained still long enough to become the first humans captured in a photograph. Who was missing from Daguerre's photograph? What many things happened that day that were not recorded? If Daguerre were to photograph this tree today, the turbulent waters of the bayou carrying clothes, toys, brush, animals, and rubble, all in the wrong place at the wrong time, would appear calm.

This St. Martinville flood is nowhere as high as the one in 1927, when waters rose to the rooftops and streets became tributaries; people in boats rescuing all those they could. Floods have happened in this town before and will happen again, yet this is not the kind of scene I'd expected to find when I set out to make pictures for Charis Wilson—it is not picturesque or even remotely ordinary. The oak is standing in three feet of water; its limbs spread in every direction like the snakes of Medusa. Soaked Spanish moss covers its arms, and tendrils of ivy form an untamed beard around its midsection. The tree seems alive and ready to uproot itself.

I was here to fill an absence, to make a photograph that was missing, that had never been made, for a person I would never meet. For many months, I had thought about the picture that I would make of the Evangeline Oak. A picture for Charis.

I use the belly-edge of my t-shirt to wipe perspiration from my upper lip as Betsy packs the puzzle of our things into the car. She enjoys finding the ideal spot for each item based on its need and function. Our things, which we have lugged down the stairs from our second-floor apartment, line the curb. I climb into the front seat and turn the air conditioner on high. The artificial breeze is a welcome respite from the humidity that hangs in the mid-June air. I am looking forward to the temperate California coast and the dry heat of the Southwest.

Buckled in the backseat is my Pentax 67 II medium-format camera and a Toyo four-by-five CF field camera. My over-the-shoulder camera bag houses two lenses, a light meter, a loupe, and an extra-large black t-shirt. I purchased the four-by-five from a friend, and it is his t-shirt, now soft from years of use, that I use as a makeshift dark cloth to pull over my head to see images as they appear on the ground glass. My sketchbook, laptop, a binder of images, and books about Charis Wilson (pronounced CARE-iss) and Edward Weston sit in a crate for quick reference. A bag of groceries and a cooler filled with film rests on the backseat floorboard within arm's reach. Betsy's denim jacket, which sports a Sophia Wallace clitoris pin and a glittery black button with the word ARTIST on the lapel, is slouched atop her messenger bag. Inside, she's packed a sketchbook, an art supply box, and the memoir of the poet Lucy Grealy. Neatly arranged in the hatch are two

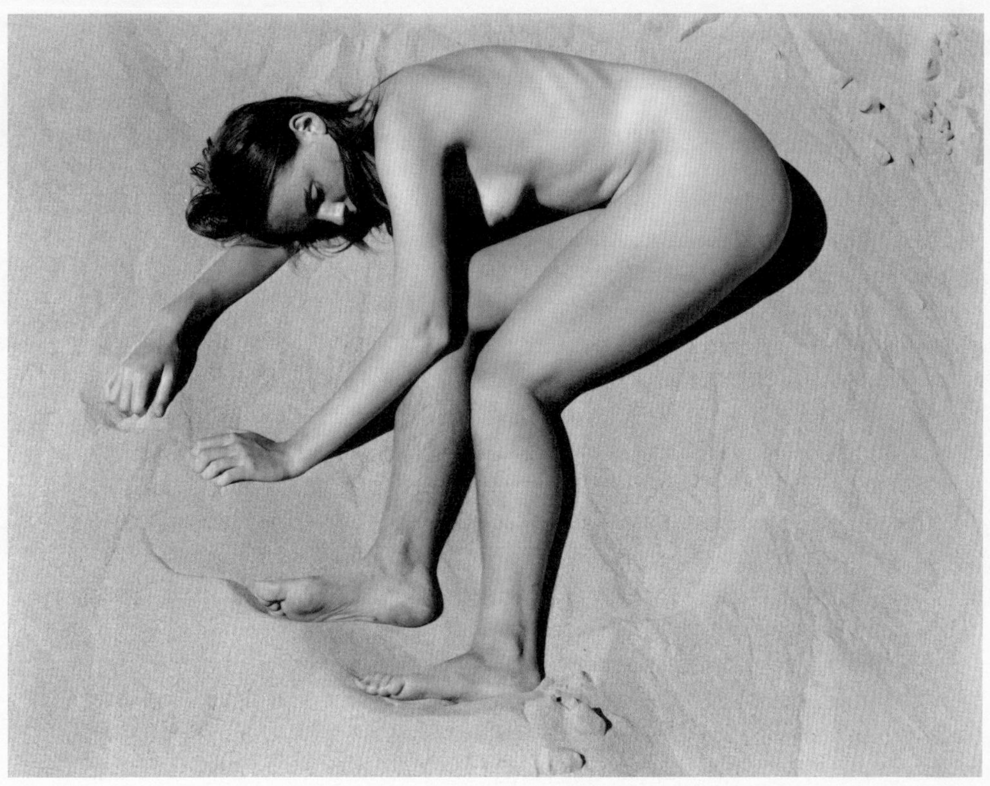

suitcases, a beach bag, bottles of water, a portable electric typewriter, hiking boots, a hiking backpack, cowboy hats, and a case of Diet Dr Pepper for Bets.

Leaving Chicago takes a good hour, as the widespread arms of the city's grid stretch for miles. Drab brick-and-mortars, corner neighborhood bars, drive-through car washes, and streets lined with two flats, three flats, six flats, and courtyard-style apartments eventually give way to bungalows and single-family homes. The highway runs parallel to train tracks that head toward the airport. We reach an endless strip of suburbia before our view finally surrenders to fields.

We listen to NPR until the reception is replaced by the hum of static. A crop duster swings figure-eights over an adjacent field. Rural Illinois is pleasantly unremarkable, impressionless. Slowly my shoulders relax, my mind opens, and I begin to feel more like my true self. Blank landscapes offer a productive space for my thoughts; they are where vivid ideas take form and my priorities as an artist become clear.

———————————————

A few years ago, I made a portrait of Betsy as she lay on a bed at an inn, the wrinkles and folds of the comforter creating what looked like diagonal rises of sand. As I looked at her from across the room, I recalled Edward Weston's photographs of Charis Wilson on the dunes in Oceano. Charis's smooth skin stands out in contrast to the textured sand beneath her, while the glaring, direct sun traces a faint black outline around her body. Betsy's suntanned skin is evidence of a long summer spent outdoors. She is sleepy and patient, but unlike Charis, she is stretched out on a scratchy comforter on a queen-sized bed, with our breakfast rolls, her can of Diet Dr Pepper, and my coffee on the bedside table. When I get back home, I search online for images of Charis at the Oceano Dunes, print them out, and glue them in my sketchbook.

The images from Oceano weren't my first encounter with Charis. It was Chas, a college crush, who first introduced me to her. Chas and I were photography majors together at the University of North Texas. The summer before I graduated, we spent a lot of time together. Before my lifeguard shifts, we would lie on the floor of Chas's apartment, poring over piles of photography books. The charged space between our bodies was compounded by the excitement we felt from devouring those images. We were enamored with Larry Sultan's *Pictures from Home* and shocked, yet fascinated, by Larry Clark's *Tulsa*. We returned often to *William Eggleston's Guide*, delighted by his sense of humor and delectable use of color. We studied picture after picture in monographs by photographers like Diane Arbus, Sally Mann, and Francesca Woodman.

That summer Chas gave me a postcard with a picture of a woman floating in a pool. She looked as if she had been there for a long time, swaying gently on the water's surface. Her legs rested on the pool's shallow ledge. I didn't know this was a photograph of Charis then. The title simply read *Floating Nude*. I also didn't know that the image was made by Edward Weston. I had yet to see images of Charis posing nude in Edward's studio or sunbathing on their deck in Santa Monica Canyon or rolling down the dunes in Oceano. And I was not yet aware of *Charis, Lake Ediza*, which I consider one of the most compelling portraits ever made, taken while Charis and Edward were hiking together in the Sierra Nevada.

I immediately fell in love with the image on the postcard, and maybe with Charis, or perhaps I just recognized something of myself in her. As a teenager, I would often finish my swim team workouts by floating between the red-and-white striped lane dividers, heels propped on the edge of the pool, body exhausted, goggle impressions around my closed eyes.

When Edward saw Charis floating in the pool in the backyard of her father's house, he ran to grab his camera. The scene was documented, not posed. I first saw Charis through Edward's composition, and in a sense, through his eyes, but it was through her words, years later, that I would learn about them both.

Charis wrote three books, including *California and the West* (1940), *The Cats of Wildcat Hill* (1947), and *Through Another Lens: My Years with Edward Weston* (1998). She contributed to *Edward Weston: Leaves of Grass by Walt Whitman* (1942) by selecting the image captions, and wrote the text accompanying *Edward Weston: Nudes* (1993) that would commemorate the importance of her role in front of Edward's camera.

The first edition of *California and the West* included ninety-six of Edward's photographs and twelve chapters of Charis's text. The book begins with the news that Edward had received a Guggenheim fellowship to make landscape photographs of California and the surrounding states. The first Guggenheim given to a photographer, the fellowship marked a turning point in his career. For the first time in his life, he had enough funds and time to fully develop a project. He was free from the constraints of running a commercial portrait business and the worry of making ends meet during the Depression. As Charis set out to record their travels, it was the beginning of a new relationship, the beginning of her adult life, a path full of hope and the potential to shape a career of her own—she knew that her writing would be used either for the manuscript to accompany Edward's Guggenheim photographs, or for the *Westways* articles she and Edward had been commissioned to produce while on the road.

In *California and the West*, Edward's photographs of landscapes, driftwood, cacti, ocean waves, twisted junipers, and abandoned buildings punctuate Charis's account of their travels to the deserts, mountains, valleys, and beach towns of California, with side trips to Arizona, Nevada, and New Mexico. From April 1937 to March 1938, they made seventeen separate trips covering over 16,000 miles in 197 days. Edward made approximately 1,400 eight-by-ten large-format negatives, while Charis wrote more than four hundred pages, her Royal Signet typewriter propped on her knees or on the hood of their car. Charis's travelogue—vivid and clear, humorous and frank—is revealing without being sentimental. I was not yet enamored with Edward's landscape photographs; the reproductions in the book were mediocre. It was getting to know Charis that excited me. I immediately began plotting her stories on a map and making a list of places to visit and photograph. A new project was beginning to take shape in my mind.

After the success of *California and the West*, Edward accepted a proposal, in 1941, to make the photographs that would accompany a publication of Walt Whitman's *Leaves of Grass*. Edward intended to make photographs in almost all of the states in the lower forty-eight, and he and Charis planned another journey; this time, they would travel from the West Coast to the East. It was during this trip that Charis and Edward began to experience the first strains on their relationship. By the end of the trip, Edward would find it difficult to make photographs; he felt anxious about the potential impacts of war on his four sons, while the growing tensions between him and Charis became palpable.

During their last years together, Charis and Edward completed another collaboration, *The Cats of Wildcat Hill*. The book chronicles the daily lives of the many cats on their property, with Charis's writing and Edward's photographs of cats romping on still life arrangements he set up for them. The project was a refuge, even though their relationship was falling apart. Through an internet search, I learned that visitors could stay overnight on the Wildcat Hill property, on the California coast between Carmel and Big Sur, now owned by Edward's grandson, Kim, and his wife, Gina. I added it to the list of places to go.

Charis's memoir, *Through Another Lens: My Years with Edward Weston*, was published in 1998, forty years after Edward's death. It offered additional locations to visit. The book begins with Charis and Edward's first months together in Carmel,

California. Charis speaks of the vulnerability of attraction, the obsessiveness of passion, and the all-consuming nature of true love. I re-read this passage several times, each time finding myself charmed by both Edward and Charis, but especially entranced by Charis's intelligence and quick wit. The remaining chapters trace the events of their eleven-year relationship, which lasted from 1934 to 1945. Charis recounts in great detail descriptions of the places they lived and worked—Edward's Carmel studio, their rented bungalows in Santa Monica Canyon, and the house they built together on Wildcat Hill. Her memoir offers an intimate portrait of their time together—through their passionate courtship to a comfortable and compatible working partnership, to the strains on and eventual destruction of the relationship. I especially related to Charis's account of leaving someone whom she deeply loved. I had left a marriage in my twenties; it was one of the most difficult decisions I ever made.

Of all the things I discovered about Charis, I was most struck by what she wrote about her experiences of being photographed. In these accounts, we have the rare privilege of reading a firsthand account of what it means to be a subject. Charis did not feel as though she was taking direction from Edward, but as though he was recording her choreography, her movements, with the camera. She often found locations for photographs, came up with ideas for images, and was as pleased as Edward was to find herself transformed into a work of art. For her, as with many other well-known models, the act of posing was itself a medium for making art.

———————————

In the passenger seat, I look over our itinerary and make notes of things to photograph in my sketchbook: a mirage, granite faces, intertwined junipers, breaking waves, a bed of pine needles, endless dunes, Betsy sunbathing, a "hot coffee" sign in the Mojave Desert (if it was still there). The pages of our route lightly graze my legs as I flip through them. I want to follow Charis's words, trace her footsteps, on this trip with Betsy. It feels like a crusade of sorts to set out to make landscape photographs and portraits of Betsy from my own perspective and experience as both an addition to known histories and a reclamation of lost ones.

When traveling for *California and the West*, Charis and Edward took their time, staying several days in each place with no real pressure to move on, other than to discover fruitful locations for making photographs. Betsy and I, both professors with art careers, have limited funds and time for this quest. After three hard days of driving, we will make it to Las Vegas, and even then, we will not yet have intersected with the places where Charis and Edward had once been. It won't be until we reach California that we'll catch up with them and see the sites that had been most significant to Charis. From Death Valley, where they first stopped on their journey, we will travel to Twentynine Palms to search for their campsite. We will then hike the peaks of the Sierra Nevada above Lake Ediza to look for the place where the portrait *Charis, Lake Ediza* was made. At Lake Tenaya in Yosemite, we will hunt for Edward's famous pair of junipers before making our way to Carmel, where Charis and Edward first met. We will visit Santa Monica Canyon, where they first lived together, and the nearby sand dunes in Oceano, before heading back up Highway 1 to Charis's writing studio at Wildcat Hill in Carmel and nearby Point Lobos and Big Sur. Leaving California, we will cross the Mojave Desert on our way to Texas, where Betsy will fly from Dallas back to Chicago so I can spend a few days with my mom. From Granbury, I will drive on my own to St. Martinville, Louisiana, to make a final pilgrimage for Charis.

Betsy is anxious about the trip. Her limit for vacations is usually no more than a few days; we will be on the road for almost three weeks. And this road trip is not your typical vacation. At each stop along the way, I will be making landscape photographs and portraits of Betsy, and we will be away from our cats, the comforts of home, Betsy's regular banjo practice, her workout schedule, her studio. Betsy is a sculptor, and there is only so much she can do on the road. She has been gearing up for this trip for a while, hoping she can be at ease and just go along for the ride.

Mostly, Betsy is anxious about leaving the city, because it is a safe place for someone like her, a place for a couple like us. The towns on our route are uncertain. In these kinds of places, she worries about feeling like a pariah. She expects a sort of nastiness that is unprompted and unpredictable. In rural towns, we rarely feel relaxed among the locals. Betsy's androgyny coupled with her baggy, boyish clothes, and me at her side, with our matching wedding bands, often sends an alert to the community, "Hey, fellow neighbors, gay city folk have walked in the door." Hard faces and stoney stares often meet our shy gazes in convenience stores, Dairy Queens, and B&Bs.

Betsy has kept her dark blonde hair short for as long as I have known her. Her favorite t-shirts look like they could belong to a teenage math wizard and accentuate her broad shoulders. She wears an athletic watch on her right wrist and favors tennis shoes for the studio and boots for work or art openings. She wears her keys attached to a belt loop on the front of her jeans and tucks a leather wallet in her back left pocket, a handkerchief in her right.

When Betsy was little, her mom used to make her compete in beauty pageants. Her fine hair would be styled into contestant shapes—curled and held in place with colorful bows. She wore shiny dresses and makeup, all of which accentuated the fact that these things weren't for a girl like her. Bets has never been completely content in her own skin, mainly because there are so few people that look as androgynous as she does. A few years ago, she went to a festival for women who primarily identified as being queer, and found it a miraculous experience. There she was able to walk through crowds and be reassuringly inconspicuous, because so many women looked like she did. Without the negotiations required, the silent judgments made, by our larger society, she felt free.

I travel a lot by myself. I am unassuming and not particularly eye-catching. I wear basic, monotone clothing and have a quiet presence. I can move in and out of stores, up and down escalators, without a second glance from passersby. As an introverted photographer, I enjoy this anonymity—its shield allows me to watch people, to observe my surroundings, without being noticed.

When I am with Bets, I am no longer invisible. Learning to be okay with being seen is hard for me. No longer standing in the wings, peering at the audience, but on stage, it is my turn to perform "How to Be a Gay Person in a Way That Makes Straight People Feel Comfortable." It's a role I can never quite pull off, because it requires gestures, and, at times, conversations that I have never mastered. In these situations, I feel exposed and hyperaware of how I am in my body.

The day before their first trip for *California and the West*, Charis asked Edward to cut her hair in a short bob. He slowly cut inch by inch until it was as short as she wanted. She also bought men's shirts and pants and a pair of men's boots at an army surplus store. Charis was called "sir" once at a gas station when she asked where they might camp, and another time while she was eating blackberries on the side of the road. Perhaps this was surprising for her, to be seen as a man, but it may have also provided her with a sense of security while traveling with Edward. They often traveled with Edward's sons or other male photographers until Charis eventually requested that they travel without a group. Her androgynous attire also offered a bit of protection to offset the difference in their ages. Charis was twenty-three years old and Edward, fifty-one. In their bohemian community in Carmel, Charis and Edward were not concerned about this; Charis's own parents had twenty-nine years between them—it was only on the road, in unknown territory, that it became a concern. Charis was often the first one to encounter inquisitive folk; as Edward did not drive, she was the official chauffeur.

Bets and I pull over in a gas station parking lot to have our first roadside lunch. We eat our crackers, cheese, peanut butter, grapes, and dark chocolate facing the building and a pair of air conditioners. Their loud hum makes it difficult for us to hear each other talk. Bets, who is wearing overalls and Niagara Falls socks, has her feet propped up on the dash. Maid of the Mist boats swirl at the base of the falls when she wiggles her toes. As we finish eating, I look into the rearview mirror and realize that we have had our backs turned on the magnificent Mississippi River. I decide then and there that in the weeks to come, we will be sure to find more scenic places to stop and do our best to never leave a view so foolishly unappreciated.

With Betsy asleep in the passenger's seat, my mind begins to wander. I consider the open road and how it threads one moment in time with another. I enjoy the suspension, the in-between-ness of car travel. A hawk soars overhead. When I was a child, my dad would point out hawks circling above us during road trips. Ever since he died, memories of him rise to my consciousness without warning. Seeing something as simple as a wooden toothpick in a restaurant dispenser or hearing a Willie Nelson song can have me in tears in an instant. I wonder if the hawk is my dad, or my dad's spirit. He is strong and certain, gliding next to us for a while.

My dad died while I was at an artist residency in Upstate New York. A few days before, I had woken in the night to the sound of screeching—hundreds of crows chanting in unison, "Caw, caw, caw." Pause. "Caw, caw, caw." Pause. The sound was so loud I was afraid to look out the window. One by one, they settled in the trees, taking hold, agitated. The crows' cawing pulsed; they became a single force with darting eyes. The next day I bought a humidifier to drown out their cries.

My parents had both been sick with a severe stomach flu, and I thought they should go to the doctor. When I mentioned this to my mom on the phone, she insisted that a stomach bug was going around town and that they would be feeling better soon. Oddly, that week I was feeling anxious and unwell myself and spent far too many hours on the internet looking up heart attack symptoms for women. One particularly bad night, I woke up every thirty minutes drenched in sweat and completely out of breath. The next day I learned that my dad had passed away from a heart attack. Thinking back on this, it seems the murder of crows were a sign, a warning of what was to come.

I imagined my dad in the hospital bed looking as if he were asleep, my brother and mom sitting close at his side. I am glad that I was not there, that I did not have to see my dad, who was so full of life, lying there motionless and still. We create a last, and lasting, portrait of ourselves in the minds of those who are present at our deaths. I am sure my brother and mother will always carry that portrait of my dad with them. For me, I will remember the self-portraits my dad often took, a mischievous smile from ear to ear, on family vacations when no one was looking, a picture known only to himself until the roll of film was developed.

I look through my sketchbook and read my notes as Betsy takes a turn behind the wheel. In the months preceding this trip, I had scoured articles by critics, curators, and photographers for details about Charis. I traveled to the Center for Creative Photography in Tucson, to sift through Charis and Edward's separate archives. I read their personal letters to one another, to family and friends. I carefully touched the memorabilia that had once belonged to them. I held each of the figurines Edward had given to Charis in the palm of my hand. I picked up a shawl Edward had given to Charis from one of his trips to Mexico and tenderly ran my fingers across the intricately woven pattern and fringe at its edges.

Charis would not have written a memoir at all if it were not for her gnawing frustration with how narrowly Edward and his work were interpreted in the decades after his death in 1958. She had carefully cut out the articles that had so aggravated her, annotating the margins with passionate exclamation points, question marks, and x's, underlining text, often in red, sometimes twice. Later in her life, Charis was increasingly invited to give lectures on Edward and her time with him. In her notes for one of these engagements, she outlines her initial response to the invitation to speak:

> *No, of course not!*
>
> 1) *I'm not a speaker.*
> 2) *I'm not a photographer.*
> 3) *I'm not an expert.*
> 4) *I don't have theories about photography,*
> 5) *… I don't even have slides!*
>
> *Then I thought of some "Yes, But…'s"*
>
> 1) *Haven't you been complaining, in recent years, that Edward's image was getting more and more unrecognizable?*

*2)   Shouldn't you try to correct some of this growing mythology before
it gets any farther out of hand?*
*3)   Why leave it to people who never knew him to furnish fanciful accounts
of what they assume he was like?*
4)   Why, Indeed?[1]

Sifting through her papers, I found notes for another such talk:

> *Most of what is written and said about him leaves me somewhere between
> mildly amused and violently outraged. I know that I overreact, and that the
> work of history is simplification. We collapse centuries into the Dark Ages and
> we gloss over years and decades as "the Roaring 20s" or "The Depression"
> and as history gets simplified, so must individual lives. All the sharp,
> significant incidents that we've lived through and been shaped by eventually
> settle into a soft, generalized image, as if what was once a dazzlingly sharp
> photograph, full of fine detail, faded to a thoroughly pictorial mist with barely
> a discernible subject.*
>
> > *This simplifying process is at work today, transforming the real EW
> > into an imaginary historical character. And there is no stopping it. I'm aware
> > that it isn't possible to set the record straight. I hope, however, to produce a
> > memoir in the coming year that will stem a little of the tide of nonsense that's
> > been pouring E's way ever since big money and the photo market made him
> > an easy target for the game of Revelations.*[2]

How hard it must be to see someone so important to you, with whom you spent a
significant part of your life, reduced, in a few paragraphs, to a person you don't recognize.
When we lose people close to us, we become aware of the utter failure of language to
describe the reality of who they were. And we realize the ways in which the stories people
tell have the ability to reshape our understandings. And if the person is as well-known
as Edward Weston, their lives and art can readily be interpreted, used, by other people to
advance their own narratives, their own agendas.

"Unlike a photograph, a life is not immutable once the person who lived it has died.
The life is remade by those who remain," Charis writes. "[I]n article after article, I watched the
man I loved being transformed into someone I could never have loved. This flesh-and-blood
man was becoming a cliché-ridden myth created by people who had never known him."[3]

But photographs, too, create myths, shape perceptions. They allude to company
kept. They portray a choice of dress, a mannerism made in one brief instance. They offer
clues. But they, like words, fail to deliver the embodied essence of someone—what it was
like to be in their presence, to meet their eye, smell their scent, feel the warmth of their
body in an embrace. They are distilled to an image and transferred to a piece of paper.
A static likeness. A still photograph. A shadow.

From Illinois to Iowa to Nebraska, the scenery is interchangeable. The travel plazas we stop at each have a large map on the wall, a gift shop filled with state-specific souvenirs, a Starbucks, a handful of fast-food restaurants. Outside, people pace the periphery with miniature dogs; truckers pass by in workday trances; and teenage girls, who uniformly seem to wear sweatpants with PINK across the seat, walk in and out of the plazas, all with cellphones in hand.

Near Lincoln, Nebraska, we eat dinner side by side on top of a picnic table outside of a Wendy's, where a bird's nest rests in the S. As the sun begins to set, a soft warm glow illuminates a thirty-foot inflatable gorilla on the lawn of the restaurant across the street, his teeth in a fierce snarl as he holds up two gigantic burgers, one in each hand. For some reason, the gorilla makes Bets think of her brothers and the wild times they had together in hotels when they were kids. She tells me about having water fights and wrestling matches and racing on luggage racks until her parents received warnings from the management. I knew that she was thinking of her older brother, Andy. I give Betsy's knee a gentle squeeze as she wipes her tears away with her handkerchief. I realize that we are closer now, in our grief, her having lost her brother, and me losing my dad, within the same year.

Charis stayed nestled up, while Edward made coffee and thought about the
photographs he wanted to make that day. When it was really cold, she would scoot to the
bottom of her sleeping bag, curled tight. Betsy is the same way. She sleeps late. I wake
first, snuggling into her heat for a few minutes, then I get going. I drink coffee and make
lists of things to photograph or walk around to see if anything catches my eye. It's a
good hour, usually, before Bets rises, hair in a jumble, popping the top of her first Diet
Dr Pepper for the day.

We are ready to leave Lincoln after the free breakfast buffet, served in a room
where the news blares from flat-screen televisions. As we walk outside, I ask Bets if we
should repack the cooler with ice, to which she replies, "Say 'cooler' again." *Cooler* is one of
her favorite words because of my Texas accent. Bets repacks our supplies, fitting everything
into place, even with the challenge presented by the rather unwieldy electric typewriter.

Charis brought a Royal Signet typewriter with her to record each day's happenings
as she and Edward traveled. She was interested in local lore and history and was especially
delighted when she found a good storyteller to interview. Edward, absorbed in making his
work, preferred to stay away from people who might disturb his concentration. Charis
would often stand by, talking with folks as he worked. She would find moments after they
set up camp, or more often than not, in the morning when Edward was photographing

nearby, to type her accounts of their travels. The electric typewriter I had purchased in honor of Charis was already becoming a cumbersome relic, but the night before I had tapped out a poem about her, and despite it being a rather poor one, I enjoyed the accompaniment of the keys as I typed.

Bets takes the first shift driving so that I can finish my coffee and spend time with Edward's pictures of Charis and the landscapes we would soon see. I think about what I had learned of their relationship, and search for clues, of love, desire, comfort, strain. I look out the window at the North Platte River and imagine it from the sky, our path intersecting with its tributaries here and there, as I-80 follows the river for more than three hundred miles.

We stop for lunch in Crook, Colorado, across from an open field and the first of the foothills. Tall grass moves like ocean waves, undulating and rolling in a strong wind that whistles and hums. Betsy is already feeling homesick. Every time we take a long trip, there is an adjustment period. For the first two days, Bets is filled with a palpable anxiety, but if we are lucky, everything is okay by the third day as she adapts to the routines of the road. A bird on a wire sings its heart out while we eat the muffins and yogurt we saved from the breakfast bar.

Depression isn't something you wear, it wears you. Depression picks Betsy out and slides in through her arms, her chest, her stomach, her thighs, her calves. When it arrives, it can stay for days, weeks, or months at a time. Her skin becomes a one-piece suit for her depression. Sometimes the depression is too heavy, making it hard for her to walk, talk, eat, or even move.

Back in the car at a rest stop, I look over at Bets to see tears running down her face, one drop on the tip of her nose. She shifts in her seat and stares straight ahead, not looking at the mountains as they push up through the flat line of the horizon. Betsy's depression is not to be confused with grief. The grief I felt when my father died was all-consuming, but manageable, and with it were moments of love and peace.

We stop in Grand Junction, named for the place where the Colorado and Gunnison Rivers meet. Settled in our room, we decide to exercise, hoping it will help Bets feel better. The workout room has exactly enough equipment for two people. Bets runs on the treadmill, and I use the elliptical while we watch a television show about what celebrities like Zsa Zsa Gabor and David Coulier are up to now. Back in the room, we quickly slather each other with suntan lotion and head outside. We sprawl on some lounge chairs near the modest pool, just in time for the bottom tip of the sun to begin to sink behind the building across from us.

The San Rafael Reef is a hogback ridge that abruptly interrupts the surrounding landscape—a wall of jagged layers of earth, once horizontal, now nearly vertical, tilt like skyscrapers uplifted by a huge geologic dome. Early pioneers found it impossible to cross this section of Utah because of the height of this dramatic anticline. It is here that I make the first landscape photograph of our trip, a view of I-70 cutting through the reef from east to west. This picture is the first four-by-five landscape photograph I have ever made with any intention. I feel a little like an explorer, albeit one with every modern convenience. A few feet from this astounding view is a historical marker, but better yet, I use my cellphone to find out more information. Near the scenic overlook, a woman is selling necklaces carefully displayed on a blanket, and travelers are taking pictures of friends and family, or themselves, the reef serving as mere backdrop. I must have looked out of place standing there in the parking lot, several yards from the actual overlook, my large camera mounted on a tripod, my head disappearing under the black t-shirt as I focused the scene on the ground glass.

      After spending three days driving across the United States, on the day before we would begin to intersect with the places where Charis and Edward had traveled, I was beginning to wonder about my reasons for coming on this trip. I was reconsidering the importance of this quest: Could I actually get closer to Charis by spending time in the places she had been, the places where Edward had photographed with her nearby?

Edward's most accomplished work was made in the context of modernism. For him, Ansel Adams, Imogen Cunningham, Sonya Noskowiak, Willard Van Dyke, and other members of Group f64, as they called themselves, this meant photographing with a small aperture, f64 if possible, to capture a scene with great depth-of-field, in sharp detail, from the foreground to the background. Purists of Group f64 believed in presenting their work as it was photographed. This meant no cropping, no multiple exposures or combination printing. Dodging and burning techniques in the darkroom were to be kept to a minimum, or if possible, not used at all. Edward made finely detailed images of isolated natural forms, such as peppers and nautilus shells, with exposures that often lasted several hours. Eventually he worked directly in nature, photographing trees, driftwood, kelp, and seaweed as they were found in the landscape.

The tenets of Group f64 were formed in opposition to Pictorialism, an aesthetic movement preceding straight photography and known for its soft-focus, surface manipulation, or combination-printing techniques. Pictorial subjects were often directed by the photographer in staged scenarios. Edward had been a successful Pictorialist before he became convinced that the best way to make a photograph was to use the camera in its truest sense, as a machine to record and represent a subject in sharp detail.

Elements of my own contemporary photographic style could be traced back to Pictorialism. For almost two decades, I had been working on *Double Life*, a suite of images that depict the intimate interactions between two women who are in fact the same model: my friend Kiba Jacobson is seen doubled in each scene. These digital composites allow the multiple selves that Kiba plays to interact with one another. We, as viewers, are voyeurs to their routines, the moments they share. In *Double Life*, I found a way to give some power to the model, and to implicate myself in the photograph. For each scene, I set my camera on a tripod, pressed the self-timer, and then moved in front of the camera to act as a stand-in for the second character Kiba would be playing. Kiba followed my direction as we responded to one another, in character, between timed takes. We would shoot several images, Kiba acting one part, and me the other, until it was time to switch roles. I then erased myself in post-production, compositing together a believable image with Kiba as both figures in the scene. In using the same model to portray characters in a relationship and by focusing on body language, facial expressions, and clothing, *Double Life* raises questions about the complexities of identity, sexuality, power, and gender while presenting a more fluid definition of *self*. As a person who feels uncomfortable with labels, I have always been interested in interrogating societal definitions of beauty, gender, and sexuality, as well as the dynamics and expectations of our roles in relationships.

Akin to the photographs made by Group f64, my images look believable—if images are to be believed at all—but not unlike the methods used by the Pictorialists, they are composites of staged, choreographed scenes in which every element has been carefully considered. I am the director, choreographer, stand-in, prop designer, and stylist. More importantly, this level of control allows me to create personal work that has an emotional tone that resonates with the larger questions I want to explore as an artist.

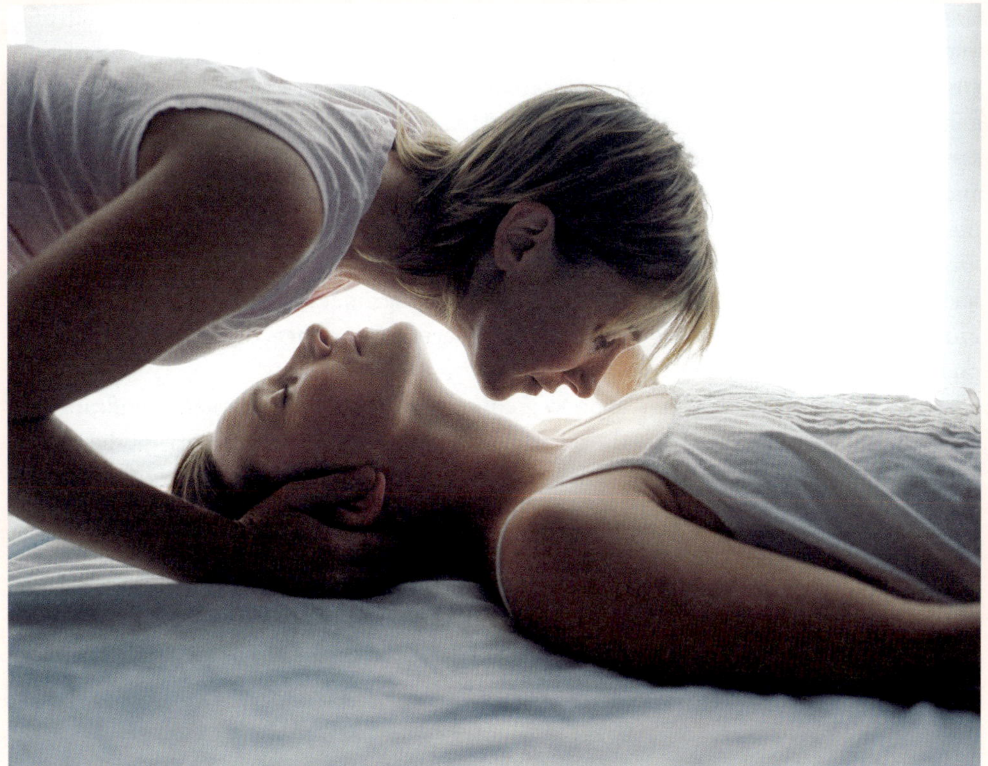

My new portraits of Betsy are not composites constructed in Photoshop. The interaction is completely different. Betsy is the sole subject in the frame; I regard her from the other side of the lens. I thought that turning my camera on her would be an easier way to work. But it is not. I find myself troubled by the power the photographer has over the sitter. I have seen enough projects where subjects are caught off-guard, captured by stealthy photographers without their consent. And I am profoundly aware of the implications of the male gaze that I have learned so much about in articles and lectures by critics and scholars and other artists. The dynamics of making this new work require me to look through the lens at a subject who can decide to meet my gaze or look away. That Betsy can make direct eye contact with a viewer beyond me is something I have not contended with before. The characters Kiba played never looked into the camera's lens—they were less subjects than actors in a scene.

In taking up this quest, my main interest was in Charis and Edward's relationship, as photographer and subject, and how it related to mine and Betsy's. But I wondered, too, what it meant to be on the same side of the lens as Edward—to make portraits of Betsy and then landscape photographs in the places that he had, sometimes from precisely the same spot. This time, the images would be made by me, as a woman, photographer, partner. There was a weight to this project that I hadn't fully come to terms with yet. Perhaps I could learn something from grappling with the tension between these different intentions.

So here I was, in the middle of this parking lot, getting ready to follow the path of one of the most quintessentially male photographers in the canon. I hadn't driven across the United States to walk in Edward Weston's footsteps but to try to find the places where he and Charis had been together. Even so, I would be standing where he stood, seeing what he saw. As I had done in *Double Life*, Betsy and I would try on multiple roles, that of Charis and Edward, photographer and subject, self and other. Would Betsy and I be able to find the places that Charis had written about—and Edward had photographed—in *California and the West*? In the time that had passed between then and now, what had changed and what had remained the same? I was interested in ideas of pilgrimage and homage. Yet, what I most wanted was to look through the lens of Charis's experience, to have her guide my photographs for this book.

There is a long tradition of photographers making portraits of their significant other. In *California and the West*, the portraits of Charis intermittently interrupt the landscape photographs. What was it about her occasional presence that so captured my interest? What did these portraits made of her, along with the ones taken throughout the time they were together, say about their relationship and who Charis was in relation to Edward? I wanted this new work to explore a female-to-female dynamic. Perhaps my photographs with Betsy, defined by our intimate relationship, could raise questions about the image and the nature of intimacy—of power, agency, and the direction of the gaze.

We pass over Hoover Dam as Bets grabs a box of Nerds from the driver's side door and shakes a tiny mound of purple and pink globules into the palm of her hand. She collects a few clusters with the tip of her tongue and lets them dissolve for a while before crunching them. The dry desert that spreads out before us is soon replaced by the suburbs of Las Vegas. By the time we reach the old strip, my face and forearms are lightly sunburned even though we haven't spent any time outside of the car except to pump gas and buy snacks.

By the Golden Nugget hotel pool, we languidly soak up the Las Vegas sun, an ice bucket of Coronas with lime between us. The pool has a three-story, see-through waterslide that snakes through an aquarium of fierce-looking fish, including a live shark. Vegas is surprisingly uneventful. We go unnoticed in a sea of people as DJ Vixen's music pounds and subliminal stimuli beg us to think only of sex, drinking, and gambling. For the next two hours, we lie on our lounge chairs, eyes closed. Every once in a while, I peek through the shutter of my lids: a lifeguard walks by holding a two-foot-high pile of used yellow hotel towels; a woman in a string bikini rolls over to expose two rose tattoos on each cheek; a couple takes turns oiling their brown, leathery bodies until they glisten.

Death Valley demands respect. We open the car doors. The air is hot and dry. Swarms of bees greet us as they buzz among the shadows of parked cars at Dante's View. We apply sunscreen, mist ourselves with insect spray, and congratulate each other on remembering to bring our straw cowboy hats. Betsy wears maroon shorts and a light green tank top with CHINATI on the front, a souvenir from Donald Judd's expansive art compound in Marfa, Texas. I brag about dressing appropriately for the desert as I pull on a lightweight, long-sleeved denim shirt and adjust the cuffs of my jeans. There is one serious drawback to this perfect desert attire, my jeans are black. With my camera in a backpack, I carry a tripod in one hand and an eight-by-ten photocopy of Edward Weston's *Dante's View* in the other as we join a group of tourists at the overlook. There is no way we could have prepared ourselves for the immensity, the sheer scale, of the scene before us.

Dante's View provides a bird's-eye perspective on Badwater Basin, six thousand feet below. The basin is wide and flat, with the Panamint Mountains to the west and the Amargosa Range, where we are standing, on its eastern edge. As these mountains rise, the valley floor sinks at a rate of one-fifth of an inch a year. More than two hundred feet below sea level, the valley creates a natural trap where heat hovers. Everything is a shade of white. The glare from the sun glistens off the glittering, lacelike salt beds below, creating the illusion that we are standing in an overexposed photograph. This reflective white light hurts

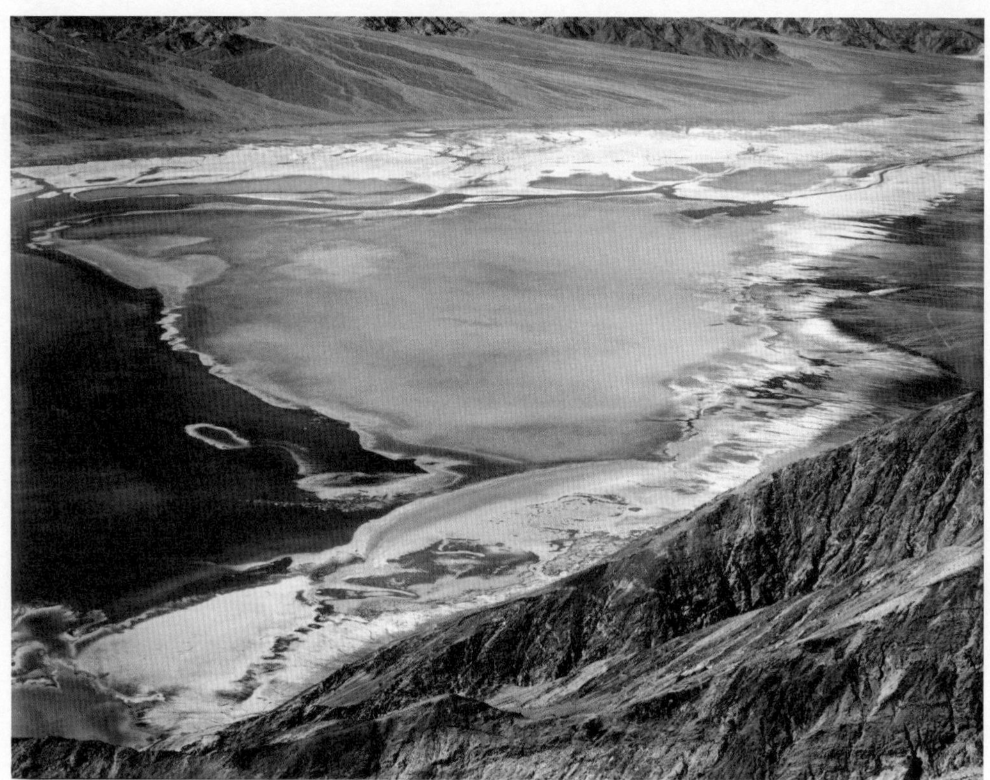

the eyes, and as I put on my sunglasses, I think that this could be either heaven or a white-hot hell. Death Valley feels *wrong* in some strange way—the temperature is off, the color is off. On this precipice, we feel like we're floating, suspended in a place where nothing is secure or familiar, as if Earth as we had known it was gone. Death Valley is wordless. I feel present, not in a place but a state of mind.

The heat surrounds us. Five crows circle overhead.

Death Valley was Charis and Edward's first stop on their travels for *California and the West*. I imagine Charis standing at this overlook, taking it all in, transfixed: "A hundred miles of desolate geography spread out below us in the weighty silence peculiar to deserts. We might have been on a lost moon world where time and motion had ceased to exist. Edward was so shaky with excitement he could hardly set up his camera, and all that any of us could say for some time was, 'My God! It can't be!'"[4]

As I draw my gaze from the Panamints to the ribbons of salt shimmering across the valley floor, I put my tripod on the ground and take the copy of Edward's photo from my pocket and unfold it. Holding the image at arm's length, I am surprised that the view below is so strikingly similar. I notice a road hugging the rise of the Armagosas, just as Charis had described it: "At the base of the cliff we stood on, the neat arc of an alluvial fan was rimmed by a fine black line which we presently realized must be a highway."[5]

Edward's eight-by-ten camera had been tilted downward to crop out the sky. The base of the Armagosas met the wide salt bed that poured, like an abstract painting, across the valley floor to the base of the Panamints. The flattening of space into two dimensions created an instant fiction, like all landscape photography does. I walk around slowly, looking for the spot where Edward had stood to make his photograph. Betsy moves ahead, examining cacti with hot pink tops and lizards rushing from rock to rock. Seeing her there reminds me of how differently Charis and Edward experienced the scenes they encountered when traveling for *California and the West*. The way I'm looking is different from Edward's: he was photographing scenes without reference. As part of this pilgrimage, I am revisiting the views he photographed to discover what looking again, through my eyes, has to offer. I know that some of my images will be made from Edward's vantage point, while others will be from my own, to see what he chose not to photograph.

Technically speaking, Edward's challenge was to assess each scene and make informed decisions about aperture, shutter speed, and exposure times to create negatives that would be rich with details in both the shadows and highlights. Under his dark cloth, Edward studied the image projected upside down and reversed left to right on the ground glass. This process, which requires tremendous concentration, causes you to lose a sense of your surroundings. While Edward was moving his tripod and heavy camera equipment here and there, lost in the act of translating each scene in his mind into a possible black-and-white photograph, Charis was paying attention to the geology, the flowers and fauna, the weather and temperature, the tourists they encountered. In her text, Charis takes note of all these details, and what they ate, who they traveled with, what they talked about, what supplies they bought, and what mishaps unfolded over the course of days.

> *Often after making a picture, Edward would say to me, "Do you want to look?"*
>
> *It wasn't really a question. There was no doubt by this point about my wanting to look on the ground glass, to see the colored shadow of the picture just taken. Rather, this query was a statement of relinquishment. He was officially letting go of his private connection with that selected image: I represented the public it now belonged to, potentially at least.*
>
> *The ground glass was just as it is named—a piece of glass with the surface finely ground to remove the shine. Like a view finder, it allowed the photographer to see the image, although it was upside down. I was carried away right from the start by that wonderfully shimmering, opalescent color the ground glass provided. But I had to learn to disregard those lovely shades and to start reconstructing the image in black-and-white, with all the grays between. It helped that the image was upside down, providing the first step in abstracting from the "real world." I never mastered the trick entirely, nor did I ever get sharp enough to read negatives to make the whole switch (from*

Edward took several pictures at Dante's View, five near the overlook and one
from a lower precipice on the ridge, where Betsy now wanders. Hot winds lick at the rim
of my cowboy hat, and I pull the drawstring tight. I only remove it to lift the black t-shirt
over my head. I move a few feet, look, adjust, and repeat this sequence until the scene on
the ground glass appears to line up with Edward's image. I slide a four-by-five film holder
into the camera back, pull the dark slide, and cock the shutter. I hold onto the tripod,
shoes dug into the dirt, to steady myself against the wind. I feel a sense of elation by
finding the same view. Perhaps it is this feeling, the hunt and discovery, that captivates
other people's interests as they embark on quests to revisit a particular place based on
someone else's account.

Zabriskie Point is our next stop, where the parking lot is filled with rental cars, camper
vans, and two large tourist buses. The heat from the black asphalt radiates up our bodies.
A swell of people with cameras around their necks make their way back to one of the
buses. Charis calls this phenomenon "the passing human stream that Came and Saw and
(usually) Clicked."[7] She and Edward became used to curious glances from tourists as he
photographed, head beneath the dark cloth, while they clicked the shutters of their Kodak
box cameras.

Betsy and I reapply sunscreen, this time sparring about the definition of SPF, as
the sun's intensity is already evident in the red patches of skin we failed to adequately cover
at Dante's View. At the top of a steep slope, we look at the beige mud hills; on film I know
they will be a glorious range of blacks and whites with every shade of grey in between.

As I wait patiently for an opportunity to photograph with the sun directly overhead,
I notice a man in the near distance who looks like my dad—he appears to be about the
same age my dad was when he died, sixty-seven. He is wearing beige slacks and a beige shirt
as if in camouflage—he blends right in with the sandy ridges behind him. I watch as he veers
off the path, searching for his own view. He stops and takes a picture with his point-and-
shoot, the hot breeze flapping the ankles of his slacks.

The picture I make is like Edward's—it is from the same vantage point and easily encountered by anyone visiting Zabriskie Point. What's different is that it is also a record of my grief for losing my dad. I imagine that I'll think about him every time I see this photograph.

With the lure of an air-conditioned hotel room ahead, we drive along the scenic loop at Artists Palette. Betsy is feeling better; she sings along to Andrew Bird as we pass mud hills in colors I have never seen in a landscape before. The seafoam-green, salmon-pink, Dreamsicle-orange, and lavendar hills look as if they have been spray-painted. I look at my hair in the visor mirror. The dried sweat and salt make it impossible to run my fingers through it, and yet it has never looked better. I make a mental note to buy salt spray upon returning home.

We pass the Furnace Creek Visitor Center where a large digital sign announces that it is 127 degrees. At Furnace Creek Ranch every air conditioner is battling the triple-digit heat. Their loud hum is a symphony of never-ending whole notes. Inside our room, the curtains billow in frantic shapes. I set my gear and the cooler of film as close to the air conditioner as I can.

The outdoors is practically uninhabitable. Large ravens walk around the grounds with their beaks wide open, as if stuck that way, a mechanism for cooling themselves down. We take every opportunity to find shade on our way to the pool, speed walking from one tree's shadow to the next. Charis and Edward stayed at the Texas Springs Campground up the hill and often swam at the Furnace Creek Ranch pool, which she describes as "clear blue water, soft as jelly, and gently warm."[9] That Charis mentioned the 83-degree water feeling gently warm is a clue that they visited Death Valley in the cooler months. But she was right about the pool feeling soft as jelly.

Bets and I get in just as the first stars are making their debut. We swim like teenagers, doing underwater flips and racing the length of the pool. We let our bodies slide up against one another, but we aren't really comfortable being one of those couples with their legs around each other's waists, exchanging wet kisses for all to see. Betsy looks more feminine in a bikini. I find it amusing that she can transform from math wizard to swimsuit model in a matter of a few seconds. We float like Charis with our heels resting on the edge of the pool, our eyes closed, our faces soaking up the late sun.

Back in our hotel room, I secure the curtains before unloading and reloading film. I carefully place exposed film holders and an empty film box inside the changing bag before zipping it shut. I reach my arms, up to the elbows, into the bag. A mist of perspiration forms on my forearms as I carefully remove each sheet of film and place it inside the box. I wonder if my sweat will fog the film as I carefully remove the slide of each holder. My arms smell like chemicals when I pull them from the changing bag. I quickly rinse them off. I am exhausted. Near my side of the bed, I see a gigantic cockroach. I wake up Bets, "Babe, I'm going to sleep in the other bed, not because I want to but because of a roach." "Mmhmm," she hums, without opening her eyes.

EXTREME HEAT WARNING: WALKING AFTER 10:00 AM STRONGLY DISCOURAGED, reads a sign at the entrance to Golden Canyon. It is 6:30 a.m. as we meander through the mustard-colored curves of the canyon. A spiny bush covered in downy bird feathers glows in the first rays of daylight. A few steps further on, we find the bird's bones, bleached white from the sun, a few white feathers still in its rib cage. Betsy climbs up on a flat rock and sits there, legs splayed nonchalantly, playing a game on her phone while I photograph.

Edward favored bold, diagonal compositions in Golden Canyon. Interestingly, his negatives, housed at the Center for Creative Photography, looked like positives; the scenes in front of me look like negatives, save the constant color of the blue sky overhead. The curves of the canyon captivate me—the golden hills rise, warming in the sun. I decide to photograph the valley, not the diagonal wall as Edward had done. In no time, the heat reflects off the bright canyon walls with an intensity that makes us breathless. We make our way out of the canyon's narrow oven, mouths open wide like the ravens.

We spend the rest of the morning in a tiny town called Rhyolite, which is located a few miles outside of the Death Valley National Park borders.

> *Here is the western ghost town at its nakedest. Rhyolite's gold boom came in 1906; its death in 1907. The town was deserted and everything movable in it was carried away. Parts of the walls of a three-story hotel, a two-story bank, and a grocery face each other across a weed-bordered desert road. Sections of worn adobe wall rise here and there from trash heaps of broken bottles, old shoes, rusty metal, and tin cans.*
>
> *We had judged our weather wrong. A cold wind beat on us savagely from the moment of our arrival. I held the tripod anchored while Edward worked to get the ruins against the pale storm clouds that were drifting up the sky. The town is set up on a slope of bare colored hills, and while Edward worked we could look down on an arm of the Amargosa Desert that was being rapidly transformed to a sea of blowing sand. Edward was fascinated with the town—Nevada's Athens, he called it—and would doubtless have found more to do in better weather. But there is a saturation point in a wind like this; after an hour of constant buffeting, or sand and gravel slapping into your face and eyes, you can't breathe and you can't see and you can't stand up any longer.*[10]

Several of the structures Edward had photographed are still standing, although many of them look as if they could collapse into a pile of rubble at any moment. In the middle of the road, I adjust the camera on the tripod, wind whispering through the cracks

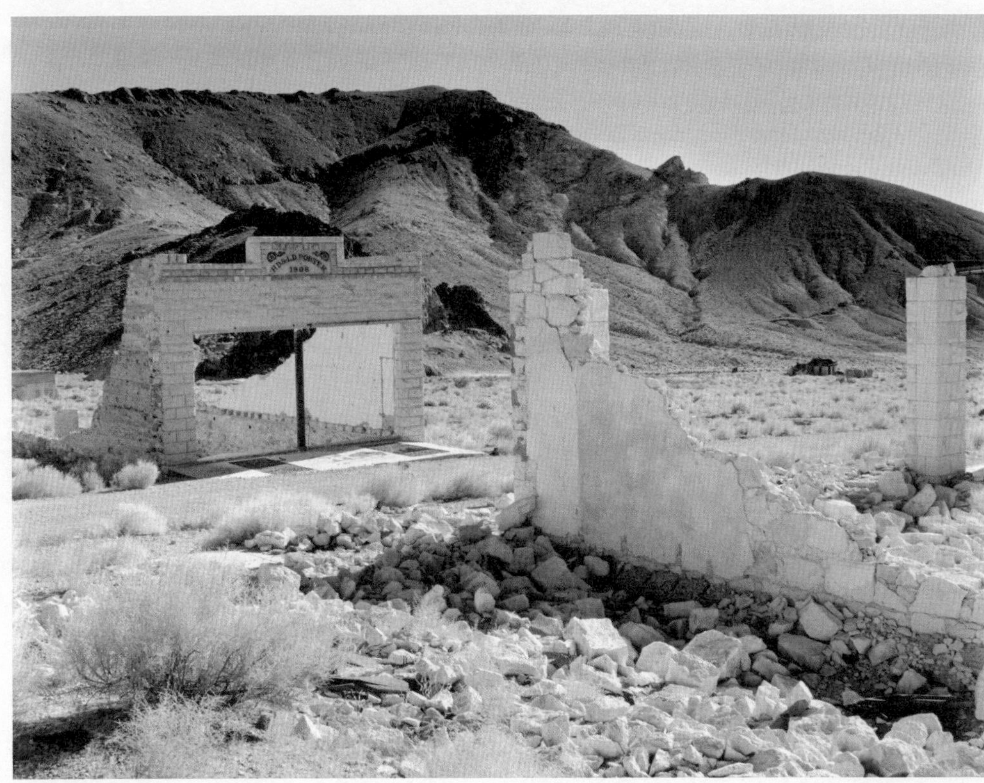

Edward Weston
Rhyolite, Nevada, 1938

of the old buildings, when a car begins to make its way toward me. The driver rolls down his window and asks, "Is this where Charles Manson's hideout was?" The air conditioner inside the car is on high, and the woman in the passenger seat is doing her best to keep her hair out of her eyes as blonde strands whirl around her face. I wipe perspiration from my forehead with the t-shirt hanging around my neck. "I don't know, it's possible." I later learn that Manson had finally been found at Barker Ranch in Death Valley, three hours south.

A visit to the Wildrose Charcoal Kilns promises to be much cooler. The kilns, located near Wildrose Peak at the southern end of the Panamints, sit eight thousand feet above sea level. Bets is feeling carsick, so we pull over at a gas station in Stovepipe Wells. I jump out of the car to take a cellphone picture of a sign with the words *SAVAGE SUMMER SUN* painted an alert orange hue—the sun's rays are emblazoned with cryptic messages about the dangers of being stranded in Death Valley in the summer. All travelers are warned to be prepared in case of an emergency.

 Bets prefers to drive when she feels carsick and takes the wheel as we leave Stovepipe Wells. Another sign by the road warns, "Avoid overheating, turn AC off next twenty miles when over 100 degrees." We oblige, but just one mile marker on, sweat is rolling down our backs. We pass another mile marker. I collect a drip of sweat from Betsy's chin before turning the AC back on.

We turn onto Emigrant Canyon Road and wind through the sharp curves of Wildrose Canyon. The terrain changes dramatically as we ascend. The landscape becomes more familiar, less like that of another planet, more in line with our definition of a desert. Dusty-rose-colored scrub brush paints the hills. The dirt is a light shade of red instead of a stark white. Pale sage begins to make an appearance as we climb. Bets points across the car dash, "That cliff looks like a wild mushroom."

The plastic cover of my binder sticks to my bare thighs as I flip to find the photos that Edward had taken of the hills we are passing. Although he preferred photographing in the midday sun, his images of the Panamints were taken late in the day, with long shadows falling across the hillsides and wispy clouds floating overhead. Today there is only blazing sun.

At the top of Wildrose Canyon, we are surprised to see evergreen trees. We pass a makeshift campground. Two tents sit propped in the shade of a parked truck. For the remaining two miles we follow a rough dirt road, our speed barely breaking five miles an hour. Finally, the kilns come into view. Magnificent in scale, these carefully built beehive-shaped structures look new and ancient at the same time, and they are such a wild thing to see after crossing miles of dry, sparse desert. We feel like we have discovered ruins from a lost time.

We open our car doors and welcome the temperate 90-degree heat. The smell of pine is mingled with the scent of charcoal, which is surprising given that the kilns have not been used since the late 1800s. I grab the four-by-five and we tentatively walk inside one of the kilns. We stand in the crisp coolness until our eyes adjust. About three feet up on all sides of the kiln are modest holes to promote air circulation. Inside one of the vent holes is a full bottle of water. I wonder who put it there. A lizard slowly slithers about on the floor as Bets sits on a rock close to the door. With black all around us, except for the light falling on her in chiaroscuro, I make her portrait.

From behind the kilns, I try to make a match of the picture that Edward took here. Bets quietly draws in her sketchbook as I work. A single pine tree has grown there in the years between us and interrupts the continuity and rhythm of the kilns as seen in Edward's picture. But then I am reminded of the images of lone trees Edward made over the years while working on *California and the West* and *Leaves of Grass*. Perhaps this tree is meant for Edward after all.

We picnic a little way up the hill under a canopy of pines. The shade is a welcome shield. We take off our hats and sunglasses, and to our surprise, on the ground before us is an elaborate city built of sticks, stones, and pinecones. From afar, the city looks like a map; this magical city is so sophisticated and intricate that its maker must have spent hours creating it. I think about making a photograph of this secret world, but Bets says it is a gift, something only to be experienced in the moment. We eat in contented silence until drops of sap from the pine limbs begin to drip on our shorts. It is time to go.

I offer to drive, but Bets climbs back in the driver's seat. Looking a bit pale, she turns to me: "The gas light is on. We will be out of gas in twenty-one miles." "How long have you known this?" I quiver. "Since we first pulled up at the kilns," she says gravely. "I wanted you to find your picture first."

It is thirty-four miles to the gas station where we had stopped earlier for Bets to buy Gatorade as I photographed the *SAVAGE SUMMER SUN* sign with its warnings to be careful about things like this. By the car's estimate, the tank would be empty thirteen miles from the gas station, in the middle of the unforgiving desert in 120-degree heat. We think about seeing if the campers we passed earlier are still there. We could ask them to follow us out of the canyon. But we decide against it. We talk about turning the air conditioner off but decide against that as well. We didn't want to end up in bad shape too soon. The drive out of the canyon is a near-continual descent; we might have a chance if we coast.

No music. Full concentration. Everything sharpened. The severity of the stark desert stretches before us. We set off and coast two miles of rough dirt road, no problem. Both of us keep an eye on the gas gauge. "Some people study how to drive best while coasting in conditions like this, only pushing the gas when necessary, to get optimal speed for gas mileage," Bets says. I look at her with raised eyebrows.

We pass the campsite and the truck with the two propped-up tents and continue onto the paved road. Around a bend we see two wild burros, and Bets sheepishly jokes, "We can ride them out of the canyon if we run out of gas."

Charis and Edward had also been in trouble in Death Valley: "Off down the road we rattled and banged until—a plunge, a lurch, a sagging stop—and there went a rear wheel bouncing away among the greasewood." After she, Edward, Cole (one of Edward's sons), and Curry (a ranger who was guiding them) learned that they didn't have the necessary tools for the situation, Charis continues, "It was a cheering discovery to make in mid-desert, with Bennetts Well ten miles away by then and nothing around but greasewood, horseflies, and heat."[11]

> "*DESERT CLAIMS FOUR*," *I saw the splendid headlines and read on, "A grim tragedy of the desert was unfolded here today as . . . " Curry was calm about it (and he should have been, since his nightly lecture at Furnace Creek always mentioned the fact that there was plenty of water in Death Valley if you knew where to look), but I noticed his first impulse, like ours, was to reach for the comfort of the full canteen.*[12]

The temperature quickly climbs. Soon, there are no more pine trees, only wide-open desert with measly patches of scrub brush. I'm acutely aware of how much water is in the car, two and a half liters. As for food, we have a package of saltines, a few tablespoons of peanut butter, two sticks of Betsy's beef jerky, and a handful of nuts. The *SAVAGE SUMMER SUN* sign advises stranded motorists: "Stay in the shade of the car, pop the hood of the trunk to keep the car a little cooler, don't walk to get help, wait in the car for someone to come."

We vow we will never tell our families about this.

As we descend, Betsy barely brakes or touches the gas. I think about the full bottle of water we had seen earlier—with that water and the food we had with us, we could have survived a few days in the kiln. As the temperature climbs to 100 degrees and then to 115 degrees, we are alert and silent. I remember something that I had read the day before, when we first arrived at Dante's View. At the gate of hell, Dante pauses briefly to read the following inscription: *Lasciate ogni speranza, voi ch'entrate. Abandon all hope, ye who enter here.* Betsy is gripping the steering wheel with both hands, and I grab her thigh as I think about the last picture that I made of her in the darkness of the kiln and the last picture on my cellphone of the winding road into the canyon. The cellphone would overheat, but the film might make it.

We finally cover the twenty-six miles to the main road. There are eight more miles to the gas station, down a steep grade. We are going to make it. And if not, we should be able to flag someone down. We joke again about riding the wild burros out of the canyon, and how the hell we could have let this happen. By the time we pull up at the pump, we would have happily paid twenty dollars a gallon for gas. $7.50 a gallon? No problem. I am grateful to be going back to the droning air conditioners of Furnace Creek Ranch, to our room with the dead cockroach and all of his friends, the cool safety of civilization.

Large ravens sit on a tree stump, their watchful eyes on us, as we unload the car. We sit on the edge of the bed eating packaged salads for dinner while Bets tells me about the people she saw at the grocery store—blue collar workers, bohemians in flip flops, and well-groomed military personnel—a microcosm of the diverse neighbors who coexist in this desert town, home to both Joshua Tree National Park Headquarters and the largest Marine Corps training base in the world, and about how she stopped to get a better view of a coyote on her way back to the inn. Their eyes locked for a few moments before he crossed the road and went on his way.

Charis and Edward traveled through Twentynine Palms in 1937. "The center of town was two gas stations—one active, one passive—and a drugstore. A mile or so north was the post office, half a mile south the grocery; between lay vast numbers of attractive homesites, if one had a weakness for uninterrupted vistas of greasewood."[13] Bets and I find Twentynine Palms looking rather rundown. Buildings once home to businesses that had experienced a short-lived heyday in the early 1950s were now repurposed or vacant. A few lone wanderers walk around the relatively empty streets. An old man sits in the shade outside the Cowboy Thrift Store. A number of barber shops offer *MILITARY HAIRCUTS*, with the exception of one salon that boasts *CIVILIAN HAIRCUTS TOO*. We reach the military base, where a chain-link fence is festooned with yellow ribbons and red plastic drinking cups that spell out *WELCOME HOME JACK*. Sun-blasted plastic flowers bloom beneath the words.

We stop at The Jelly Donut, where a banner advertising *DATE SHAKES* flaps in the wind. Charis and Edward drank date shakes every chance they got while on the road for *California and the West*. Bets and I have never tried one. The woman behind the counter talks on her phone as she scoops ice cream and then dates into a blender. A faded glamour shot of the same woman with her daughter, taken at least twenty years earlier, adorns the wall next to the register. Above the donut display, droopy Christmas decorations cling to yellowed tape. On another wall, framed photographs, arranged salon style, serve as a tribute to a man in uniform, medals pinned to his chest; in the center is a framed copy of the Declaration of Independence.

Charis and Edward had the right idea; the date shakes are delicious. We linger outside for a bit as I photograph the store with my cellphone and make plans to come back in better light.

<hr>

At the Joshua Tree National Park Visitor Center, I show a young ranger photographs that Edward made in the area. One image, made in Wonderland of the Rocks, depicts a stack of monzogranite boulders. Edges of these once angular rocks, smoothed and rounded over time by the wind, look like large, sandy marshmallows. The other image was made in Rattlesnake Valley and labeled "our campsite" in Edward's handwriting. The young ranger looks half-heartedly at the images. I tell him more about Edward until he says, "Not to discourage you or anything, but finding these rocks is . . . " I fill in, "Like finding a needle in a haystack?" At this point an older ranger walks up and joins the conversation. They, with a comradery between them, urge us not to go into the Wonderland of Rocks. They explain that many boulder piles look confusingly similar and that it is easy to get disoriented out in the desert. They take turns reiterating the impossible odds of finding either location, pointing us toward the Barker Dam Trail instead. "It's an interpretative trail, a short loop, you'll love it." I can tell they are concerned that we might expire in the relenting heat, so I tell them we will go to Barker Dam Trail in the morning. We aren't going to give up on finding Charis and Edward's campsite though.

While at the Center for Creative Photography, I peered through a loupe at the negatives Edward had made on the road, many of them never published and only seen by a handful of people like me, wearing white gloves, hunched over a light table. The eight-by-ten negatives were in the order they were taken on the trip. Charis mentioned in her memoir that she had developed a "new record-keeping system, listing every negative as it was made and adding the where and when, as well as what was included or excluded compared to other views, particularly for a series of pictures taken in one place."[14] Before this, Edward labeled his negatives with an alphabetic code—"N for nudes, T for Trees, R for rocks, S for shells, Cl for clouds (C had already been used for cactus)."[15] Looking at Edward's images, one after the other, I analyzed the landscapes he had made and noticed that several subgroups emerged: old shoes, dead animals, abandoned cars, burned trees, twisted torsos of junipers, crevasses in rocks, surf rushing in and out, and closeups of driftwood. Only three images out of the entire set identified campsites. One was made at Deadman's Point, another at Texas Springs Campground in Death Valley, and the third one, at Rattlesnake Valley, was the so-called needle in the haystack that Betsy and I were hoping to find.

Back at Twentynine Palms Inn, we take cold showers before going outside to lounge on our private patio. The sun's rays work quickly to dry our hair and warm our skin. We both have faint tan lines outlining the ghosts of socks, shirts, and shorts. Fine, feathery clouds move above us. As time goes on, the clouds form a large horseshoe. When Bets points out that the clouds look more like a large C instead of a horseshoe, I run inside, grab the four-by-five, and try to photograph them, tilting the camera skyward. Dressed only in cowboy boots, I let the black t-shirt around the bellows engulf my head. Edward, who took pictures of clouds, their cat, and Charis on their sundeck in Santa Monica Canyon, may have often been nude when he made those images. He once professed, "I hope to plan my life so that one hour every day can be spent naked in the sunlight."[16] By the time I focus and am ready to shoot, the clouds have dispersed.

After dinner, we drive the short distance to Indian Cove Boy Scout Trail just inside Joshua Tree National Park. We have no intention of hiking far. At the trailhead is a register for overnight campers to sign, but no names are listed. The desert is open and exposed. We meander slowly. We pass cholla, creosote, Mormon tea, and prickly pear cacti, their spines backlit and bright. We peer into a Mojave yucca, entranced by its spidery, fibrous threads. Industrious ants follow each other into mounds. We are exhilarated to be away from city life, the crowds and congestion. All we have to think about out here are expansive vistas and the cycles of the sun and moon.

    Charis had become enamored by a book called *California Desert Trails*, written by Joseph Smeaton Chase in 1919. The book details Chase's journeys on horseback through the Mojave Desert, including stops at Death Valley and Twentynine Palms. His writing made an impact on Charis, and after buying a copy I could see why. To my surprise, the book included photographs Chase had made on his solitary sojourns—dried up washes, thirsty riverbeds, solitary stone structures in shambles, and cacti that had been cut down for an emergency water supply. Imagining Chase alone in this harsh landscape on horseback with his camera gear and supplies in tow, miles from civilization, was both frightening and romantic. The photograph was an important record for Chase; it served as proof of his experience in this remote place. Beyond acting as reference for his future writing, I wondered if making pictures had allowed him to imagine the audience who would see them, maybe even feel their company. Perhaps the promise of sharing them made him feel less alone.

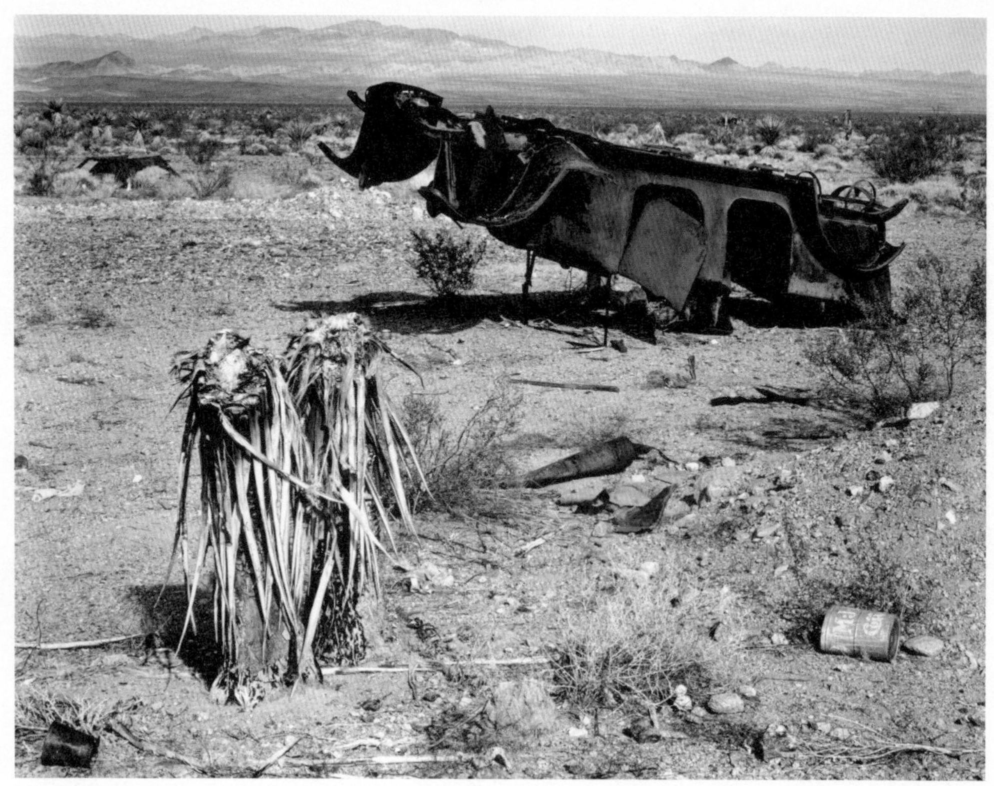

Thinking of Chase and the dangers of the remote desert, I remember that while traveling across the Colorado Desert, Charis and Edward found themselves in extreme heat, miles away from any help, as their car began to sink in the sand. They were able to stay moving, but as the temperature climbed well over a hundred degrees, Charis writes, "sweat poured off us and we drank water continually. All animal life had retired from view on the ground, and only the occasional buzzard sailed past overhead."[17] They continued on until "finally, around a bend the parched dusty land gave way to greenery and the wonderful sound of running water."[18] As they turned off the main road, they saw a note attached to a stick with a crosspiece that read, *PLEASE HELP SICK MAN AT CARRIZO STATION.*

We found the man on the stream bank under the trees. He lay on his back on a piece of worn tarpaulin, his open eyes aimed at the sky and already being investigated by two or three desert flies . . . a bottle of milk and a can of water sat alongside his small bundle, which was tied up in an old blue bandanna with a pencil through the knot. The man was short and emaciated, with red hair clipped close and a stubble of beard. He might have been around fifty.

We stood a long while looking at him, only the creek running below us making a soft sound in the hot silence. I had never seen a dead person, and

Edward made a few double exposures during their travels, an easy mistake when working with sheet-film holders. The most evocative of these accidents was of the man they found. Earlier that day, Edward had made a wide-angle view of cow bones in a field of flowers, the sunlight outlining each blossom. This exposure became overlaid with one of the dead man, so that his body now glowed with flowers and light. A second image Edward took of the man was printed in *California in the West*, although I like to remember the double exposure that now resides at the Center for Creative Photography.

After an eighteen-mile drive to the closest town, Charis and Edward reported the man's death to the local sheriff. They had begun "to see how easy it would be—if the gas ran out or a tire went flat—to die out here in the desert."[20]

Betsy and I head out early the next morning to beat the heat. Lanky outlines of Joshua Trees gambol in the light of dawn. The spiny trees, which aren't really trees but belong to the Agave family, are tall with wild arms that curl in unexpected ways. Charis often made drawings to accompany her typed text. From their time in this area, there was a flat-bottomed cloud that looked like a hat, a thunderhead that resembled two people on a ski lift, and a rather expressive rendering of a lewd Joshua tree with three arms.

Barker Dam Trail is a disappointment. The footpath is overly prescribed. Gnats are everywhere, making it impossible to walk without winding your arms into fans. The dam itself is closed off while the park restores a five-hundred-square-foot rock that is covered, almost every inch, with graffiti. I am beginning to wonder if the rangers sent us here as some kind of joke, or punishment, but I take a picture of a jubilant Joshua tree as Bets reads her Lucy Grealy book. Her patience with me and the gnats is impressive.

Not far from the dam is the entrance to Wonderland Wash, where we spot the remnants of a crumbling pink adobe. The walls had fallen in years ago but the chimney is still standing. This reminds me of *After Forest Fire, Bandon Oregon* in *California and the West*, which, depicts the wide mouth of a chimney, a dark cave with fallen brick teeth. There are no signs left of the house, just the chimney surrounded by charred trees, their eerie, leafless branches rising like smoke in the background. As Charis drove away, she "kept trying to search out a great philosophical truth from the fact that when a house burns only that part which was meant for the fire remains."[21]

We pass Mojave yucca, Parry's Nolina, and prickly pears as the sandy wash leads us toward Wonderland of Rocks. Across the way, a striking scene of boulders and brush presents itself; Betsy immediately titles the view "Grotto." We take off our packs. I'm relieved to be underneath my t-shirt shroud if only to get a break from the gnats. I take my time photographing the scene. When I emerge, Betsy's body is covered by dozens of gnats. She has taken off her t-shirt and put it over her head to cover her nose, ears, eyes, and mouth. She is also wearing her cowboy hat, which adds some humor to the scene.

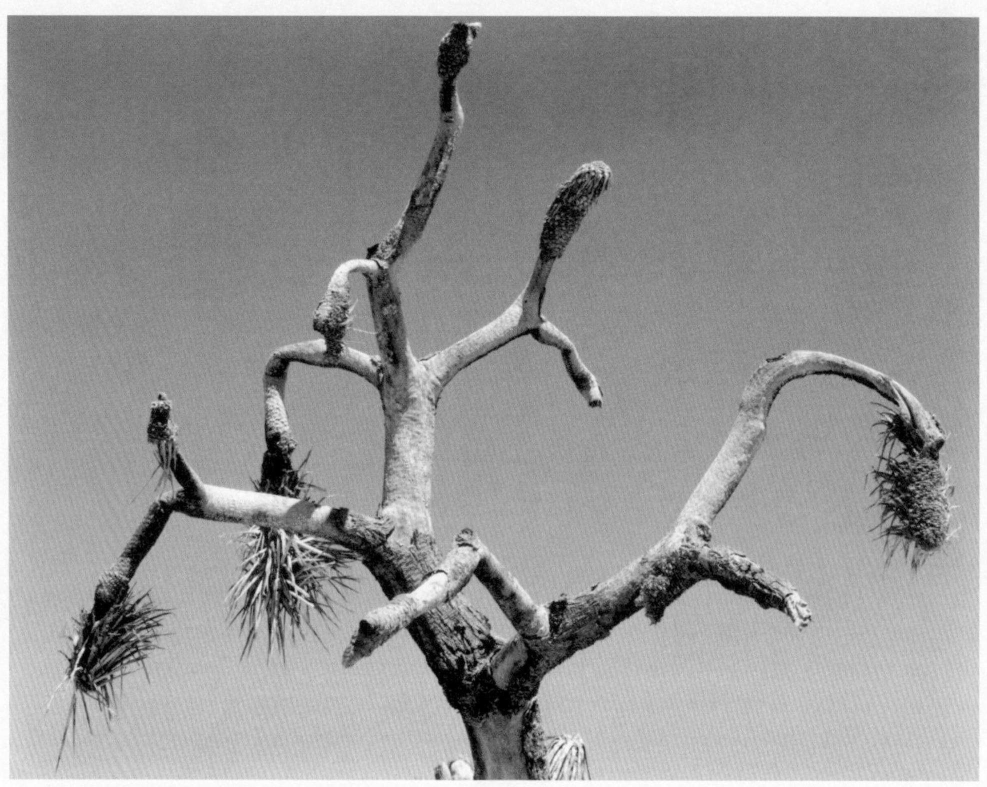

We wave, slap, and scurry our way back to the car. I stop once when I see Betsy standing beneath a magnificent Joshua tree. I ask, "What about this one?" But she has reached her limit. She raises one eyebrow, and I know we need to keep moving.

The Jelly Donut is closed, but the light is right. Bets waits in the car with the windows down. I meter the scene, check the focus, and am ready to shoot when a woman in her forties wearing a red, worn-out basketball jersey and long gym shorts enters the scene.

Leaning against the building, she props a leg up and says, "Hey, want to photograph a thug?"

I lift my head from under my black shroud and say, "No."

She walks closer to me and asks, "What are you doing? What are you photographing?"

I grab a four-by-five holder and slide it into the back of the camera. "I'm photographing the sign. A photographer made several images around this town in the late 1930s."

She comes even closer. "What photographer?" she asks.

"Edward Weston," I reply curtly.

"Oh. Doesn't he have, like, two books? He talked with my grandmother out in Amboy."

I was shocked. Charis and Edward had driven to Amboy, thirty miles north, where Charis described her and Edward as having "the unsettling experience of being completely surrounded by mirages."[22] It was possible that Charis and Edward had spoken with this woman's grandmother. I wondered if I should strike up a conversation with her about it. Most photographers would have, but the shutter is cocked, and I bristle, determined to keep working. She gets the message and walks to the other side of the building, where Bets is waiting in the car. The woman says, "I'm just a character," before sitting on the stoop next to an open sack of donut mix to make a call on her cellphone. I click the shutter, push the dark slide into the holder, and pack up the camera.

The next morning, we make our way to Rattlesnake Valley in search of Charis and Edward's campsite, despite the rangers' warning that it will be next to impossible to find. I am hopeful. There are no trees for shade, just stacked boulders in various arrangements to offer a modest reprieve from the hot wind. A cloud of dust rises behind us as I hold Edward's campsite photograph out the rolled-down passenger-side window, comparing the stacked rocks in his image to the ones at each numbered site. We roll slowly past every site before venturing down one last road marked by a sign that reads, "For day use only." We follow around a bend to the last site, near a secluded area. And there it is!

Edward must have taken the image while standing on top of a rock directly across from the site. He often stood on whatever he could find to make himself taller while photographing. I climb on top of the rock and adjust the legs of the tripod before looking at the scene on the ground glass.

Edward, Charis, and Edward's son Brett camped here for two nights. They saw jackrabbits, quail, and mourning doves. At night they lay, backs on their rolled sleeping bags, feet to the fire, smoking their pipes, having learned that the desert wind makes cigarettes burn too quickly.

While Edward and Brett photographed, Charis climbed the rocks at Rattlesnake Valley wearing only her boots. Near us, high on the rocks, are Bighorn Sheep, many of them. Their hooves clack as they jump from rock to rock. Peering between these rocks, Charis saw a dry riverbed down below. I stand still for a moment, taking in the scene. The quiet desert is waking up. A fox trots among the underbrush. A jackrabbit lifts her translucent ears to listen. Shadows seep beneath the boulders as the sun rises. Rattlesnake Valley looks like a pile of minimalist sculptures. My shadow merges with that of my camera as I walk back to the car.

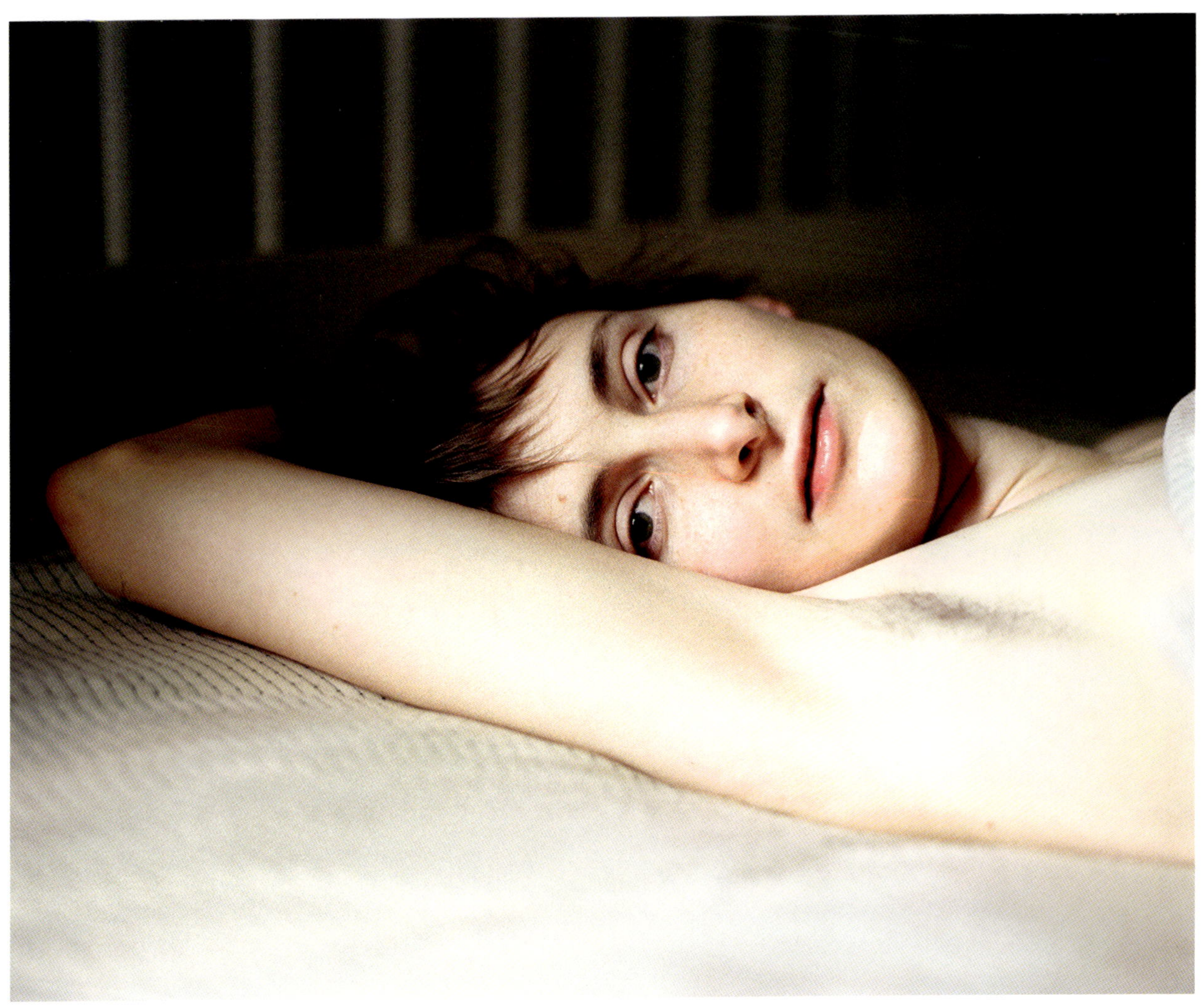

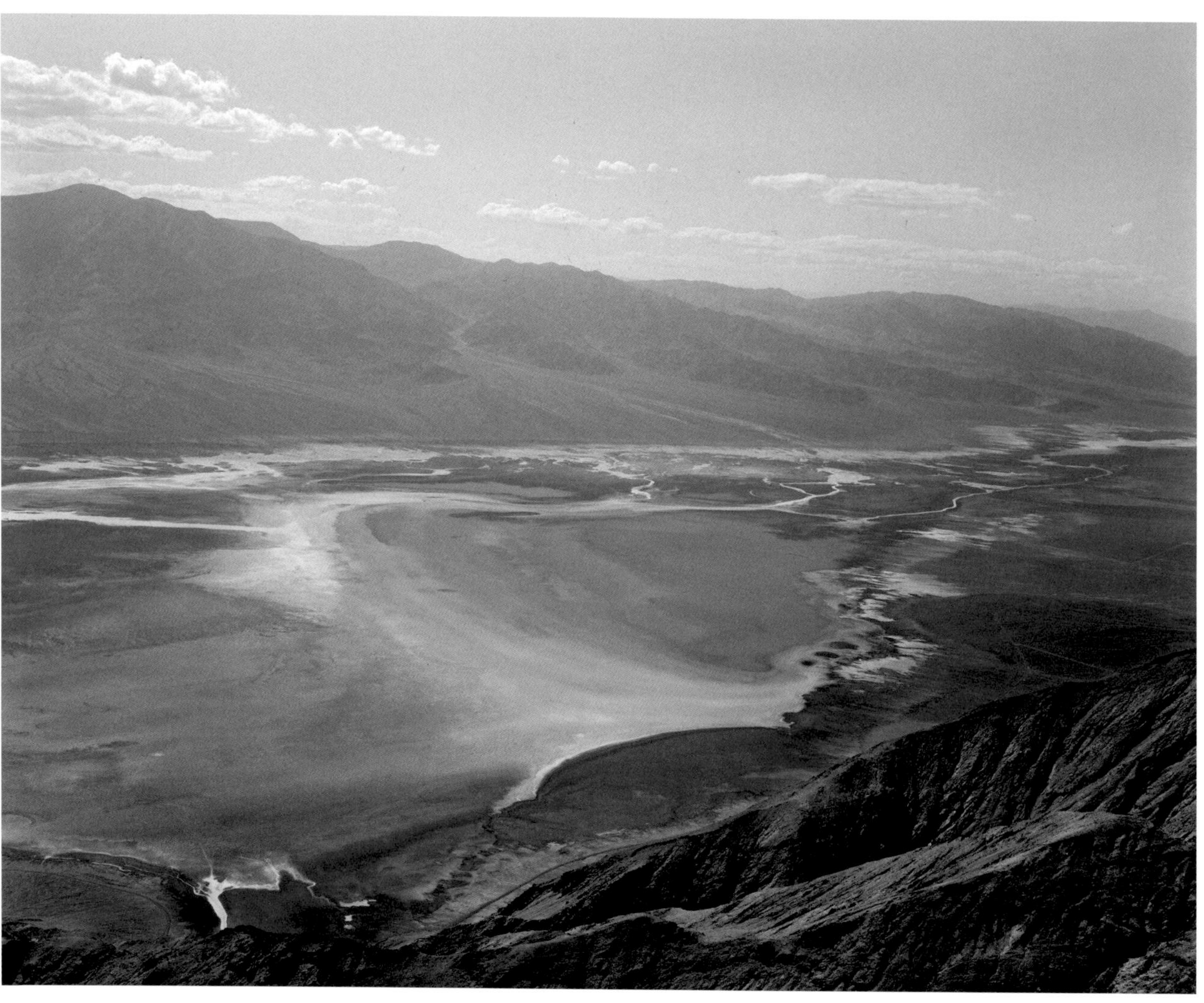

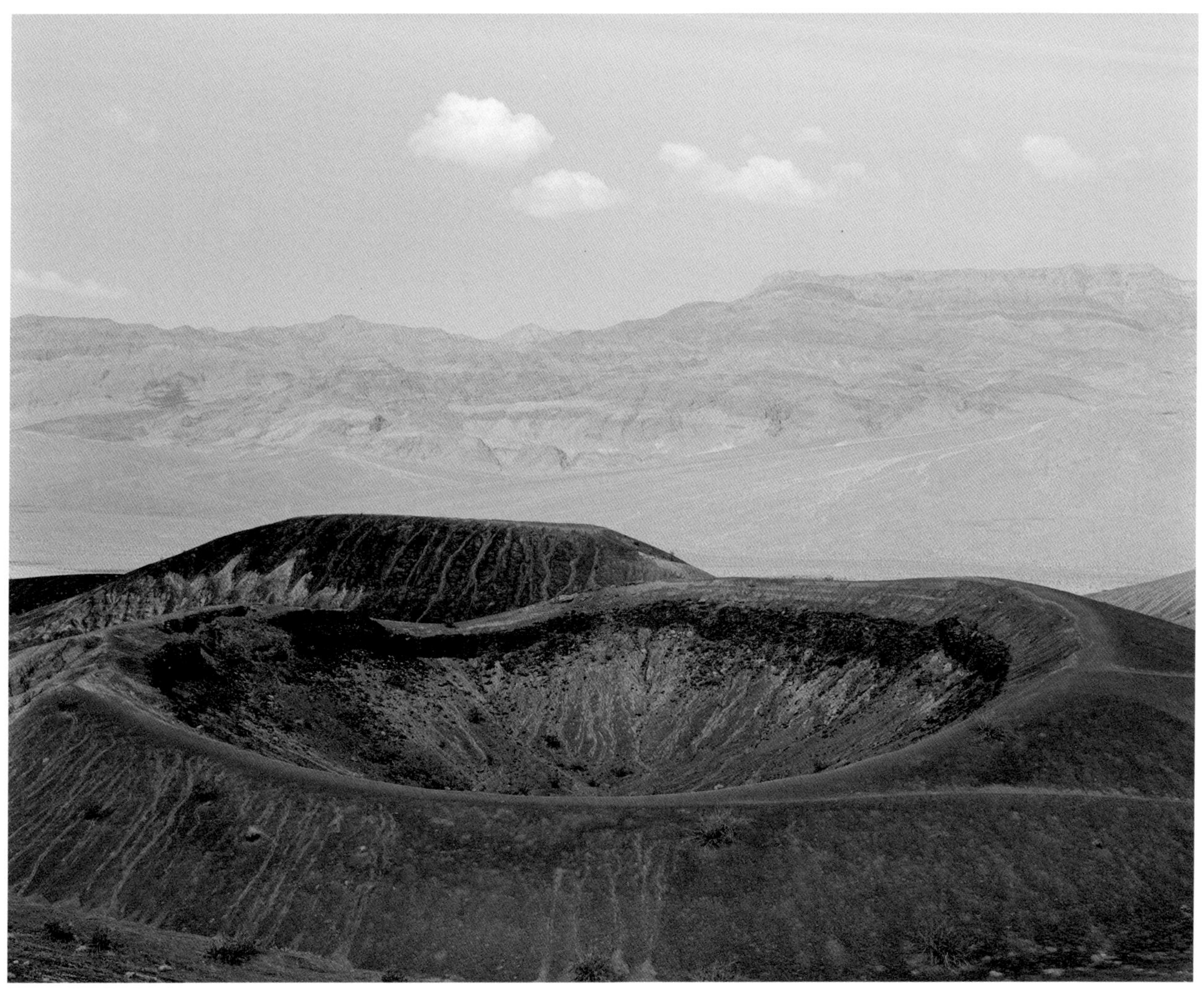

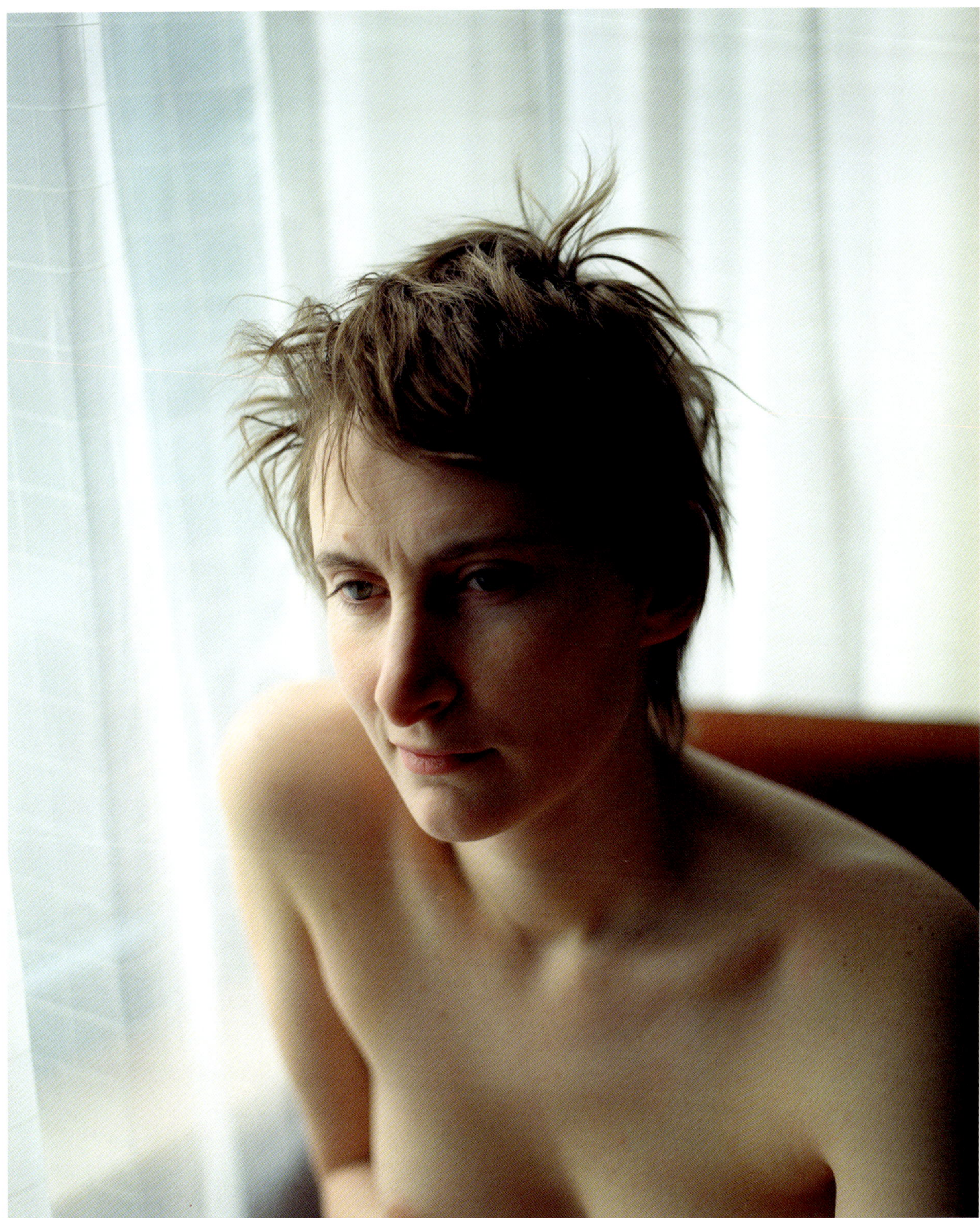

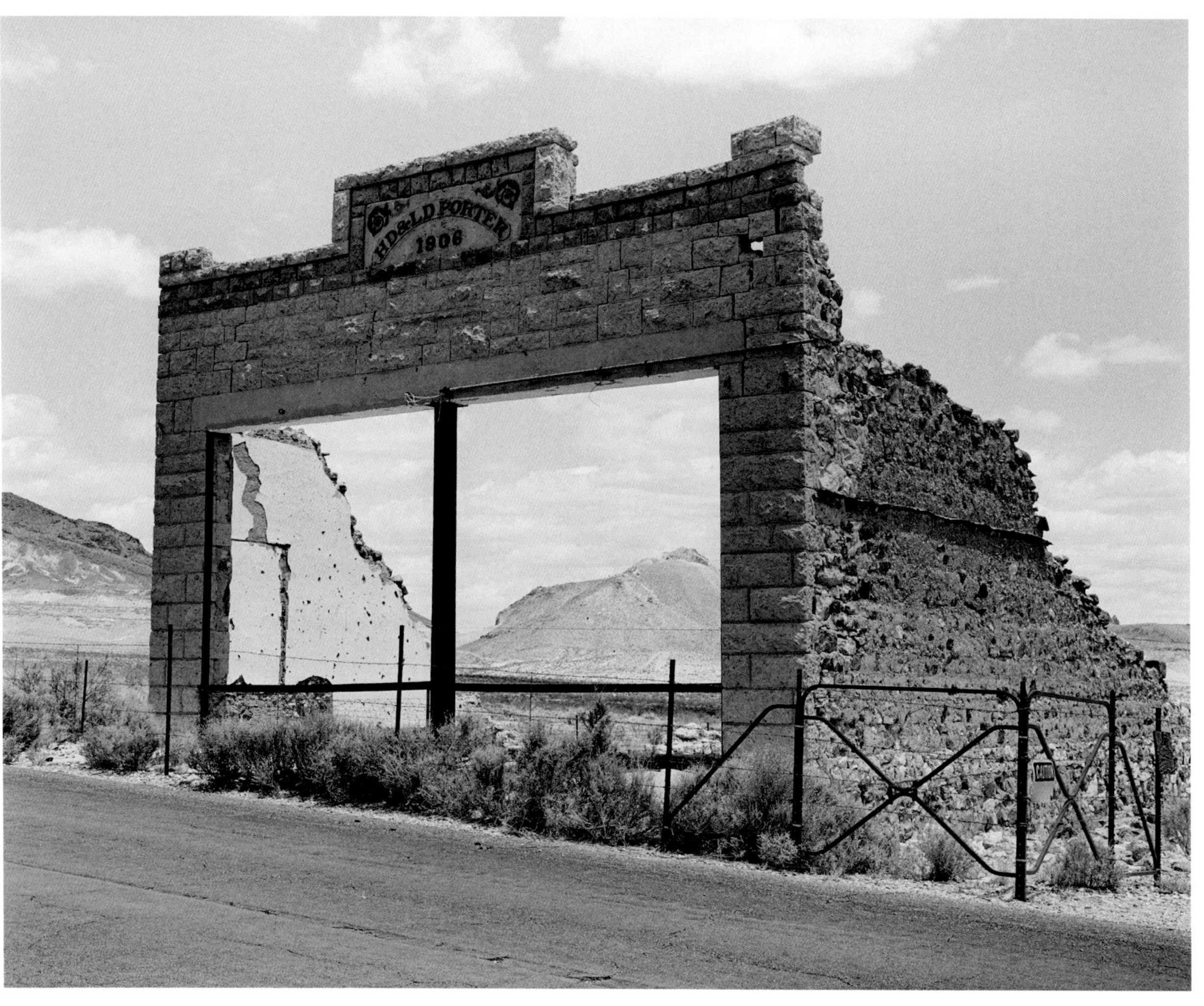

H.D.& L.D. PORTER
1906

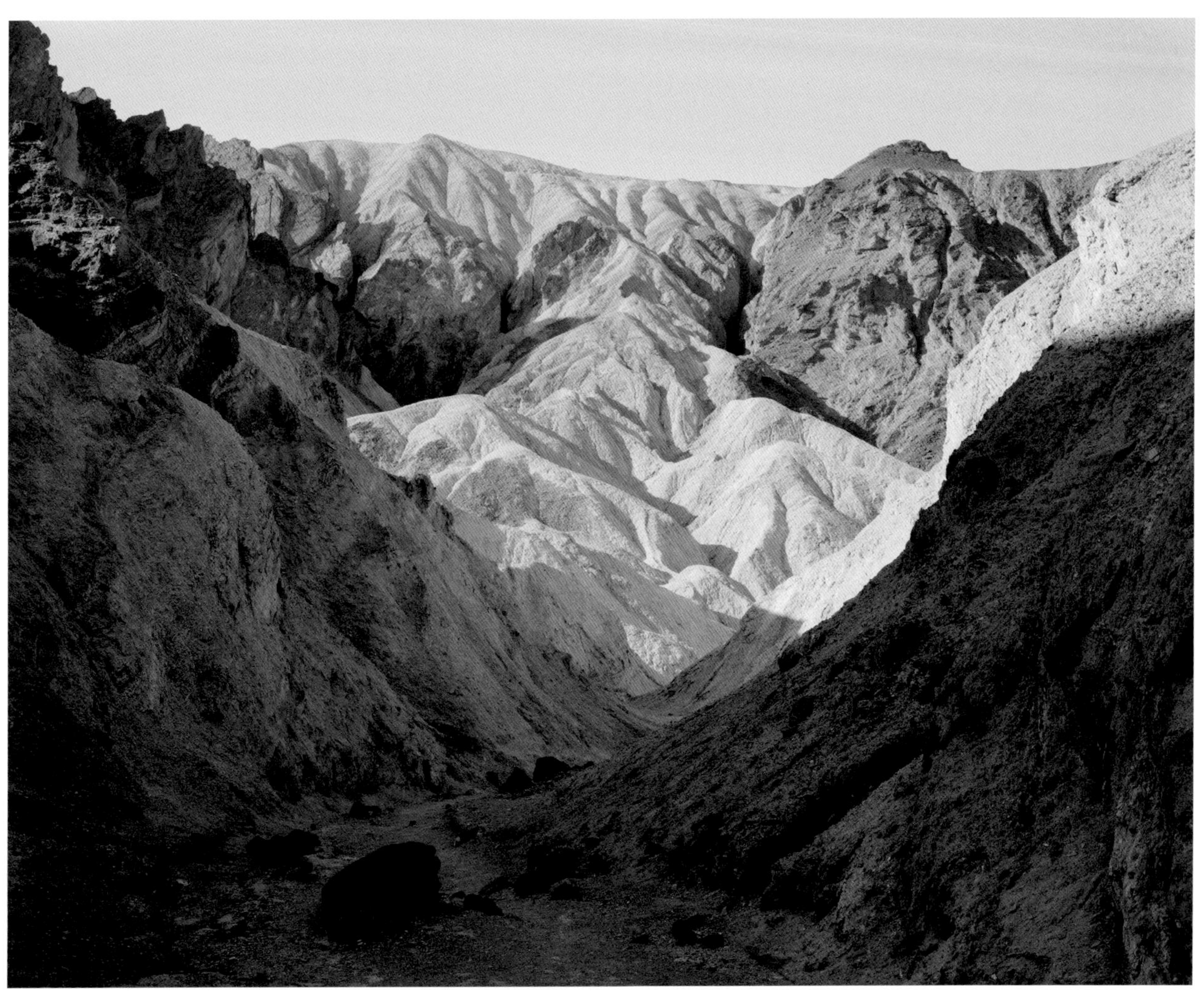

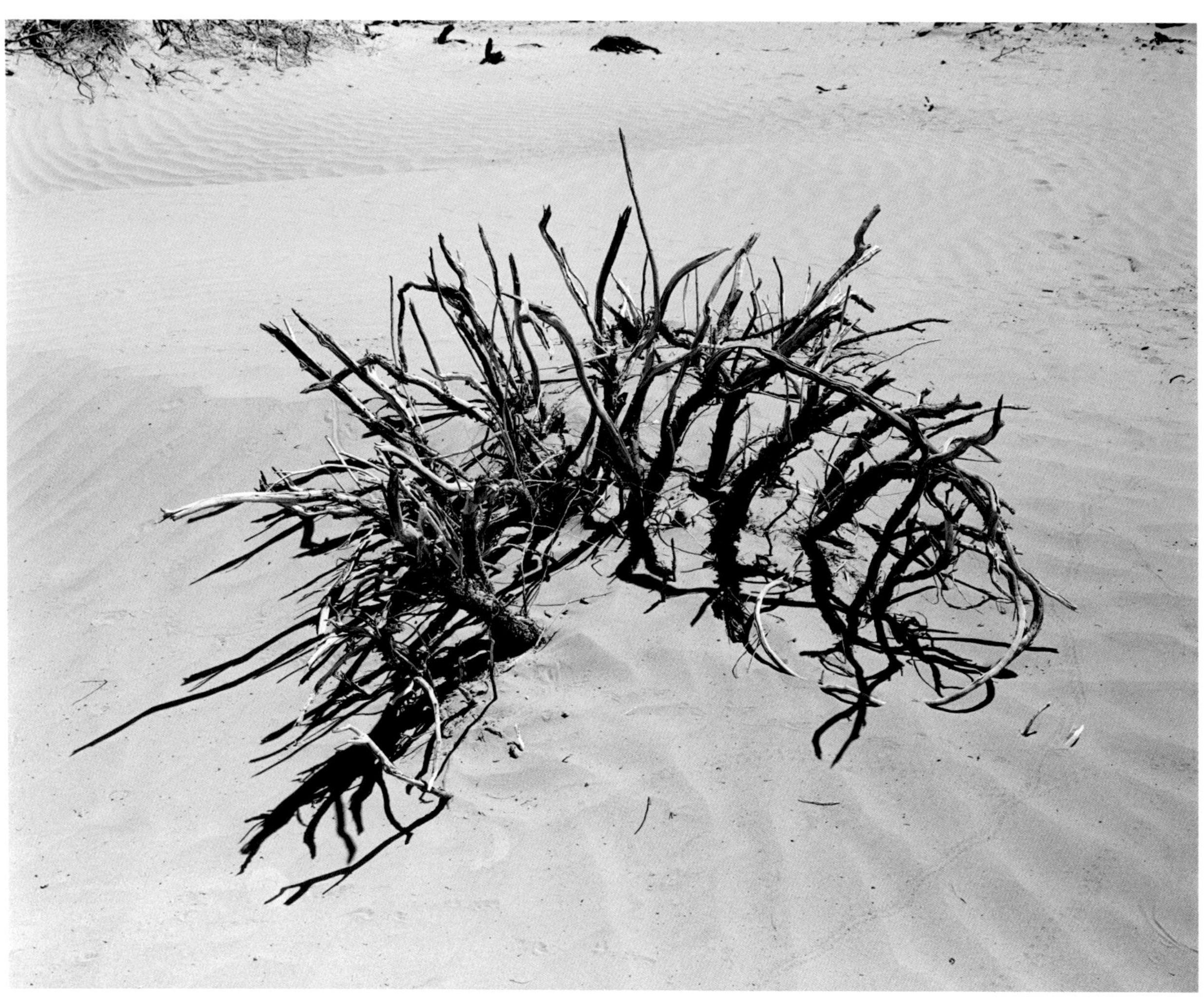

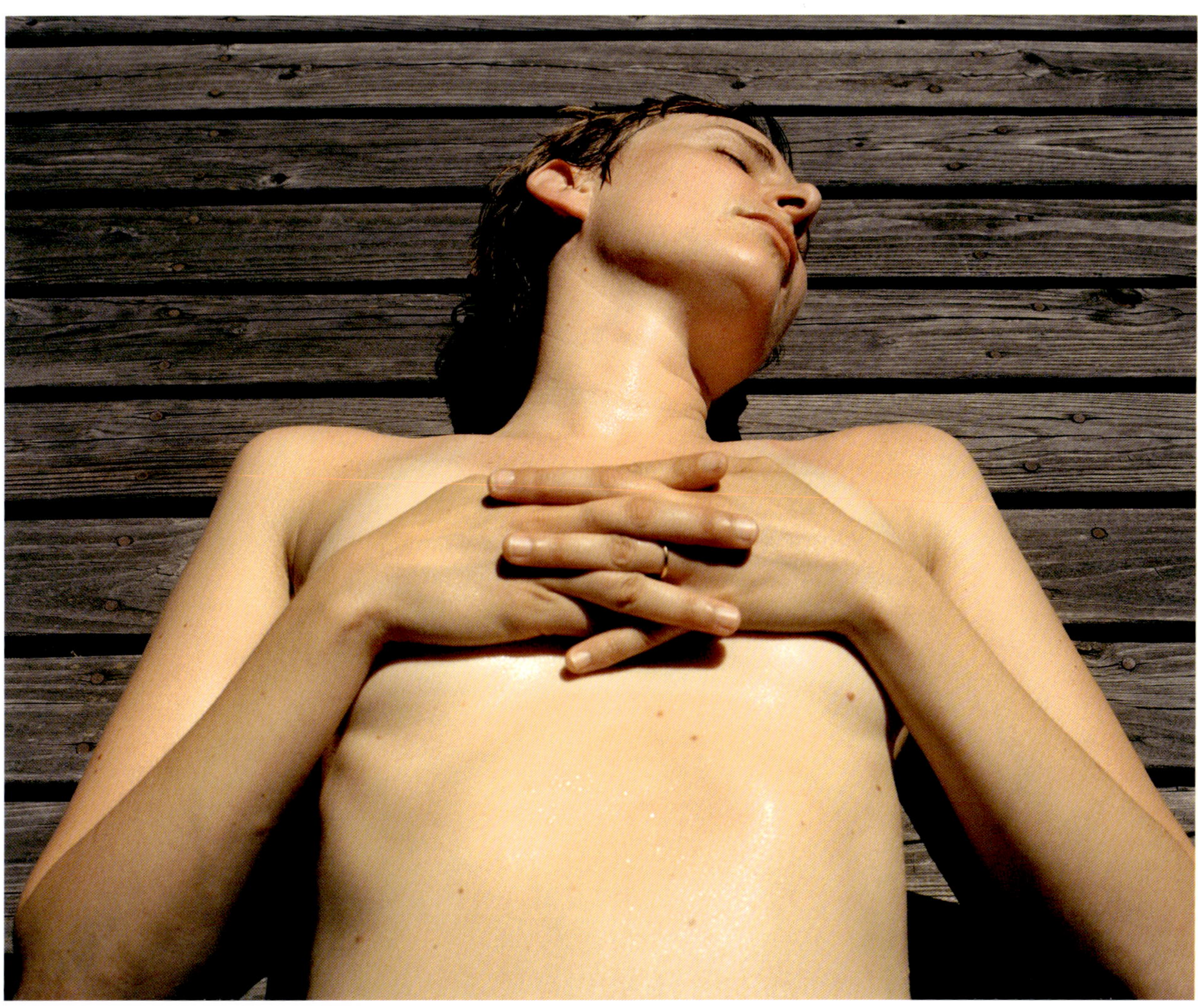

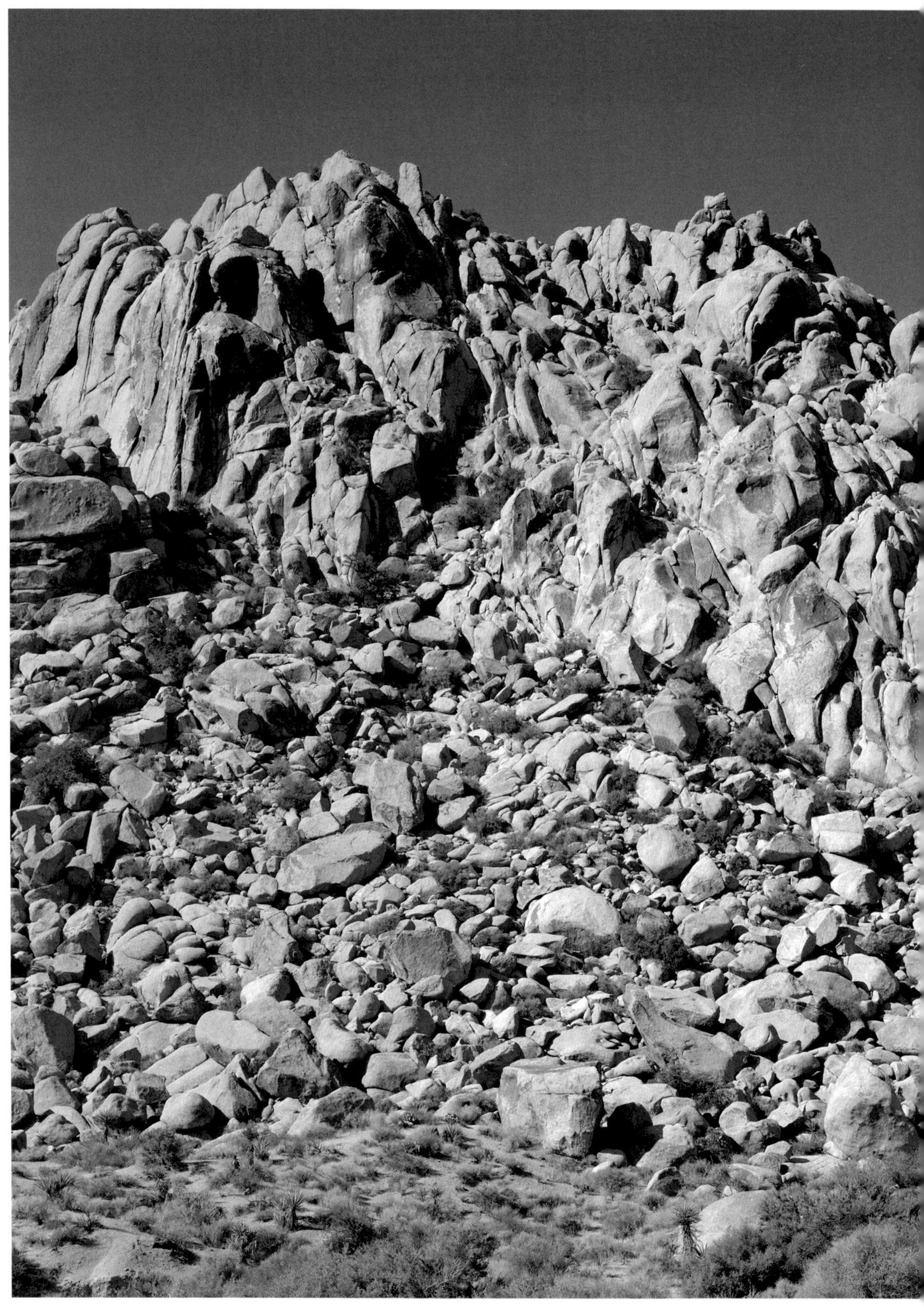

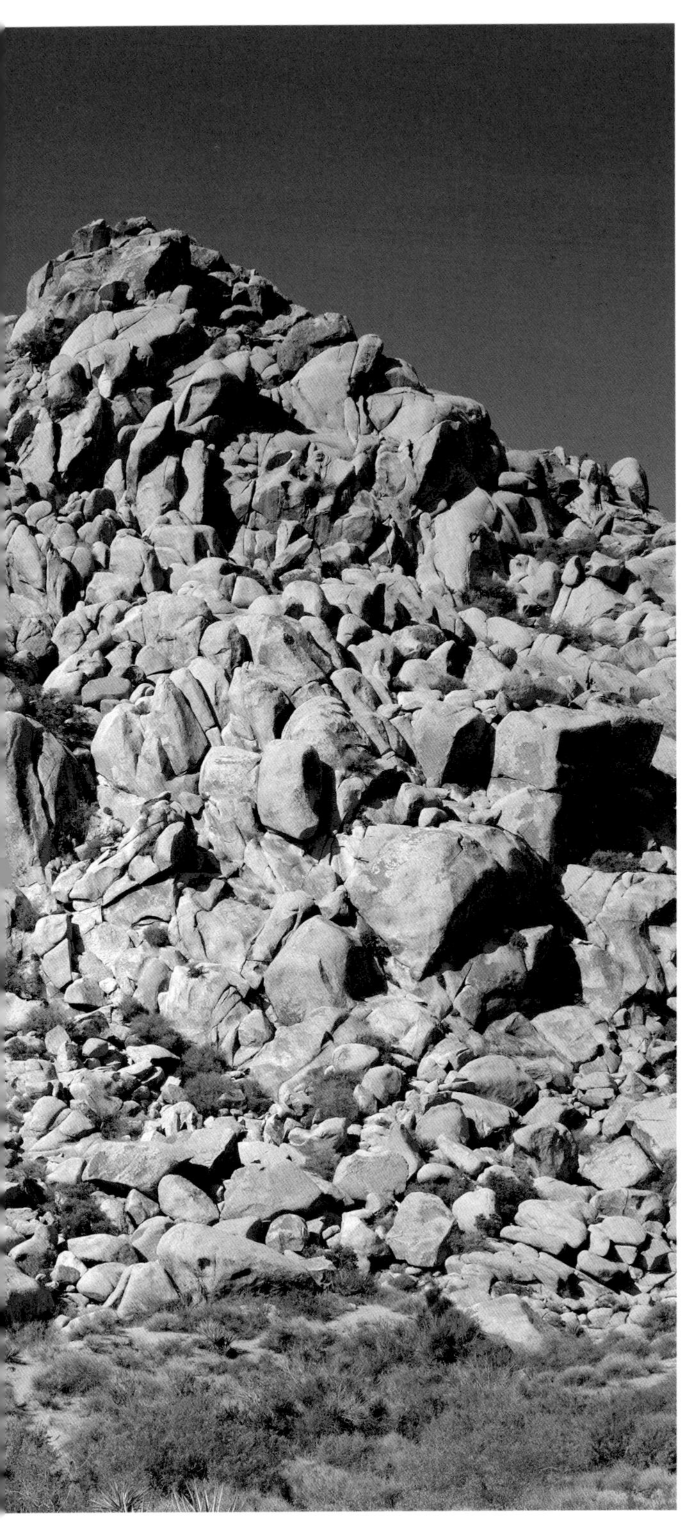

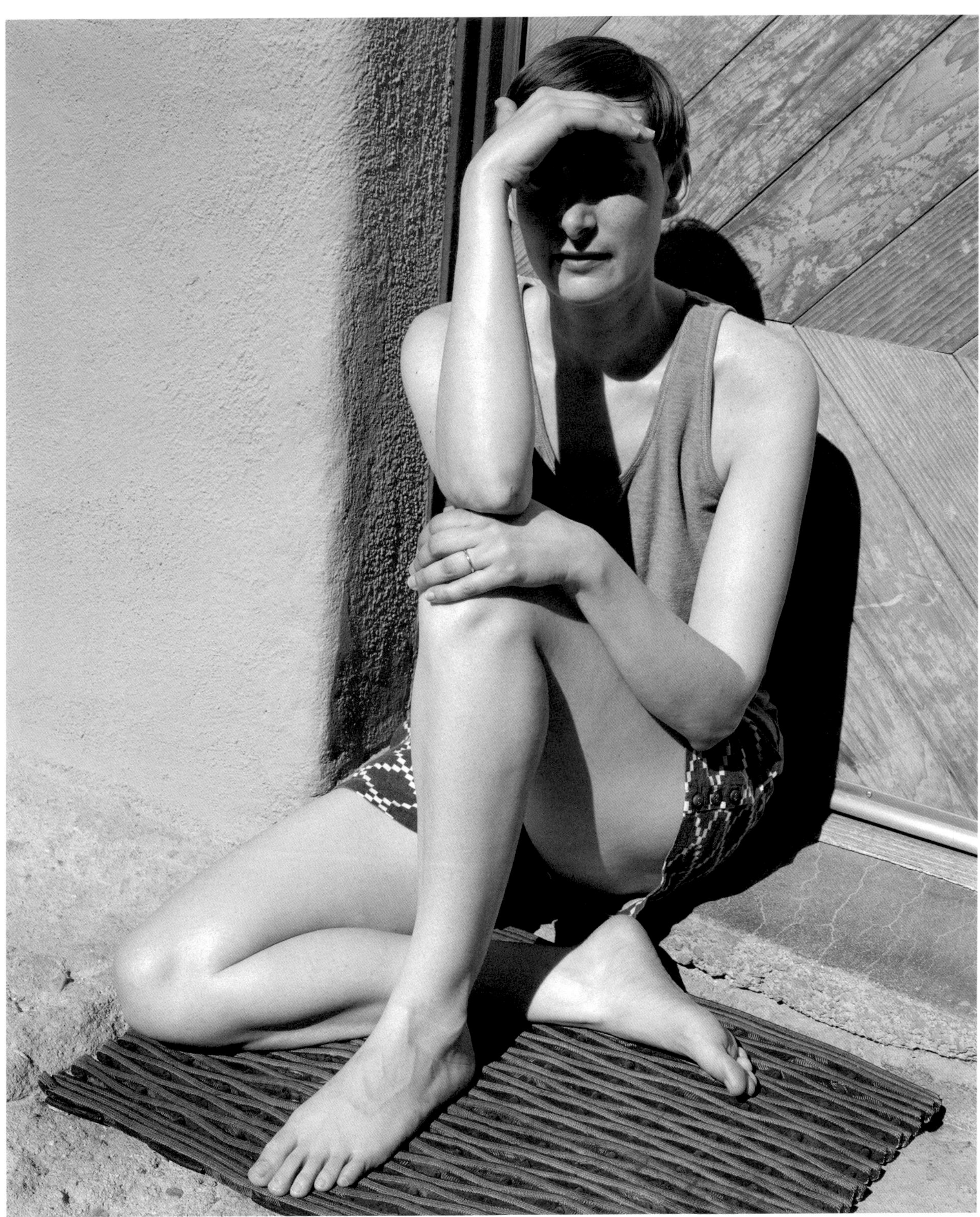

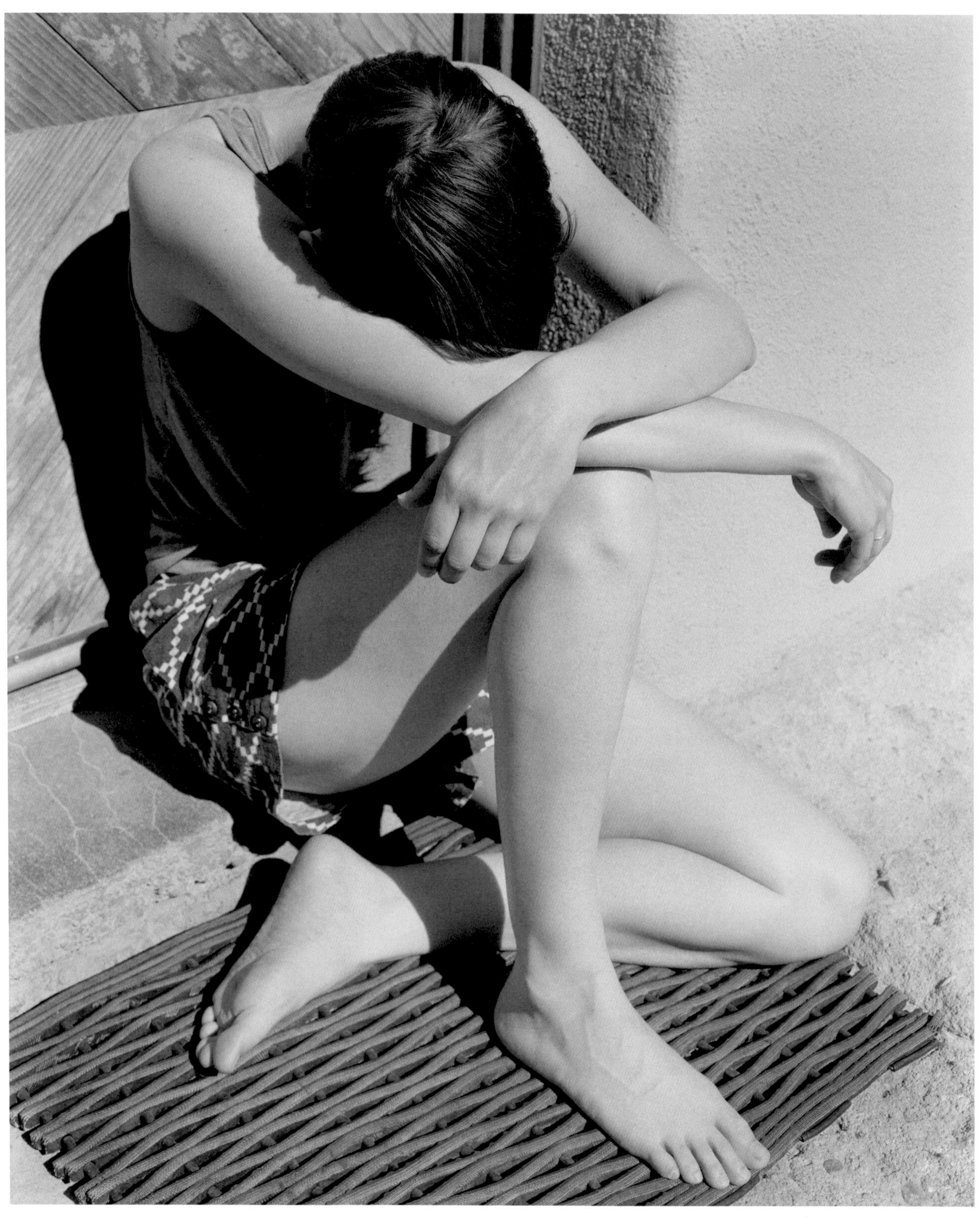

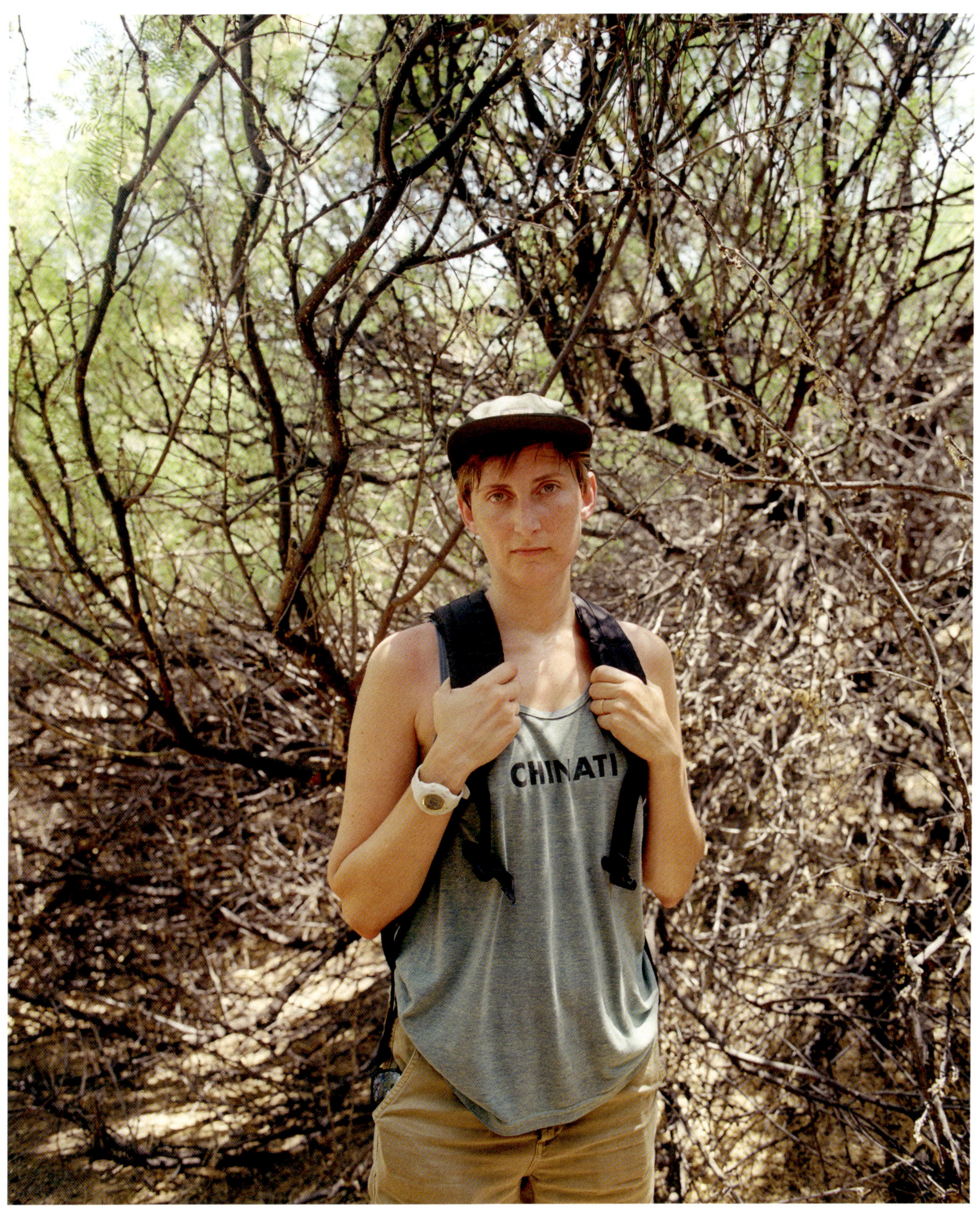
CHINATI

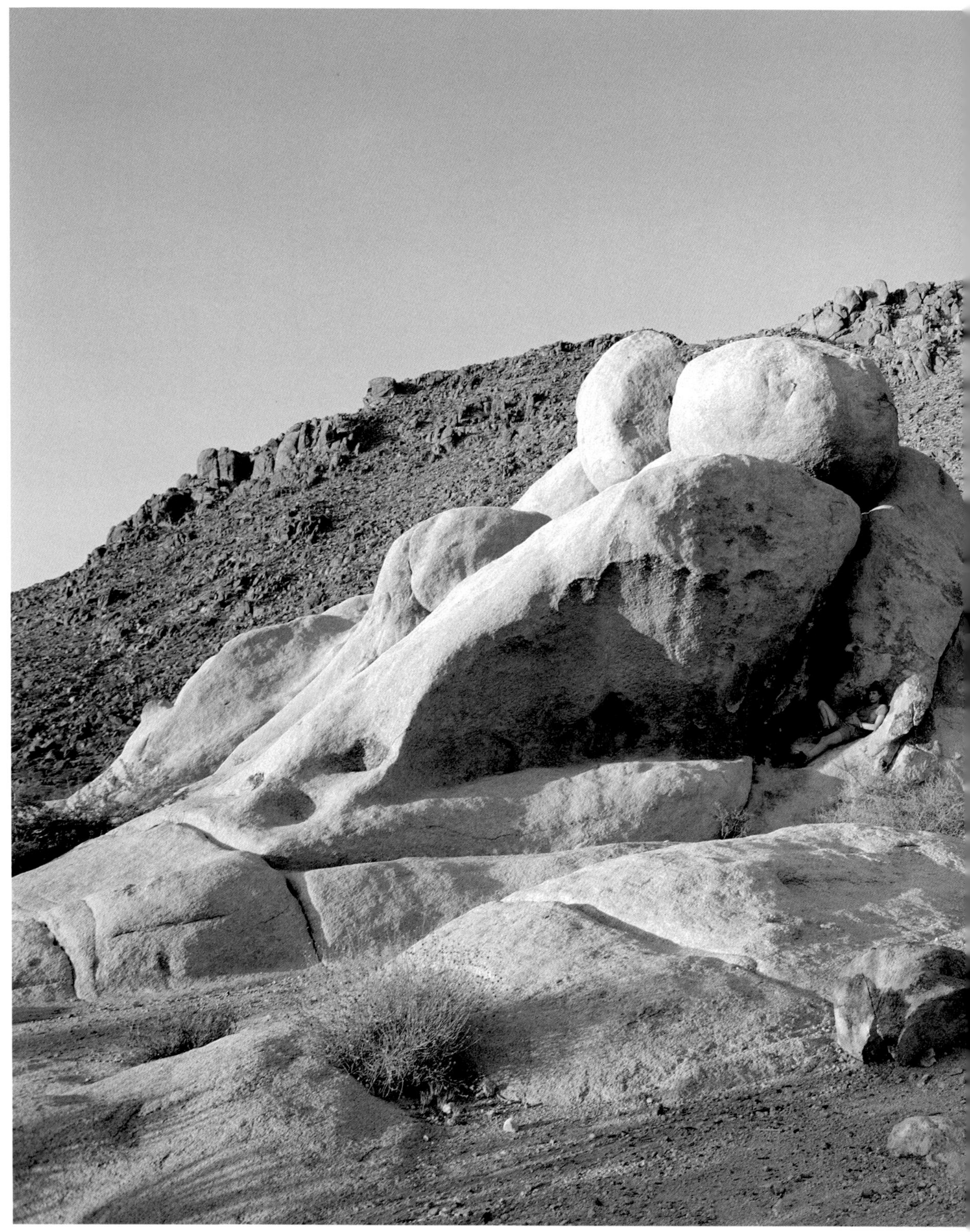

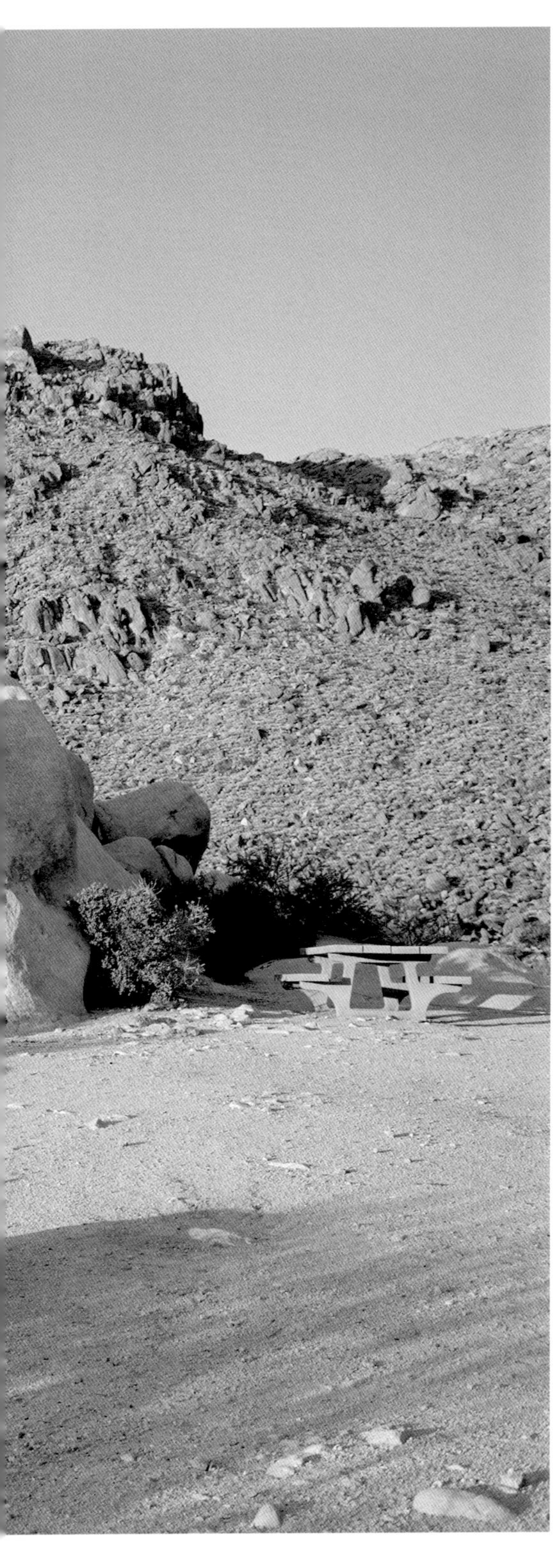

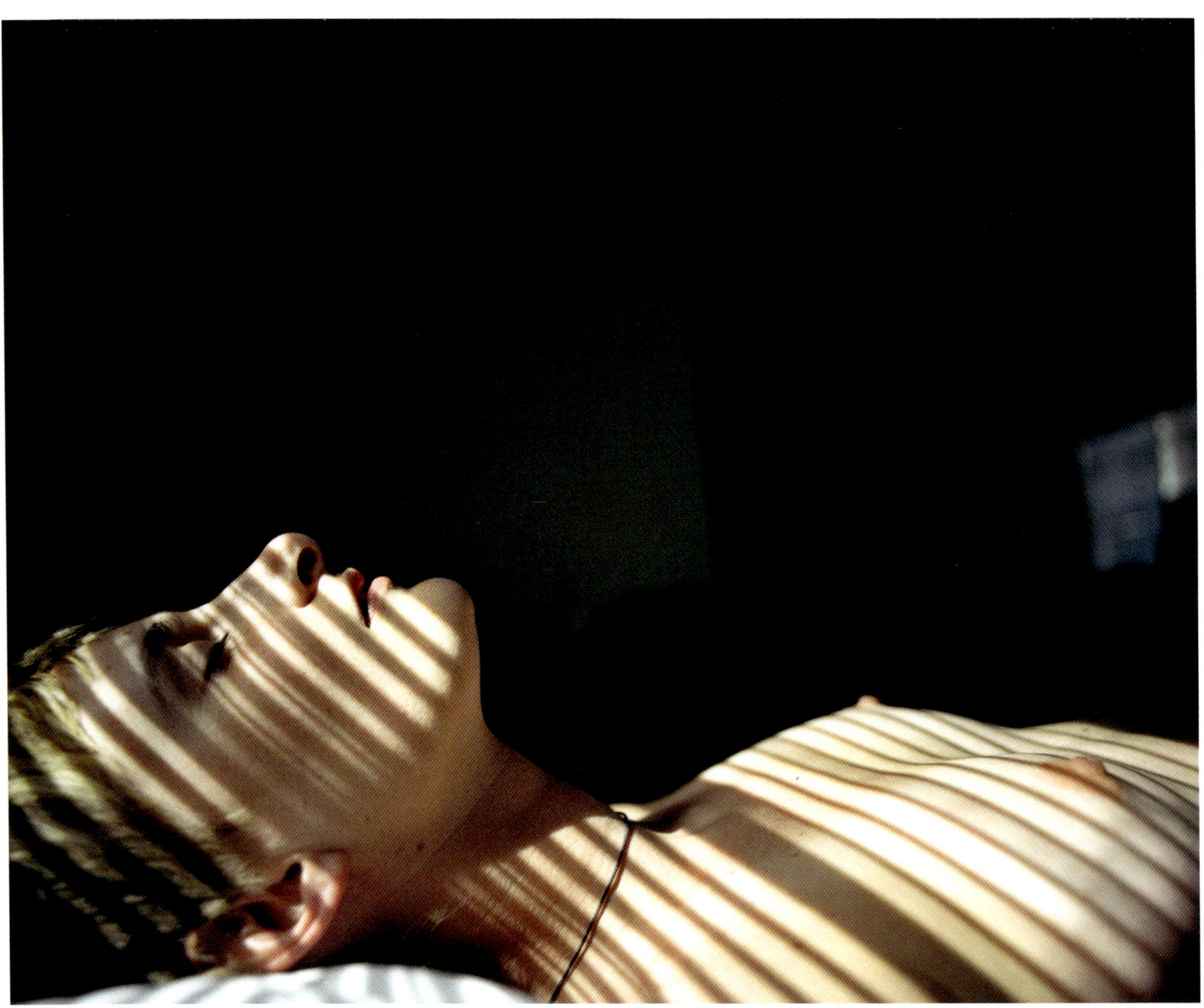

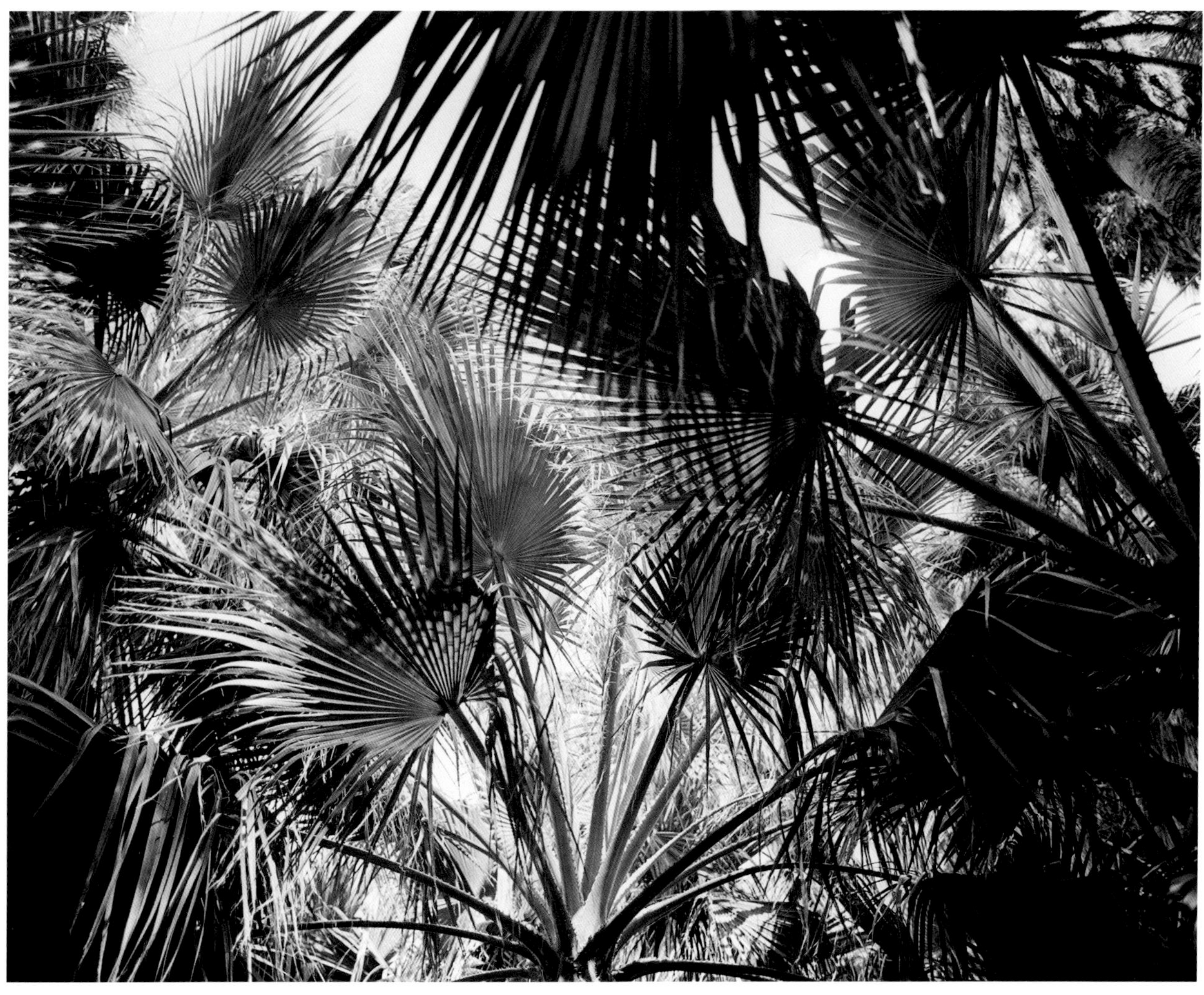

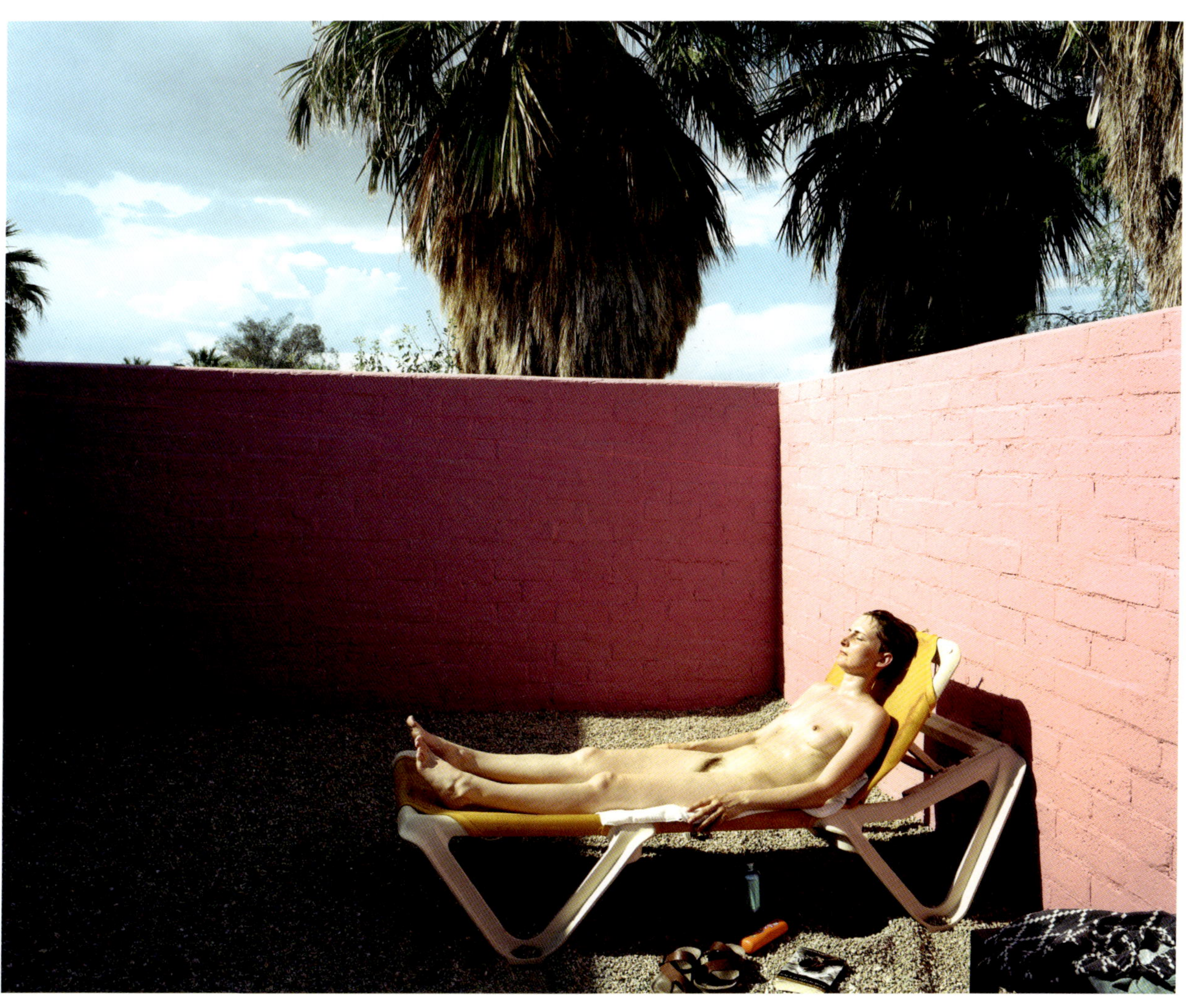

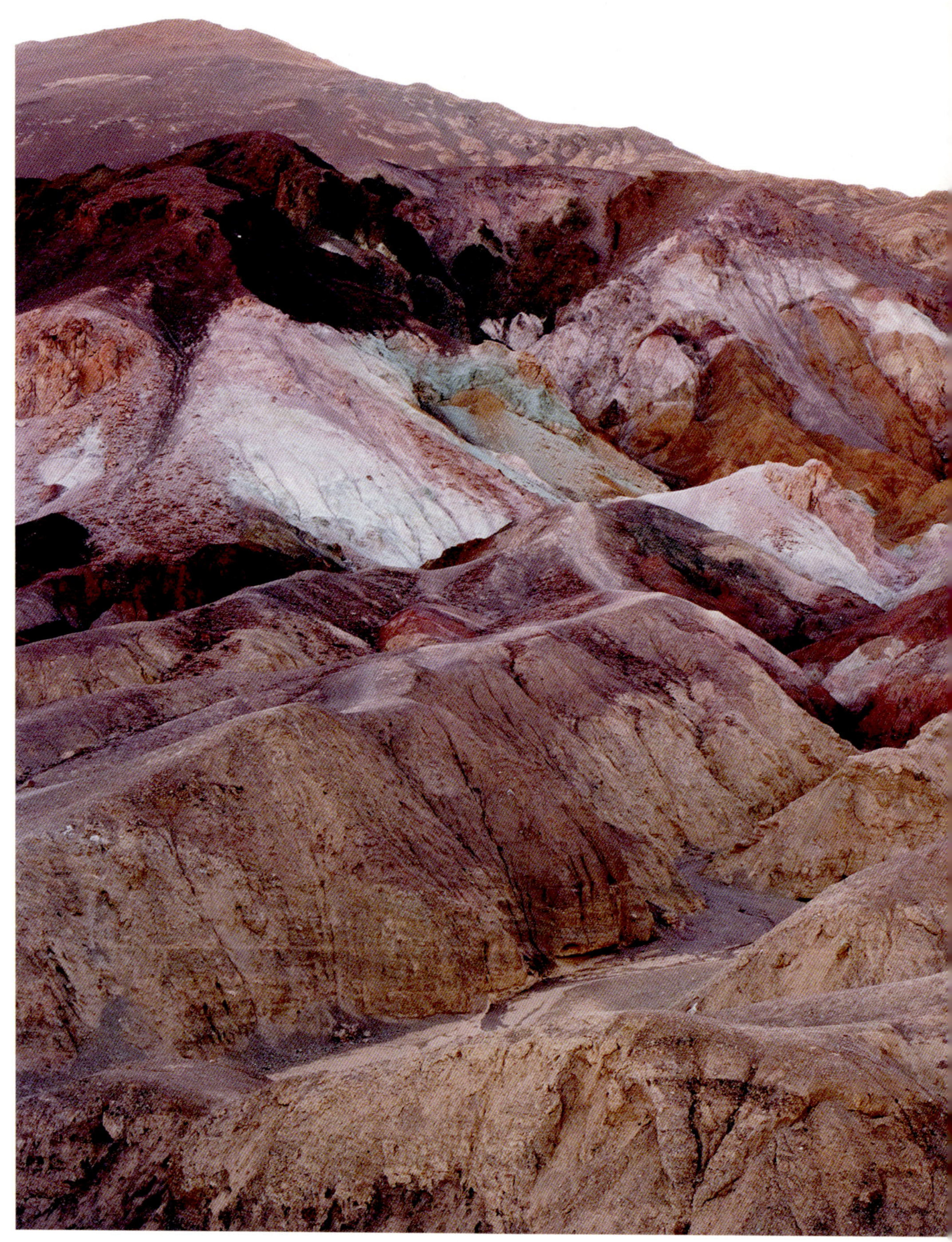

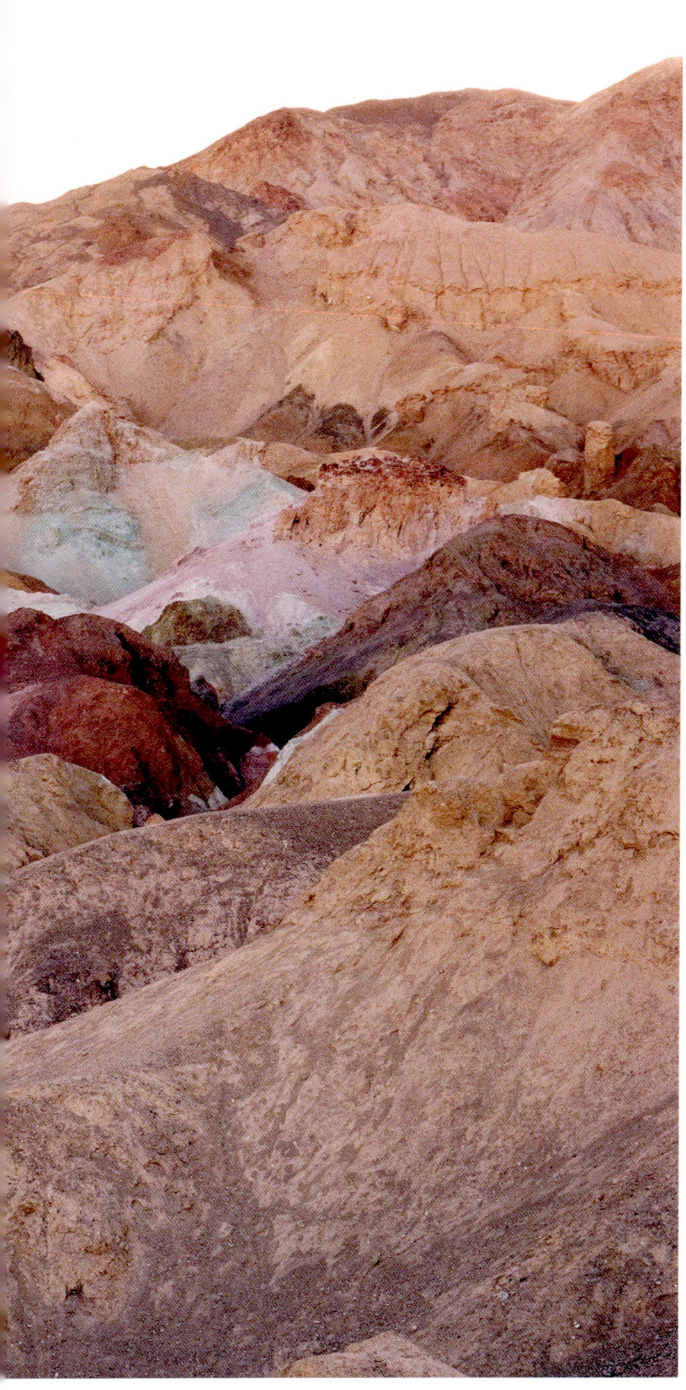

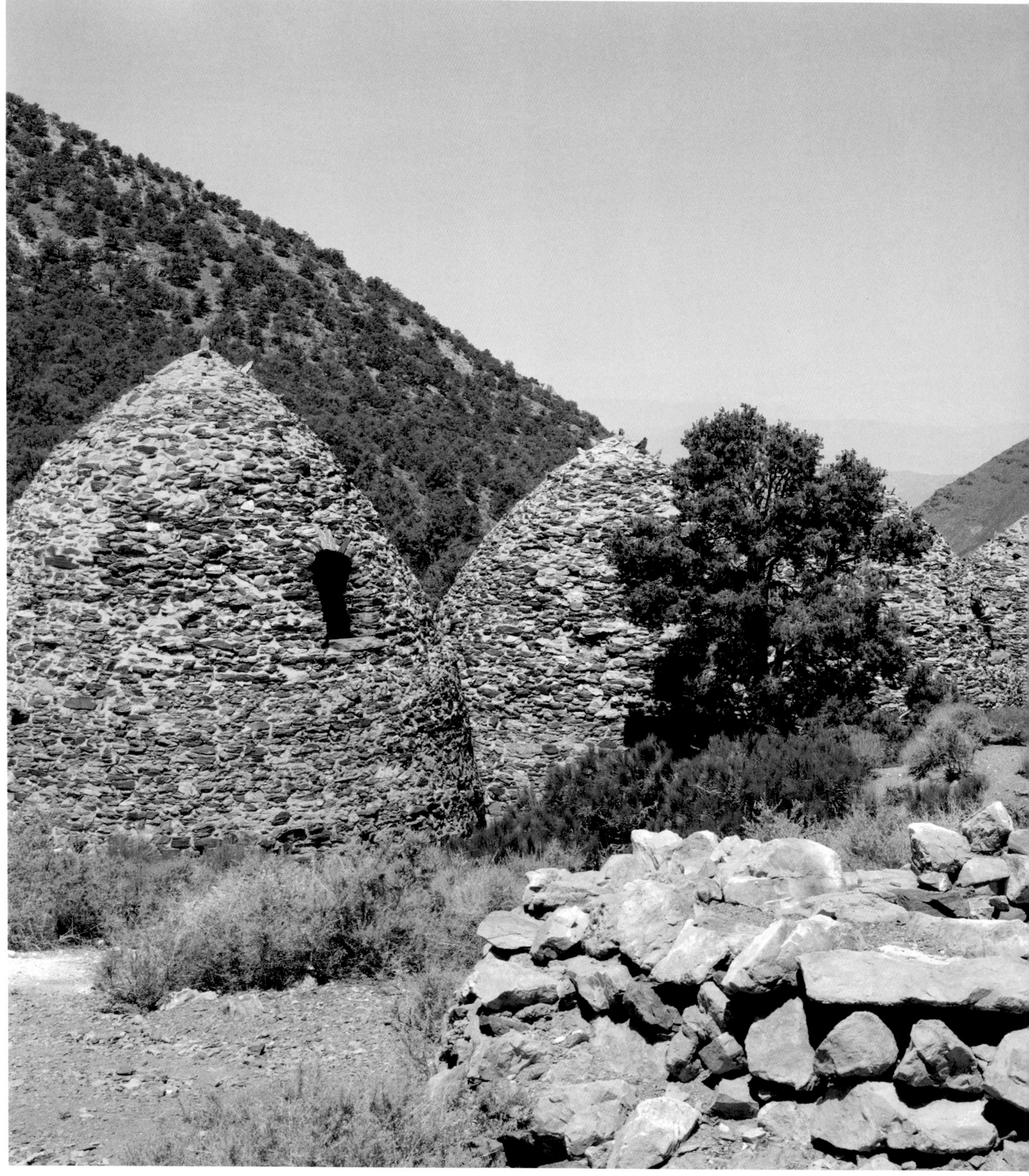

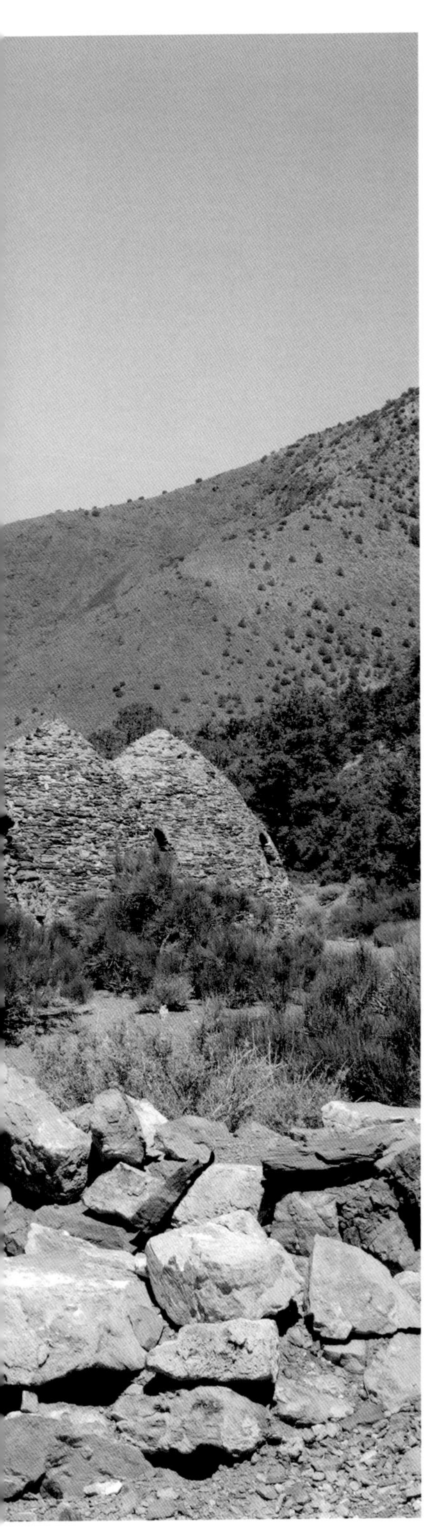

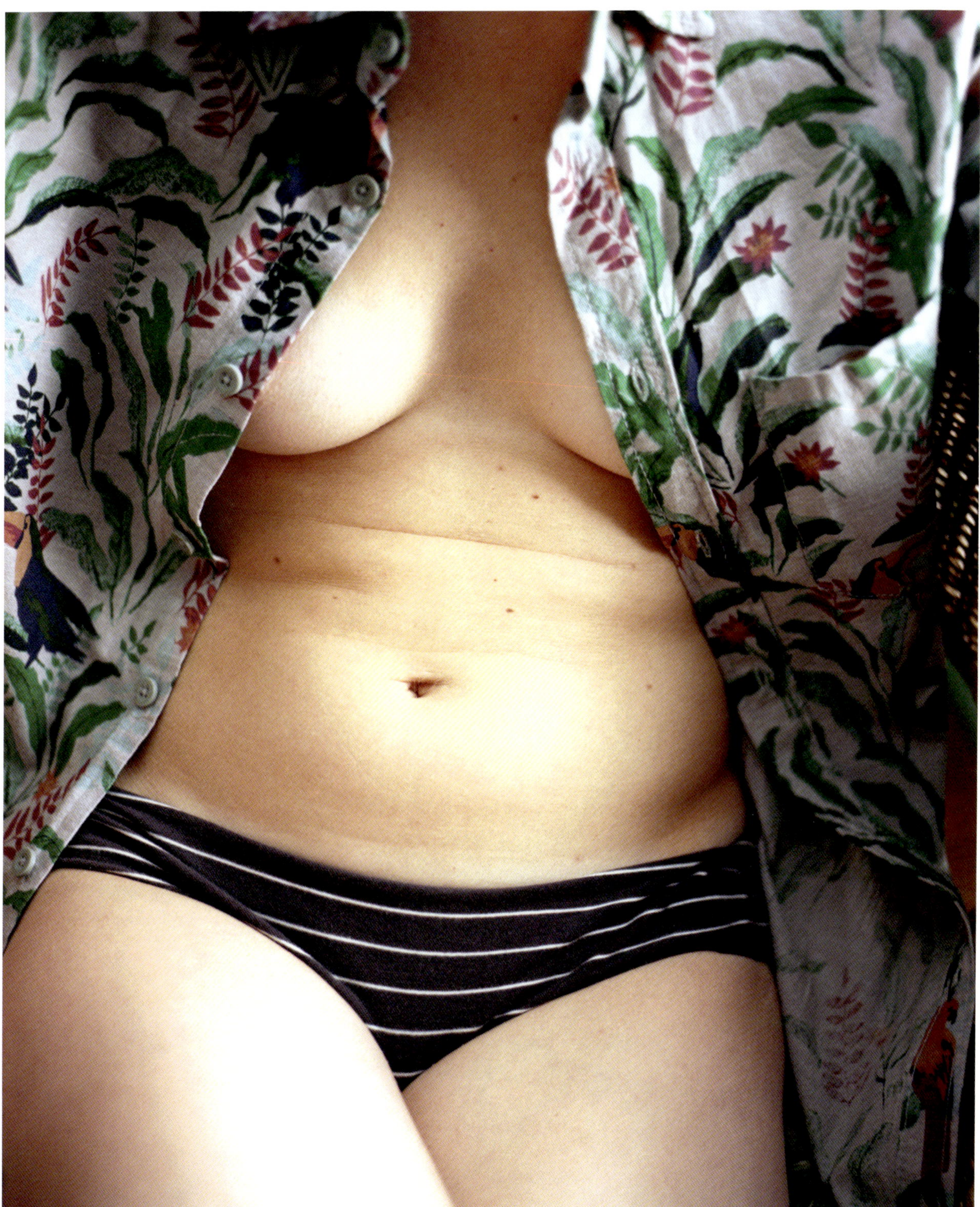

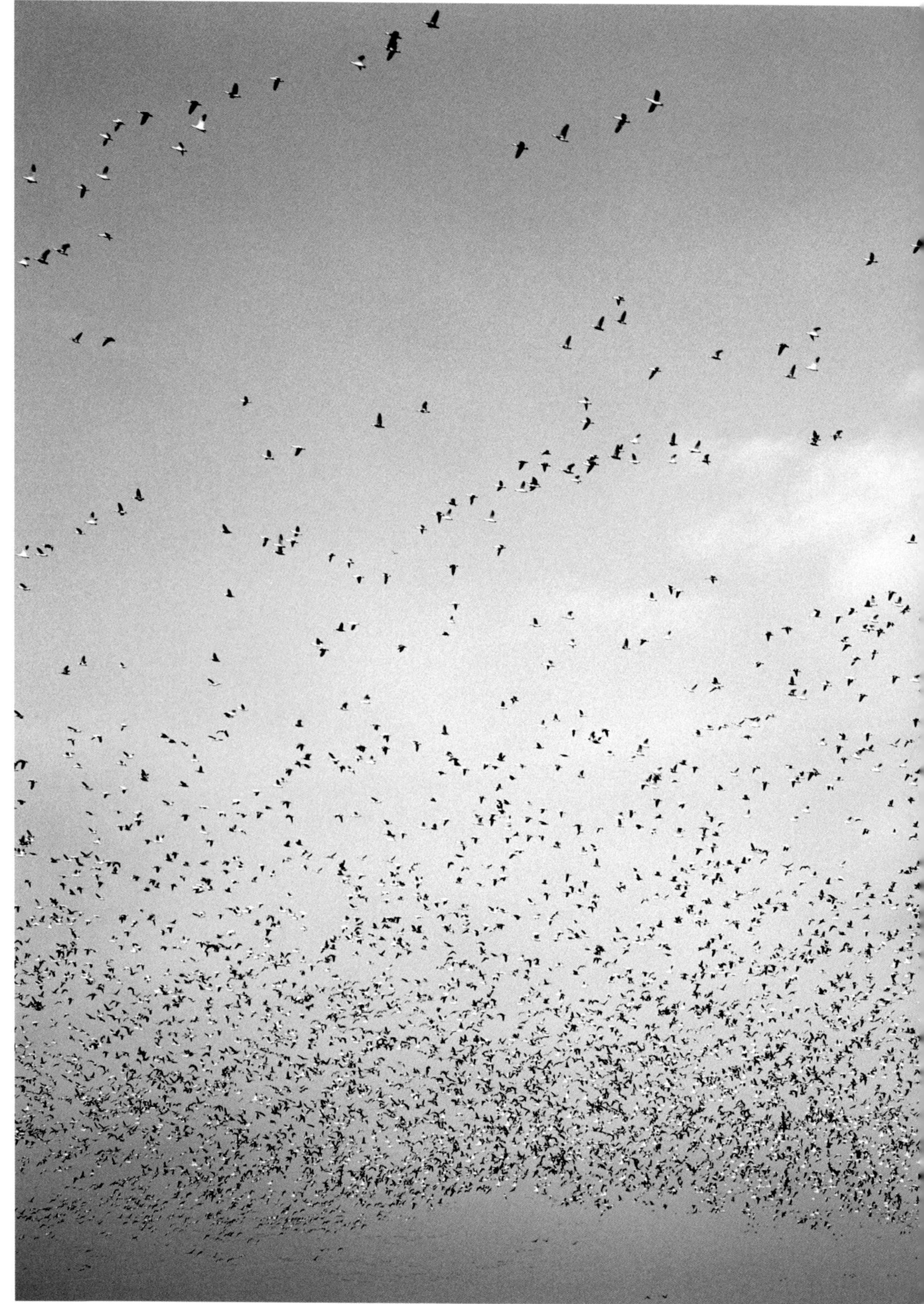

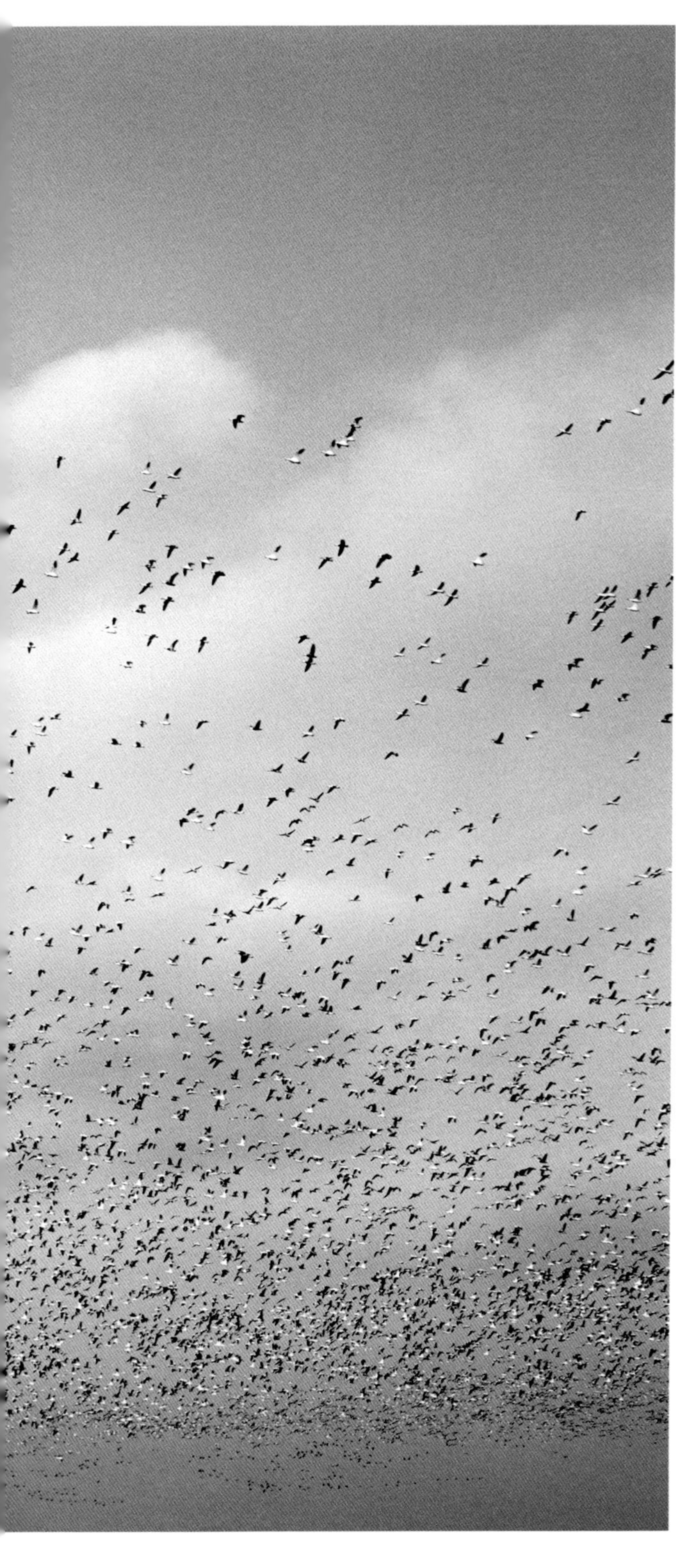

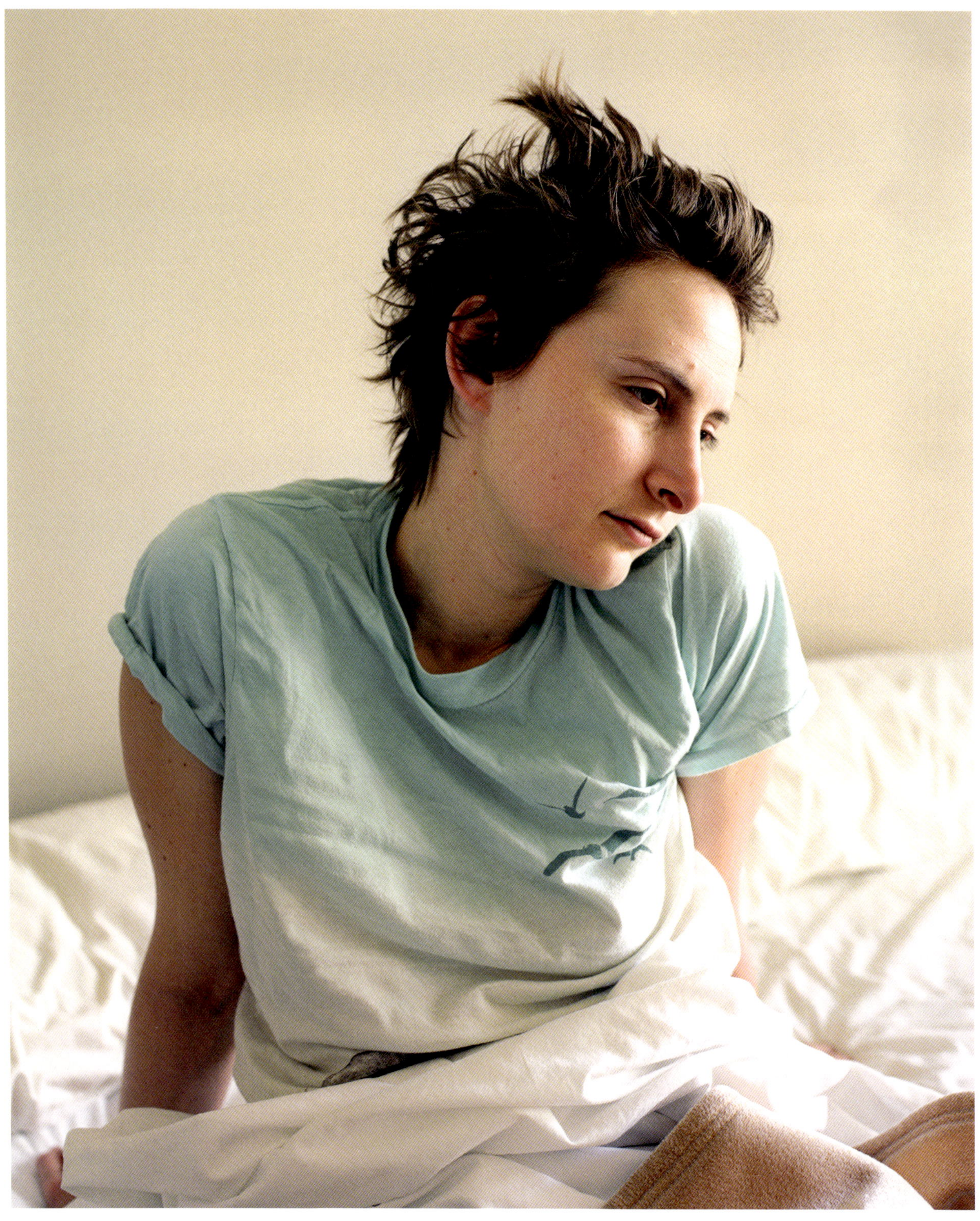

As we drive north on US 395, clouds hover over the Sierra Nevada with enough distance between them for the sun's rays to extend long arms of light toward the fields below. We pull over at the Still Life Café in Big Pine for lunch. I tell Bets about when Charis, Edward, and a group of friends stopped in nearby Lone Pine so Edward could use a darkroom. Back then, some inns were equipped with darkrooms for dedicated photographers and hobbyists. I also recount a story about Charis ordering a strawberry milkshake at a bar and the bartender obliging by serving it in a beer stein. An instant craving prompts Bets to order her own milkshake for the road.

     We arrive at Tamarack Lodge as the last light retires behind Mammoth Mountain. The air is crisp and smells of pine needles; it's fifty degrees cooler than the temperatures we experienced in the desert. In the parking lot, with goosebumps on my arms, I rummage through my suitcase for a sweater. When I turn around, I see Betsy by the car's open hatchback with practically all of our things loaded on her body: two backpacks, a tote bag full of food, a camera bag, my purse, the cooler, and a suitcase. "Do you need some help?" I offer as she rushes up the gravel drive. She has made it up the dozen steps to the lodge when her legs begin to shake, threatening to buckle under the weight of our belongings. I grab the suitcase and our room key and rush past her to open the door. We both marvel at the human tendency to attempt a single and unreasonable feat of strength simply to avoid

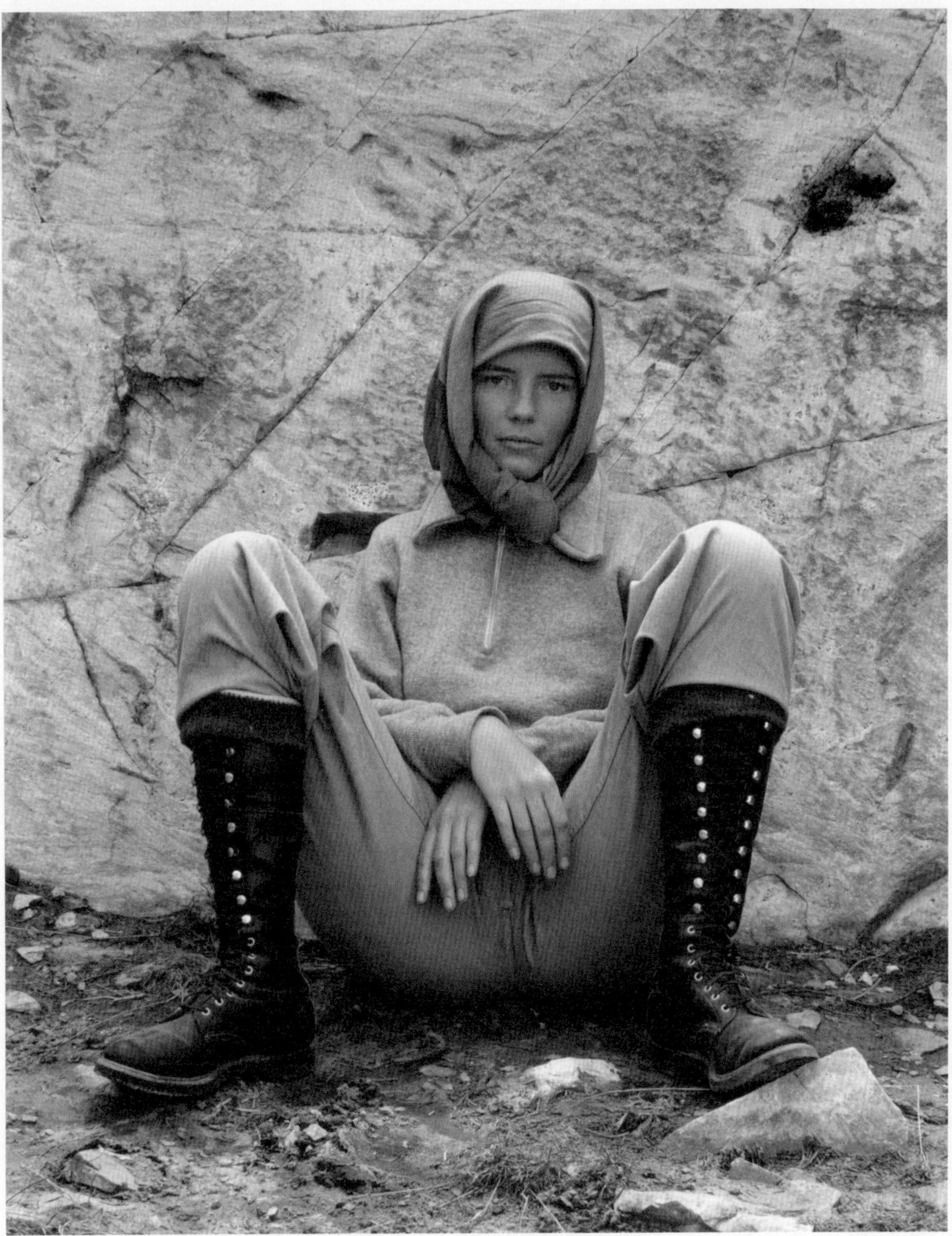

Edward Weston
*Charis, Lake
Ediza*, 1937

a second trip to the car. We hurtle up two narrow flights of stairs, our laughter filling the stairwell, until we finally collapse on the bed to catch our breath.

Our room is cozy with knotty-pine paneling on the walls and ceiling. The bed is covered with a quilted blanket of bears and trees, a theme matched by a painting of a bear and her cubs on the wall above the headboard. A framed Mammoth Mountain ski trail map from the 1980s is the only other decoration in the room. Slight pings and hissing noises come from the steam heat rising through the vents along the floorboards, as the wind above Twin Lakes, directly across from the lodge, begins to howl.

We unpack our things and then re-pack our backpacks for the fourteen-mile roundtrip hike to Lake Ediza. In my backpack are a camera, film and film holders, a light meter, photocopies of the pictures Edward made on their trip, two rain jackets, sunglasses, a liter of water, and my cellphone. The tripod is attached to the outside of Betsy's backpack. Inside, she has packed her phone, a flashlight, a mirror, a whistle, a miniature first aid kit, a pocket knife, sunscreen, a bottle of Tylenol, her long-sleeved thermal shirt, my long-sleeved denim shirt, two bandanas, snacks, two liters of water, and a Gatorade. At my request, she also packs a lemon, in honor of Charis who used lemon juice as mosquito repellant on the Ediza trip, and jellybeans, in honor of Ansel Adams who believed that the only food necessary for outdoor excursions were coffee, bacon, flour, salt, sugar, jellybeans, and whiskey.

I have never hiked more than a couple of miles in one stretch and begin to worry about the difficulty of making it to Lake Ediza and back. I unpack some of the four-by-five film holders to save weight. I won't be able to make many exposures along the hike anyway. We will need enough time to locate the granite rock that Charis leaned against in *Charis, Lake Ediza*, 1937, the sole purpose of our hike.

Charis sits with her back against a granite facade—her legs make an elegant M, knees akimbo, heels pulled in close to her body. Charis's gaze is locked on us as if we are sitting directly across from her, conversationally close, intimately close. And she, in turn, is held by our intense gaze, through Edward's lens. Charis is wearing a scarf to protect herself from the mosquitos that are everywhere at Lake Ediza in late summer. The scarf that frames her face is middle gray in tone, in perfect balance with her light-colored sweater and pants and dark-colored boots. The toe of Charis's left boot rests on a triangular tip of rock. The prominent lines that cut across the granite divide the background into four sections, one that frames her head, one that frames her lower body, and two on the upper left and upper right that call attention to the textures, indentations, and striations of the rock itself.

Some people feel a thrill when being photographed. Others feel dread. Thrill-seekers are really good at knowing how to perform for the camera, how to put their best selves forward; they turn their head slightly to showcase the beauty mark on their cheek, to present their good side. They know how to smile their best smiles, mouths closed and curling at the edges or wide to show their teeth, or with only their eyes, just enough to win us over. They are relaxed and they are comfortable in their own skin.

It is Charis's expression, along with her gesture and dress, that makes this a portrait about her as a *person*. Previously, Charis had been photographed by Edward in a formal studio setting, performing for the camera as a model. Many of the early images of her are simply titled *Nude*. In those images, Edward cropped in close with the camera, focusing on

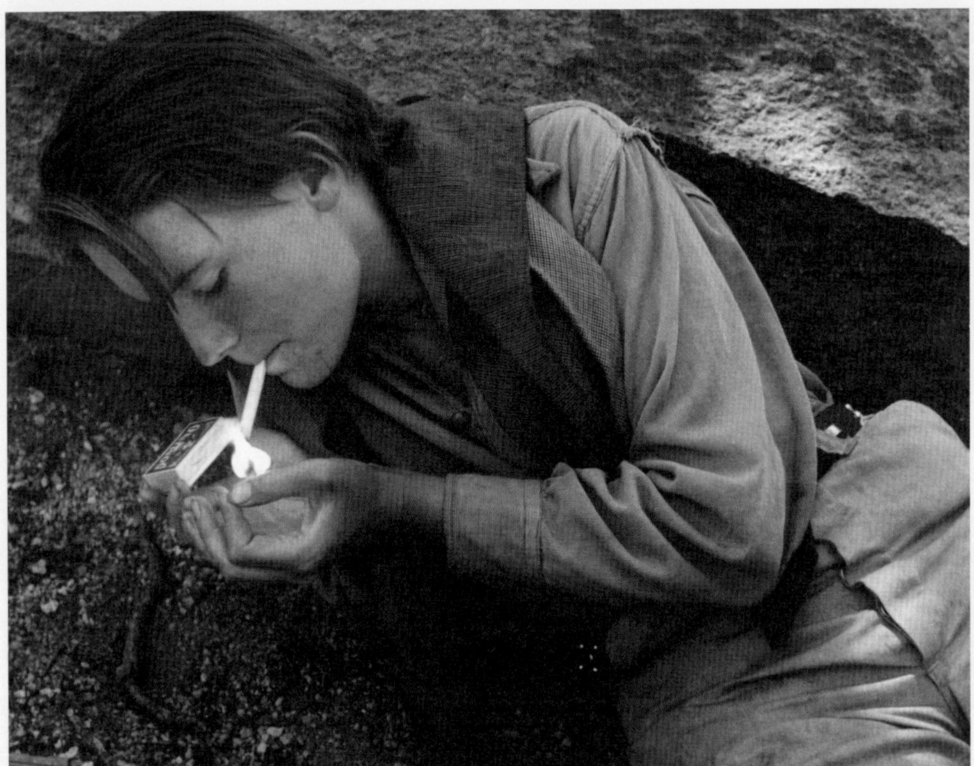

the form of her body, creating photographs that he believed had a universal appeal because of their anonymity. If there is a performance in *Charis, Lake Ediza*, it is that of Charis being herself in relation to Edward. This is one of the first photographs of Charis that was published in a book or shown in an exhibition that used her name in the title; it is a document of a specific person in a specific time and place. Charis Wilson. July 22, 1937. Lake Ediza.

This was the first time he had turned his camera on Charis during their travels for *California and the West*. She speculates that this was because of her short haircut:

> *I caused a minor trauma when I asked Edward to crop off my hair to simplify our life on the road. As he cautiously removed half an inch at a time I kept insisting "More! More!" In retrospect I see that this was a difficult act for him to carry out. His December 1934 Daybook entry describes me with "golden brown hair to shoulders," suggesting my aesthetic appeal. Edward didn't want me looking like a boy with sawed-off locks. It may even explain why he made so few pictures of me during the Guggenheim trips—he did only one in the first eight months, and then my head was covered by a scarf. However, I think a more likely explanation is that he was thrilled to be doing new work in new places and it made no sense to spend time on a subject he could just as well photograph at home.*[23]

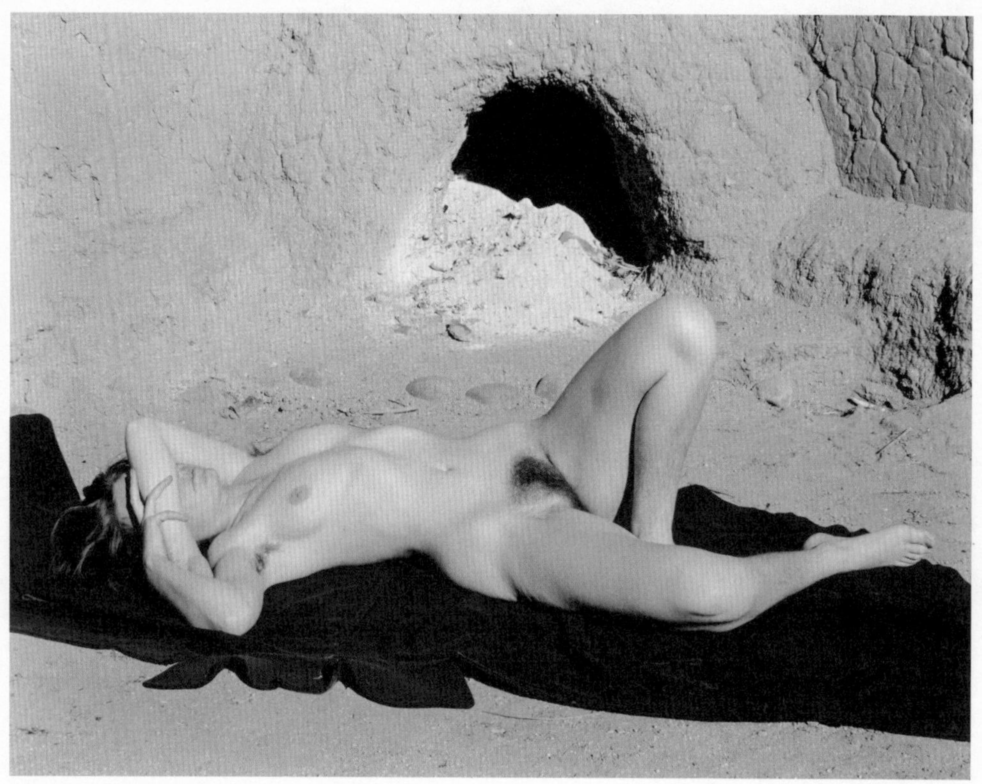

One of my favorite pictures of Charis was taken at Devil's Postpile, made while on the same trip to Lake Ediza, by Ansel Adams. Her short hair is slicked back. She looks handsome in the men's clothes she is wearing. She leans on her side and cups her hands to block the wind to light her cigarette. Here, she is a heartthrob. This image is an interesting comparison to the more overtly sensual depictions we are offered by Edward's lens. Charis included this image in her memoir; every time I flip to see it, I swoon. Charis's ease, not only in front of Ansel's lens but in herself as a woman, is evident. She was free to cut her hair short, wear men's clothing, smoke, and earn a living (or try to), despite the conventional expectations for women in those days.

Flipping through Ansel's contact sheets at the Center for Creative Photography a few months before our trip, I was pleasantly surprised to learn more about Ansel's relationship to both Charis and Edward through a series of pictures. In addition to his large-format camera, Ansel had brought along a 35 mm Contax camera. He made a photograph of Edward nude by the edge of a stream, posing like a Greek statue, and another one of Edward wearing a goofy expression as well as a scarf underneath his hat, double indemnity for fighting off mosquitos. He photographed Charis and Edward making their way up an incline in knee-deep snow, and Charis and Ron Partridge, Ansel's assistant, lying on their bellies to watch a group of chipmunks put on a show, a tree trunk as their stage. And he photographed Charis a lot. He photographed her peeking out of the tent, her smile gentle and open. He also photographed her in a striking sequence of frames that depicts her as chameleon-like: melancholic, flirtatious, graceful, tomboyish.

After we finish packing, I lie on the bed looking over Charis's descriptions of the Ediza hike for any clues that could lead us closer to the places she once had been. I drift to sleep with her voice in my head.

———————————

Edward photographed Charis on only one other occasion during their Western travels. Charis and Edward "celebrated New Year's Eve by heating buckets of water and bathing in front of a roaring fire at the 150-year-old adobe house in Albuquerque where [their] painter friend Willard Nash was staying. Earlier in the day, Edward had made the only nudes of the Guggenheim."[24] He had found Charis sunbathing in the courtyard, her arms raised, eyes shielded from the sun. Her pose is natural, arranged for comfort on an uncomfortable surface. Charis is lying on Edward's old black cape, the one he wore during his bohemian days in Carmel and in Mexico with Tina Modotti, the one Tina had laid on to be photographed. For Charis and Edward, "the old black cape from those days was too useful to have been stored away. It served as a dustcover for whatever was packed in the trunk of the car, a foot warmer on cold nights, a picnic cloth for al fresco dining, and a blanket for sunbathing."[25]

Edward took four negatives of Charis sunbathing on the cape. In the first three, the cape's unruly shadow merges with Charis's, as the sun, high in the sky, beats down on her. Each of the images he took that day creates a relationship between her body and the adobe fireplace behind her, with its cracking and dry surface a textural contrast to Charis's soft skin. In the fourth image, we see Charis in Edward's black cape as she leans against the adobe fireplace. The cape is two sizes too big for her, and two decades too old. This image is the only one in which her boyish haircut is visible; as she leans forward, a curl lies against her right cheekbone.

———————————

We arrive at the trailhead to find a glittery mist hovering over Agnew Meadow. A blanket of dew covers the ground. Coyotes howl in the near distance. Bets soon finds us a pair of hiking sticks, a "bear whipper" for her and an enchanted "blazing staff" with a curled handle for me. We take cellphone pictures of each other standing next to a sign that reads Ansel Adams Wilderness, so that I can digitally combine the two images of us together later. I think about Edward and Ansel's disdain for combination printing and smile as Betsy takes my picture.

Carrying camera equipment for the entirety of the trip is going to be a challenge. Charis and Edward, Ansel, Ron Partridge, and two rock climbers had mules to carry their

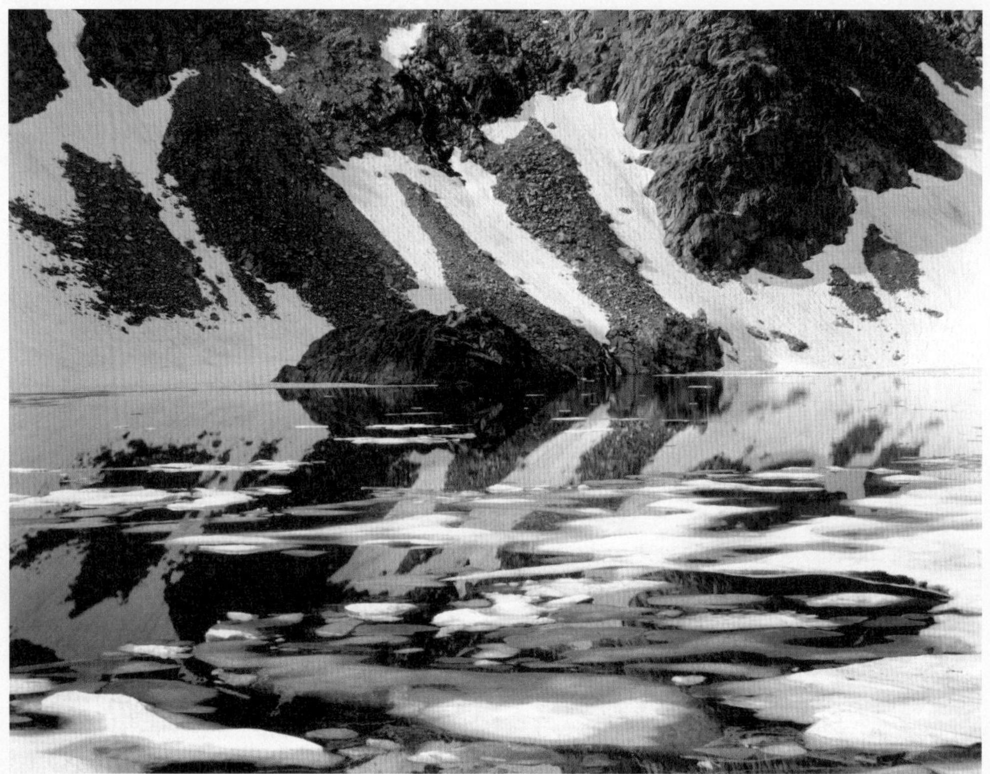

equipment and supplies. Even with this extra help, Charis had a hard time hiking to Ediza because of the altitude, she "struggled and gasped so obviously that Ron got behind me to push, while Edward went up the mountain with no trouble at all. By the time I reached Lake Ediza, I was exhausted, and stayed that way for the rest of the week."[26] A little of Charis's exhaustion might have been caused by the hangover she had from a party at Ansel and Virginia's house in Yosemite the night before. I wished that Betsy and I had a mule.

Our hike to Lake Ediza is a fourteen-mile quest to find evidence of another time, another trip, another couple. We wade through the thigh-high grass on the meadow, moving briskly through blue shadows, watching as the light slides down the mountainsides promising us its warmth. For seven miles, we wander through the woods, up and down trails that narrow and turn. We are looking for a place of apparent insignificance. A boulder. A backdrop. A setting for a portrait.

As we climb Shadow Creek Trail, we encounter many of the same spectacular views that Charis and Edward did, of the San Joaquin River Valley and Volcanic Ridge, and the waterfalls and lakes along the way. We pass a coriander-colored pine, dead and beautiful, its brittle branch skirt shedding needles on the ground. We examine the Anderson's thistle, Bigelow's sneezeweed, Mountain pride, and false hellebores that line the trail. Charis had learned the names of wildflowers from her mother, Helen, and made note of the varieties to use later in *Westways Magazine* or *California and the West*. "I still like the idea of being able to name my surroundings; to know the name of something is to see it more clearly,"[27] she writes in *Through Another Lens*.

Edward was known for his still lifes of peppers and shells, as well as the nudes and commercial portraits he made to subsidize his art practice, but he had made relatively few landscapes. I had not thought of Edward as a landscape photographer before I began chasing the pictures he made when he was with Charis, but I was beginning to appreciate his evolving interests, for mine were evolving too.

When we finally reach Lake Ediza, it is more beautiful than we thought possible. The lake is crystal clear. Flowers in bright hues dress up the base of boulders. We find a place to rest among granite rocks that shield us from the wind. I stand behind Betsy, resting my chin on her shoulder. She smells of salt, sweet sweat, and sunshine. I scan the circumference of the lake for signs of the campsite where Charis, Edward, Ansel, Ron, and the two rock climbers stayed.

> *We were camped in a fringe of hemlocks at the edge of a terrace that overhangs the south end of Lake Ediza. The grassy smoothness of the terrace is broken here and there by heaps of polished granite and cut by a dozen meandering little streams that join in groups for the rush down hill. Volcanic Ridge, a dark forbidding mass, closes off the east; south, the Minarets—a line of jagged black spires, patched with snow that looks like cut-out bits of paper—tower in the sky; to the west Mt. Ritter and Banner Peak, both around thirteen thousand feet—story-book mountains, neatly cut triangular masses of snow and rock. Only northward the views open out; above the lake and the wall of forest and cliff that shuts it in, we can look away over miles of curving mountaintops whose outlines grow softer and softer in the distance.*[28]

The six of them slept in a tent built for two and drank hot toddies during the afternoon rains. They "took turns assembling meals, although Ron and Ansel did more than the rest of us. It didn't occur to me that, as I was the only female, some of the others might have expected that I would perform domestic wonders in camp. Edward and I were so balanced in this regard that it didn't matter what situation we were in, the pattern of shared labor held."[29] Edward had the challenge of unloading and reloading film.

> *For the first time on any trip he used up all the holders (made twenty-four negatives) in one day.… No gracious Heimy* [the name of the car that they bought for the Guggenheim travels] *to toss a tarpaulin over; only a silly little changing bag the very sight of which filled Edward with dismay. Lying prone on the floor of the tent, he plunged into this mockery up to his elbows.*

The bag had been designed for something a good deal smaller than 8x10 holders; there wasn't space enough in it to shake hands with yourself and maintain any semblance of cordiality. Edward did one holder at a time, closing the film box each time so we could open the bottom of the bag, eject the empty holder and pass in a fresh one. He was muttering profanity, each moment assuring me, "Now that one's scratched." It took so long to get even the unloading done that Ansel volunteered for the reloading, saying he was an old hand at this and could do it in half the time. Having put his neck out, he got the job every night thereafter.[30]

We have about two hours before we need to begin our descent back to Agnew Meadow. We walk along a trail that hugs the edge of the lake. There are plenty of granite boulders, but none of them look like the boulder in the image. The granite switchbacks we had hiked before reaching Lake Ediza were stronger contenders than any of these rocks. We begin walking up the trail to Iceberg Lake, to trace Charis's path, looking for the slightest clue. Based on Charis's description, the place we were hoping to find was located somewhere between Lake Ediza and Iceberg Lake.

My heart told me we had climbed another thousand feet and I was thinking up good reasons for returning to camp, but just in the nick of time, there it was; a little lake with cakes of ice and snow floating over its inky water; across it, rising steeply from the water's edge, the Clyde Minaret, exposing a diminutive glacier on its chest. Rich hunting grounds for Edward; he worked away like mad, on icebergs, lake, minarets, tree stumps, snow and rocks. A few hours passed and I was debating: should I give up my most sensible principle and become a photographer so I, too, could retire under a focusing cloth and be safe from armies of half-starved insects? As we sat on a rock by the lake to eat our odds and ends of lunch (including jellybeans), we watched a little red bird hopping over the floating ice cakes, pecking frozen insects—getting his lunch from the frigidaire just like city folks.

Edward set to work again, but now at each exposure he had to wait for a reluctant sun to come out of the clouds. The waits grew longer, and at last the sun went under for good. We started back to camp as the first faint rumblings of thunder came echoing up the peaks. Halfway down we encountered Ansel; we all disposed ourselves in a hollow of rocks for rest and talk. But Edward, as I say, doesn't know the meaning of the word. He instantly found a blasted triple-trunked pine with a smooth whiteness of snow beyond it that needed his attention, and when he could find nothing else to do he turned the camera on me, mosquito-rigging and all.[31]

The trail is narrow and the rocks are slippery from a nearby brook. Grasshoppers jump, bouncing off our legs, as they search for food. We are surrounded by granite slopes, any of which could have been the one Charis leaned against in the portrait. I pull out my photocopy of *Charis, Lake Ediza*. We agree to search for thirty more minutes and follow a trail on the north side of the lake as the clouds begin to build above us.

After a most diligent hunt, we fail to find the right spot. Backtracking along the trail, I see magenta mountain pride growing at the base of a large boulder. This is not where the picture of Charis was taken, but somehow I feel that Charis had been here. Often, as Ansel, Ron, and Edward photographed around the lake, Charis spent her time writing, sunbathing, or sleeping on the rocks. This rock has a large, flat surface easily heated by the sun, a perfect spot to lie down to sleep or read. I take a few portraits of Betsy. As each day passes, she's beginning to feel better and doesn't mind the attention of my camera.

It is 4:45 p.m. when we begin our descent. The granite staircase is steep. As time goes on, I feel like my legs will give out, and I imagine robot legs made of aluminum, a control box putting one leg before the other. My pace is excruciatingly slow. Near the Shadow Lake Trail Junction, Bets looks at me with concern and says, "Our goal is to get out of here before nightfall." I nod in agreement, noticing the seriousness of her tone. "It's going to be uncomfortable, but we have to troop through it," she adds. I take two Tylenol with a swig of water, and Bets moves some of the film holders from my backpack into hers.

The next two and a half miles are relatively flat, but then there's a steady ascent up the canyon to Agnew Meadow. I concentrate on the glow of the mountains ahead; the golden scene is slowly swallowed by shadows as they creep up the mountainsides. I think about the bottle of Gatorade we had left in the glove compartment of the car. We pass each landmark with relief, Shadow Lake, the dead pine among its lush neighbors, the Ansel Adams Wilderness sign. We can barely see the trail. It's 8:20 p.m. when we finally arrive back at Agnew Meadow. Bats flitter overhead. Bets and I take a rare selfie, our smiling faces barely lit in the twilight.

Before leaving Mammoth Lakes, we stop to buy food and supplies. "Can I buy a pack of cigarettes?" Bets asks. "It'll help my anxiety. We are on vacation. We'll only smoke this one pack," she bargains. Bets and I are on-and-off-again smokers; if one of us starts, the other soon follows. I think of the photographs that I could make of Betsy smoking. I relent, "Sure." Betsy runs inside as I wait, groggily looking out the window while taking note of how good my body feels even though my muscles are still sore from yesterday's hike. Remembering that we will need the cooler, I jump out of the car and open the hatch to find it buried beneath a mountain of our belongings. As I tug on the cooler's handle, the electric typewriter flies out of the car and strikes my shin before landing on the ground. I curse the thing because bringing the typewriter was only for nostalgia's sake, really. I could have typed on my laptop or written in my sketchbook. When Bets gets back with sundries, cigarettes, and ice, she finds me with my leg propped on the dash to minimize the throbbing. She quickly puts ice in a Ziploc bag, wraps the bag with paper towels, and places it over the goose egg growing on my shin. I hold the ice there until my leg goes numb.

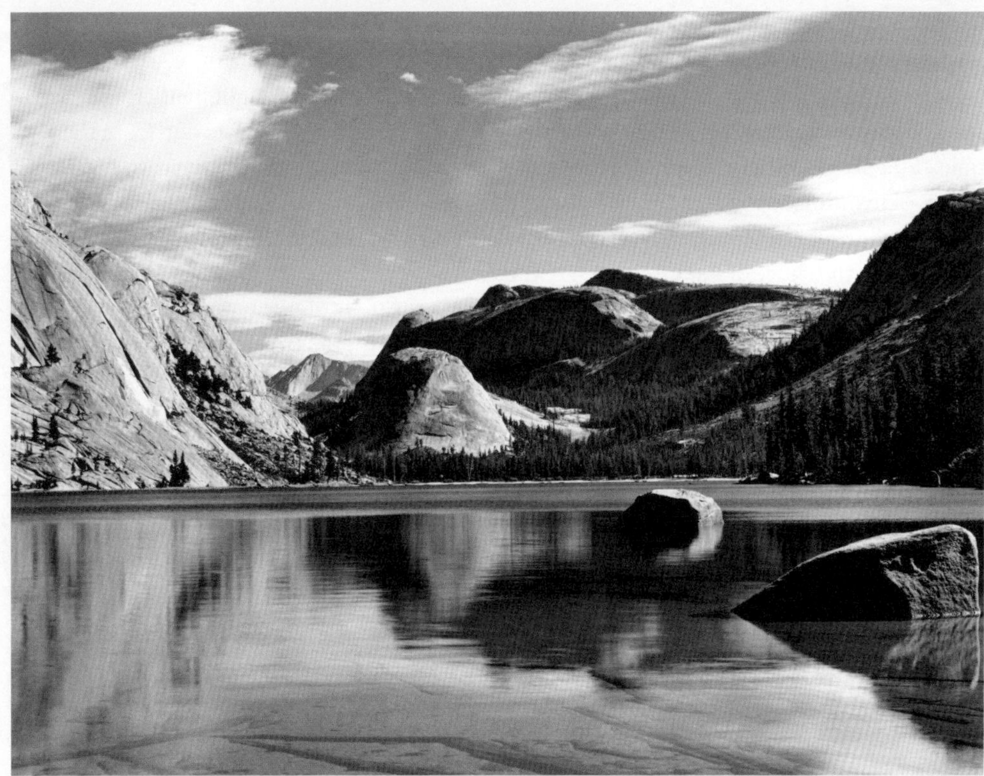

The drive to Lake Tenaya is less than sixty miles, twenty-five miles on US 395 and thirty miles on US 120, also known as Tioga Pass Road, which winds through Yosemite Valley and is the only connection between eastern and western California along a two-hundred-mile stretch of the southern Sierra Nevada. The pass is usually closed six months of the year, from the first snowfall in November to late spring.

Before entering the park, we decide to take a restroom break at a large travel center. In the bathroom, a young girl holds her wet hands under a dryer as her mom squeezes toothpaste onto a brightly colored toothbrush over a nearby sink. When the girl looks up and sees Betsy, with her short hair and boyish frame, she quickly runs to her mom and tugs the back of her shirt. I know where this is going and I watch as the mom, who looks startled for a second, looks up at Betsy, then at me, then back at Betsy again, before leaning down to quietly whisper something in her daughter's ear. I don't linger to see the girl's reaction and walk into the closest stall. When we climb back in the car, Betsy feels defeated and self-conscious.

We wait in line behind other cars, Airstream trailers, campervans, and RVs with Cruise America written on their side, until we finally pass through the entrance to Yosemite National Park. The towering, granite-covered mountains that first come into view are foreboding. The vertical angles of their facades are severe and imposing. I feel a sort of

89

instinctual sense of fear at the sight of them. There are no feminine adjectives to describe the scene, no undulating hills or soft mounds, no valleys opening before us. We pass Saddlebag Lake, and I say out loud, "That's my lake." Bets grabs my right haunch and says she loves my soft curves. We climb more than four thousand feet. My ears pop from the quick ascent. Mountains, their tops covered with snow, appear in the distance; they are sharp, demanding, proud. In Death Valley, we were surrounded by a vast emptiness. Here, it's as if we are about to be crushed by nature, the steep faces hemming us in on all sides.

On the shore of Lake Tenaya, I compare a copy of Edward's photograph with the scene in front of us. A granite dome across the lake is the main subject, pinned in place by granite hills. Two boulders play supporting roles as they emerge from the lake like stepping stones for a giant, leading our eyes toward the dome. In Edward's photograph, the clouds are thin and low and create the appearance of snow-covered mountains in the distance. The lake is calm, its glass-like surface reflecting the dome and hills.

On this summer day, a breeze ripples the water's surface as puffy clouds create the illusion that smoke signals are coming from directly behind the dome. I can tell that I am not standing in the right spot, so I take off my shoes and socks and wade into the icy water carrying my camera. I picture Charis wading out in the lake years ago for a morning swim that consisted of "a quarter-mile walk out to where the water was waist-deep, and a frozen-footed walk back."[32] She and Edward camped here for four days while he photographed the juniper trees.

> *Nights were sharply cold; days drowsily hot, except up on the mountain where a little breeze was always circulating. The few campers at the other end of the lake were screened off from us by trees and distance. Oh yes, this was the life—the life, and the place to live it. This was the desert island everyone dreams of, where existence is a poem and nature all benevolence. No radios or newspapers or watches, no buildings or telephones or mosquitos.*[33]

As I wipe gritty mud off the legs of the tripod, Bets and I are surprised to see a bundle of sage resting on a nearby rock. A thin red ribbon is wound around its leaves. The tips are charred. We wonder who smudged this spot, why they felt the need to cleanse or bless this place. "It's the Weston curse," Betsy jokes. I laugh and take the camera out to make a picture. But before I do, I hesitate. Taking the picture feels wrong—someone chose this place for a private ceremony. As I click the shutter, I remind myself that I don't believe in curses and unwanted spirits.

Back at the car, Betsy and I eat lunch together on a rock. We consider throwing away the film with the smudge stick, its latent image waiting for development. Photographers all too often feel the world is theirs, to hunt and capture. Taking souls, naming things. I later learn that there was indeed a curse put on Yosemite Valley, not by Edward Weston, but by Chief Tenaya, after whom this lake was named.

Yosemite Valley was known by the natives who lived here as Ahwahnee, or large gaping mouth. In 1849, the Ahwahneechee who lived along the western Sierra Nevada foothills became alarmed when miners looking for gold invaded their land. A war between the tribe and the miners ensued, leading to the Mariposa-Indian War. The federal Indian Commission convinced several tribes, some peacefully and some with force, to move to reservations. The Ahwahneechee, also known as the Yosemites, or grizzly bears, refused, retreating deep into the valley. The Mariposa Battalion was sent to find them, and it was then that white men first entered the valley. Chief Tenaya, the leader of the tribe, was captured on May 22, 1851. After hearing the news that one of his three sons was killed while trying to escape, Chief Tenaya is reported as saying:

> *Kill me, Sir Captain, yes, kill me as you killed my son, as you would kill my people if they were to come to you. You would kill all my tribe if you had the power. Yes, Sir America, you can now tell your warriors to kill the old chief. You have made my life dark with sorrow. You killed the child of my heart. Why not kill the father? But wait a little and when I am dead I will call my people to come and they shall hear me in their sleep and come to avenge the death of their chief and his son. Yes, Sir America, my spirit will make trouble for you and your people, as you have made trouble to me and my people. With the wizards I will follow the white people and make them fear me. You may kill me, Sir Captain, but you shall not live in peace. I will follow in your footsteps. I will not leave my home, but be with the spirits among the rocks, the waterfalls, in the rivers and in the winds; wherever you go I will be with you. You will not see me but you will fear the spirit of the old chief and grow cold. The Great Spirit has spoken. I am done.*[34]

Lafayette Bunnell of the Mariposa Battalion renamed this place Lake Tenaya, even though the Chief insisted that the lake already had a name, Pyweak, or Lake of the Shining Rocks.

———————————

Camping is no longer allowed on the shores of the lake as it was in 1937. Bets and I check into Tuolumne Meadows Campground, a few miles up Tioga Pass Road. We put our food in a bear box near the parking lot, our toiletries in a bear box near the bathroom, and the rest of our belongings in a wheelbarrow that we push to our cabin, which has a white canvas roof and sides, a concrete floor, and a green door with the number 51 stenciled on it in white paint. Inside is a wood-burning stove, a bucket of wood, and our choice of four twin-sized beds. A cold night is forecast, so seeing that each bed comes with two wool blankets, we choose to sleep at the back of the cabin with the wood stove nestled between us. Towels, washcloths, cups, a plastic carafe, a Tuolumne Meadows matchbook, and a brochure about the hantavirus sits on top of a folding card table in the middle of the tent. A laminated poster with more information about the virus is located on the wall next to the stove. I secretly survey our canvas walls and assess the likelihood of a bear trying to rip through them.

The last night of their stay on the shores of Lake Tenaya, Charis was woken up by Edward roaring fiercely at bears who were growling outside of their tent. Everything looks pretty safe, and it seems like our greatest chance of encountering a bear will be on the walk to the bathroom in the middle of the night.

We eat dinner at the Tuolumne Meadows Lodge, where we sit at a round table with other campers. After only talking to each other for several days, Betsy and I feel awkward. The conversation has an uncomfortable air as we share where we are from (California except for me and Bets) and what our occupations are. We are all teachers of some sort except for an older gentleman, who tells us about his sailing trips to exotic locales. Bets orders a glass of wine, which we share between snippets of small talk.

When we get back to our cabin, Bets puts a fire starter and two logs in the stove and lights a match from the Tuolumne Meadows matchbook. The heat fills our room so completely that we consider sleeping in the nude. Bets falls asleep underneath a window flap she has lifted to release some of the intense heat. A single sheet is pulled up just enough to cover her hips. Bets has been more relaxed over the past few days. Her anxiety has begun to subside. Ansel Adams often talked about the power of nature to improve mental health. I watch the orange glow from the stove move across the floor, flickering wildly. The embers burn quietly down until their glow fades from sight.

The next morning, we drive back to Lake Tenaya and sit in the car for a few minutes discussing where we think the junipers in Edward's photographs might be. We cross Tioga Road and walk through pine trees until we come to a clearing where granite shelves rise forming a modest hill.

For hours, we climb in search of the junipers. Some of Edward's most recognized photographs are of these trees. As we scale the steep granite slope, I think of Charis and Edward.

> *All day we climbed cautiously up and down the slick rocks, passing the camera and case back and forth, as one or the other of us achieved a securer vantage point. Late in the afternoon we limped into camp, exhausted from the hazardous climbing, maddened by the spectacle of beautiful junipers always above us, unreachable. A reviving swim in the lake, a hot supper, a long sleep; next morning we took up the search with renewed vigor. Almost at once we found what we were looking for: an old truck trail leading back to the base of a cliff where the climb was broken into comparatively easy stages, with at least one good juniper on every shelf.*[35]

Ansel had photographed many landscapes in Yosemite, and Edward laid claim to his own territory by focusing his efforts on the twisted trunks of these resilient trees. In Edward's photographs of natural forms, they are often made monumental and seem to metamorphose into something humanlike. The trees look frozen in a twisted reach or sensual grasp. He vehemently denied this, professing that what he captured was the true

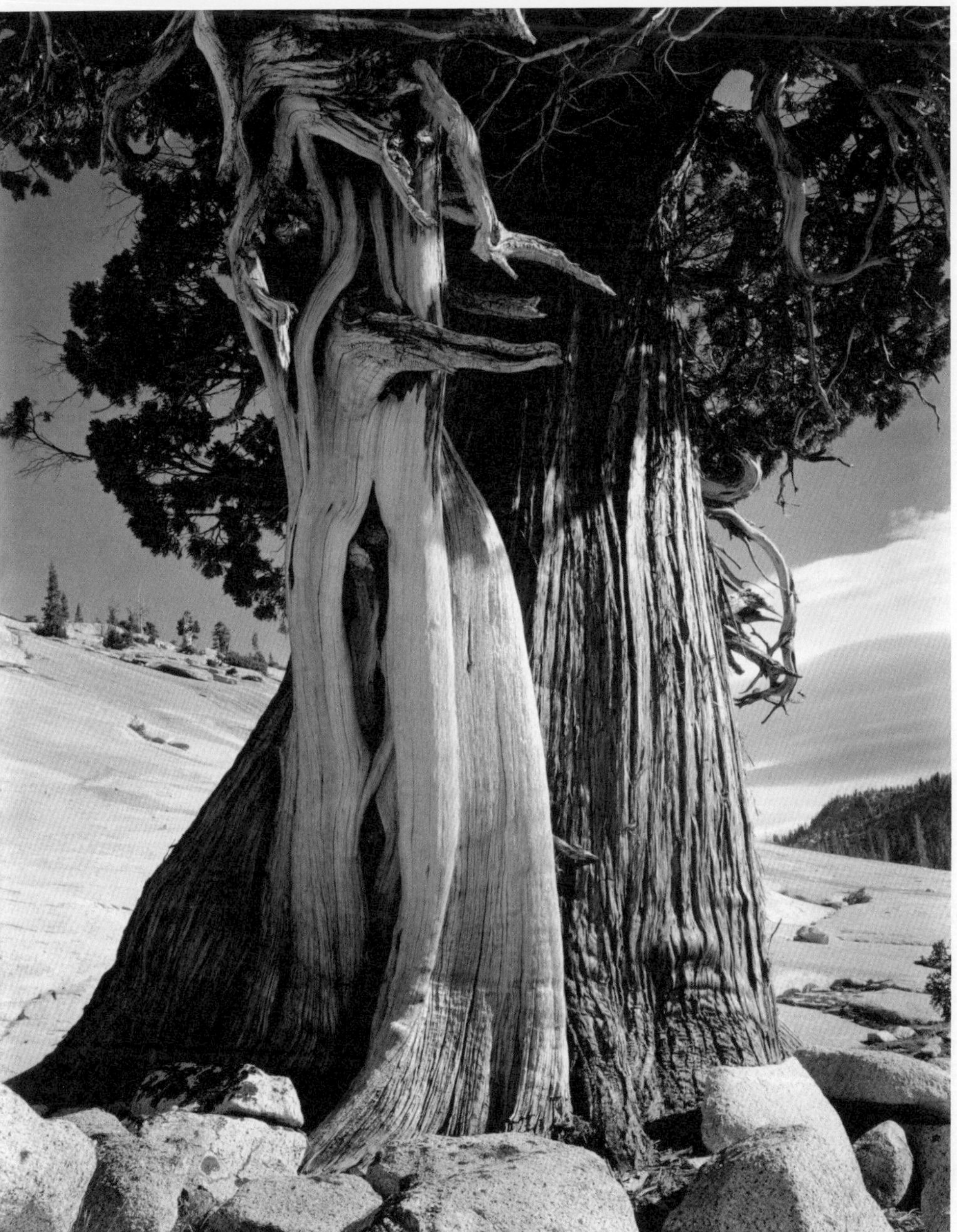

Edward Weston
Juniper, Lake Tenaya,
1937

93

essence of the thing itself. I even wondered if Edward, who was so awake in his sexuality, was subconsciously searching for the erotic. But as we climb, I realize that anthropomorphizing the junipers is inevitable. We pass trunks of junipers that look like torsos, others with arms raised high, and an intertwined couple in a tangle of rough wood.

Halfway up the hill, we discover a twelve-foot granite crevice lined with bright pink flowers that we see as a woman in repose. We stare in disbelief; it's as if we have found the vagina from which all nature was birthed. "Arbus Vaginalis," Betsy offers. I photograph the scene and feel as if I'm photographing something obscene, which is crazy, because it's of summer flowers growing in the intersection of two granite plates.

I had been calling the junipers "vagina trees" in honor of the most famous junipers that Edward photographed. In his image, the trees look like a couple locked in an embrace: the broader and sturdier of the two presses against the slenderer one, its vagina-shaped trunk complete with a clitoris at the top. Edward made thirty-four negatives of nine different trees, and out of the compositions made of these two trees he wrote "favorite" on the back of this image.

We hop across granite cracks large enough to swallow us and see wildflowers in what looks like places too harsh for life to thrive. Water trickles down between the granite slopes and pools for birds to bathe in and for marmots to drink. I find a feather on the ground that reminds me of my dad.

We are high enough now to see Lake Tenaya from above. The sun shimmers off its surface, glinting. I understand now why Pyweak is the perfect name for this lake. I stop frequently to look at reference images, match horizon lines and slopes of hills with the view I hold in my hands. I check an email exchange between two photographers, Mark Klett and Byron Wolfe, who made a piece entitled *Above Lake Tenaya, Connecting Views from Edward Weston to Eadweard Muybridge*. Their image, which was made in 2001, links the junipers I am seeking from Edward's 1937 photograph with an image Muybridge made in 1872. They've included a Google Earth image with two pins—one pin based on memory, the other, on plausibility. There is also a friendly back and forth between them about their recollections of finding the junipers. Memory is a strange thing, and each of them remembers the trees being in a different location. Charis, too, found the junipers again in 1982 when she was working on her memoir. She "was amazed to see that hardly a twig had changed in forty-five years."[36]

We walk apart from one another, Bets looking over a ridge or through some pines in one direction, and me in the other. We pass a few fallen junipers along the way, and I begin to wonder if the famous vagina trees are no longer standing. Junipers can live for thousands of years, but who knew how old they already were when Edward photographed them.

Then, off in the distance, I see two junipers close to one another. The more petite of the two trees leans at an unfamiliar angle, so at first, I don't believe that this is the pair we are seeking. But as I make my way to the other side of them, I know that these are the junipers in Edward's photograph.

While I move the camera here and there, two deer appear, as do two lizards who lie together, sunning themselves. In a flat area surrounded by rocks, I disappear under my black shroud and see upside down on the ground glass what Edward had seen so many years ago. In an intense rush, I have the sensation that I am standing in the exact place where he had stood. I could see him with his boundless energy jumping from here to there with his camera, framing the scene. I pictured Charis sitting nearby, eating fruit and nuts from the little pouch on her belt. And I envisioned them resting in the shade of this magnificent pair of trees and taking a siesta on the warm granite rocks nearby.

The junipers witnessed one of the most memorable and happy times in Charis and Edward's life together. As Charis would later write, "This was the highlight of all our travels. I would have been happy to spend a month swimming, sleeping, observing wildlife, scaling the granite fastnesses (to my limited capacity), and encouraging Edward to find more reasons for lingering. Even now, I feel deprived that we spent only four days in that magnificent setting."[37] Charis and Edward had been together for four years now, past the stage of infatuation and new desire, having arrived at a comfortable companionship as artists dedicated to their work. Here among the junipers and at their campsite below, they had fallen into their own rhythm, away from other people and the long lines of cars winding their way from one spectacular roadside view to another.

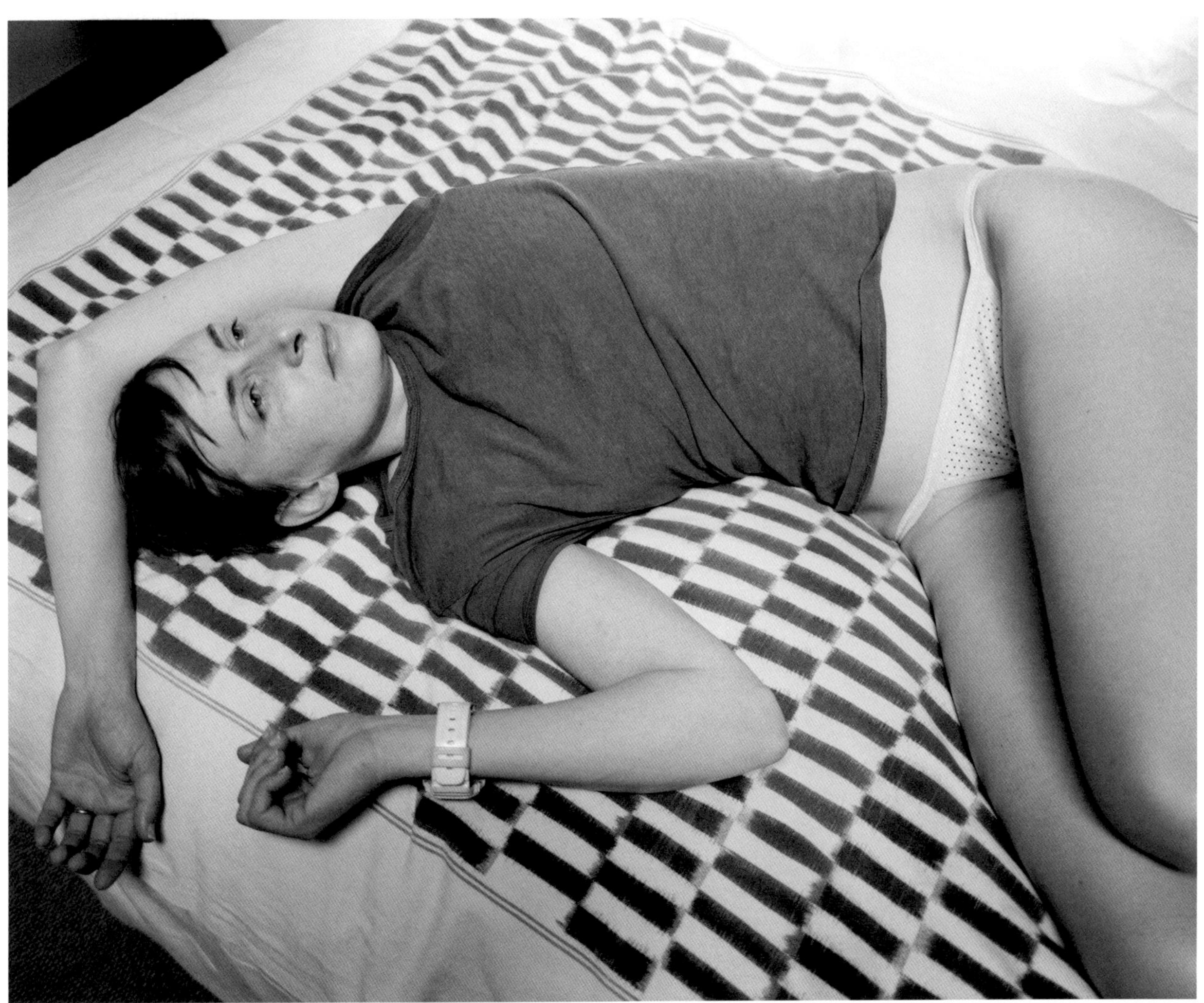

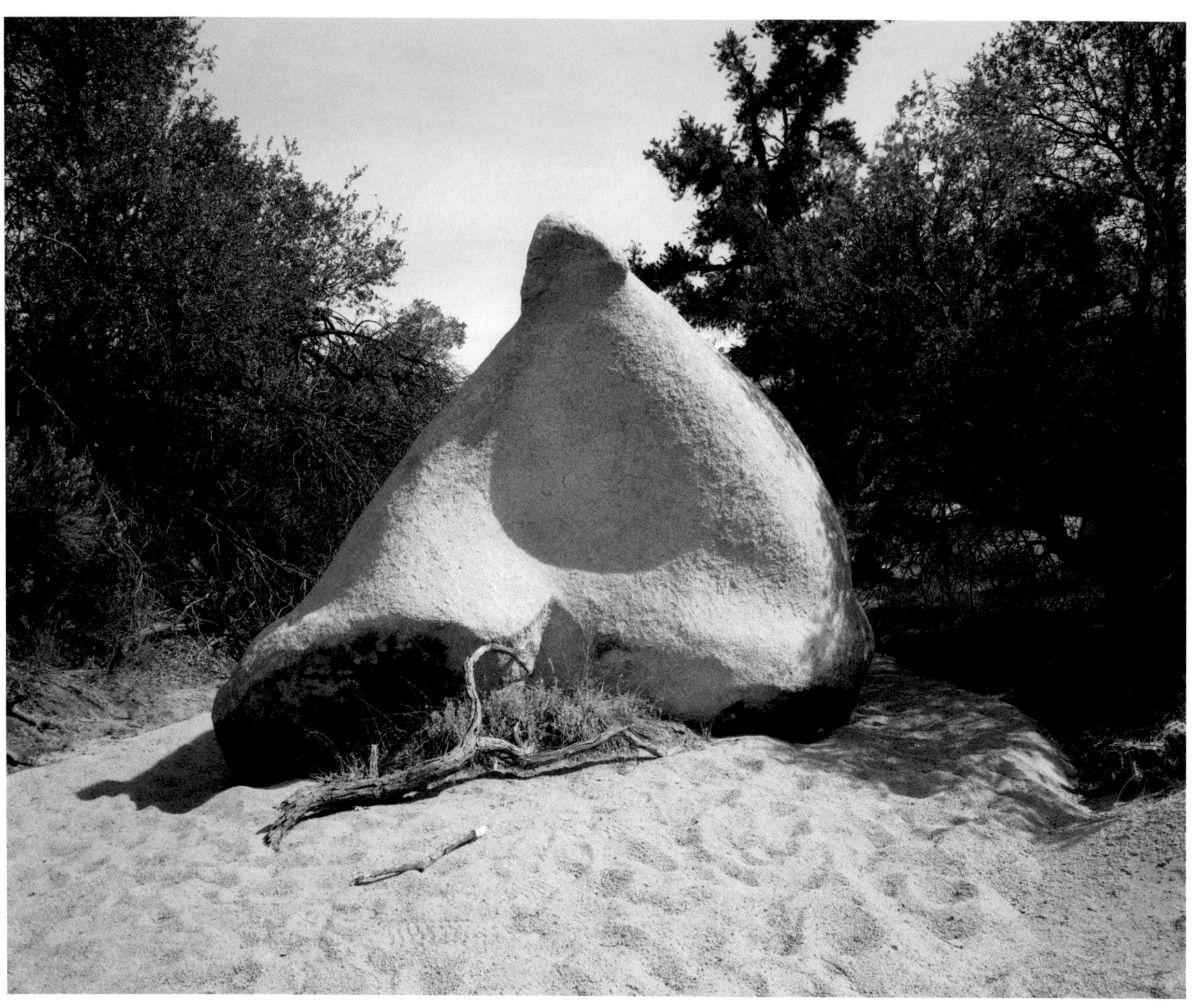

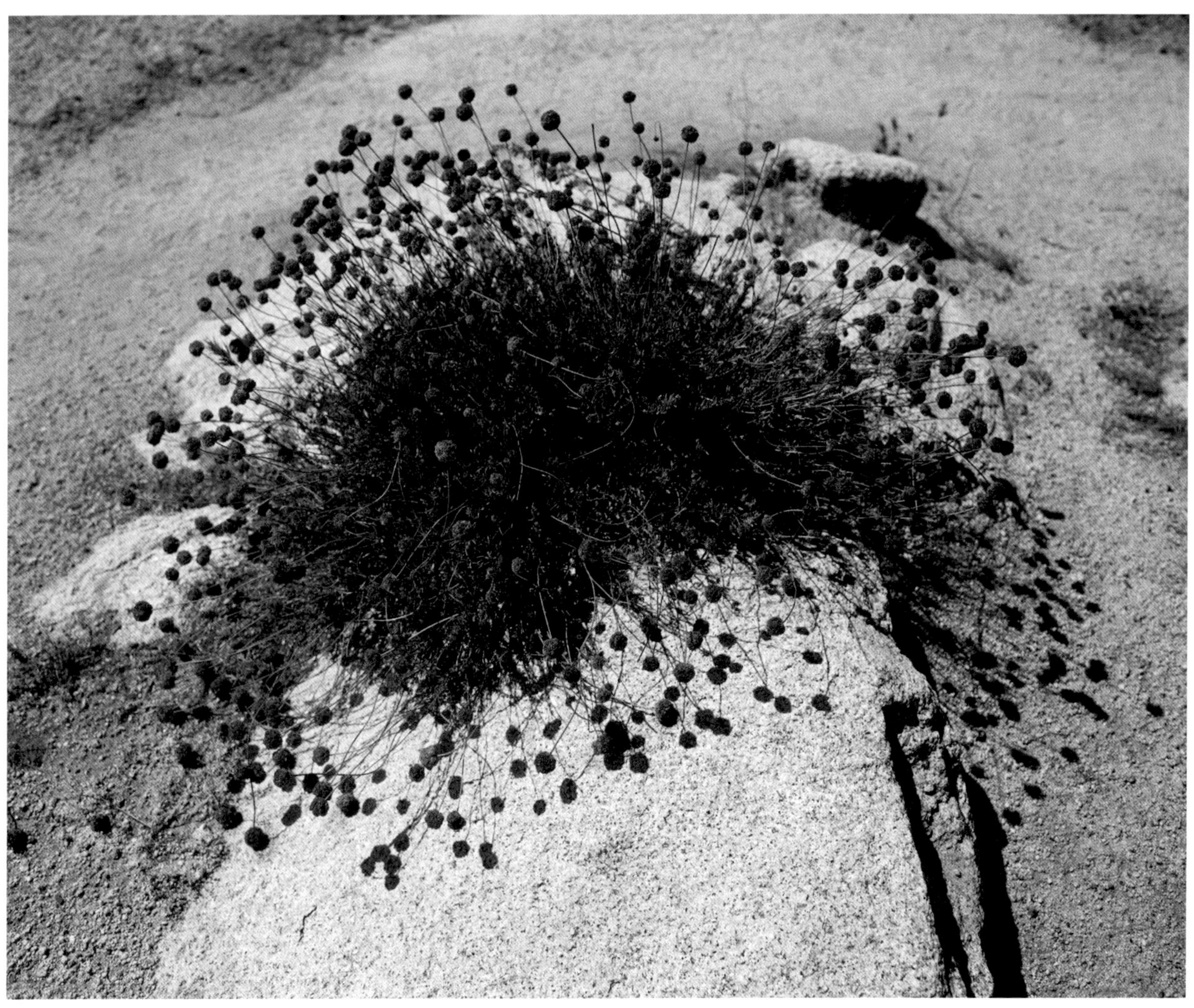

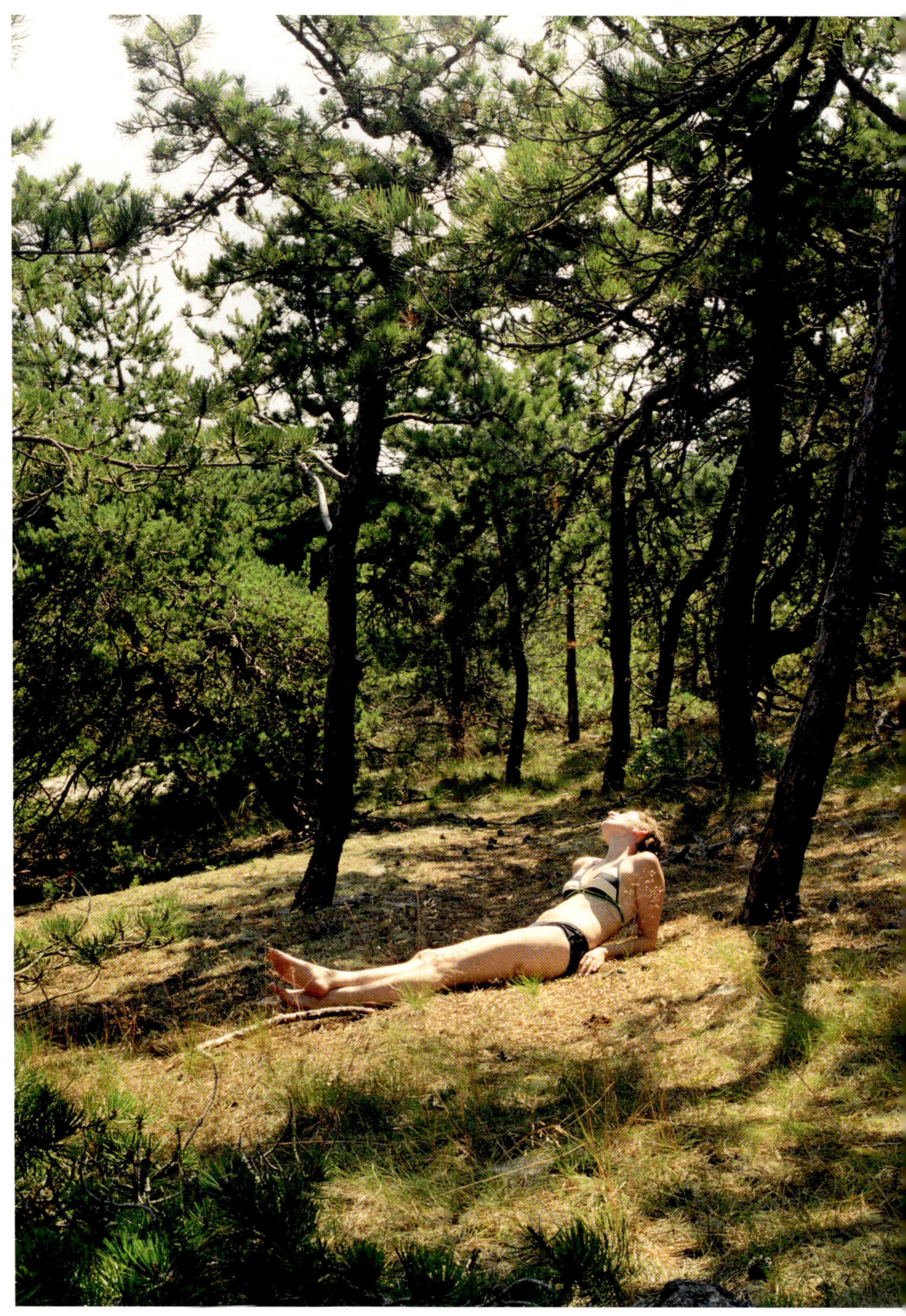

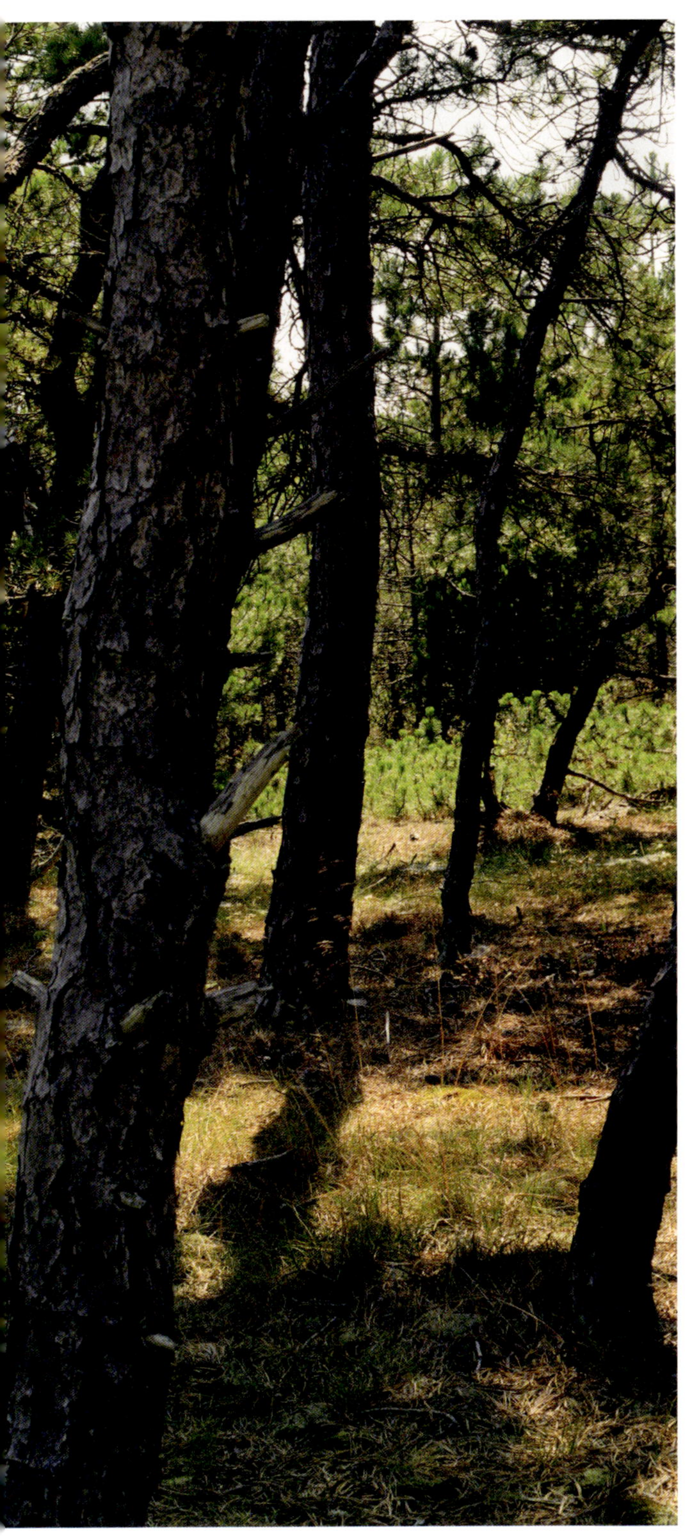

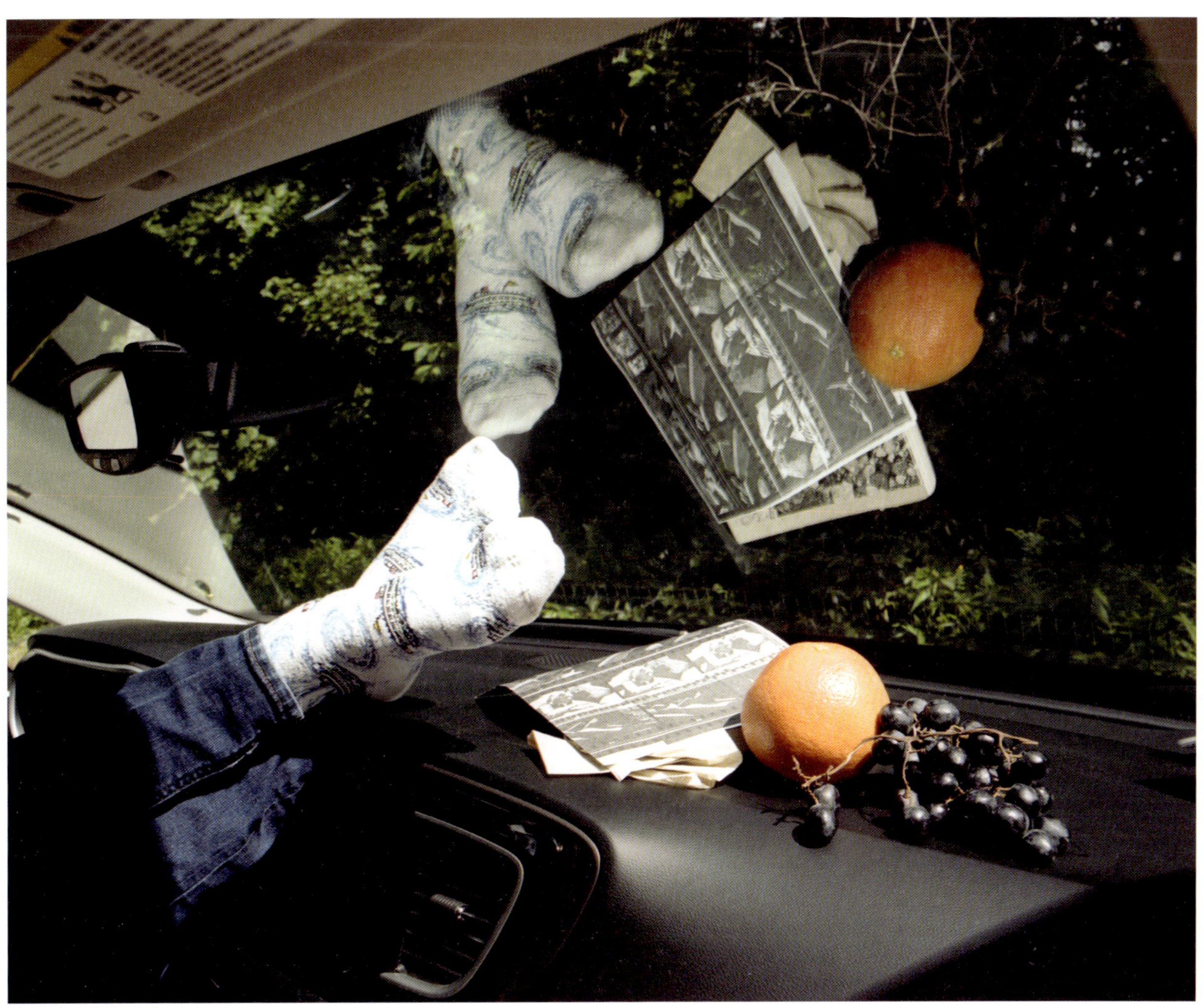

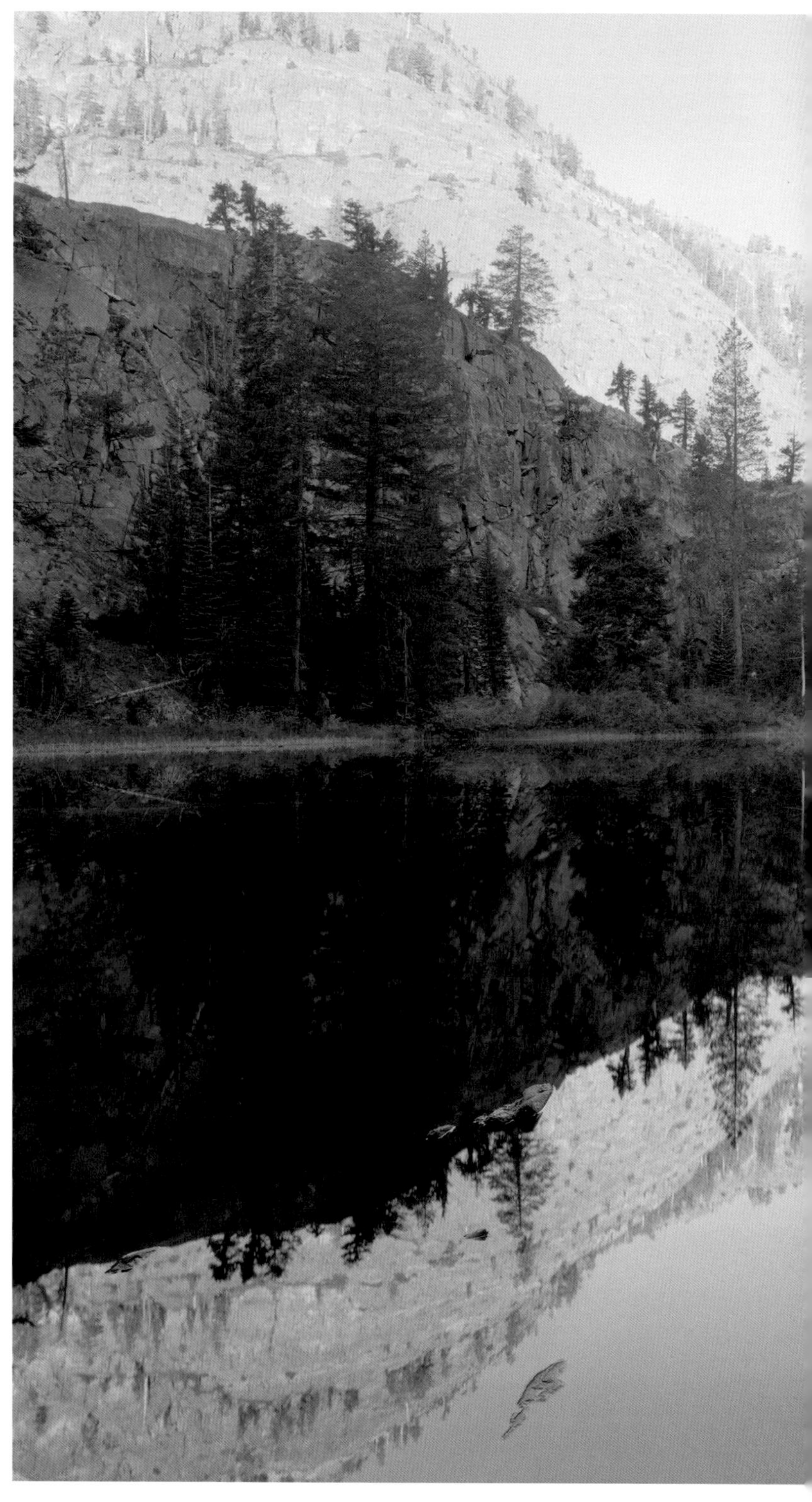

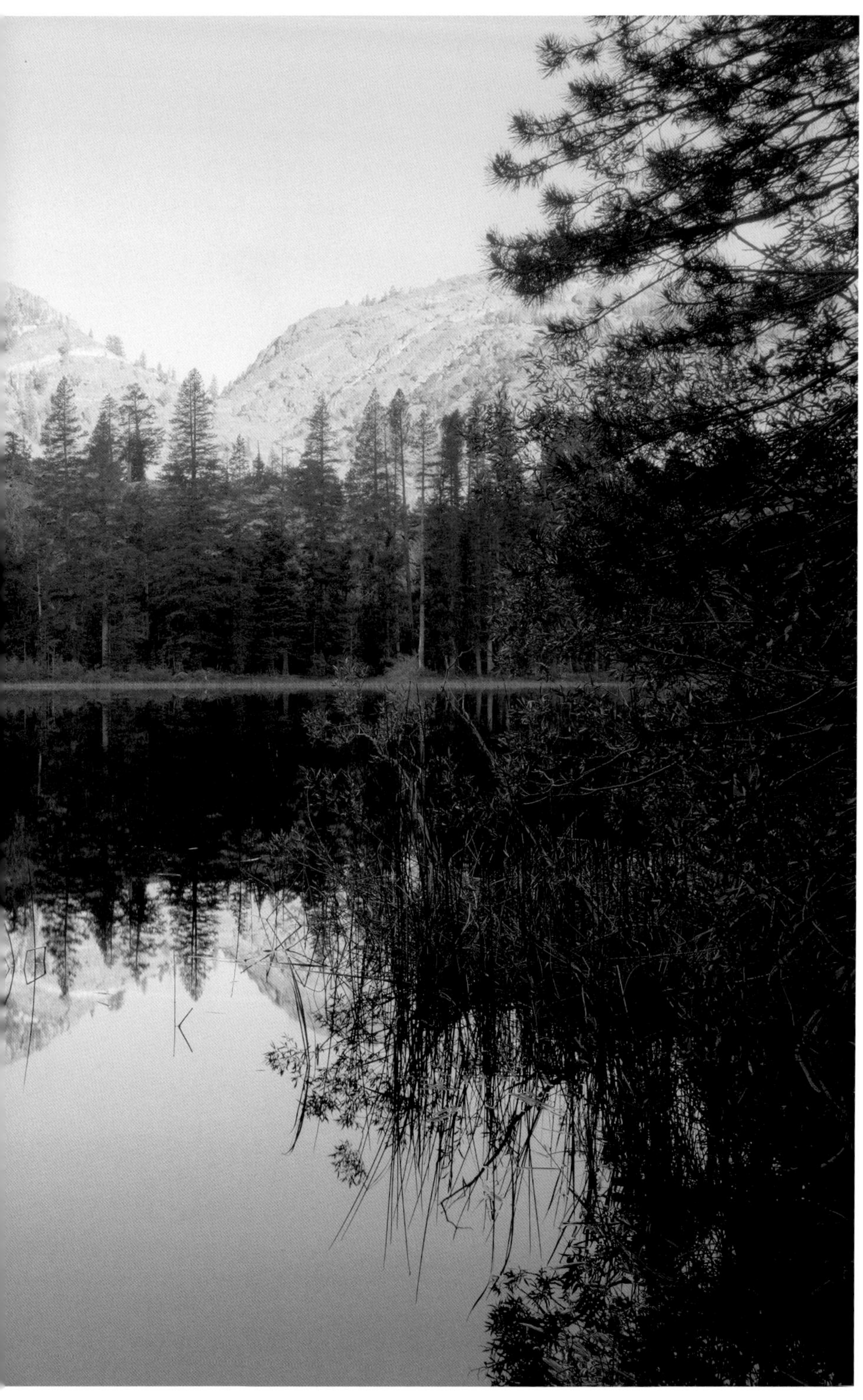

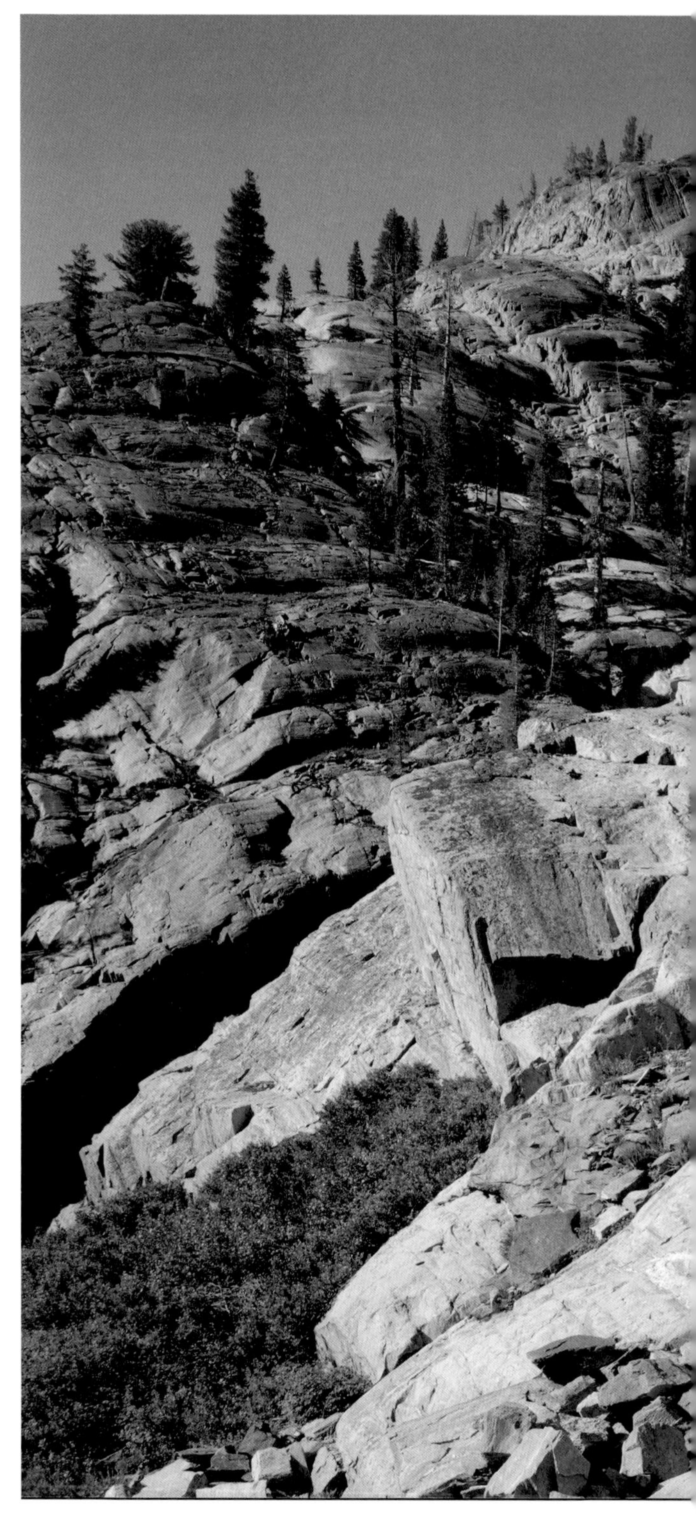

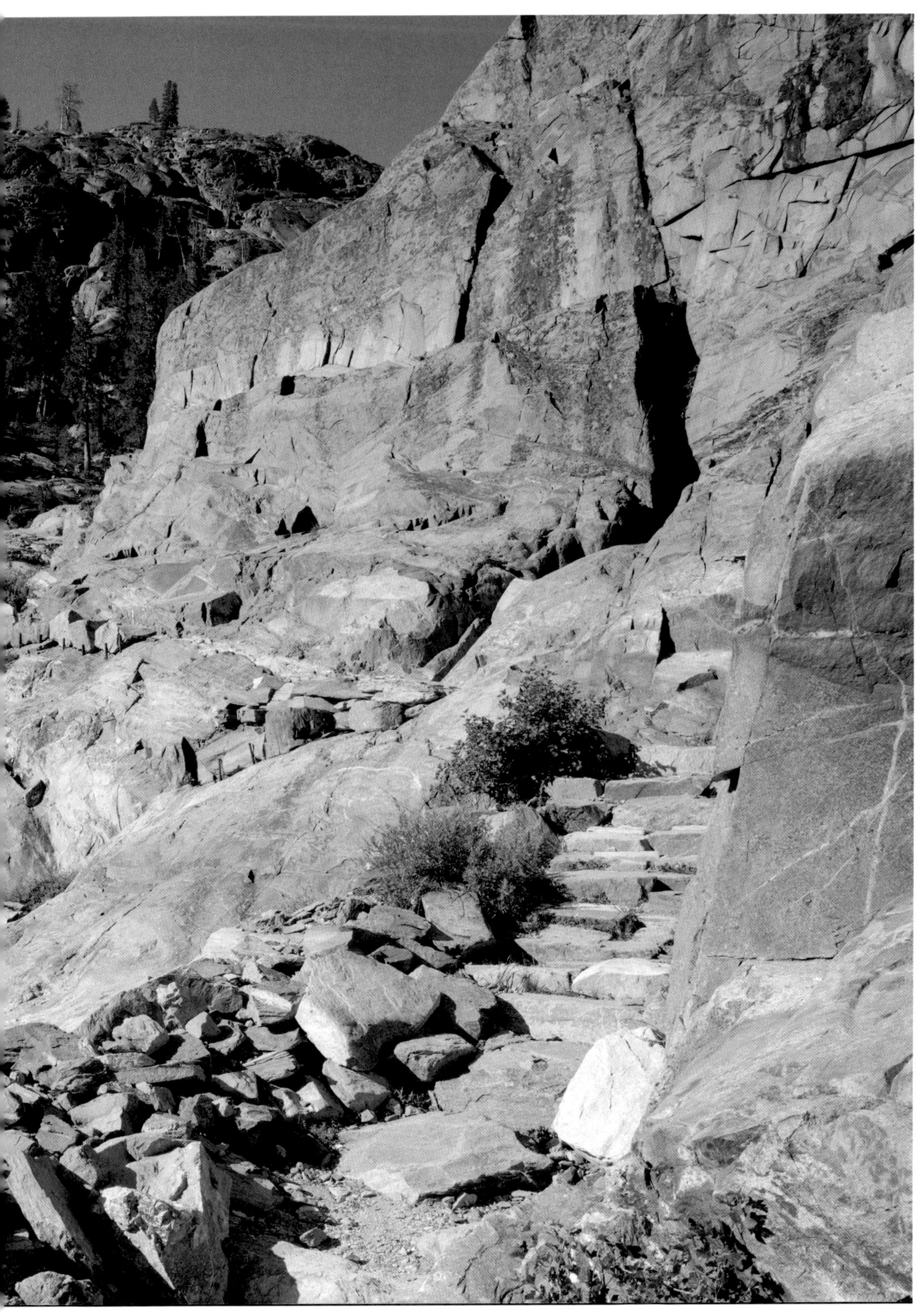

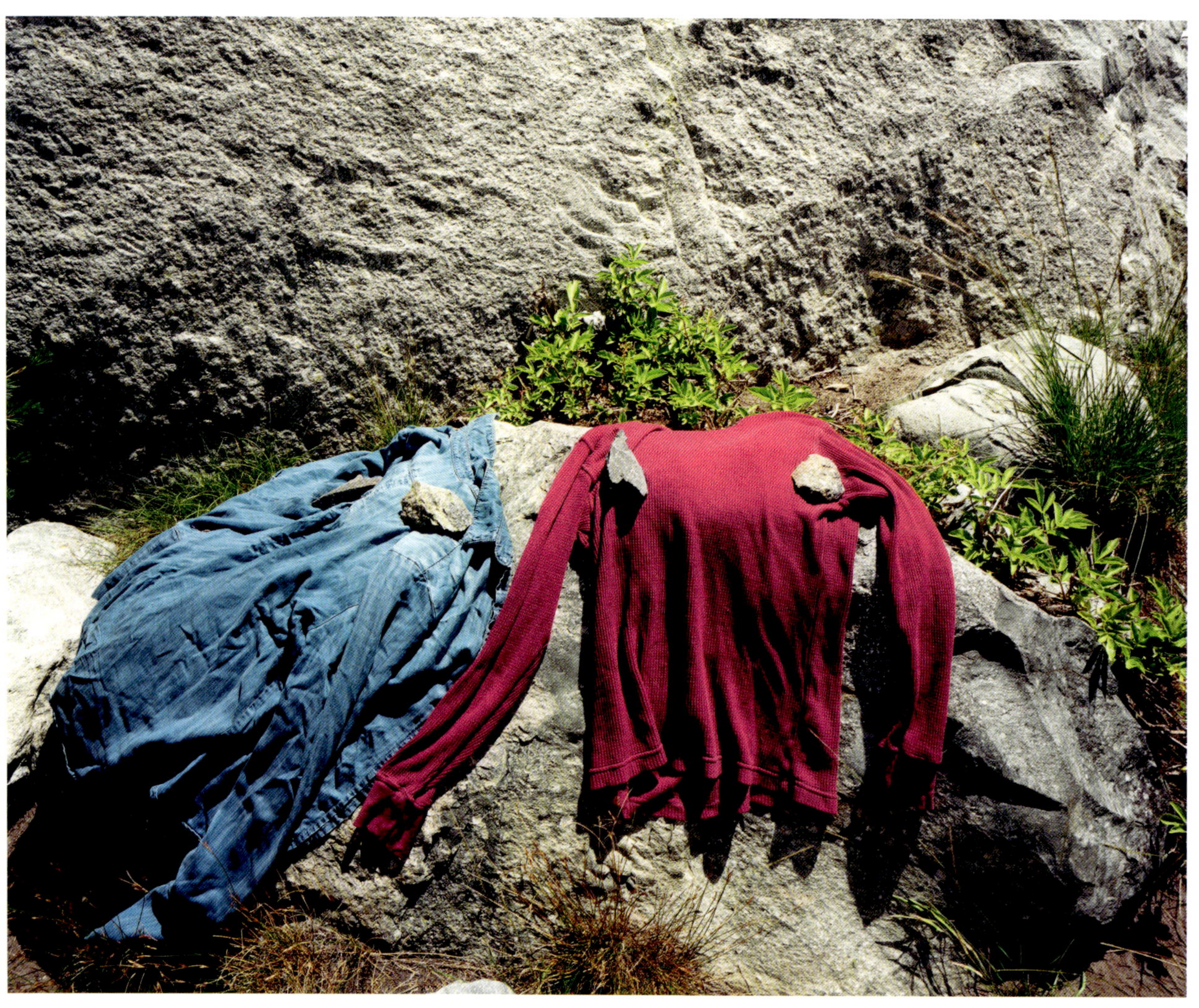

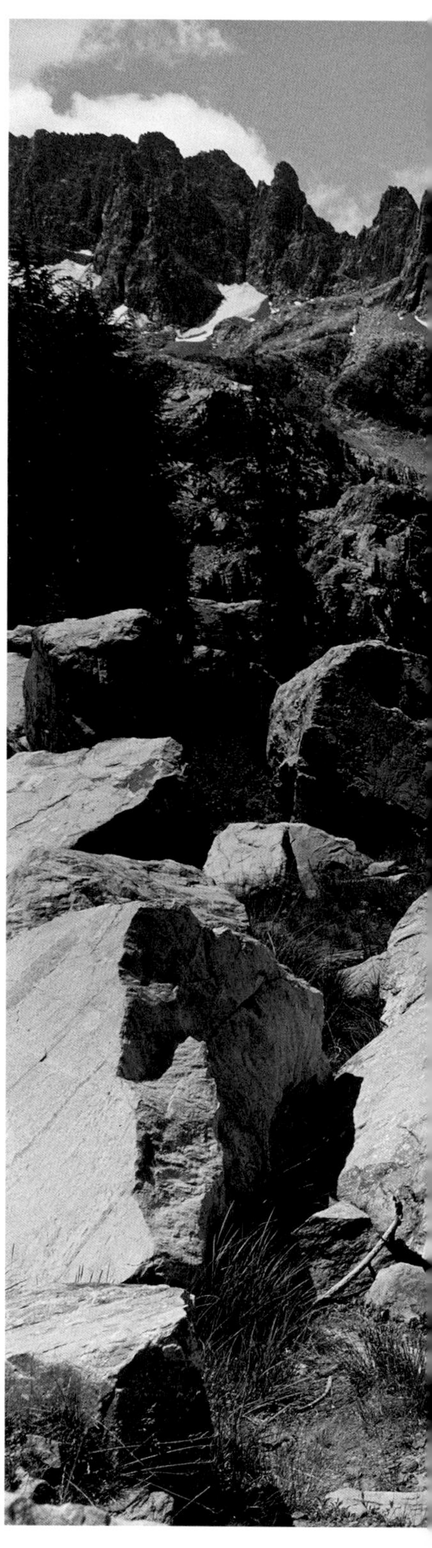

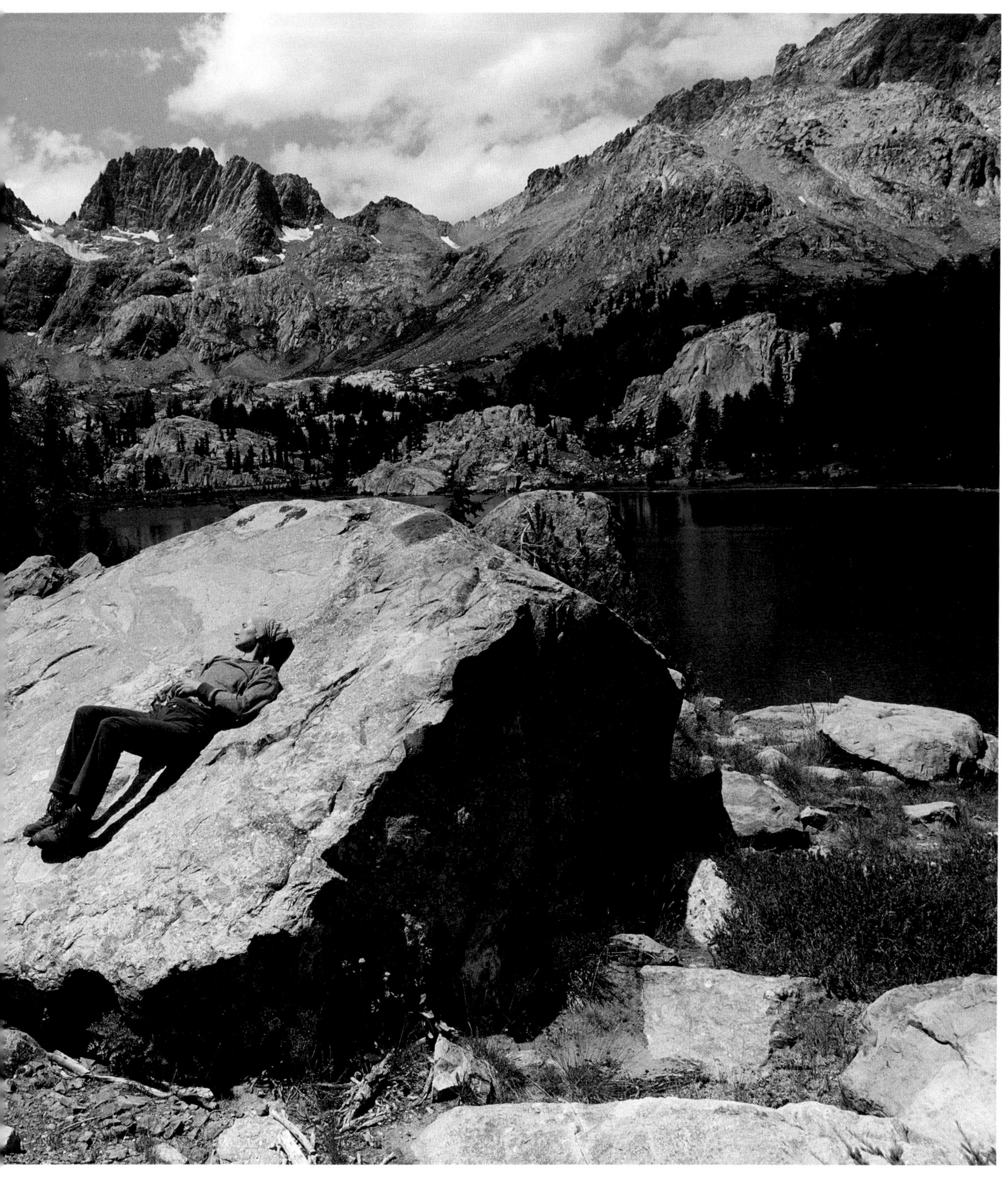

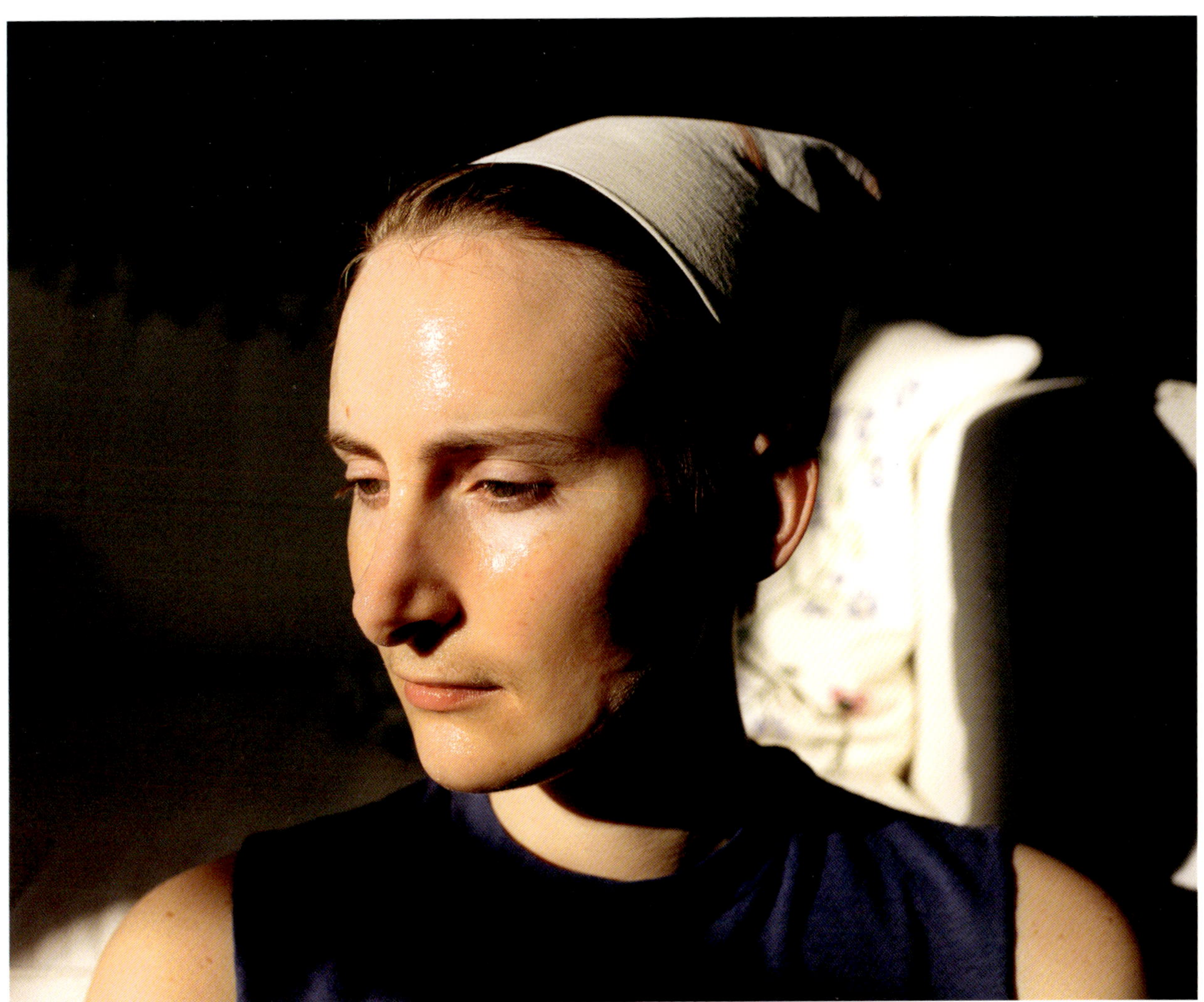

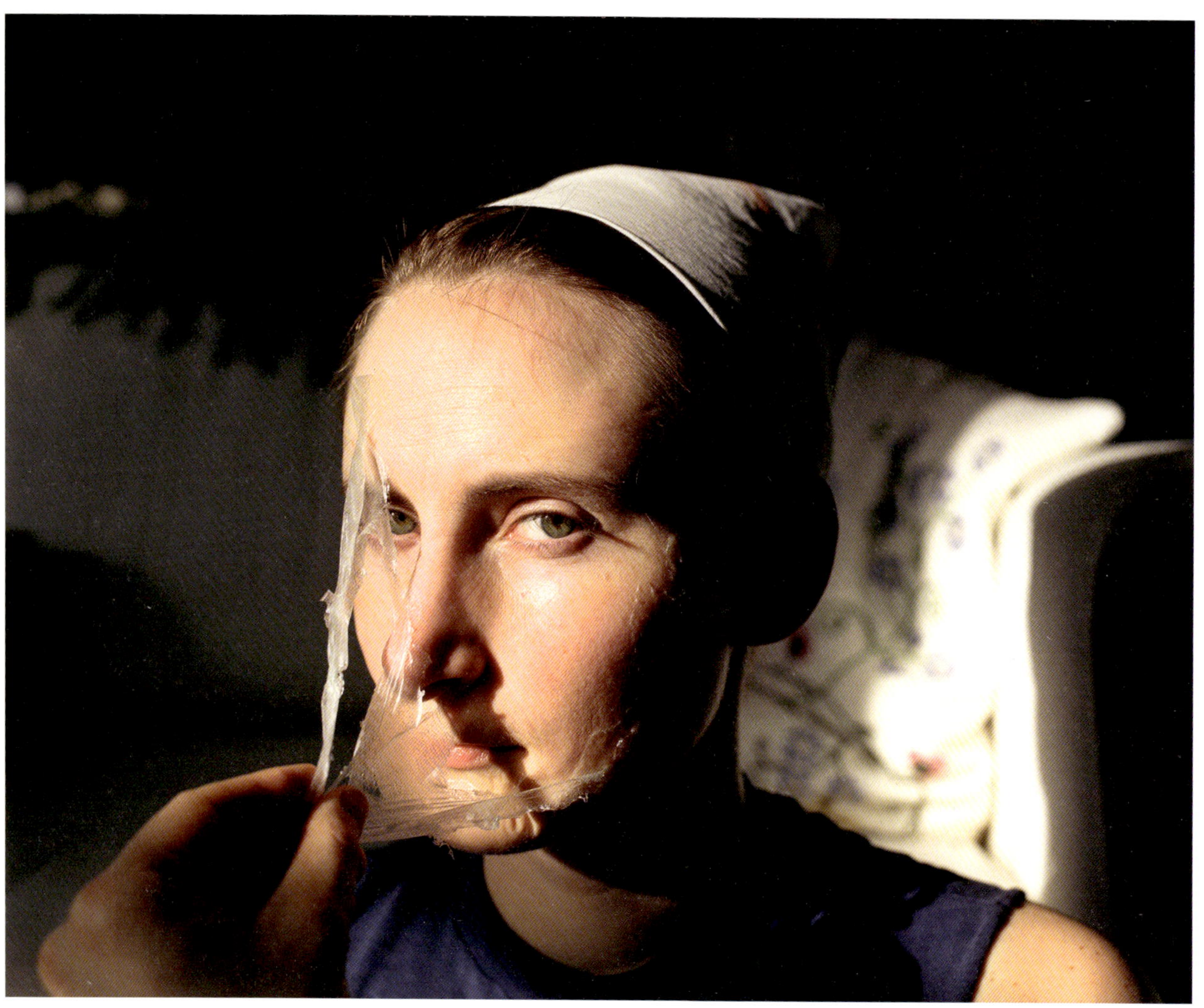

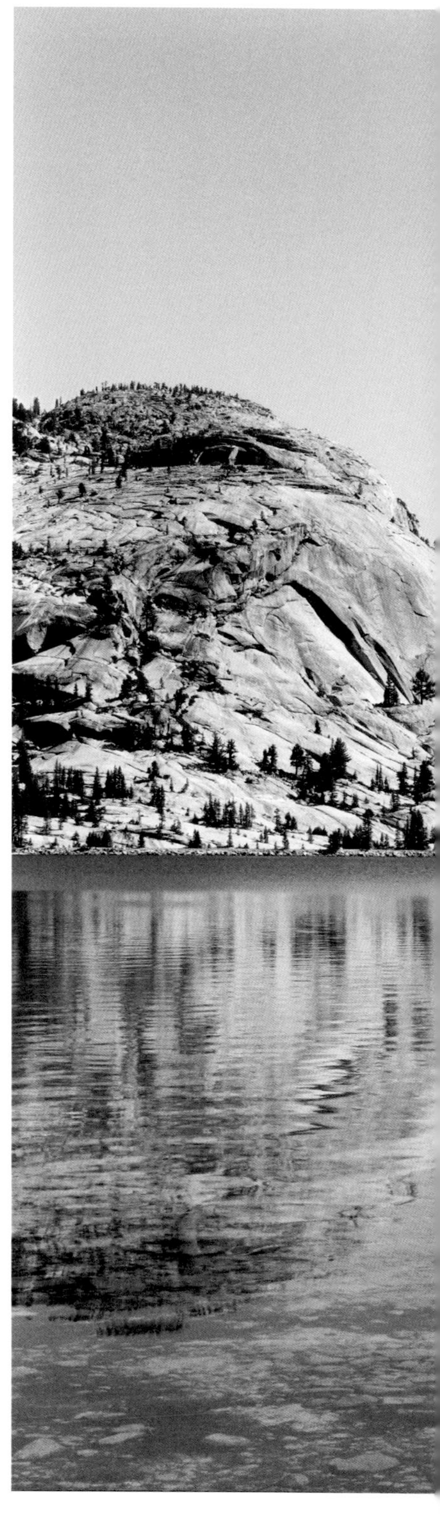

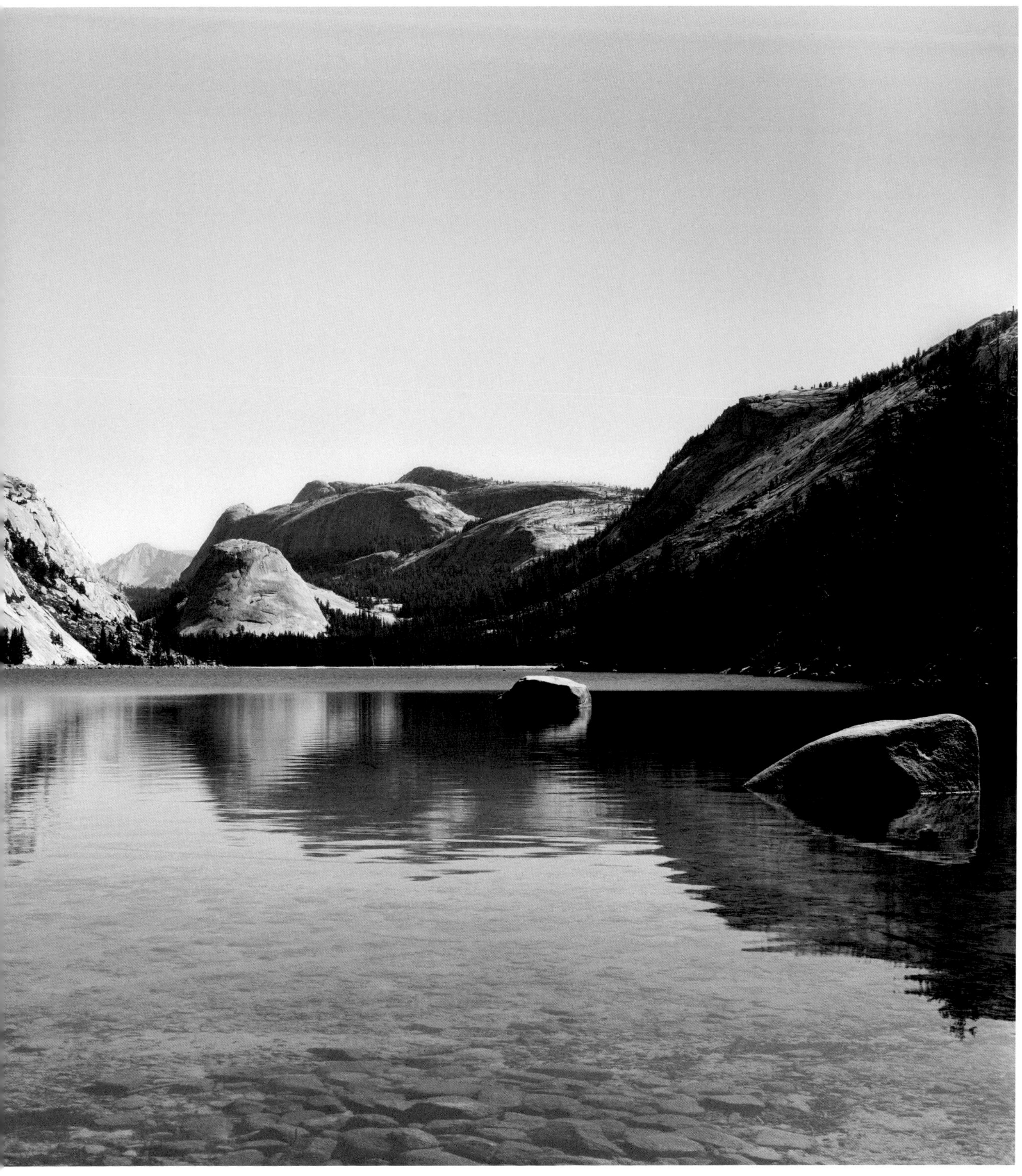

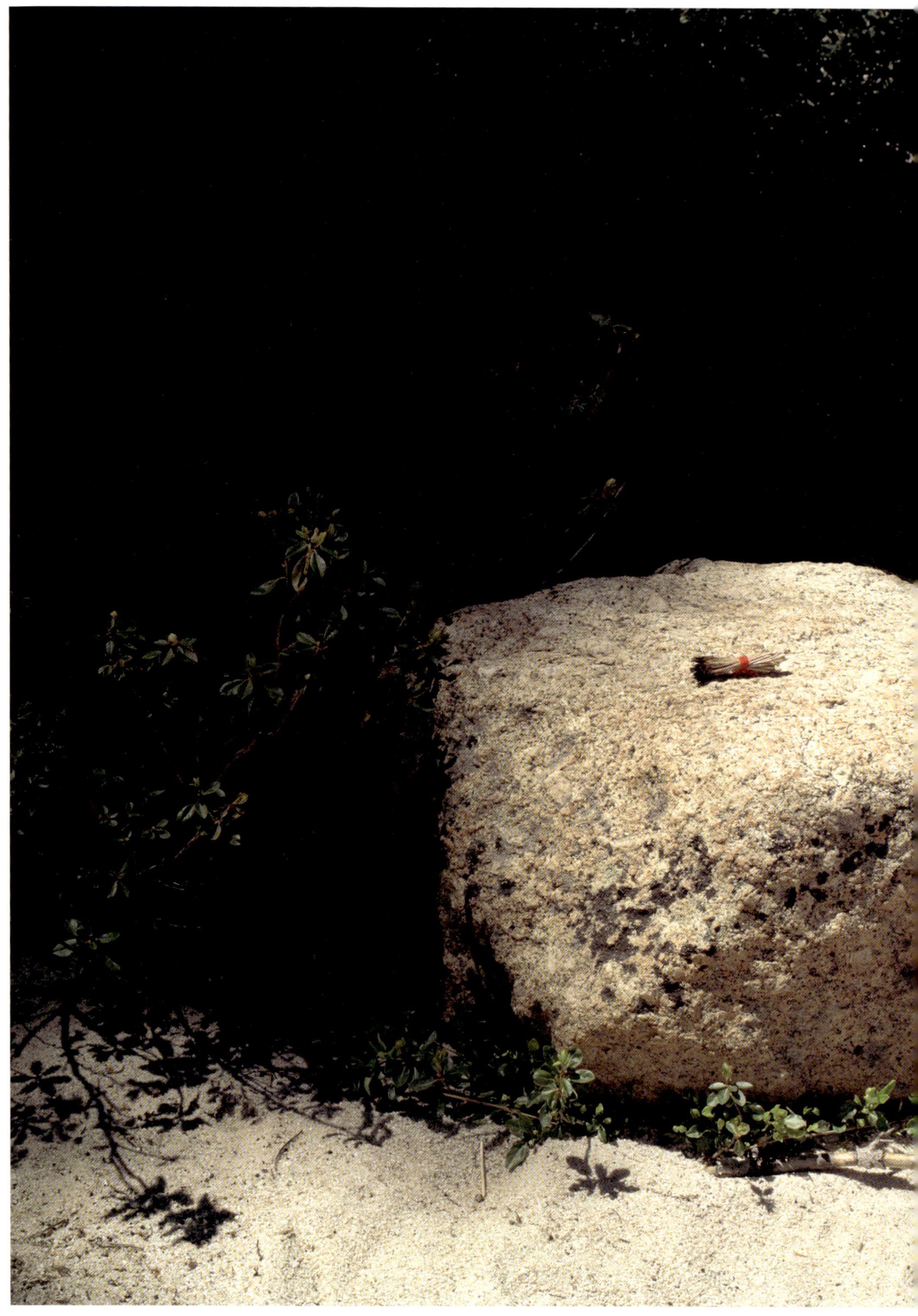

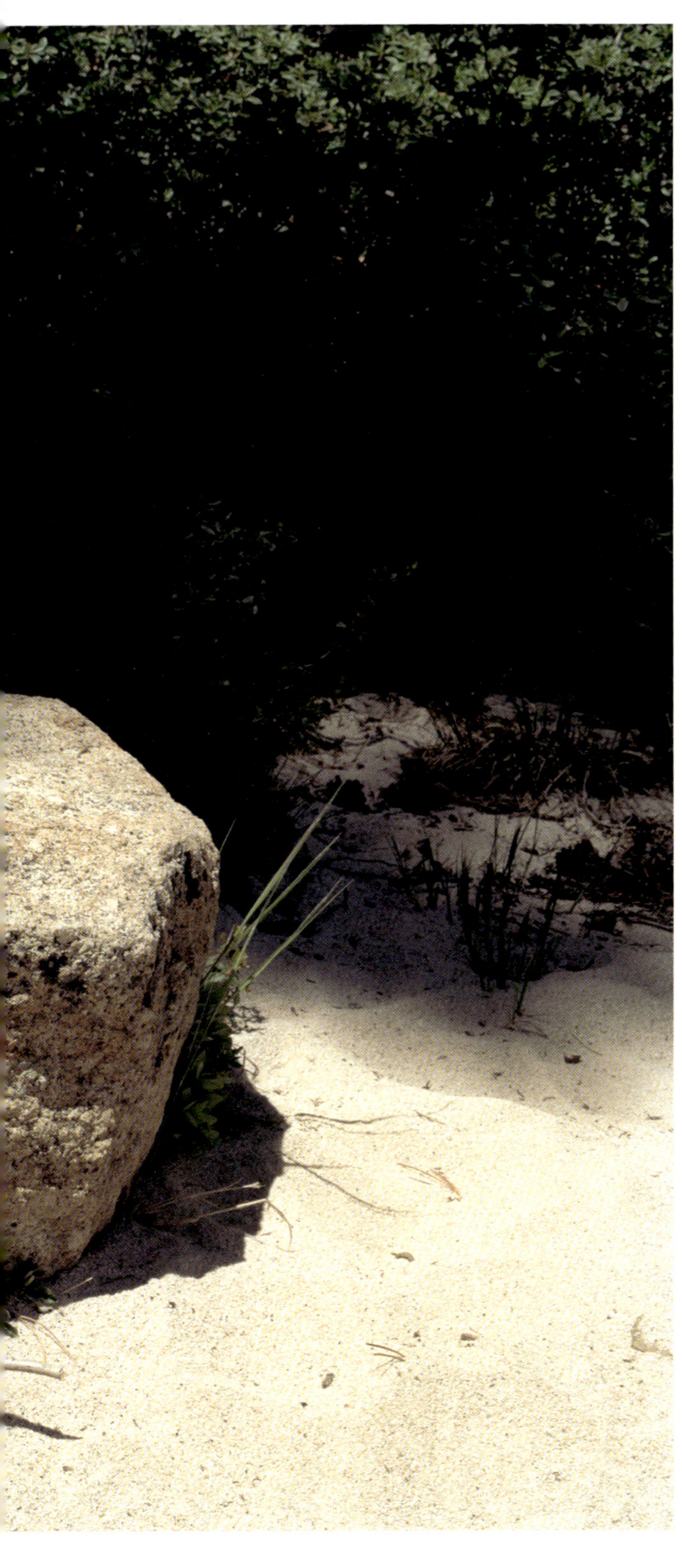

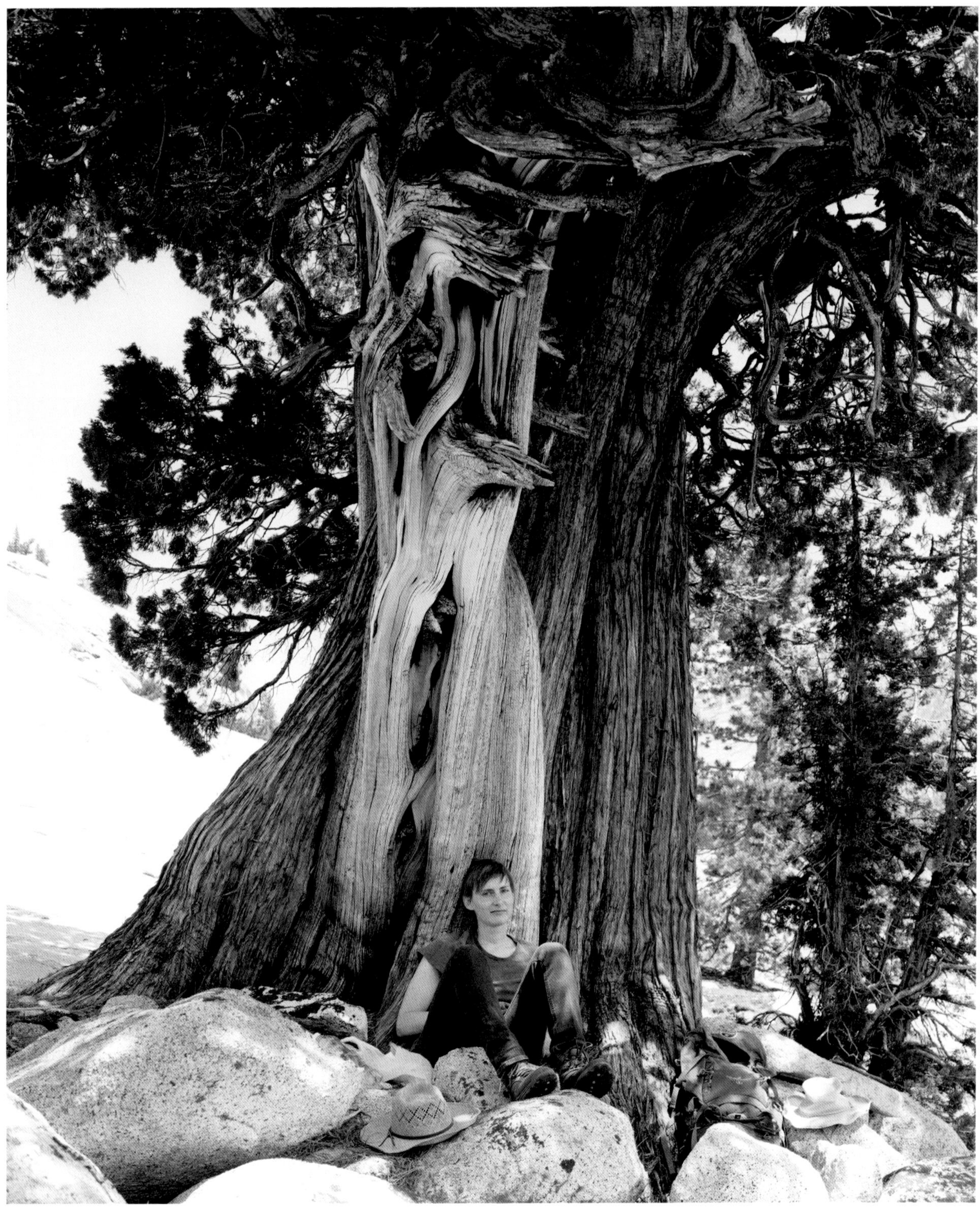

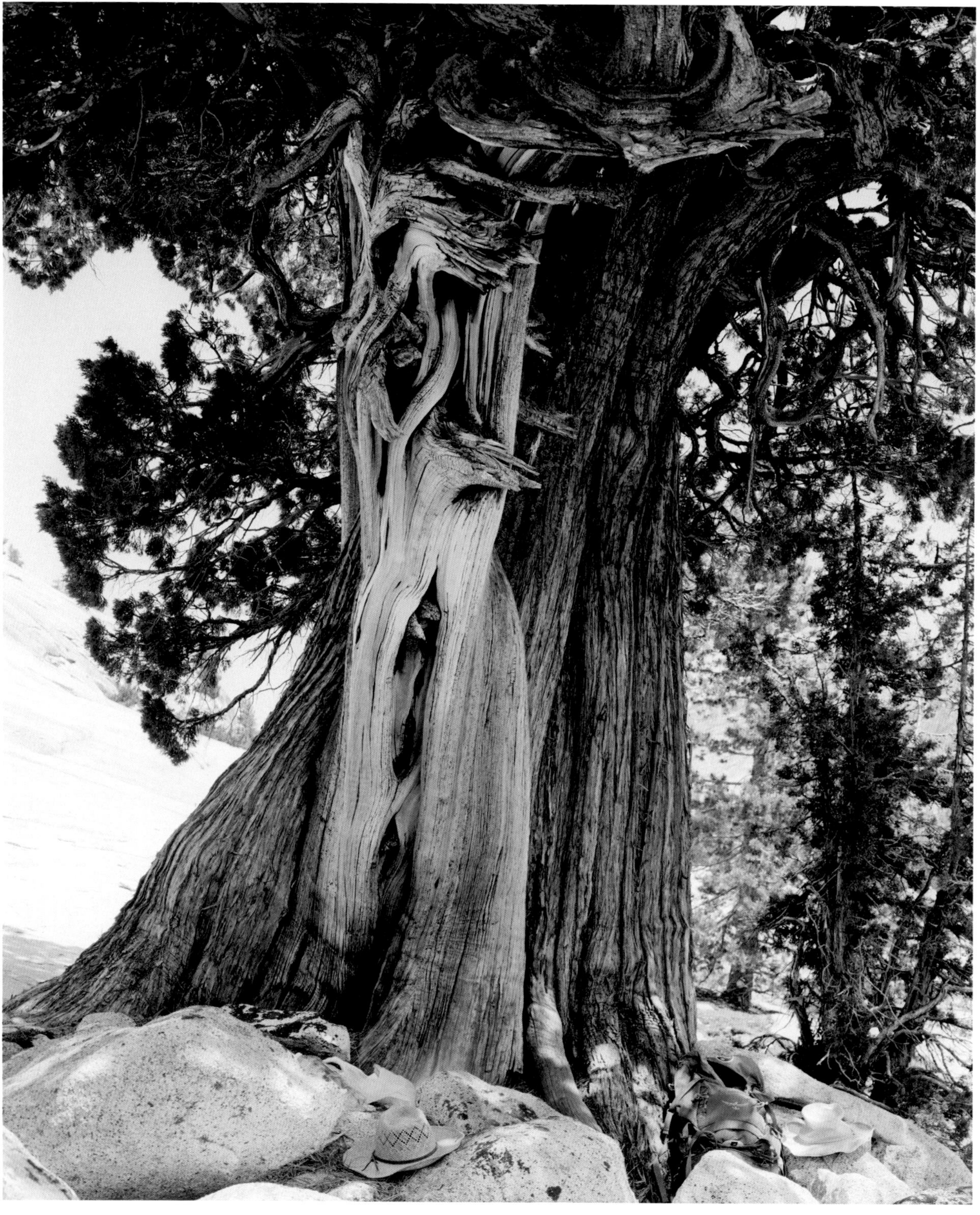

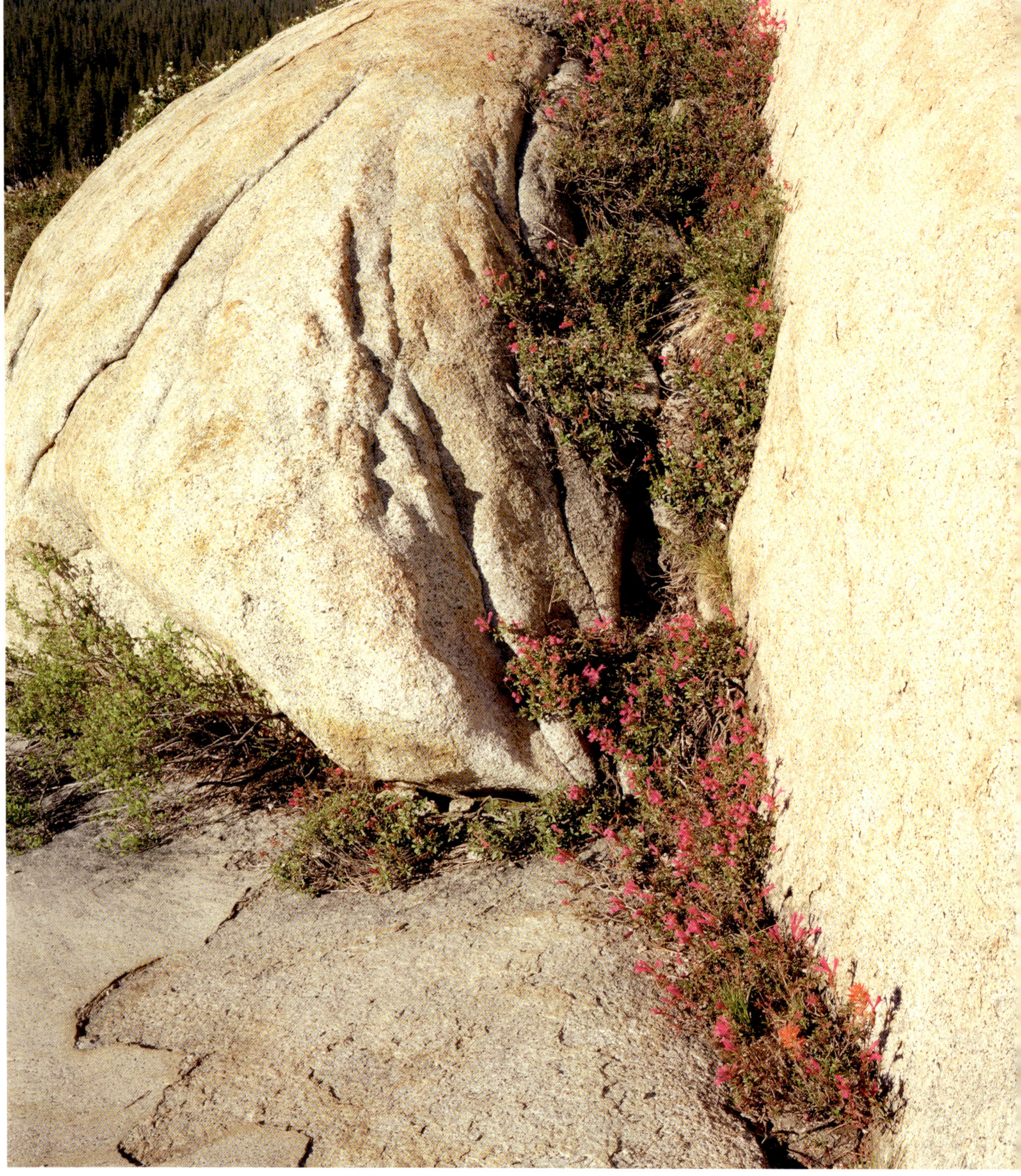

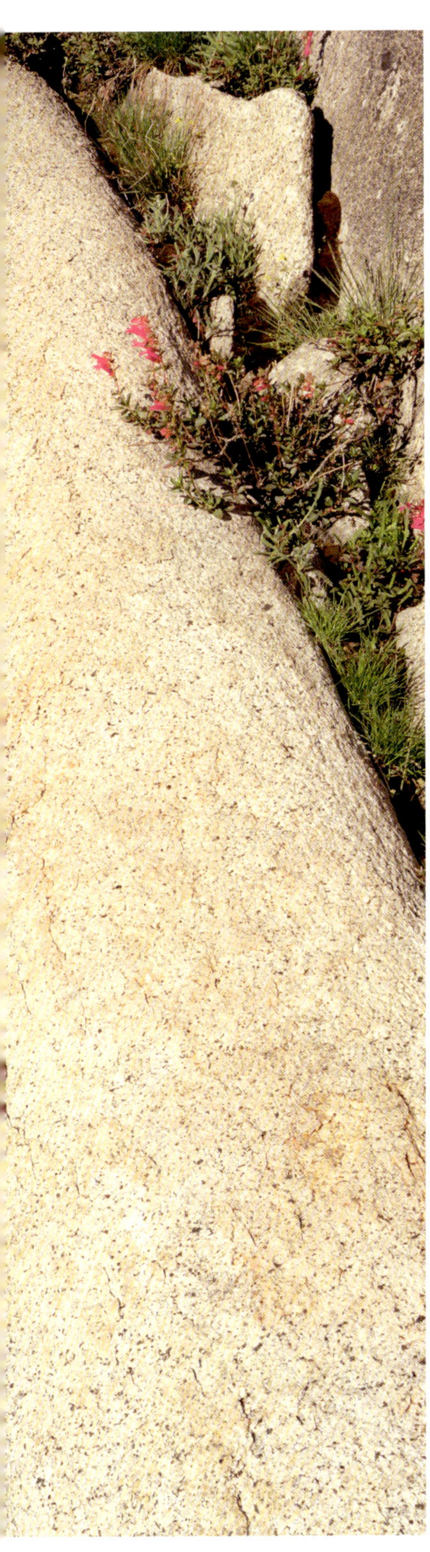

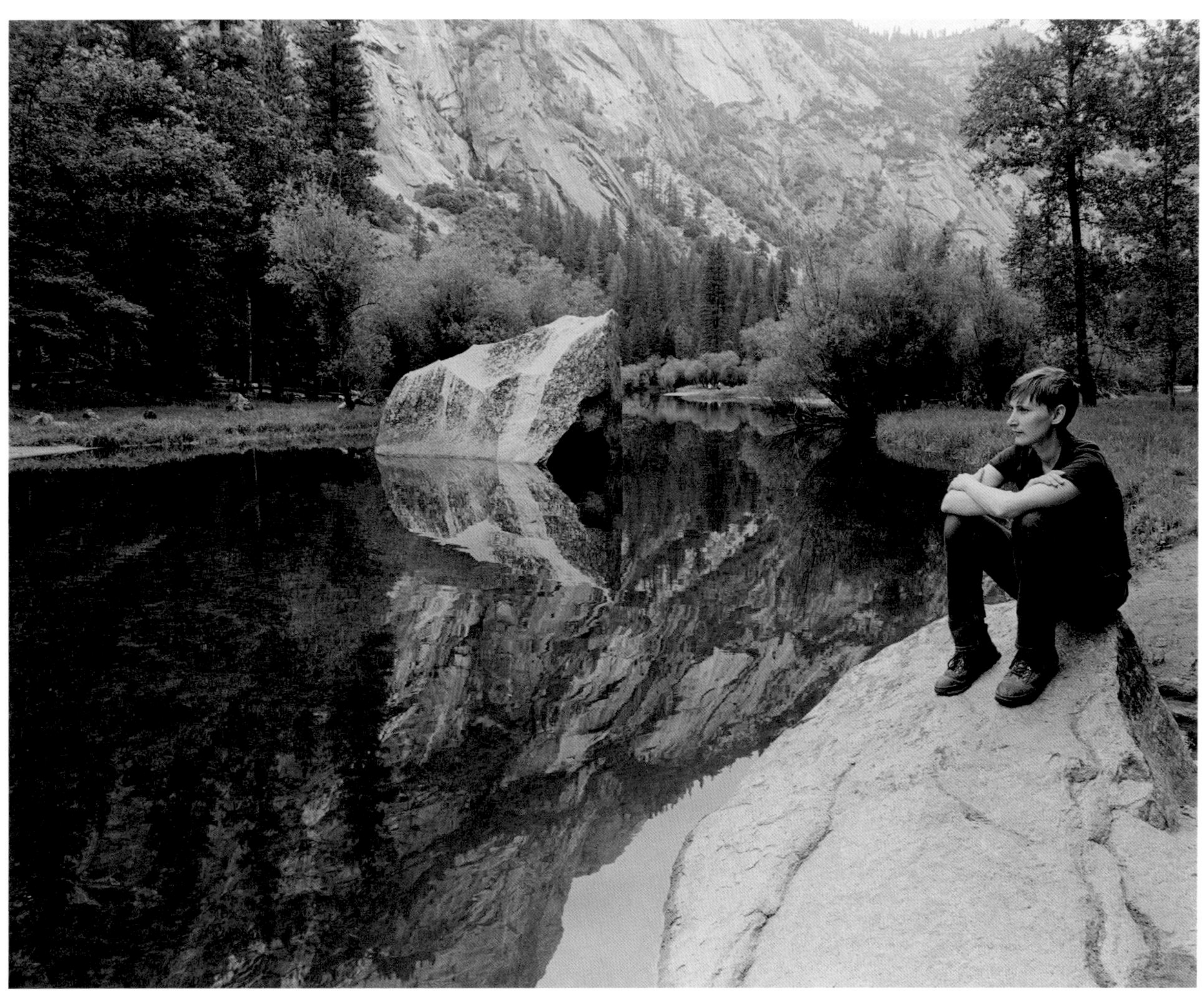

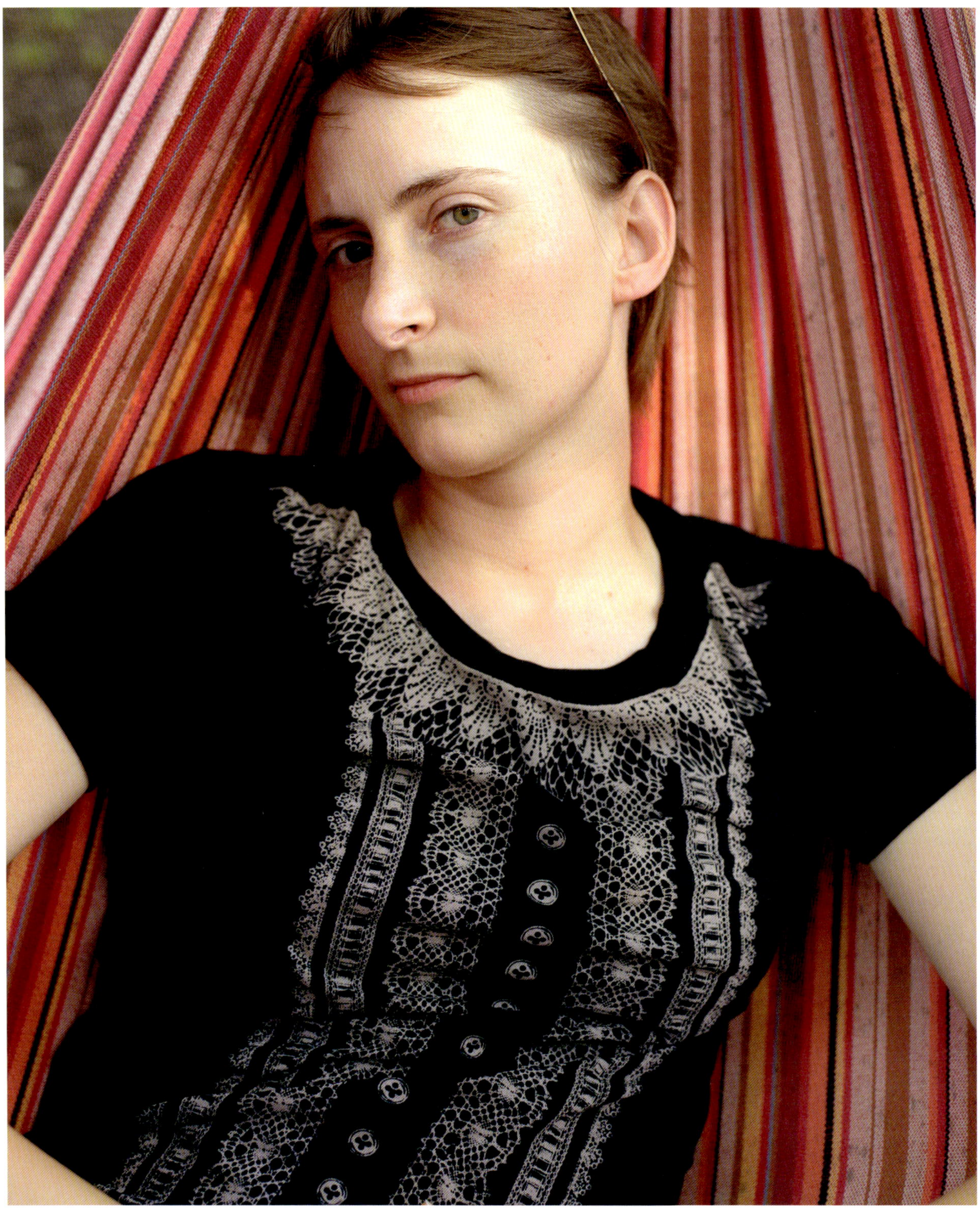

My Texas hometown was built around Lake Granbury; it had almost dried up by the year Dad died. After months of drought, docks stood on bared stilts and boats hung in their marina stalls two stories above the lakebed. The tributary where my brother and I used to swim was ankle-deep muck.

When I was growing up, I spent countless hours doing backflips into the water with my friends. The lake was so high then that I could swim under a dock, hold onto a rusted metal pole, and wrap my legs around my boyfriend's waist, so that unseen by anyone on land, we could make out, wet lips, wet cheeks, wet hair. Sometimes, I would just sit and look out over the lake, the full moon reflected on its surface, as gentle waves lapped against the dock's ladder. Sometimes the lake was choppy and the wind fierce. Sometimes it was still as glass and eerily silent.

As the lake continued to recede, the muddy bed below the dock was revealed; it was littered with things people had dropped into the water over the years. The summer after Dad died, my mom and I found old tires, fishing wire, rusted fishing poles, a pink bike, a floral makeup case with a sandwich bag of old weed inside. A week later, after I'd gone back to Chicago, Mom sent me an article from the Hood County newspaper about the fire department rescuing a kid who had gotten stuck in the sludge—he'd walked out in it until he was waist deep and unable to move.

The sun appears as we descend more than 4,400 feet to the valley floor. We see a coyote
running, creating a line across a field with his body, which is a beautiful sight in the morning
mist, dew hanging off every blade of grass. We pass burned trees that look like sharpened black
pencils. We pull over at designated scenic views brimming with tourists taking quick snaps in
front of Tunnel View, El Capitan, and Glacier Point. Shoulder to shoulder, click after click, the
visitors capture the scenes before us. Tunnel View does not disappoint. Bridal Veil Falls,
however, looks more like Bridal Veil Trickle because of the extreme drought California has
endured the past three years.

Deborah Bright writes in her essay "Of Mother Nature and Marlboro Men: An Inquiry
into the Cultural Meanings of Landscape Photography":

> *The federal government published popular National Park Portfolios during
> the 1920s, which prepared the general public for its first views of Yellowstone
> and Yosemite.*
>
> *As automobile travel became widespread in the 1920s, the Park
> Service's Landscape Architecture Division engineered the wilderness to
> accommodate the new mobility with planned roads and numbered scenic
> turnoffs, sited and designed to conform to conventional pictorial standards.
> Nature was redesigned, we might say, for middle-class convenience and
> efficiency. With the active participation of government and private enterprise,
> wilderness scenery became good business. In this enterprise, photography
> rapidly surpassed other modes of graphic illustration to play a central role
> in merchandizing landscape for public consumption.…These views became
> the established "standards" against which all future visual records of these
> landscape spectacles would be measured. It was these "mechanical
> reproductions" of the chosen shrines that lured tourists into making the
> journey to find the Real Thing.*[38]

Breaking from Charis and Edward's path, Betsy and I become two of the many
tourists making their way to Mirror Lake. The trail is so crowded, I feel claustrophobic
and annoyed. Evidence of our fellow travelers is everywhere—all the things they've left
behind, from soda bottles and chip bags tucked in tree crevices to a pair of pink panties
precariously draped on a rock. The boulders we pass almost look fake from the touch of
so many hands over so many years. We have to scurry off the trail to let horseback riders
pass, and we watch with dread as a group of kids on BMX bikes rush up a dry stream.

When we get to Mirror Lake, it is as I imagined, with the impressive North Dome
on one side and Half Dome on the other, their reflections playing tricks on the eye, like
some monumental Rorschach test. The lake is lower than usual. A dam near the south end

holds the interest of a family of ten, complete with a grizzly bear of a grandpa, who is shouting about how easy it would be to cross the lake on the logs instead of walking around the edge. As I focus the scene on the ground glass of the four-by-five, I am shocked to see the reflection of Mirror Lake rippling, not from rain, but from the family walking across the dam. Grizzly grandpa has made it to the other side and is barking orders at his family to hurry up. They hold hands, some with babies on their shoulders. In no time, one of the older women falls into the lake with one of the grandkids. One of the dads almost falls in trying to help her up. As I impatiently wait for the lake's reflection to settle, a pair of older women come around the bend in time to see the last family member make it to the other side. They decide to follow, and sure enough, one of them falls off the dam and up to her waist in the cool water. When she gets out, she takes off her wet shorts and underwear, and in a flash, fashions a skirt out of her scarf. By this time, Bets and I have sat down on a boulder to eat Pringles and watch the action.

It takes us a long time to make our way out of Yosemite. Traffic is close to intolerable until we turn onto CA 140, which hugs the Merced River. We wind down the meandering road. Light brown and yellow grasses, brittle and bright and thirsty, cover the dry mountains. I wonder if this area is more susceptible to landslides because of the drought. The Merced River, which supplies water to more than 150,000 acres of farmland, is barely three feet deep, not its usual seven at this time of year. The river depends on snow, and rainfall from the northern Sierra Nevada, and both are at their lowest levels since records started being kept in 1920.

Mountains become hills, and hills give way to open space. Parched farmlands are pierced with For Sale signs, but other farms, perhaps receiving irrigation from the Merced River, seem to be doing all right, with fields of corn and orchards of olive and almond trees. We stop for fresh strawberries at a stand by the side of the road and eat them as we go, listening to my limited selection of music, this time in alphabetical order by song title, from *The Albatross, All I Want, All in my Grill, American Girl, And She Was, Anyone's Ghost, Ashes to Ashes,* and *The Avalanche* to *Back of Your Head, Basic Space, Bitter Memories, Black Beauty, Black Lake, Blackhawk, Blue,* and *Blurred Lines* until we reach *Brandy,* which we sing at the top of our lungs, on repeat, until we reach the ocean.

Charis and Edward met in 1934 at a concert at the Denny Watrous Gallery in Carmel.
Founded by two women, Dene Denny and Hazel Watrous, the space was Carmel's first fine
art gallery and was also used to showcase theater and live music performances. During
intermission, Charis noticed Edward from across the room.

*At nineteen I am a very self-conscious young woman. I have recently returned
from a wild year in San Francisco to start work in my mother Helen's dress
shop. My lavender piqué dress with stand-up ruffles around wide armholes
is a present from her, or perhaps on extended loan; I am taller than she is, but
we usually wear the same size. The dress makes me feel glamorous, and I'm
looking around to see if anyone else thinks so. My eyes keep returning to a
short man in brown clothes who is talking with friends across the room. He
is wearing a jaunty corduroy jacket, tan slacks, and a pair of Mexican
huaraches, and has about him an air of poised vitality suggesting readiness
for instant action or total relaxation.*

*We have been keenly aware of each other for several minutes before
he surprises me by making his way through the crooked lane of chairs
and asking my brother to introduce us. Only then do I realize that he is the*

photographer Edward Weston, and that he and Leon have already crossed paths in this small town and become friends. Close up I find him even more attractive, and take him to be in his late thirties. His handshake is firm and his voice has a dry huskiness. His features would seem homely were it not for the liveliness of his expression and the probing restlessness of his brown eyes. His springy red-brown hair is brushed back from the top and side of his head, with no effort made to conceal the prominent bald dome, which is scattered with freckles and deeply tanned.

He looks at me with admiration, and the openness and intensity of that look would be embarrassing if he didn't, at the same time, make it seem playful—as though we were sharing a private joke. As the three of us stand chatting, I can feel his attention focused on me even when his comments are directed to Leon. I say that I would very much like to see his work, and before the lights blink to end the intermission we arrange for me to visit his studio the following Sunday to look at prints.[39]

As it turned out, Edward was out of town taking pictures for the Public Works of Art Project in Los Angeles the following Sunday. His portrait studio business, like Charis's mother's dress shop, was not doing well during the Depression. He had taken on the job to help make ends meet, and in his absence, Sonya Noskowiak agreed to show Charis some of Edward's photographs.

Edward had been in a relationship with Sonya for five years at that point and they were living together. Edward's wife, Flora Chandler, was aware of his relationship with Sonya. She and Edward had separated in 1923, when Edward moved into his Tropico studio with Tina Modotti. Flora and Edward would eventually divorce in 1937, after sixteen years of separation. Sonya was a photographer and one of the founding members of Group f64.

In the studio that Sunday afternoon, Sonya set up a painter's easel and proceeded to show Charis contact prints that Edward had made of an artichoke cut in half, rows of lettuce in a field, ocean-smoothed rocks, and wild cypress trees from Point Lobos.

I had seen some poor reproductions of his photographs, but nothing had prepared me for the real thing. Perhaps no preparation is possible for such a shock to the senses. I felt as though I had turned a corner into a cleaner, sharper, more exciting world—one in which any rock or cloud or weed patch might convey a message of cosmic significance. At first I tried to comment on the pictures as we went along, but I was soon reduced to occasional exclamations as one overwhelming image supplanted another. There were shells whose pale nacreous radiance made them self-luminous; inland ranches baking under the summer sun; bas-reliefs of wave-washed rocks on a Point Lobos beach; the classic structure of a barn at Castroville holding sky and earth apart; green peppers whose complex topology seemed to hide secrets of creation. By the time we had gone through fifty prints I was exhilarated, but also exhausted.[40]

Sonya also showed Charis some of Edward's nudes and explained what it was like to model for a photographer rather than a painter; she asked if Charis would be interested in modeling for Edward sometime. Charis agreed.

After the studio visit with Sonya, Charis drove to Cooke's Cove, which was named for her grandmother, Grace MacGowan Cooke, who owned a nearby cottage. When Charis was young, she often stayed there with her grandmother and grand-aunt, Alice MacGowan, who were both prolific writers. Charis learned about the complexities of writing by watching and listening as Grace and Alice read aloud, critiqued, and rewrote their works in progress. Charis's father, Henry Leon Wilson, known as H. L., was also a writer, but he would write feverishly for long spans of time, during which Charis and her brother, Leon, learned from experience not to bother him.

Charis had always wanted to go to college, and when she was awarded a modest scholarship to attend Sarah Lawrence, she was elated. Upon hearing the news from her parents that even with the scholarship they could not afford for her to attend, Charis became depressed and reckless. She moved to San Francisco and had been living there for eight months when she experienced severe stomach pains. Charis's mother, Helen Cooke Wilson, suspected that Charis might be pregnant, and came to pick her up. The doctor in Carmel confirmed that not only was Charis pregnant but that she also had appendicitis; he agreed to perform two surgeries as a favor to Helen. Neither Charis nor her mother spoke of it again. Charis was left feeling hopeless about her future.

Cooke's Cove was the place she came to think about things, to sit in the comfort of the car watching the morning fog hover over the bay or the sun set. Charis went there on the Sunday she met with Sonya to think about Edward's images.

Where had I been all my life to have missed so much? I didn't mind conceding to Edward the rights of discovery to the Castroville barn and the Salinas lettuce field; I had driven past them often enough, but with my head full of other matters. Point Lobos was something else. This was my childhood playground, where I had climbed through the great jaws of the whale skeleton, dabbled in tide pools, picnicked in the cypress groves, and swum in the icy green water of China Cove. Later I wrote poems about the shore rocks, etched with ripple wave patterns that echoed the salt tide which shaped them; poems about life and death in the tide pools, whose inhabitants I observed by the hour; poems about the twisting inlets I swam through, where purple urchins and bright orange starfish were lodged in beds of pink rockweed and waving green sea lettuce. What could I have to learn about a place I knew so well from someone who had lived in Carmel for only five years?

A lesson in humility, for one thing. I fancied my own eye to be rigorously sharp and penetrating—that it could be superficial was a bitter pill to swallow. But worse, my Point Lobos poems now seemed unsubstantial when compared with Edward's strong, precise, evocative images. His picture of kelp on the Carmel beach hung in my mind, testifying to my blindness; how

The day finally came for Charis to model for Edward. She climbed the wrought-iron
stairs to the second-floor studio. She was nervous, not about being nude, as she felt
comfortable with her clothes off, but about how the camera would see her. The nudes Sonya
had shown her a few weeks ago were of closeups, fragments of the bodies, rarely showing
the models' faces. Some of the bodies were muscular, some petite and slender. Charis was
nervous about how her soft features, her untoned arms and curvy hips, would photograph.

The studio was arranged differently than it had been on her previous visit. The
easel and table were moved to the side, and the couch was in the center of the room so that
light from the high window fell on it. A four-by-five Graflex camera was mounted on a
tripod, its long legs extended, across from the couch. Charis writes that it was "a big barn
of a room, almost empty of furnishing, so that it seemed to be all space and light."[42]

Their attraction to one another was intense. The camera gave them permission
to look unapologetically at one another and to move physically closer to each other in the
process. The act of seeing Charis was exhilarating for Edward, and the act of being seen
made Charis feel significant—to be photographed is to experience a form of adoration.
Many of Edward's relationships were directly connected to his art making: all of the
significant women in Edward's life, Flora Chandler, Margrethe Mather, Tina Modotti,
and Sonya Noskowiak, had modeled for him. He had been attracted to the newness of
his relationships with these women and the discoveries that came with them. And now
too, he felt more alive with Charis. He enjoyed the intensity of her gaze: he was also seen,
adored, and held in her sight.

Charis and Edward did not have sex the first time she modeled for him, but it was
on their minds. The following day they ran into each other in town, and Edward asked if
Charis wanted to see the pictures he had made. They walked the short distance to Edward's
darkroom. In the semi-dark space, they could feel each other moving, the air between them
charged, electric, as they watched the photographs develop. Neither one of them made a
move as Edward pulled each print from the wash.

Seeing a photograph of yourself can be anywhere from exhilarating to awful.
Charis was surprised to learn that she photographed better than she had expected. She
thought the images were far more beautiful than their subject.

*I returned to my office in a state of euphoria inspired by an entirely new view
of my body. How silly to have agonized over how big my hips were when I could
see from the photographs that they were just the right size for the rest of me.
For years I had been self-conscious about my height; in those days 5'8" was
conspicuously tall for a girl. Now I saw clearly that my height was just what it*

*should be. Of course this perfection was really a trick of Edward's camera, but I
was utterly happy to be the subject and to feel I had been made into a work of art.*[43]

A portrait not only documents the likeness of someone at a particular time in
a particular place, but it also records the photographer and model's relationship to
one another in that moment. Their combined energies are projected and preserved. The
most captivating portraits contain an energy that is palpable—an intense desire or an
active and revealing awkwardness that peels off a surface layer to show something raw
underneath. We can change dramatically in the presence of another person. Sometimes,
we see ourselves in them, and they in turn, see themselves in us: we become mirrors.

When Charis and Edward were first seeing each other, they would meet at Edward's
studio before sunrise. During the day, while working at the Carmelita Shop, her mother's
dress shop, Charis often found it hard to concentrate. As she sat at her desk on the second
floor, where she balanced the books, she would try to catch a glimpse of Edward walking
by on the street below, which he did several times a day.

*Edward's studio on Lincoln was one block away from his house on Monte
Verde, and the Carmelita Shop faced Ocean Avenue halfway between the two,
so he passed below my office window several times daily. Because his trips were
irregular, and my view was limited to about ten yards of sidewalk, I would
miss him if I wasn't looking out at exactly the right moment. The sight of this
amazing human being striding along as if he could have been just anyone gave
me the satisfying sense of having a great secret.*[44]

In a letter to him she writes, "A glimpse of your shoulder has tantalized me—
I wish one of us lived somewhere else then life would be simpler—or it's nice to think it
would. I think I'll break down and mail this—then I'll be sure to see you—the law of
incidence has never failed us yet."[45]

Betsy and I walk up Ocean Avenue past a coffee shop, two restaurants, a sweet
shop, and a hair salon, in the hopes of finding where the Carmelita Shop had been. These
buildings are all too close to the sidewalk for someone at a second-floor window to spy on
people below. But the White Rabbit, a gift store on the second floor of a Thomas Kinkade—
like cottage, has a picture window with the perfect view for watching passersby—someone
standing in the window could easily see me and Betsy. Charis would have had an ideal perch
from which to catch a glimpse of Edward. Betsy and I stare at the window of the closed
shop. Night is falling, and a cool breeze from the sea four blocks away curls up our bodies as
we inhale the fresh salt air. We walk back down the avenue watching our shadows converge,
time and again, beneath the streetlamp light as we make our way back to the hotel.

At 5:30 a.m., I wake and quietly change clothes before leaving Betsy, who is comfortably sleeping in our hotel bed at the Pine Inn; I want to photograph Edward's old studio before sunrise. Built in 1925, the building included Carmel's first bookstore and the Carmel Art Association, but Edward's old studio is now home to the Carmel Bay Company Store. The wetness of the sea air makes my hair curl as I search for the right angle to frame Edward's old studio window on the second floor of the Seven Arts Building. Photographing this early allows me to stand in the middle of the street, free from the interference of the tourists and residents who regularly pass along Ocean Avenue. Charis and Edward would never have imagined that decades later a woman with a four-by-five camera would stand in the street making a slow exposure of the studio window in the first light of day.

Not far from Edward's studio is Cooke's Cove. I grab a cigarette from the pack and lean on the hood of the car, watching the ocean waves undulate, the backdrop to a theater of beach joggers and morning dog walkers beginning their daily routines.

After a late breakfast, Betsy and I head back to the Carmel Bay Company Store, which is now open. We join other tourists milling about the aisles of books, dinnerware, candles, handmade soaps, and home furnishings. We walk up a wide staircase to the second floor and enter Edward's old studio, an airy room with a high vaulted ceiling and exposed wood beams. A picture window is the focal point of the east side of the room. Virginia creeper has made its way across the window and frames the scene outside. Another large window hovers high above Ocean Avenue. The space is bright, and even though it is large, it feels cozy. The worn hardwood floor moans softly as we walk across it. I try to imagine the placement of the couch and camera, along with the nearby model stands, the day Charis came here to model for Edward for the first time. Edward's old bookcase-topped desk would have been somewhere in the room, as well as his bed, covered by a black and red serape that "gave the room a brilliant splash of color that kept the place from looking somber."[46]

I could see them there—him making her feel comfortable by letting her look through the lens as he posed first, sitting calmly on the couch, and her, overcompensating for her nervousness by undressing in front of Edward instead of in the bathroom down the hall as he had offered. Edward confidently moving behind the camera, peering through the pince-nez glasses he kept around his neck to see if the image on the ground glass is in focus, before quickly glancing back at Charis to make an exposure. Charis reveals, "You were always aware of the latent energy in Edward, but in speech and movement he actually was a calm, quiet man. When he was working, however, all the vitality came fully to the surface; hands and body moved with astonishing speed and grace."[47]

The camera is a powerful tool—a veil to hide behind, a window to see through. A photographer has been granted permission to observe things that even a close friend might miss—little moles or freckles, a scar, a slightly drooping eyelid. The sitter allows themselves to be *seen*, to be the focus of the photographer's intense attention and curiosity.

Maybe having the camera's eye on her was innate to Charis. Helen, her mother, had also been a famous muse. In 1908, Arnold Genthe had photographed her, Charis writes,

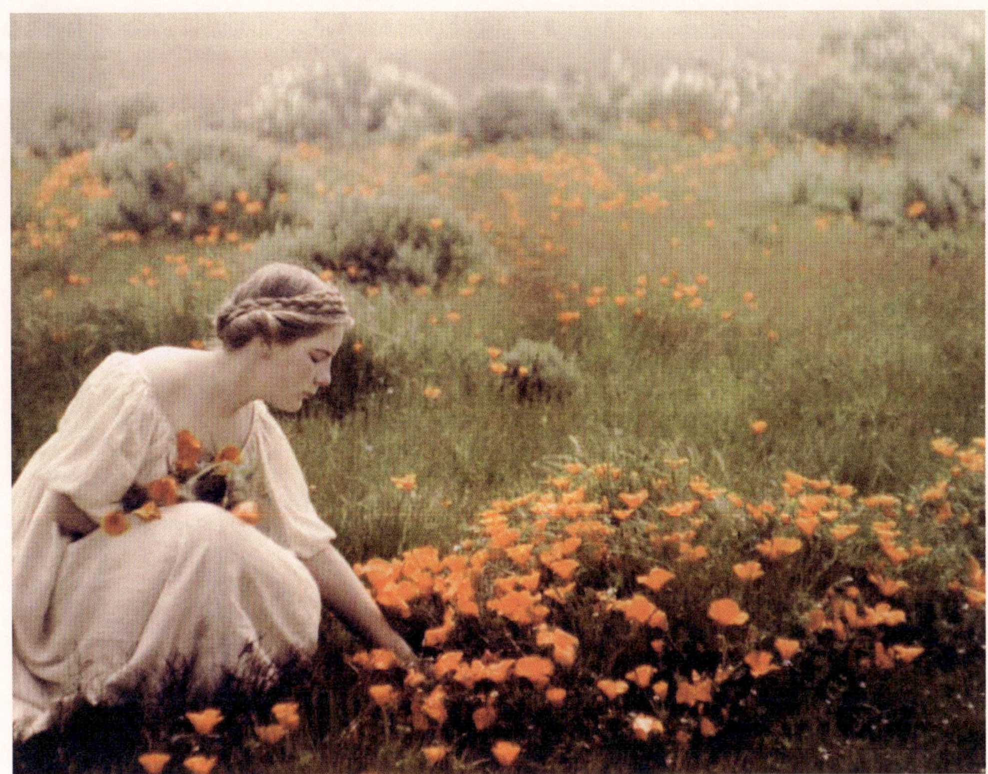

"in a pictorial style—clad in billowing draperies at Carmel Point and kneeling in a field of golden California poppies."[48] I first saw this image of Helen in a history of photography class in the early 1990s. We were learning about Genthe, who was known for being one of the first photographers to use the autochrome color process. Little did I know that I would discover more about Genthe's graceful model as I learned about Charis. Helen was considered by many to have a beauty, poise, and maturity beyond her years. Writer Sinclair Lewis, poet William Rose Benét, and Arnold Genthe all hoped to win her affection, yet it was H. L. Wilson, then a well-known writer, whom she chose to marry. So perhaps it was a natural thing for Charis to pose for Edward, just as it had been for Helen with Arnold Genthe.

When Charis went to model for Edward a second time, they were much more comfortable with each other, and were able to hold conversations effortlessly as they worked. One of my favorite pictures of Charis was taken during this session. During a break, Charis sits with her legs crossed, her robe falling loosely about her body. She holds a cup of wine in one hand, the other gently rests on her shoulder. Her head is turned in profile, and she appears to be in deep thought. This photograph is significant because it diverged from the intentions Edward had for the other pictures he was making that day. Charis was captivating enough to make him jump up, put down his wine, shout for her to hold the pose, and photograph her—her face, her gestures, her body language—as Charis, rather than as a fragmented nude.

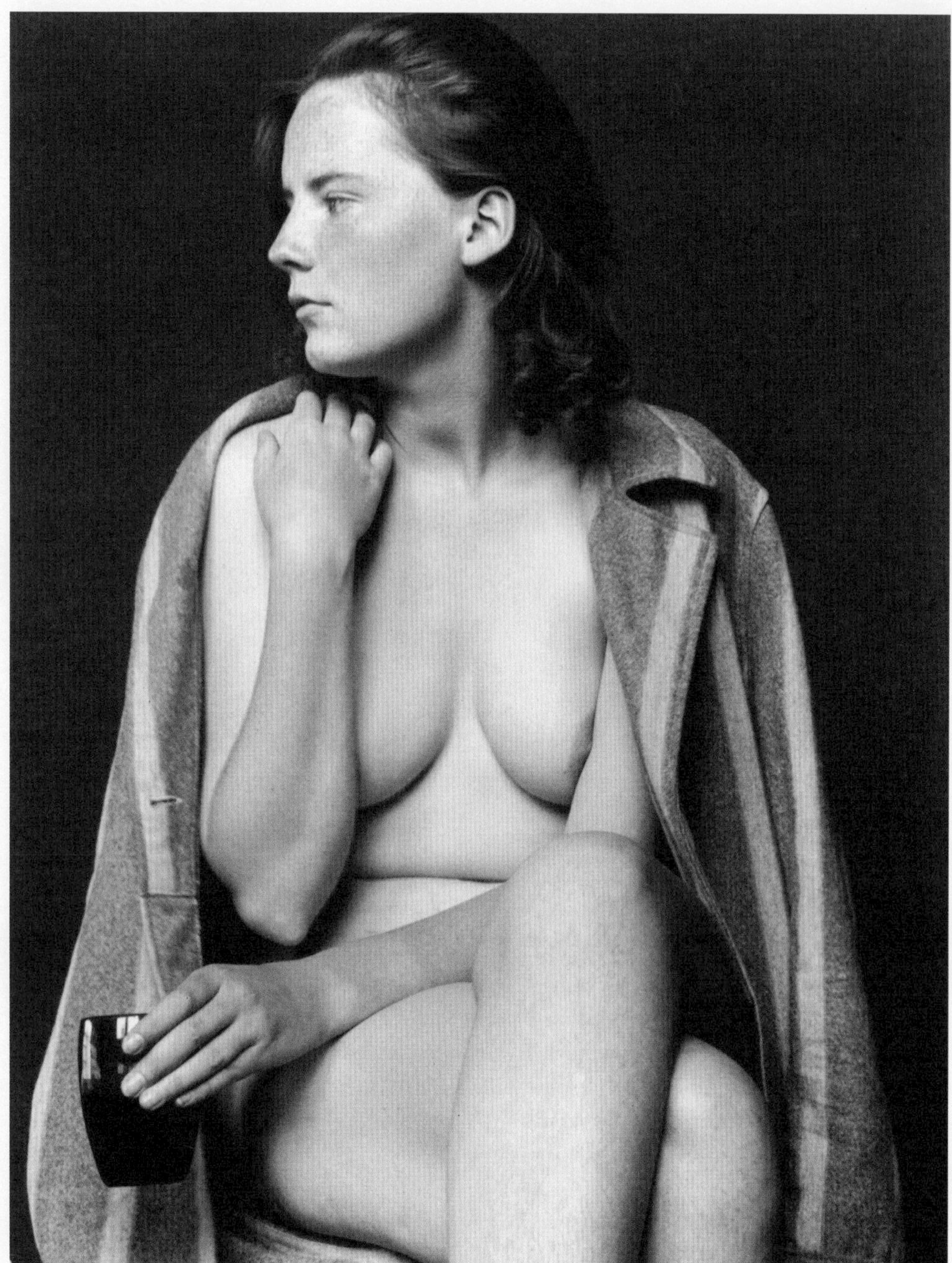

As Edward made his last exposures of the day, Charis knew that she would make the first move:

> *After all this loosening up I looked for a change in Edward's behavior, but he remained as circumspect as before, and I realized that his reputation as a Lothario was wildly exaggerated. I would have to take the first step. I did so, even though it was only a very compelling look, it soon brought photography to a halt. What followed was as great a revelation as Edward's photographs. I thought of myself as a sophisticated woman of the world, but now I learned how limited all my previous experience had been, as what had always seemed to me to be a branch of playacting became unmistakably real.[49]*
>
> *My sexual experience in the three years since I was sixteen had been notable for quantity rather than quality. As a result, I was less than optimistic about ever finding "the right man," and I had acquired a rather cynical view of the male sex.*
>
> *Meeting Edward changed everything. With the first nude session, I had to revise my views on men—they weren't all alike in the matter of sex. Here was one who could spend an afternoon in a room with a nude female and never make a move. In a very short time we achieved a degree of intimacy I had never before experienced: Edward was the person from whom I need have no secrets, the person to whom I could tell anything, no matter how foolish or embarrassing it might be. He was the person from whom I could expect understanding, sympathy, acceptance, and love. As for making love, with Edward I discovered right away that, while I had an extensive acquaintance with the mechanics, the deep exchange of feeling that can transform the mechanics into a profound fusion of two individuals was entirely new to me. With patience and tact, and without ever commenting on my lack of erotic presence, Edward gradually broke down my resistance to real participation. In loving Edward, my heart had found a home.[50]*

In the months that followed, Charis and Edward met at his studio in the pre-dawn hours. Before the blue hues of morning signaled the impending workday, Charis and Edward lay on the bed, their bodies lit by the light of a single candle so as not to alert anyone of their presence. Edward had always reserved these early morning hours to write in his *Daybooks*, but now he spent this time with Charis, getting to know her body as she was getting to know his, and taking pleasure in not just sex but in conversation, talking with her as they drank coffee from the matching yellow mugs that he had bought for them. The last regular entry that Edward wrote in his *Daybooks* is where their story begins.

> *December 9, 1934. I have not opened this book for almost 8 months,—and with good reason; I have been too busy, busy living. I notice the last entry was 4-20. On 4-22 a new love came into my life, a most beautiful one, one which will, I believe, stand the test of time.*

I met C. a short time before going South on the P.W.A.P. work, saw her at a concert, was immediately attracted, and asked to be introduced. I certainly had no conscious designs in mind at the time, but I am not in the habit of asking for introductions to anyone which means that the attraction was stronger then than I realized. I saw this tall, beautiful girl, with finely proportioned body, intelligent face well-freckled, blue eyes, golden brown hair to shoulders, —and had to meet. Fortunately this was easy. Her brother was already one of my good friends, which I, of course, did not know.

I left for the South before our paths crossed again. While there a letter from S. said she had a new model for me, one with a beautiful body. It was C.— Poor S.—How ironical. But what happened was inevitable.

The first nudes of C. were easily amongst the finest I had done, perhaps the finest. I was definitely interested now, and knew she knew I was. I felt a response. But I am slow, even if I feel sure, especially if I am deeply moved. I did not wait long before making the second series which was made on April 22, a day to always remember. I knew now what was coming; eyes don't lie and she wore no mask. Even so I opened a bottle of wine to help build my ego. You see I really wanted C. hence my hesitation.

And I worked with hesitation; photography had a bad second place. I made some eighteen negatives, delaying always delaying, until at last she lay there below me waiting, holding my eyes with hers. And I was lost and have been ever since. A new and important chapter in my life opened on Sunday afternoon, April 22, 1934.

After eight months we are closer than ever. Perhaps C. will be remembered as the great love of my life. Already I have achieved certain heights reached with no other love.

Domestic relations have been severely strained, quite to the breaking point, casting a shadow over my association with C. A change must take place and soon. I must have peace to enjoy, fulfill, this beauty.[51]

Bets and I eat dinner at Vesuvio, an Italian restaurant a few blocks from the Pine Inn. The restaurant is crowded, so we sit at the bar, drinking wine as we take turns wrapping our arms around each other's backs and resting our hands on each other's thighs. We could do this at the bar, our backs turned away from the gaze of Carmel residents. This is a wealthy crowd; they seem tighter-lipped and more proper than the bohemian Carmelites of the 1920s and '30s, who talked with passion late into the night and then wandered home down dirt lanes.

We share an arugula and tomato pizza as we discuss the possibilities of the bartender being the father of our child, were we to have one; he is tall and tattooed and has long dark hair. He moves with grace, like a dancer. As drink orders from servers, food orders from customers at the bar, and complaints from the well-to-do come his way, he remains calm and attentive.

Bets and I are content with the way our lives are. We know a few artist couples who have found a way to make it all work, keeping kids and jobs and relationships in balance, but we wonder if the same would be true for us. We are both afraid that at least one of us would have to sacrifice her art career in order to take care of a child. I understand parenting to be completely exhausting, especially those first few years. I can be selfish; I enjoy long, quiet hours of working without interruption. On top of this, when Betsy is depressed, it is hard for her. We both wonder what parenting would be like when her depression surfaced. We love our life together. It is simple and full of freedom, and we accept each other's eccentricities. We give each other space and enjoy the time we spend together.

After dinner, standing outside the White Rabbit, Bets and I look up at the window that we think Charis looked out of so long ago while working at The Carmelita Shop. We stand there for a while. The store is open and we wander upstairs to find that every item in the store is dedicated to *Alice in Wonderland*. Mad Hatter and Alice t-shirts, tote bags, and aprons hang from the racks. Giant antique keys, charm necklaces, and Alice figurines sit on overstuffed shelves. Hanging wall clocks adorn every last inch of space. The numbers on their faces are reversed and their hands run counterclockwise.

Through two swinging French doors, I can see the back office, where an ornate, wing-backed, gold-gilded, oversized Queen of Hearts throne sits in the corner. Nestled in this treetop office, Charis wrote and read the letters and poems that she and Edward sent to one another, even though they lived in the same town. They counted on the Carmel Post Office in the long hours and sometimes days that kept them apart. The last line of a poem Charis mailed to Edward uses her own code to date it—she references the time that she wrote it as a gesture to indicate the specific time she was thinking of him and to convey the intimacy of their connection.

> *What time ago was it*
> *I thot, hoped, began (slowly) to believe—*
> *What time ago could this have been when now*
> *I am so full of you*
> *I make no gesture freely*
> *My thots curl round your eyes*
> *And catch the clouds inside your eyes*
> *And your eyes look out of me at*
> *Me looking out of them at you*
> *And so*
> *What time ago*
> *12M4232434*[52]

Here, amid all the Alice in Wonderland clocks in the space where Charis once watched for Edward, this link to a precise moment in time seems so resonant: 12:00 midnight, April 23 to April 24, 1934.

Both the Carmelita Shop and Edward's portrait studio were forced to close because of the Depression. In January 1935, Edward moved to Santa Monica Canyon with his son Brett to take a job working for the Federal Art Project, a New Deal program that was created to support the work of artists. A few months later, Edward made a picture for Charis, a valentine. He arranged objects from their time together in Carmel for a still life: a Japanese straw slipper balanced on a white sake bottle, a coffee cup turned on its side, the back of an envelope with a wax seal, the front of a second envelope with Charis Wilson written across it, an f5.6 Plasmat lens, Edward's pince-nez glasses, a Mexican box that contained love letters, and a single candlestick, all carefully arranged on a large piece of white paper. In the lower left corner, Edward wrote significant dates to be decoded and understood only by Charis in his large and loopy handwriting. In the accompanying letter he sent with the photograph, Edward urged, "Come on down. If we are going to starve, we might as well do it together."[53] Charis recounts her reservations in her memoir.

Would running to Edward for shelter be a good beginning for our life together? What did I have to offer him that could make a strong alliance— devotion? Fidelity? The ability to work hard?

By summer's end, Charis had made the decision to move in with Edward. For the
next two years they lived together in Santa Monica Canyon. Edward's sons Brett, Neil, and
Cole stayed with them for varying intervals.

———————————

Bets and I follow Highway 101 to Malibu, where surfers change into their wetsuits on
the shoulder of the road and the unsightly backs of expensive houses block our view of the
ocean. Northbound traffic inches along as one lane of the highway is closed for repairs.
The possibility of a landslide feels frightening—safety fences seem like rickety barriers for
the sides of mountains. We pass a sign for Mulholland Drive, and I wonder how many
Mulholland Drives there are in Los Angeles. The Santa Monica Mountains come into view;
they look like the backs of horses with wide girths and velvety golden hair.

It is mid-afternoon when we reach Santa Monica Canyon. We take two quick turns
off the highway to arrive at Mesa Road, a narrow and steep residential street within walking
distance of the beach. Charis mentions in *Through Another Lens* that when she visited Santa
Monica Canyon in the 1980s, the house at 446 Mesa Road was no longer there, but we
decide to take a look anyway. I am curious about the area and want to get a feel for the place.
Perhaps I'll be able to experience a little of the atmosphere and surroundings that Charis
did when she was young and first in love.

Charis describes 446 Mesa Road as "a standard Southern California bungalow, with
the long side of the L-shaped living room continuing into the dining room."[55] There was
an old-fashioned kitchen, a laundry porch converted to a darkroom, two bedrooms upstairs,
and "although the interior of the house had a standard layout, the spacious sundeck that
covered most of the roof was unusual. Surfaced with silver-painted tar paper and surrounded
by a three-foot parapet of white plaster, the deck in full sunlight dazzled the eyes. Because
he had rejoiced in such a rooftop area for photographing and sunbathing a decade earlier in
Mexico, Edward was seduced into paying more rent than he should have."[56]

As I stand across from the house that now has the number 446, I am struck by
how closely this bungalow fits Charis's description. I can't see inside, this might not have
been her house of course, but the one feature of the house that so allured Edward, the large
sundeck off the master bedroom, is there. And although there is no silver-painted tar paper

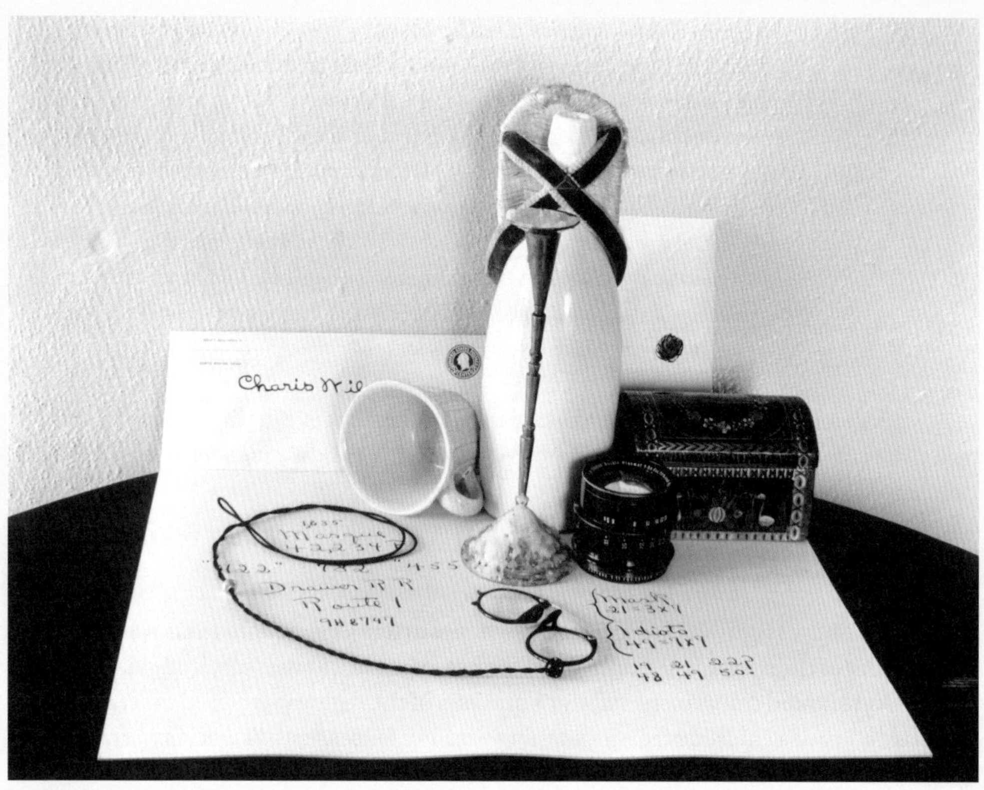

lining the deck, it is covered with the white plaster that she mentions and has an arched door that, when opened, could be where Charis sat for one of Edward's most famous photographs of her, simply titled *Nude*.

I can see it. The sizzling sun reflects off the silver-painted roof. Charis waits with her head tucked into herself like a swan as Edward adjusts his eight-by-ten camera. Though he usually uses his four-by-five Graflex, he is curious about how the eight-by-ten camera treats the human form. Charis sits on an old army blanket instead of the metallic paint that covers every inch of the sundeck. Edward likes to lie directly on that brilliant tin while sunbathing, no problem, but Charis prefers to lie on a blanket for their morning sun soaks. Edward is having a hard time fitting all of Charis in the frame while having enough room on the deck to see the image reflected on the ground glass. To allow for more distance, Edward asks Charis to scoot her body toward the open doorway to their bedroom. He knows that by exposing for the bright highlights of the light on Charis's arms and knees, the bedroom clutter in the background will fall into shadow.

Edward looks up to find Charis with her head folded into herself for some relief from the sun and asks her to "hold it." He adjusts the focus until the image of Charis appears sharp, upside down, and reversed on the ground glass. She is an elegant form, soft and curled, her arms make an oval, her interlaced fingers gently cradle her legs. Edward can only see the top of her head; her hair is parted and twisted and held close to her scalp with bobby pins. A triangle-shaped shadow stretches from its peak, behind her knee along the back of her calf and thigh, to its base, which rests on her adjacent thigh. The right edge of the shadow reaches between her crossed legs, concealing all but a tiny fringe of pubic hair.

In the image, Charis's body becomes a sensual depiction of the human form in a way that's reminiscent of the vegetables that Edward had photographed years before. Although Edward denied that his vegetables were metaphors for human beings, averring that his method of photographing was purely descriptive, it is hard to imagine that he was unaware of how the contours of a bell pepper could be interpreted as lovers in a tight embrace. While the vegetables Edward photographed seem to be striving to become more human, here, Charis becomes more of an object, a form. Though, unlike the nudes that Edward made in the studio—which were cropped tight and devoid of individuality—this picture retains elements of Charis's personality. Her hairstyle and pose are specific to her, even if we cannot see her face. This pose has been repeated by model after model, decade after decade, for professional and amateur photographers alike. None of the imitations I've seen are as elegant, graceful, or evocative as this image of Charis.

On Mesa Road, Charis and Edward struggled to make ends meet on his Federal Art Project salary of $38.50 a week. But Edward was resourceful, coming up with a Print of the Month Club for collectors and taking on freelance portrait work, photographing celebrities such as Henry Fonda, Igor Stravinsky, and E. E. Cummings for *Vogue*. Artists of all kinds would stop by for picnics, beach days, and parties, where Edward was known to cross-dress and dance a wild rhumba. Charis, who had a natural knack for conversation, often stayed up late, gossiping and talking with whomever was still around about books, art, culture, society, history, psychology, and politics. Charis and Edward attended some now-famous parties as well, including a reception for Marcel Duchamp at the house of collectors Walter and Louise Arensberg, who were close to Charis from her teenage years. I imagine how Duchamp's *Nude Descending a Staircase* might have loosely influenced both Edward and Charis as they made the images of her rolling down the Oceano dunes.

But it wasn't this social buzzing that interested me. I was impressed by the way Charis and Edward supported their passions, were true to themselves and their art, during this in-between time before life settled into a more predictable pattern. In Carmel, their limited time together had been spent in secret. While their life together in Santa Monica Canyon was new and exciting, Edward was under more financial stress than he had ever experienced. His guiding principle was to pare things down to necessities; he required only enough money to make photographs and enjoy life while doing so. Yet he still needed to make money. He spent tedious hours photographing paintings for the Federal Art Project and also agreed to make studio portraits, which at times, he loathed. They ate meals at home and drank alcohol only when visitors brought it with them. Edward bartered photographs for dentist's visits, cans of olive oil, a string quartet for a party. Charis was not in charge of managing the cooking and cleaning for the household; Edward

Edward Weston
Nude, 1936

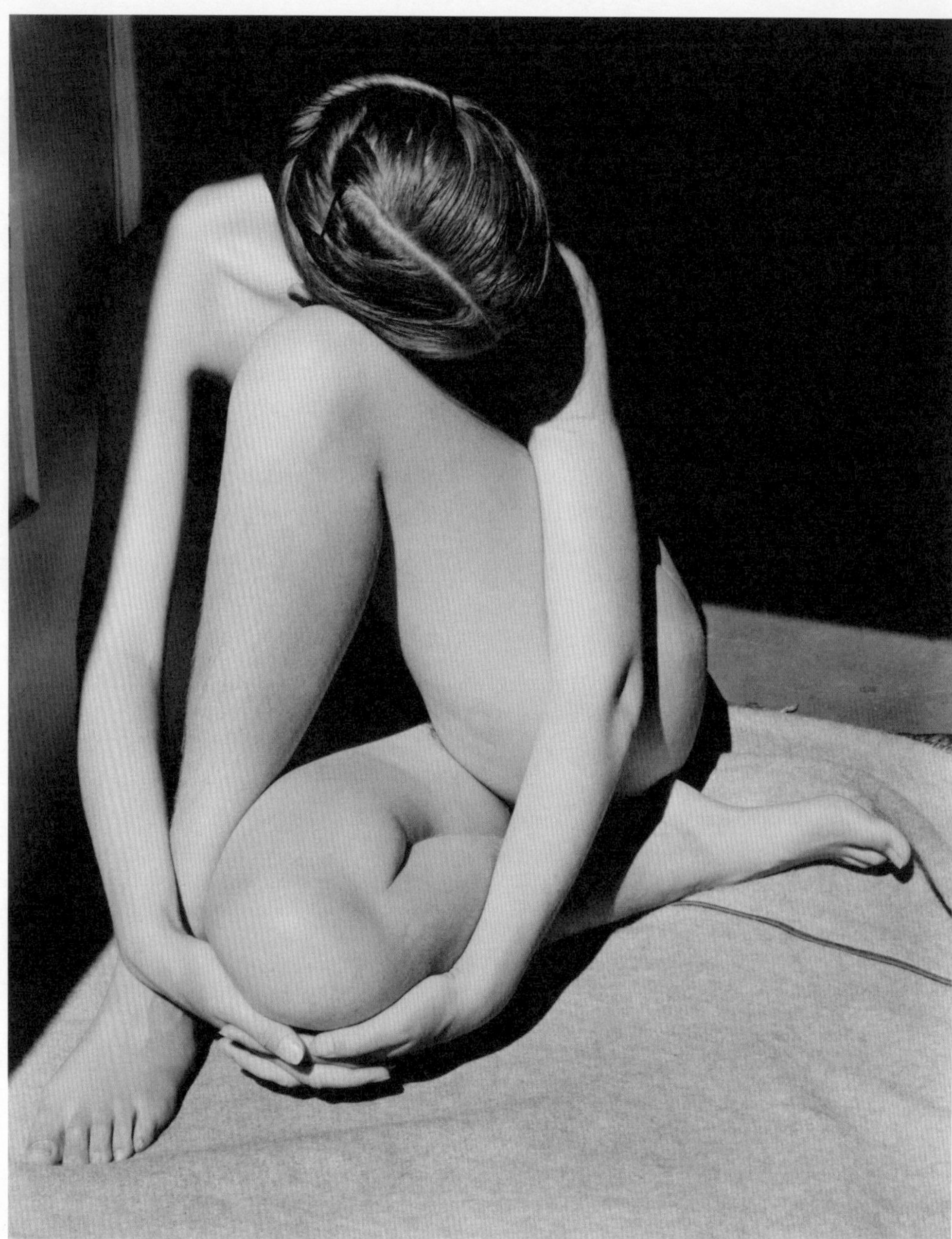

SANTA MONICA CANYON

believed that he, Charis, and each of his sons should be as self-sufficient as possible. Everyone in the house was expected to contribute to household chores.

This was a honeymoon period for Edward and Charis, a time for discovery. Charis was learning about her body, sexuality, and moods, and she was getting an education, not by attending college but by living life. She engaged in long talks with other writers and poets, receiving feedback on her work, and attended art openings and events with some of the most talented artists of the time. Charis had grown up around writers dedicated to honing their craft. Unlike the days she had spent working in her mother's dress shop doing accounting, in Santa Monica Canyon, Charis had time to explore her passions and to figure out who she was at her core.

Charis spent most of her days writing poetry and prose, sometimes even painting. Inspired by the unlocked stream-of-consciousness that can happen in the darkroom, Charis often scribbled lines of poetry while Edward developed film. I understood her compulsion. All of one's senses are heightened in the darkroom. And when it is shared with someone else, the sound of voices comes to represent the distance between bodies. The energy is felt by sound and an alertness to bodies moving in the dark. The act of developing sheet film is a meditation; it has a rhythm. Counting each piece of four-by-five film as it cycles through the developer, stop bath, and fixer is akin to counting strokes and alternating breaths to reach the end of a swimming pool. Being surrounded by the dark can be comforting—the darkroom is a perfect place for allowing strange and seemingly insignificant memories or freeform thoughts to emerge.

> *The pure blackness in a darkroom is disorienting in its intensity. At first my eyes protested by producing light shows—imaginary flashes and colorful patterns. When these subsided, and I discovered there was no difference between having one's eyes open or closed, I imagined I was poised on the ideal threshold for communicating with my subconscious where I supposed my poetic muse resided. Sure enough, words would appear against the blackness, and I would transcribe on a shorthand pad, a few words to a page, until the safety light came on and my muse quit. I would hurry to my "dark" writing, but it seldom revealed any rich poetic ore.*[57]

Naturally, Charis read as much as she could. She subscribed to *Poetry* magazine and read works by Percy Bysshe Shelley and T. S. Eliot. And she spent hours with Edward's *Daybooks*. She found his written words to be "dogmatic, didactic and judgmental, whereas Edward himself was open-minded, unpresumptuous, even diffident."[58] She learned about his struggles as an artist, his personal admissions of weakness, the evolution of his work, and his need for affirmation from Alfred Stieglitz, the preeminent voice on photography and its worth as art. His financial struggles were covered in detail: tedious portrait sessions, print viewings in hopes of making sales. His reliance on his wife Flora's financial support was especially fraught with emotion. Their relationship had been severely strained by the pressures of having four boys to raise during the Depression, as well as their differences in opinion on how to be a family—new, bohemian ideas versus more conventional and puritanical definitions and structures. All of this fueled Edward's frequent bouts of depression and his desire to live more simply—somewhere away from people where he could concentrate fully on his work.

In Edward's *Daybooks*, personal relationships and art making are completely interwoven and untangling those knots often became quite messy. Through research, I had learned not only about Edward's relationship with Charis, but also about his close and intimate relationships with Tina Modotti, Margrethe Mather (who was primarily attracted to women), and Ramiel McGehee (a self-identified gay man). Edward had been one of Ramiel's love interests, and the two of them regularly wrote letters to one another. Edward mentioned Ramiel and Tina in his *Daybooks*, "Tina and Ramiel, always linked in my mind, always clasped to my heart." I wonder why historians seem so sure that Edward was exclusively attracted to women. His Bohemian days spent with Margrethe Mather, Ramiel McGehee, and Johan Hagemeyer are described as celebrating a fluidity of sexuality. Party photos show Edward wearing dresses, participating in evenings where both men and women broke boundaries of conventional dress, exchanged gender roles, and let go of expectations defined by sex. Weston had a feminine side and a vulnerable presence that was conveyed in his letters, often sent with pressed flowers, that perhaps drew him close to women and men alike.

Each of Edward's long-term relationships brought with it a change in his picture-making style. He learned about Pictorialism from Margrethe Mather. In Mexico, Edward's work was as topical as was possible for him, taking its cues from Tina Modotti's exploration in politics and social issues. When Edward returned to Carmel in 1929, he began to photograph vegetables, shells, and other natural forms with Sonya Noskowiak. It was Sonya who showed him the evocative beauty of an artichoke cut in half—the two of them often took their time in the supermarket to find just the right peach or pear.

Edward's work changed once again after he met Charis. She was not interested in becoming a photographer, but she did want to learn as much about the medium as she could—she had a voracious appetite for learning about all kinds of things, from photography to painting, poetry to politics. Everything she learned could be put to use in her writing. After moving from Carmel to Santa Monica Canyon, Edward lost interest in making nude studio images. Perhaps it was because he did not have a studio, but more than likely, it was because his interests had changed again. He was turning away from closeups of the female form—on the rare occasion that he did photograph Charis, her body was not cropped or fragmented but depicted as part of the environment. Landscapes, often accompanied by Charis's text, became the focus of the next phase of his career.

When the landlord threatened to raise the rent at 446 Mesa Drive, Charis and Edward moved a few blocks away to 454 East Rustic Road. Their new house was quaint, with dark wood, and nestled among tall palm trees. It was while living here that Edward heard that the Guggenheim committee was interested in awarding a fellowship to a photographer. His first attempt at the application was precise and to the point, and only two sentences long:

"I wish to continue an epic series of photographs of the west, begun about 1929; this will include a range of satires on advertising to ranch life, from beach kelp to mountains. The publication of the above seems assured."[59] Charis and Edward heard from at least four different sources that Henry Allen Moe, the secretary-general of the Guggenheim Foundation, did not feel comfortable presenting Edward's statement to the judges; its brevity was regarded as pretentious and flippant. Charis helped Edward to rework the proposal by asking him questions, the two of them batting ideas back and forth before crafting a five-page document that she was proud to admit "left no doubt it was written in total sincerity by a man who believed deeply in his work."[60] They mailed the new statement in and waited to hear from the committee.

After several months, Edward received the news that his proposal had been awarded the Guggenheim. Charis and Edward soon began preparations for spending a majority of the next year on the road. They bought a new car with an advance from Phil Hanna, editor of *Westways Magazine*. In addition, Phil would pay them for monthly contributions while they were on the road—fifty dollars for Edward's pictures and fifteen dollars for Charis's writing. They bought camping gear, canned goods, and other simple foods to take with them. Charis planned to bring her Royal Signet typewriter, books to read, and a hand-carved pipe given to her by a friend. As for Edward, he would need the eight-by-ten Century Universal Camera, a Paul Ries tripod with a tilting top, a focusing cloth, a triple convertible Turner Reich lens, a lens shade, twelve film holders, a few filters, and a light meter. They had a few going-away parties where they received advice from friends about where to stay and what to bring. The last few weeks they spent in Santa Monica Canyon were filled with promise.

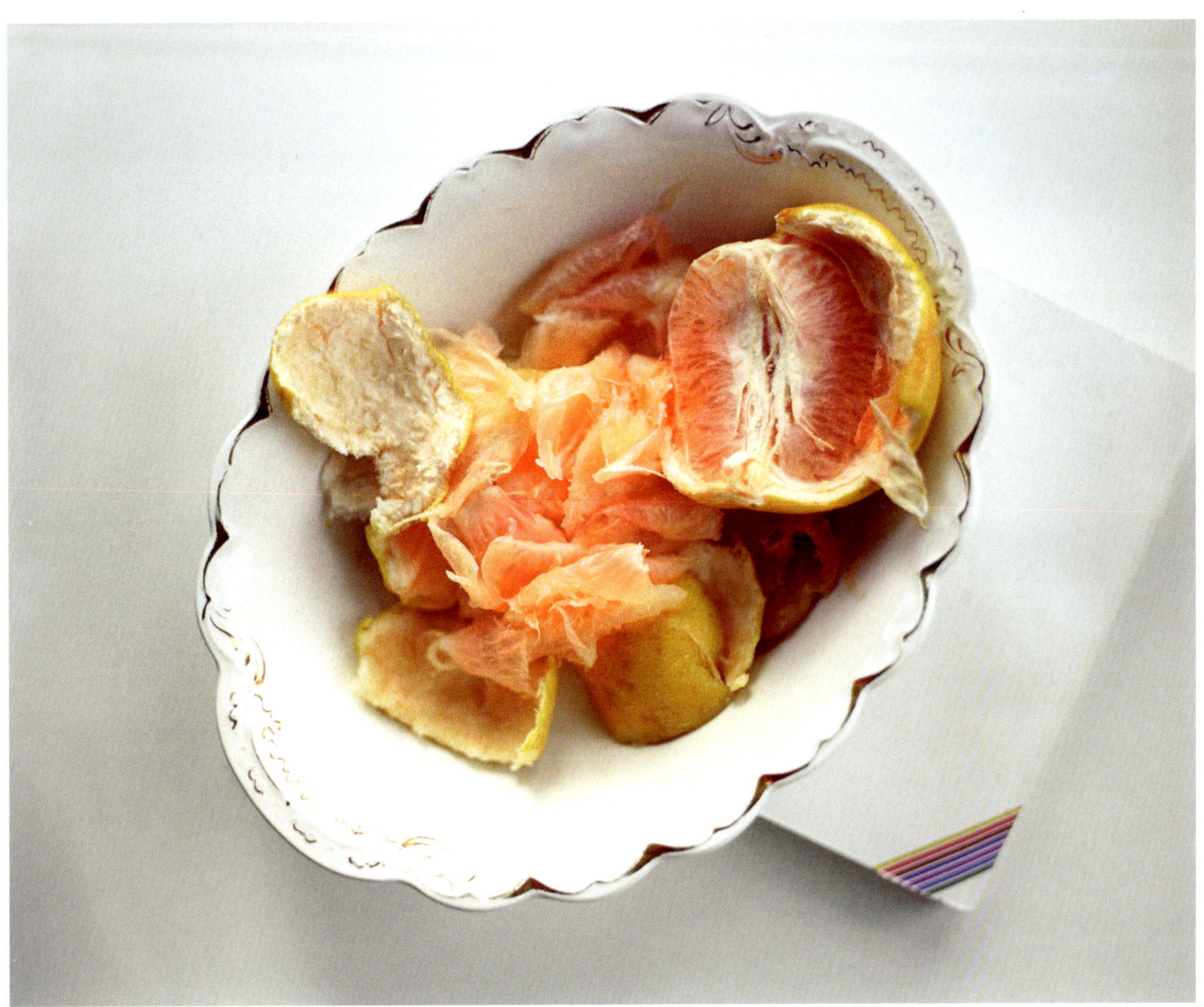

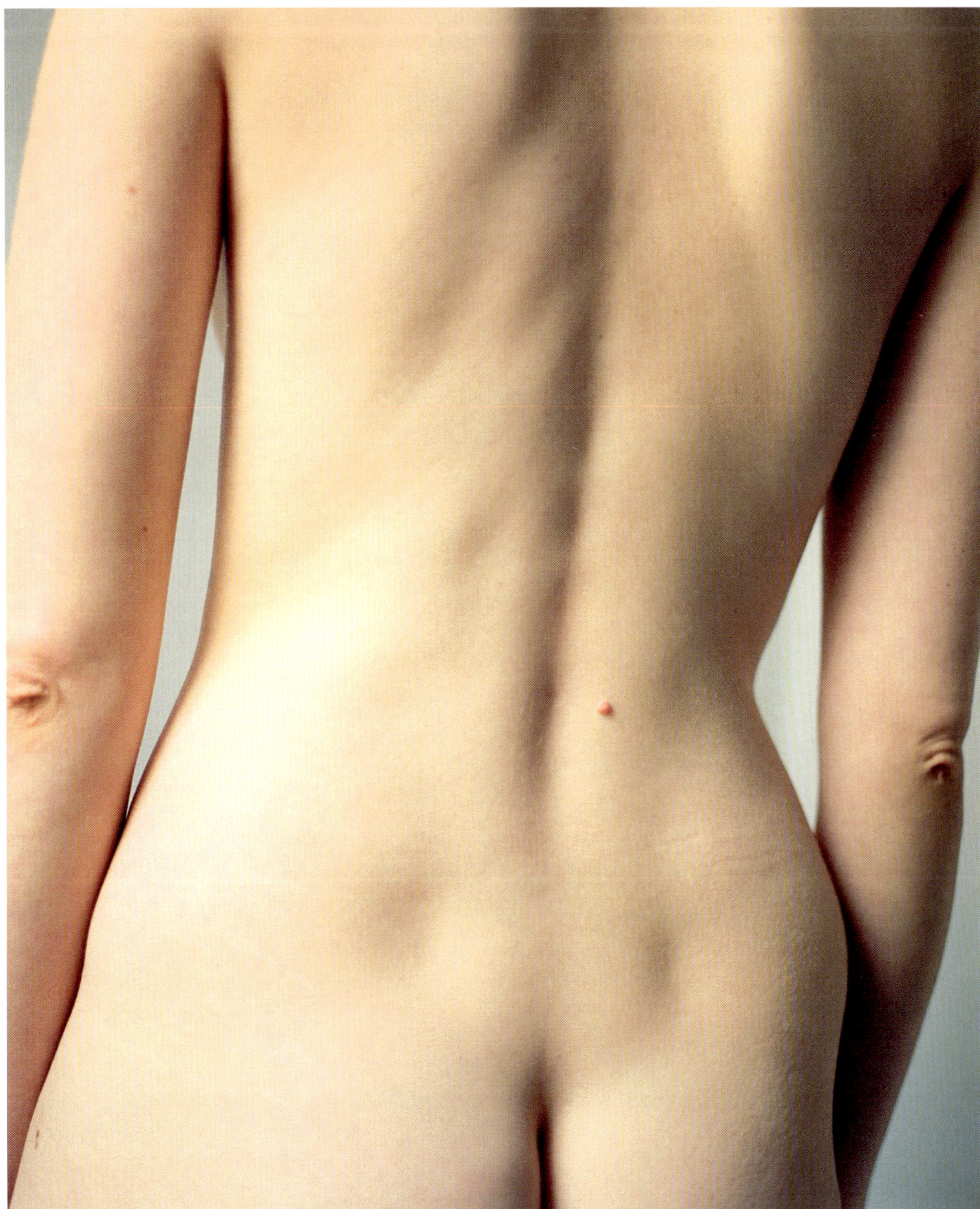

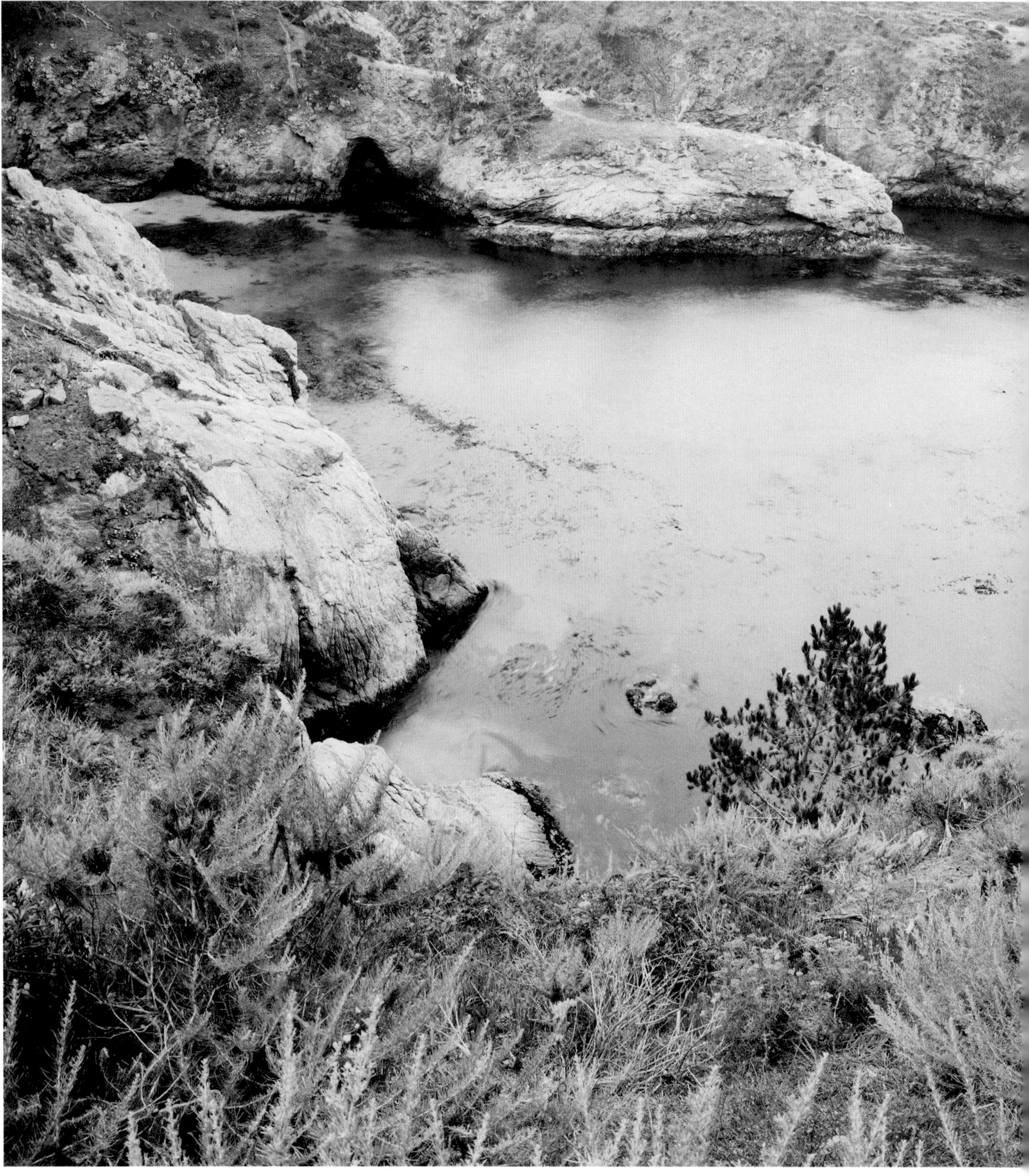

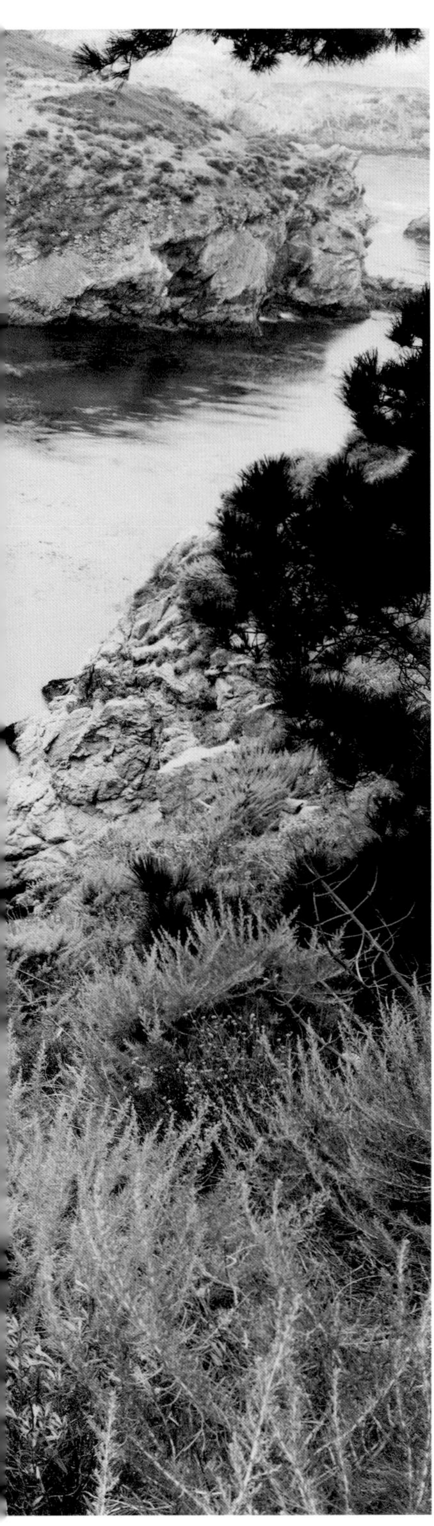

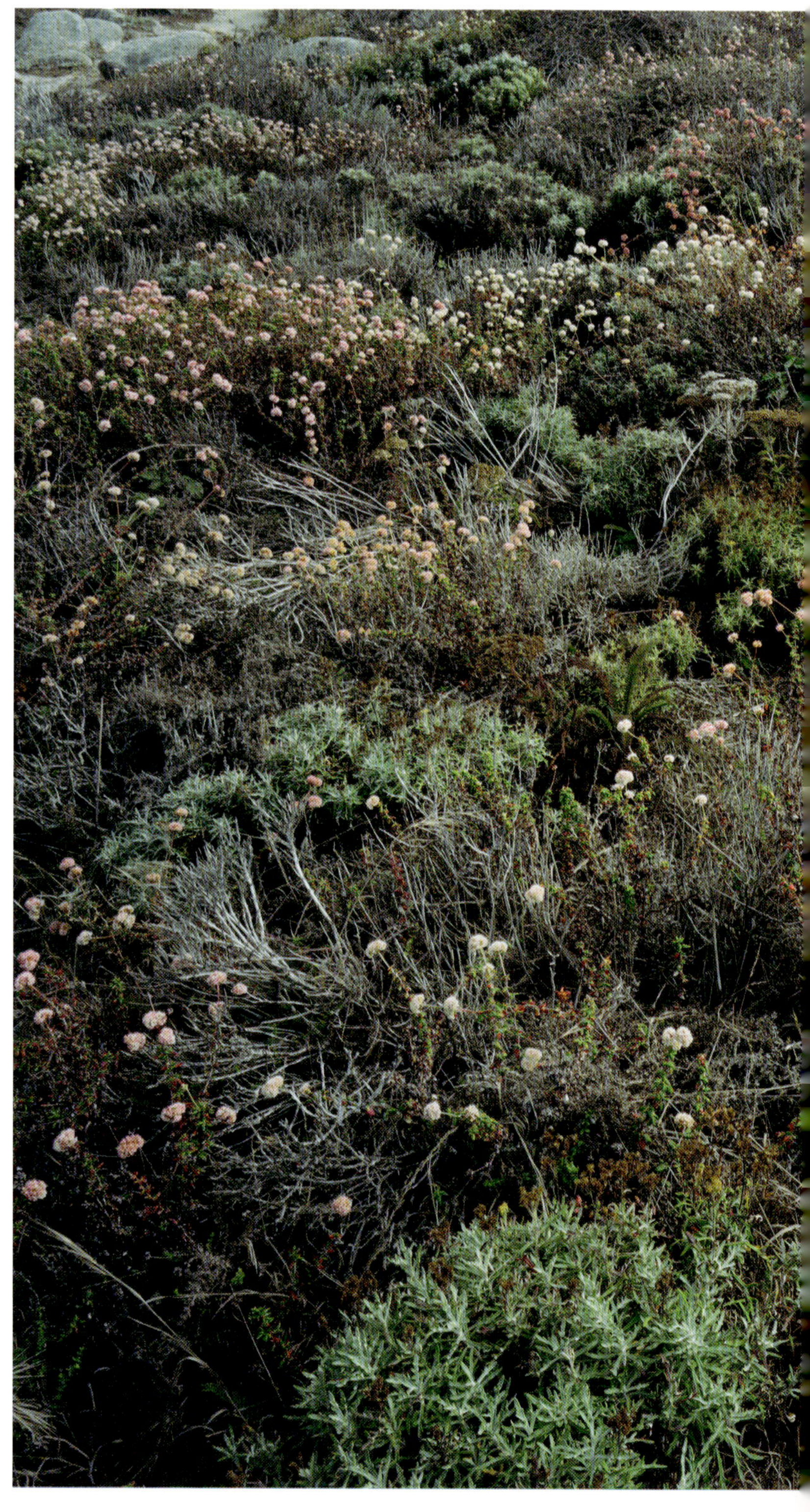

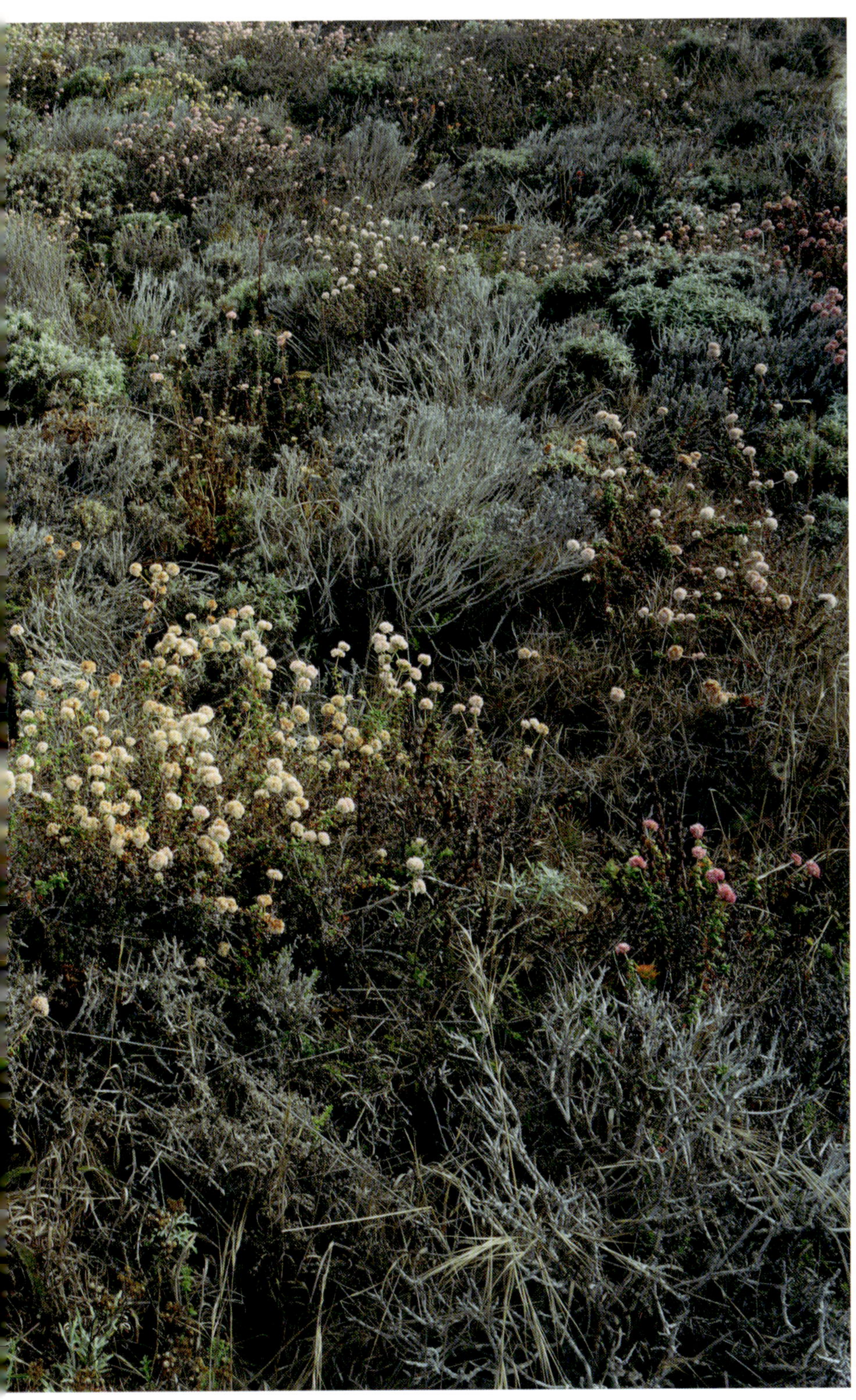

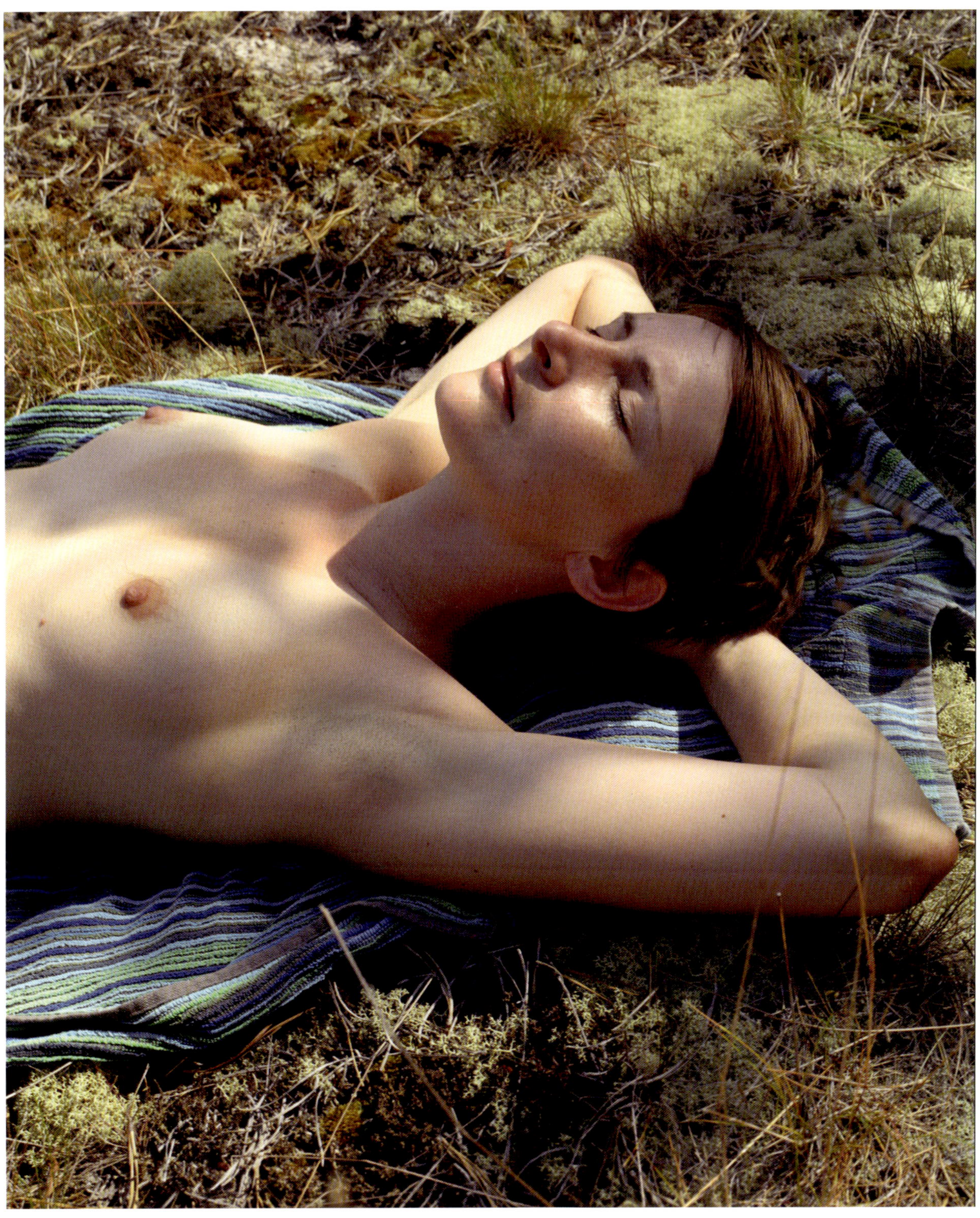

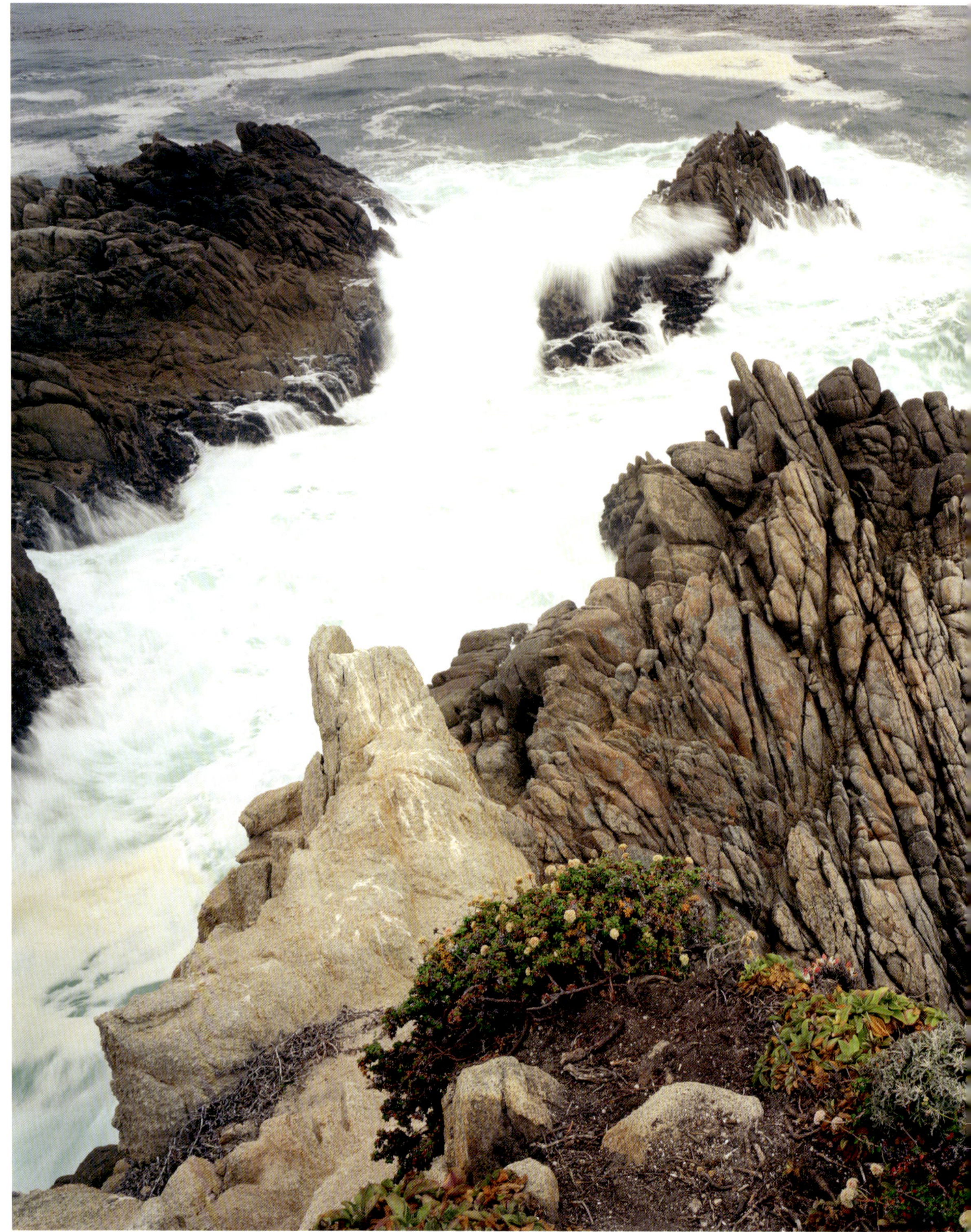

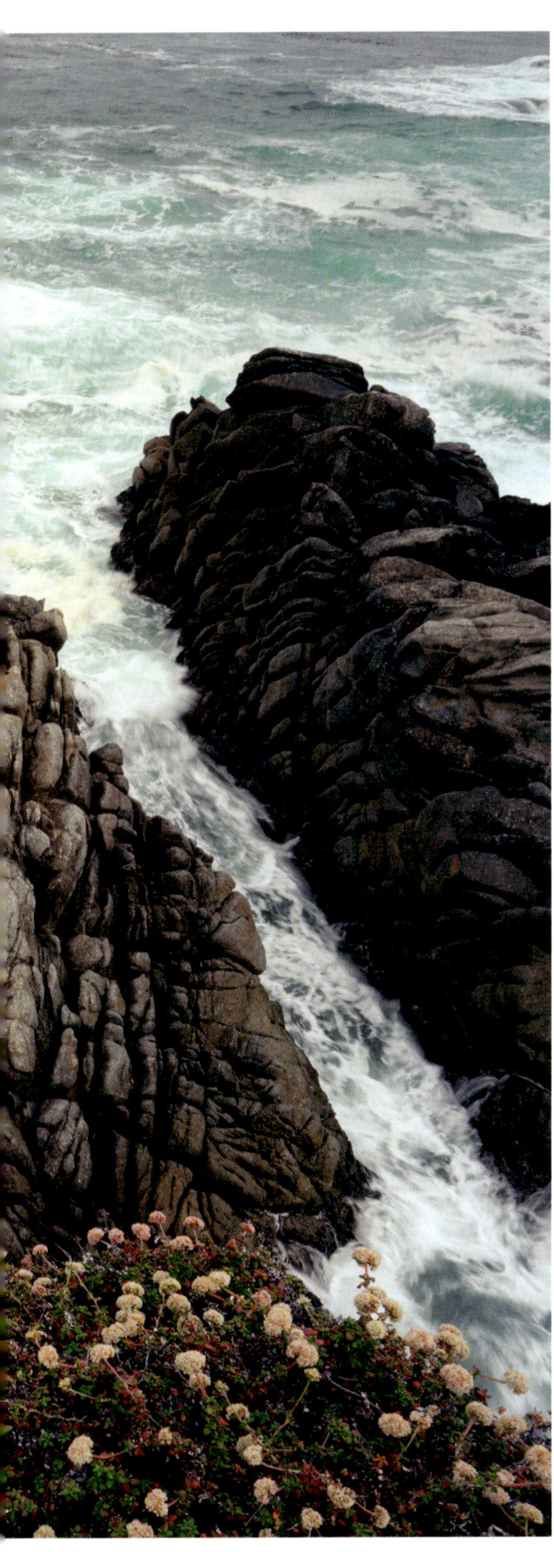

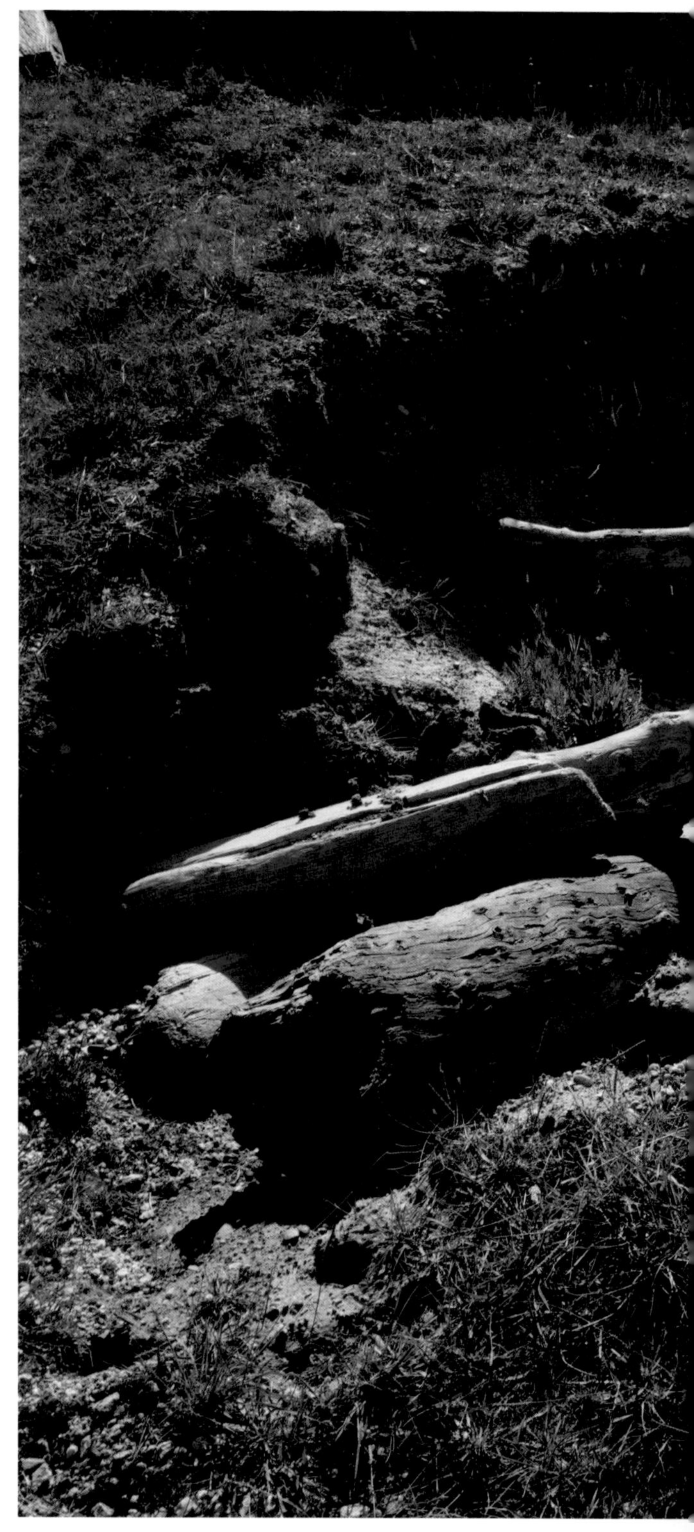

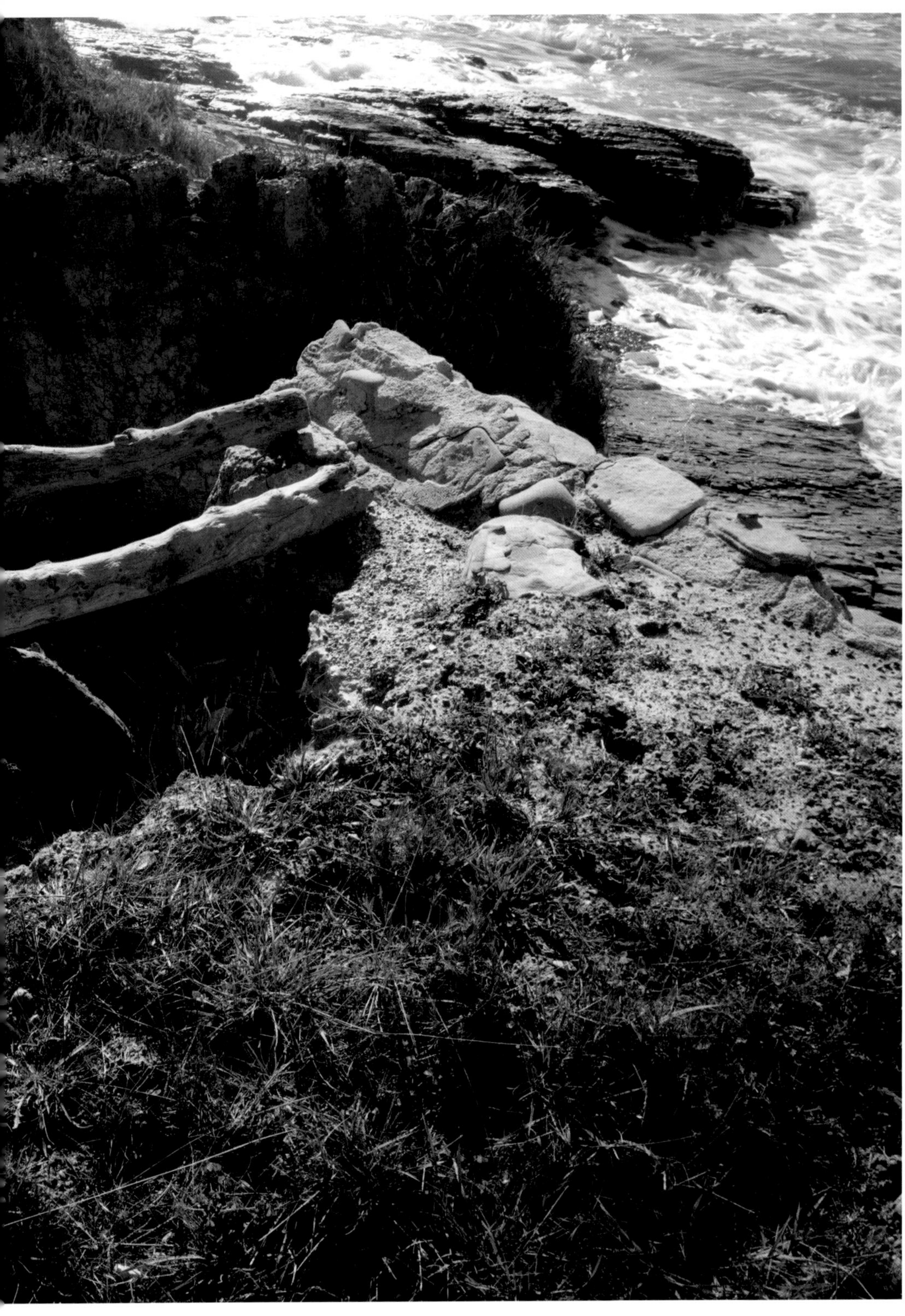

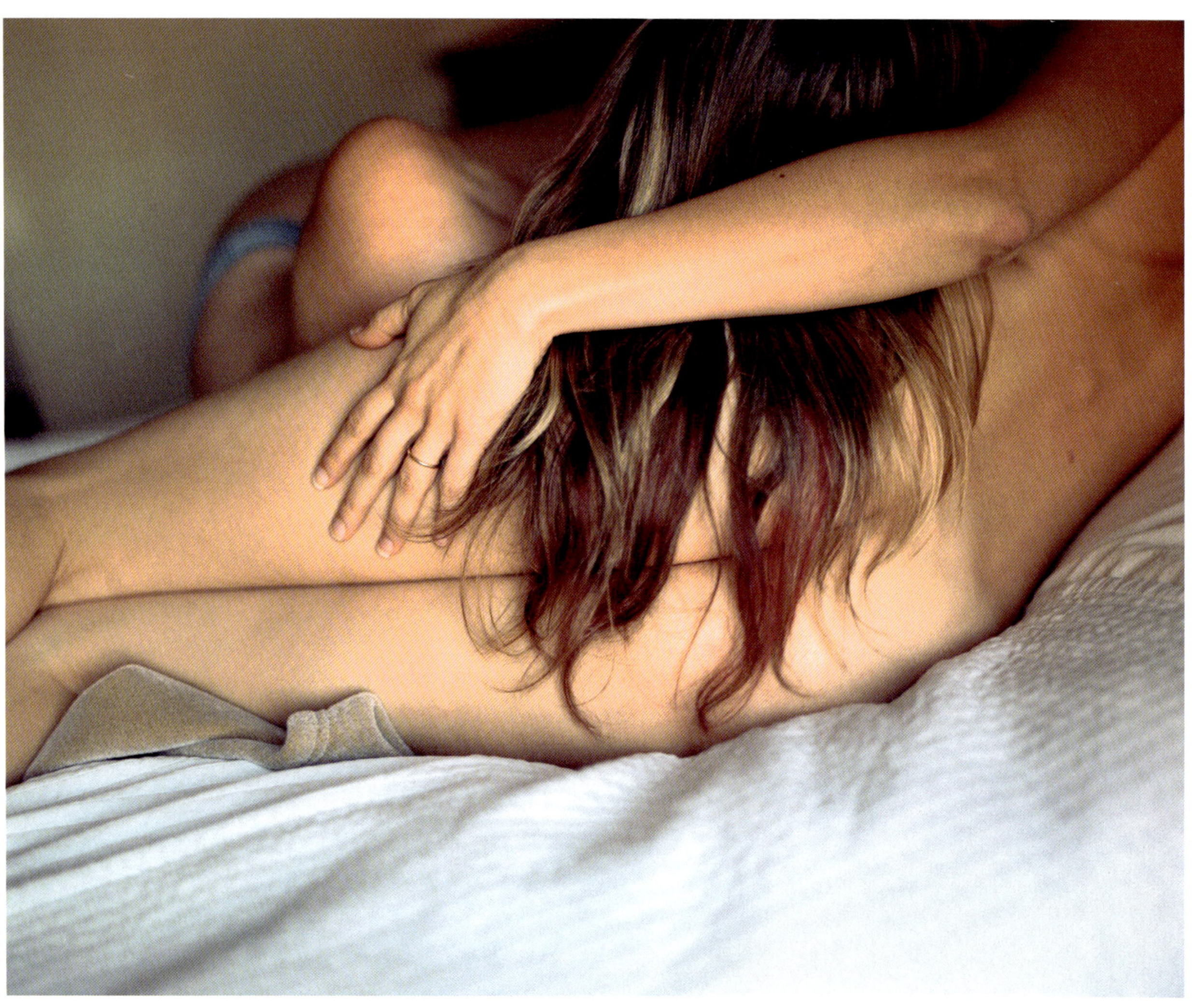

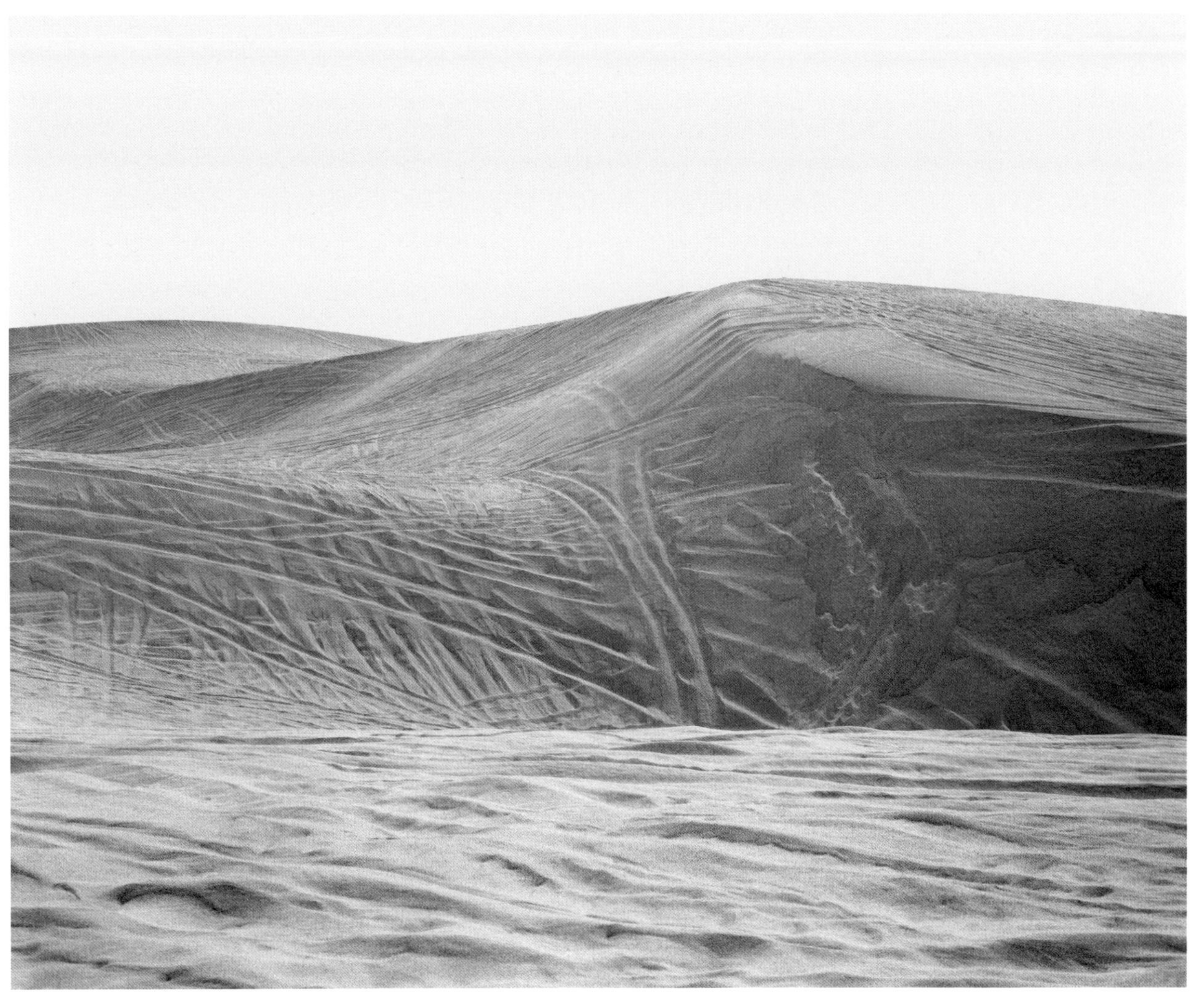

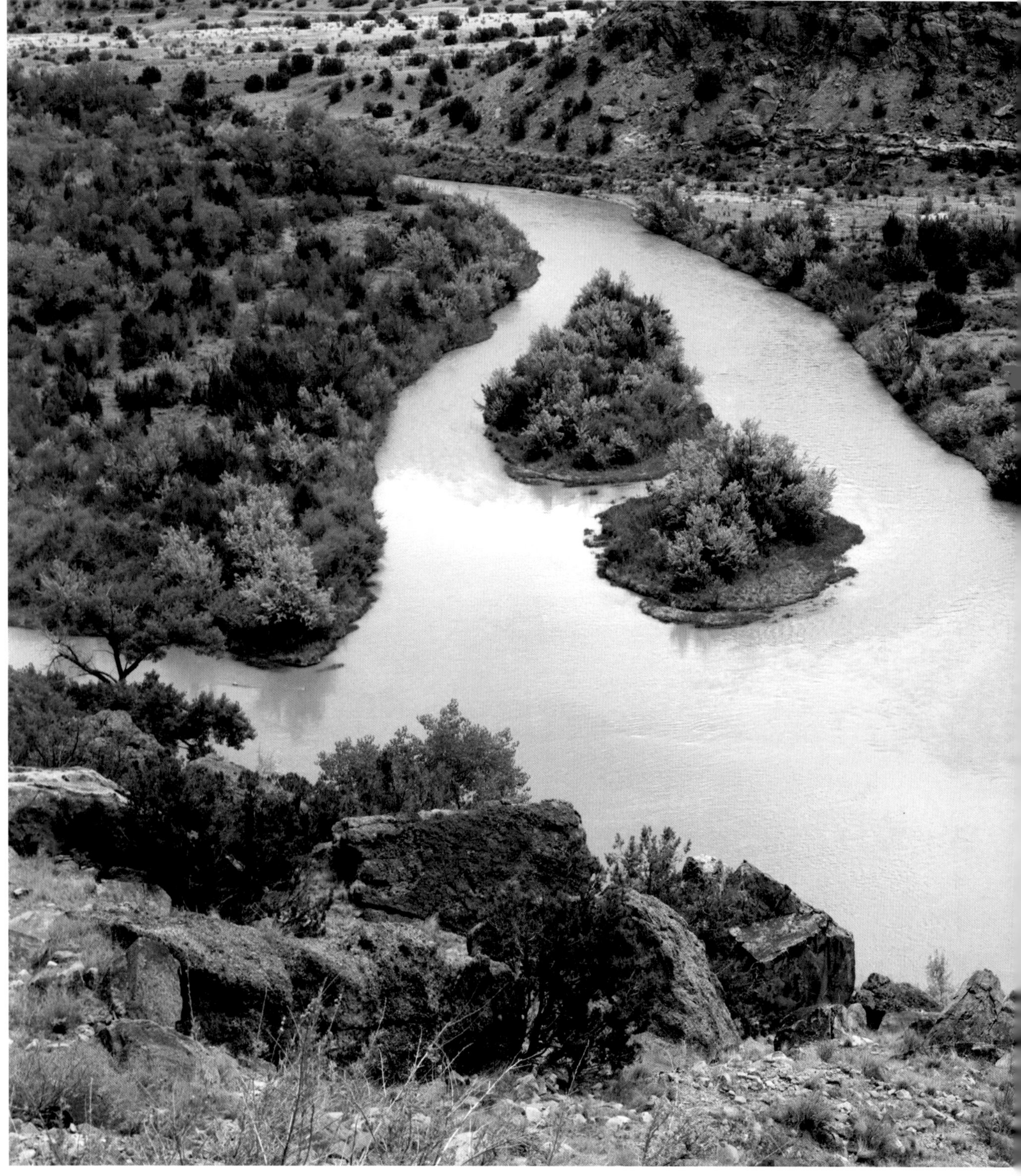

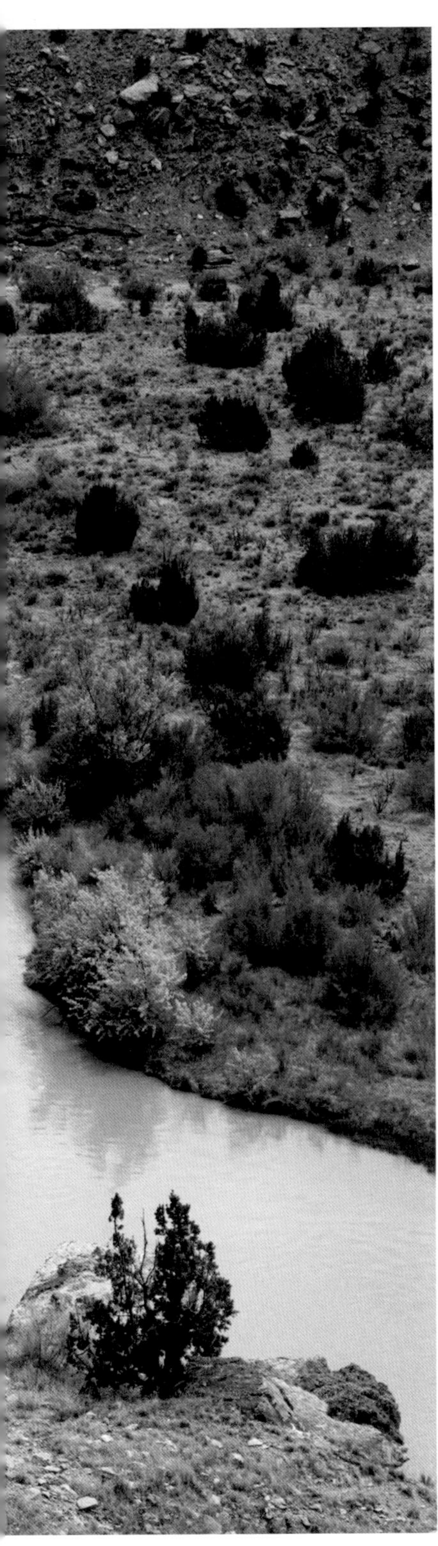

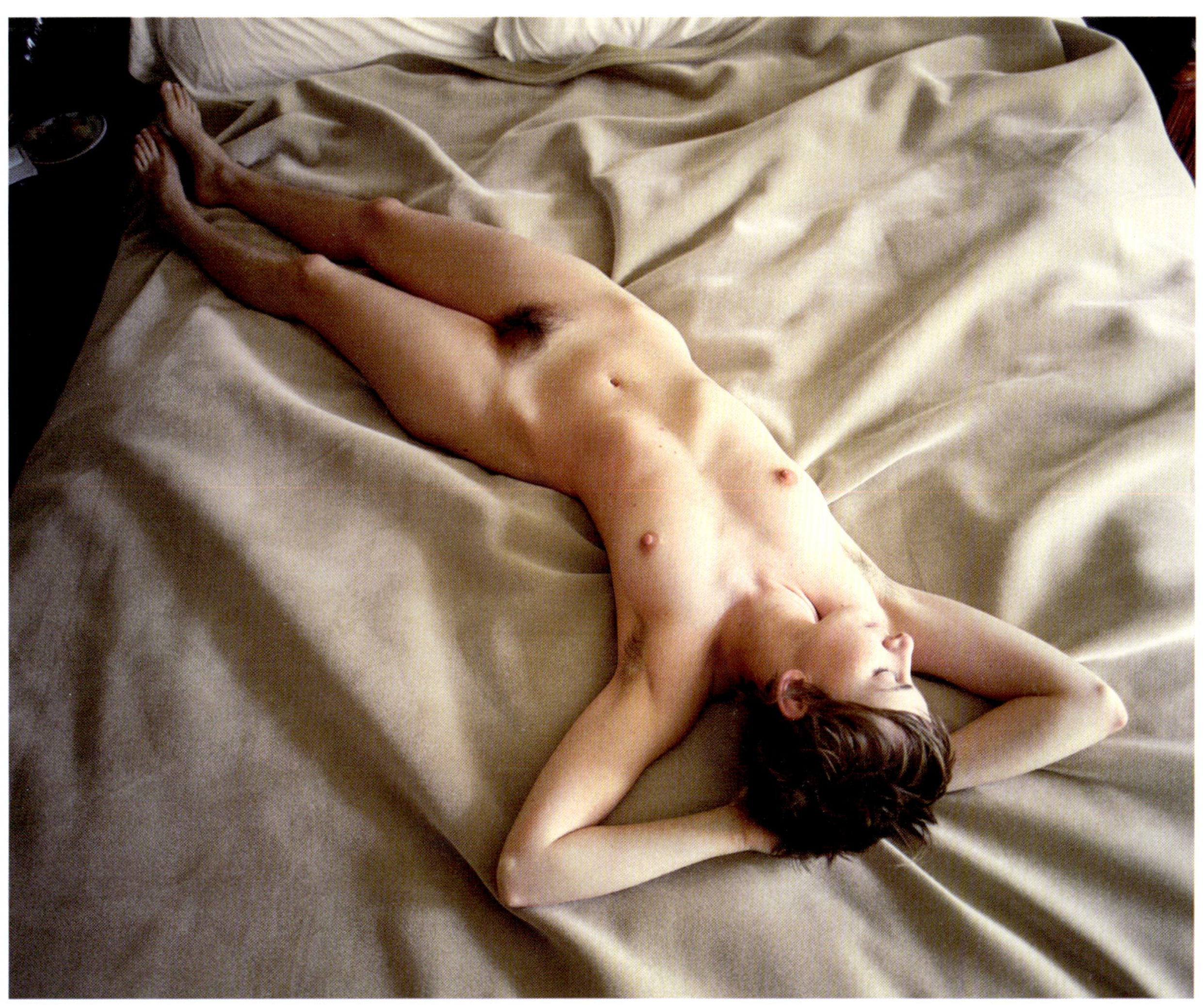

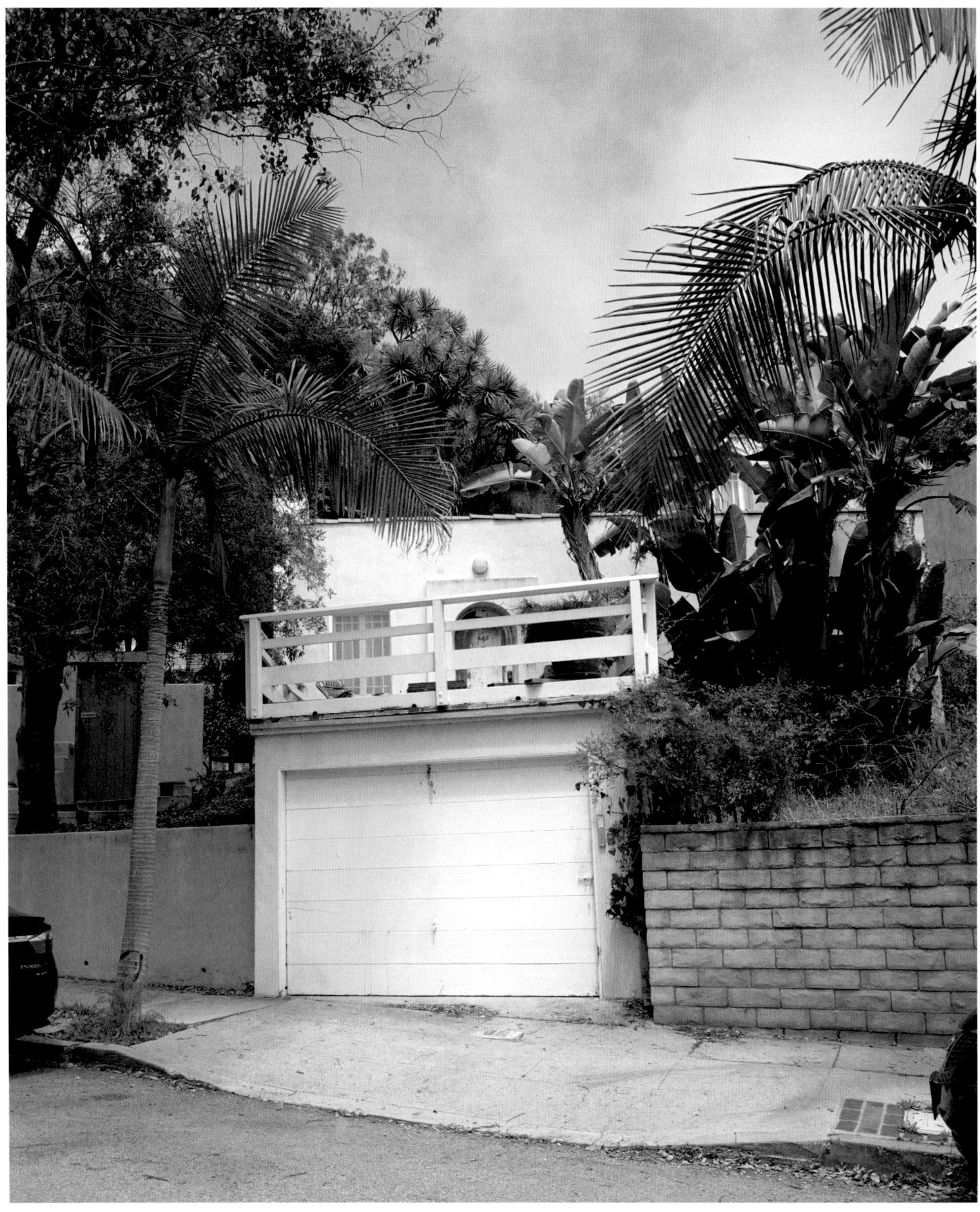

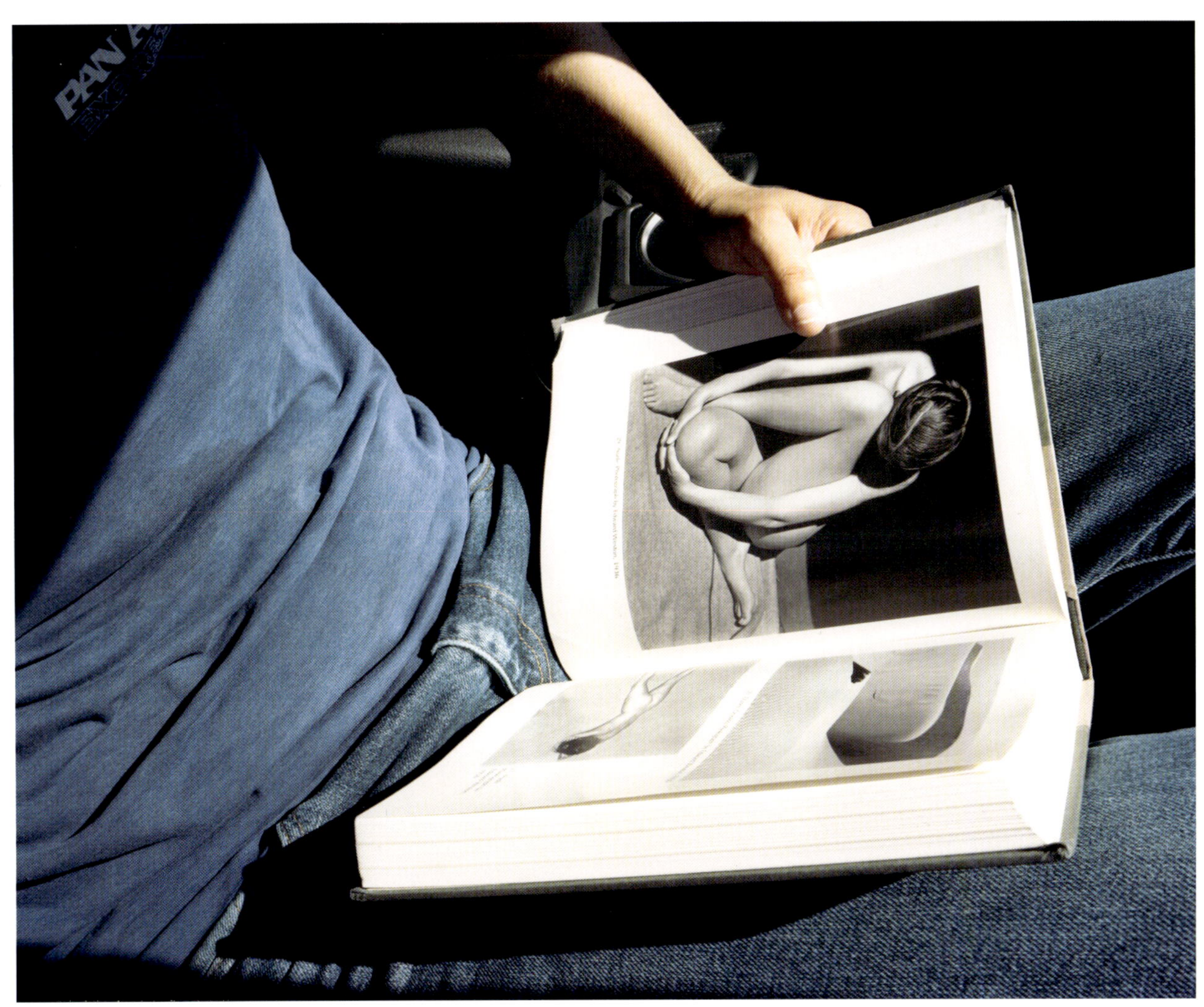

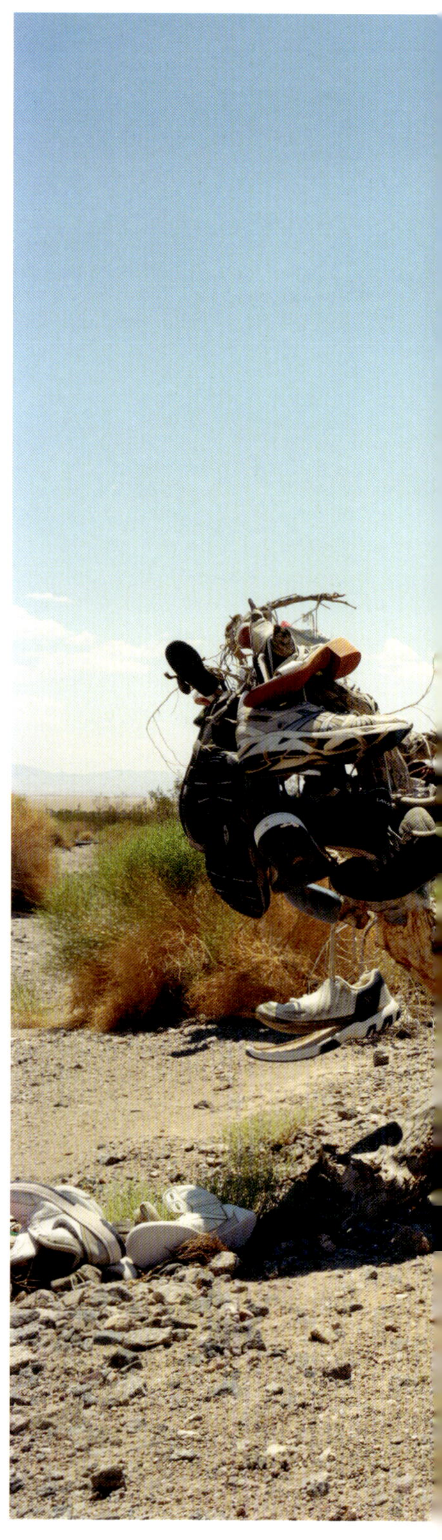

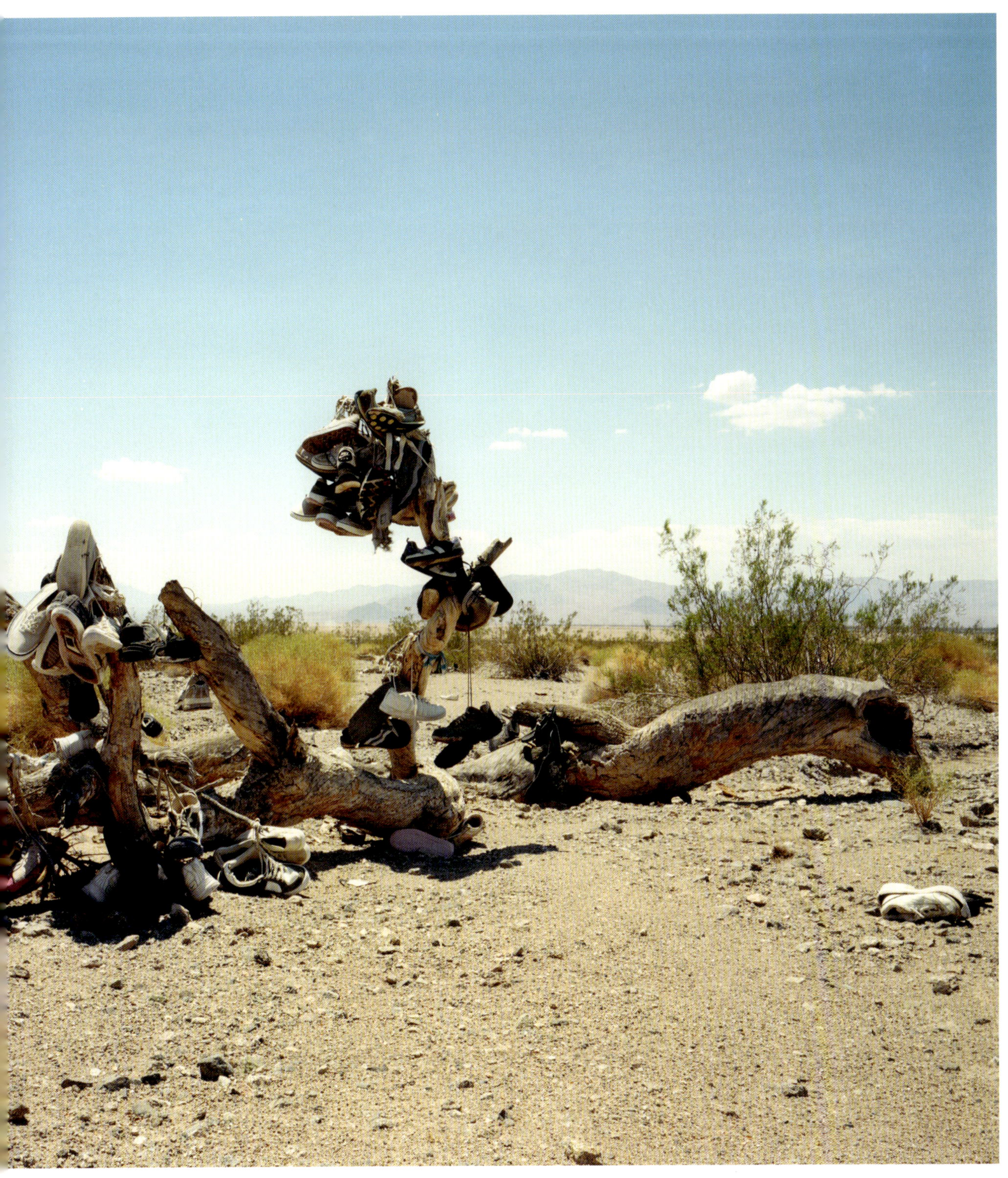

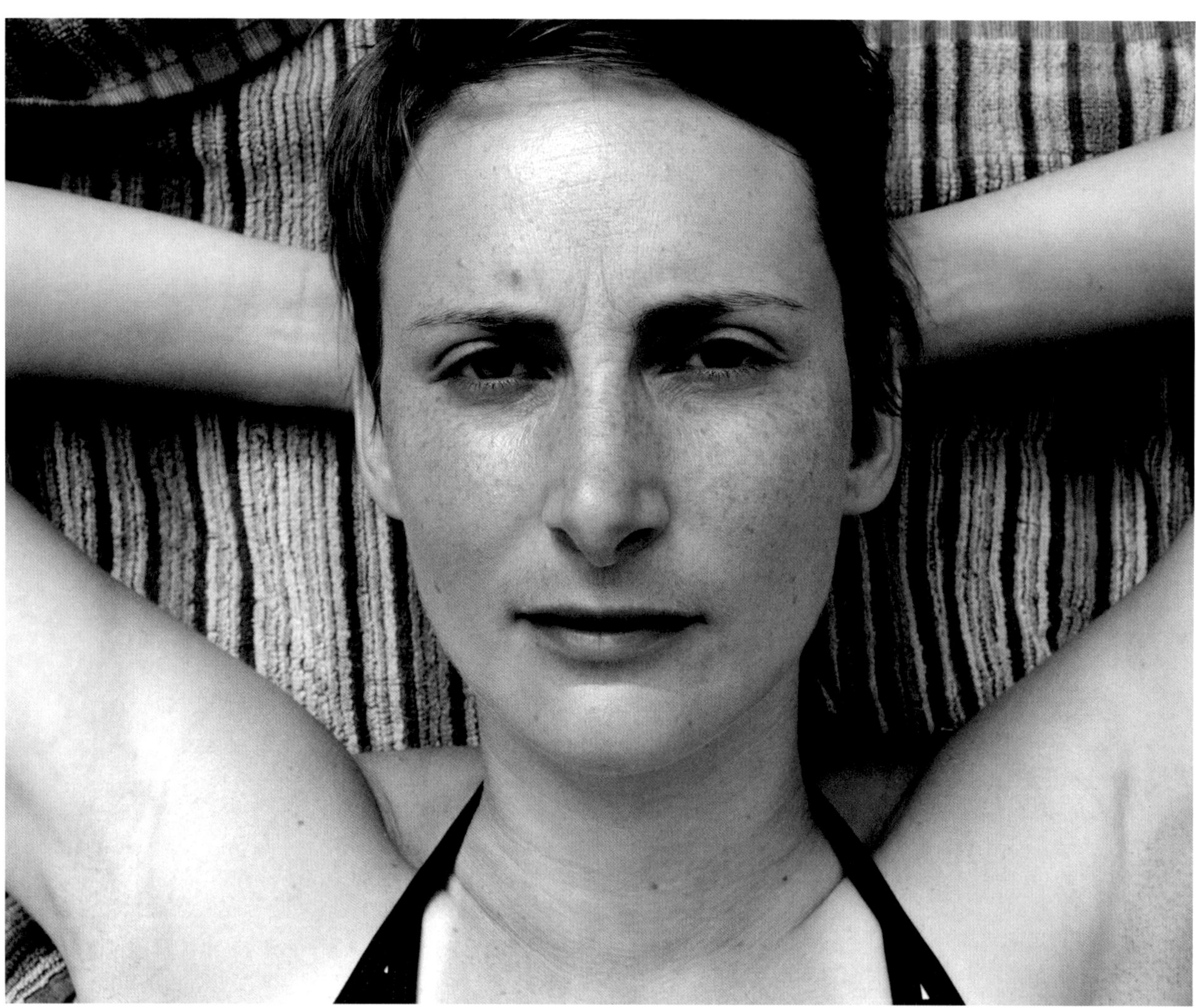

The dunes where Edward photographed Charis are not far from Santa Monica Canyon.
I flip past images in my binder of Charis and Edward's parties, friends dancing late into the
night at Wildcat Hill, picnicking with friends at Point Lobos, and landscapes that Edward
made until I turn to pictures of Charis at the dunes. From the angle, it appears that Edward
took the photographs while standing on a high dune directly across from Charis. From
there, he could focus as she repeatedly rolled down the dune face, stopping herself, body
curled or splayed out, in poses that seem difficult to hold. Although I knew that the dunes
had been continuously reshaped by weather since Charis and Edward made the images in
1936, I was curious to see them for myself. Charis mentions experiencing a profound silence
at the dunes. This, too, I wanted to experience, the silence, the sense of getting lost.

The dunes cover over 3,500 acres, from Oceano's Pismo Beach in the north to the
Santa Maria River in the south. Some of the dunes have been fenced off to protect wildlife,
particularly the Western Snowy Plover, a bird on the federal threatened species list, and the
California Least Tern, which is recognized as endangered by both the state of California and
the US government. Another approximately 1,100 acres are designated for off-road vehicle
use. Here, the highest dunes reach more than two hundred feet tall with wavelike crests.

Bets is always ready for some fun that's a little risky. As she looks into ATV rental
prices, she assures me that we will be perfectly safe. I was pretty much terrified. When I was

in my early twenties, my fiancé and I crashed while riding on his Honda Rebel in a public park at night. I wrapped my arms around his waist as we drove on a pedestrian walking path. I held on tight as the needle of the speedometer climbed. We rode through swarms of gnats, their tiny guts splatting the shields of our helmets. A full moon was out and grey-green outlines of trees presented themselves against the dark blue night. The walking path curved sharply to the right and before we knew it, we crashed hard into a ditch. The bike whirled and grounded itself deep within the muddy ground. A gash on my right ankle began to drip blood on my shoe. Other than feeling a slow creep of faintness wash over our bodies, we were alright. Since then I have had no interest in riding in any vehicles that expose limbs to the elements without the security of windows, doors, and roofs.

I am hoping that maybe we can just explore the dunes on foot. In search of an access point, we follow backroads that look promising but instead lead to private properties with high fences. The sand hills are dotted with silver lupine, deerweed, and coyote bush, and as we roll down the windows, the smell of sun on tall grass rushes in. We pass strawberry fields where workers in long-sleeved shirts, jeans, hats, and bandanas, backs bent, move row to row. Sand has all but erased the road's shoulders when we finally find a state park that is open for visitors.

The park closes at sunset, so we quickly pack up our gear. Signs warn us to look out for bobcats, giant stinging nettles, and poison oak as we pass through the gate into a wooded area where insects buzz from bloom to bloom. From the shade beneath canopies of wax myrtles and arroyo willows, we hear the sounds of birds calling and ocean waves hitting the shore in the distance. We come to a boardwalk that extends over Oso Flaco Lake, where ducks glide across its clear-as-glass surface. The air is humid and thick. We have entered a scene with an order, a certainty to things, the opposite of the surreal dune environment we have been hoping to find.

We wander through some brush and set out on an unmarked trail, probably for park maintenance vehicles. Our feet sink deep with each step. The sun is still bright, but there are no trees for shade. Bets takes off her long-sleeve button-up to reveal a skull-and-bones t-shirt. I put on sunglasses. After only twenty minutes, we are exhausted. Salt sits in the corners of my mouth. Betsy's face is turning pink and her bandana is drenched with sweat. Suddenly, I could picture us as if from a distance, two women knee-deep in sand carrying heavy camera equipment. Of course, I'm doing this because it is my passion, but Betsy is indulging me, in this moment, on this entire trip really, for no other reason than to support me. She believes in the importance of my photographs to explore her androgyny, question societal expectations, and represent our relationship as two women. Her experience as a queer artist with a background in feminist theory also keeps her along for the ride.

We make our way to a clearing where we can see the ocean to the west. We are at the south end of the dune system, close to where the Santa Maria River meets the sea. Charis and Edward's dunes must be to the north, within the thousand-plus acres now reserved for all-terrain vehicle use—Betsy can't wait for us to rent an ATV in the morning. We walk to the beach, where a teenager sits with his headphones on, and farther down, a couple relaxes together, their bodies becoming one entangled shape. Thousands of mole crabs quickly burrow under the sand as each wave is pulled back into the sea. A few gulls glide overhead as I glance over at Bets, her androgynous silhouette eclipsing the sun.

<hr>

Madonna Inn's hot-pink sign flashes its welcome as we arrive. The hotel's Swiss-chalet exterior is trimmed in bubble gum pink. I feel like we've stumbled upon an amusement park for adults only. Each one of the inn's 110 rooms is unique and designed by Alex and Phyllis Madonna, who believe that the enchantments of their fantasy-themed hotel will bring repeat customers. In reading about the inn's history, I learn that Alex favors rounded walls and curves over straight lines and corners, and that Phyllis decorates each room with lavish furnishings—specialty wallpaper, locally designed etched glass, and likes to use as much pink and gold as she can.

With Southern charm, the receptionist explains that there is a daily resort fee for use of the swimming pool, hot tub, gym, and tennis courts as she hands me two fuchsia plastic tumblers with "Madonna Inn" written on them in gold lettering. She circles various hikes and points out where to find the swimming pool, stables, and magenta tennis courts on a map before encouraging me to take a postcard from the swiveling racks. The five-by-seven-inch postcards depict the interiors of all 110 rooms, many of which are lined with rock from the local area and include rock fireplaces and bathrooms complete with waterfalls. These rooms are dark and cave-like and have names like Yosemite Rock, Jungle Rock, Lucky Rock, and Hideaway. The rooms named American Beauty, Elegance, Floral Fantasy, and Love Nest boast lavish pink interiors adorned with love birds, gaudy chandeliers, and spiral staircases that lead to private viewing towers. I pull *Room 140, Bridal Falls* from the rack and read the description on the backside.

> *Bridalveil Falls, one of the most famous waterfalls in Yosemite National Park, cascades into a valley from high above the edge of a majestic rock cliff. This room was inspired by the grandeur and splendor of this picturesque landmark.*
>
> *Surrounded in natural stone, a lovely handcrafted leaded glass window graces the entrance of this secluded room in our hilltop unit. The bathroom features the Inn's signature waterfall shower, rock wash basin and king bed.*

Bridal Falls, our room for the night, is spacious enough for a raucous party. A sectional covered in fabric that looks like rattlesnake skin occupies the center of the room. A round, plush coffee table covered in the same fabric acts as a focal point. The carpet, walls, ceiling, and doors are all painted fresh-cut-grass green, and rock walls surround the bed. Two mismatched chandeliers hang from the ceiling and an elaborate gilded gold mirror reflects back the scene in all its glory. We take turns bathing in the elaborate rock shower, which when experienced, conjured none of the excitement of showering outside. I stay up late reloading film holders as Bets sleeps nestled against a backdrop of boulders.

Sunbuggie is nestled between two other ATV rental stores. We decide to rent a RZR, which sits higher off the ground than typical dune buggies, with a metal frame and four large wheels. We're told it provides a smoother ride compared to other options, but when driven fast, it's more inclined to flip. We watch a mandatory ten-minute safety video that includes a summary to ensure that we have learned the rules, including: "Never jump RZRs. A RZR will land on its nose."

As we wait outside on a bench for a tram to take us down Pismo Beach, a caravan of trucks—windows rolled down and country music blaring—passes by hauling dune buggies and four-wheelers. One guy sits atop a three-wheeler on a trailer that's hitched to a heavy-duty pickup driven by one of his buddies. He slathers on sunscreen and chair dances at the same time. The driver sings along, his hand slapping out the rhythm on the car door.

We meet Sunbuggie staff members at a trailer, where we receive full-face helmets with elongated, pointed chins designed to increase ventilation while also deflecting debris. We check our helmets by nodding our heads up and down and side to side. Mine feels snug. The futuristic design of the helmet is accentuated by rose-colored ski goggles. Betsy and I can't see each other's mouths. Engines rev as riders on RZRs, dune buggies, and four-wheelers make their way to and from the entrance to the dunes. We will have to yell.

Zach, a Sunbuggie employee in his late thirties, double-checks the fit of our helmets. "Hold the handlebar on the dash with both hands while she drives," he says handing me a map. Black dots signify points of reference, such as Competition Hill, Tabletop, Barbeque Flats, and Worm Valley. Eyeing the camera gear as I buckle it in with a seatbelt, Zach asks, "What are you gonna photograph?"

"I'm looking for high dunes that were photographed by a famous photographer in the 1930s. Have you heard of Edward Weston?"

Zach shrugs.

"Well, he stayed in a makeshift cabin in the dunes when he came here to photograph." I hesitate to say anything more, but Zach looks interested.

"I spent a lot of time exploring the dunes with this guy, Norm Hammond, when I was a kid," Zach offers. "His son was my age. Norm would tell us stories about the hermits and wanderers who lived in the dunes." Zach points out a restricted area labeled Moy Mell on the map. "The cabins used to be here. The Dunites, as Norm called them, lived there. Maybe your photographer stayed with them."

I am amazed. Not only had Charis written about staying at Moy Mell, but I had recently read *The Dunites*, the book written by Norm Hammond. In 1972, Norm was exploring the dunes when he found a man living there in a makeshift cabin. The man was the last of a community that had been established in the early 1930s. The Dunites, a group of poets, mystics, artists, nudists, hermits, and people just beaten down by the Depression, found themselves together in the dunes, living off Pismo clams found in fresh water a few feet underground and talking around campfires under a bright constellation of stars. Norm became fascinated by the stories he heard about the Dunites and began to do as much research as he could about them. I told Zach that I had read Norm's book and that, yes, the dunes close to Moy Mell were the ones we wanted. Charis and Edward made frequent trips to the dunes when they lived in Santa Monica Canyon. On clear days with minimal wind, they would drive up to photograph in these expansive dunes. The Dunites always welcomed their company.

Zach pulls out his phone and shows us some of his best dune pics. Some are drenched in sunset glows of blazing orange and pink, others are camouflaged by dramatic shadows. He takes a quick snap of Betsy and me in the RZR, our smiles hidden by the long snouts of our helmets. "Drive to the entrance of Sand Highway," he says pointing to the map. "Sand Highway is bound by a set of markers, numbered 1 through 25, running north to south. Moy Mell is to the west of markers 11 and 12." The dunes we are searching for should be within walking distance of there. If I had learned anything about Edward from tracking his viewpoints at Dante's View, Zabriskie Point, and Lake Tenaya, it was that he did not stray far from a parked car or home base when photographing. Zach reminds us that all ATVs are required to have a whip and flag, a miniature orange flag on a long white stick, so that drivers are aware of approaching ATVs. Bets nods her pointy helmet, hits the gas, and we're off.

As we leave the crowded coastline behind, the dunes spread out before us. Light winds lift sand off the ridges of the high dunes. We reach Sand Highway markers 11 and 12 and pull over next to a sign restricting access. This is Moy Mell. I try to imagine cabins nestled near the sagebrush, a dune rat reading on a stoop, another soaking up the sun, nude. As far as I can tell, to find evidence of the Dunites would require excavating in the ever-moving sand. Charis was here in 1936.

> *To the north the dunes dropped to mere sand hills, but south of us stretched range after range of sand mountains with valleys and plains set among them—a whole sandy geography where the straight line is outlawed and the arc and parabola ruled. How did the sand continually duplicate its favorite shapes and yet produce an endless variety of forms? As puzzling a question as the role of contrast in photography. I watched Edward tramping along the sand ridge below me and slid down to intercept him. "Down that way," I reported with a wide arm sweep to the south, "the dunes are endless. You'll never run out of new subjects."[61]*

Charis and Edward walked carefully so as not to ruin a potential composition with their tracks. Their footsteps were the only intrusion on the sand, save a few tracks left by early rising birds.

On the dunes that stretch before me and Betsy, tire tracks cover every rise and fall, every bowl and swell. Some are thick, some thin, but all are tracings of speed and conquest. I had not realized how soft, even sensual, Edward's photographs of the dunes were until I see these harsh marks gouging patterns into the smooth inclines and curves. An unmarked dune does not exist.

As Bets and I make our way across this strange landscape, we lose all sense of space and scale. Each time we think we are lost or going in circles, we find our way back to the

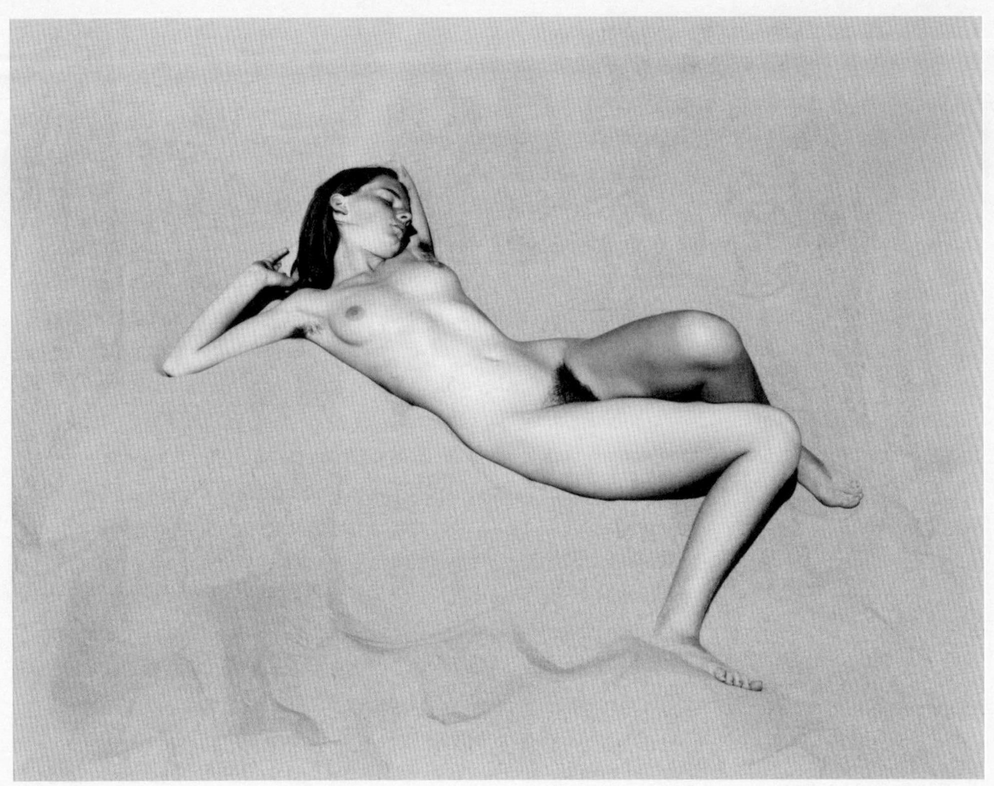

Sand Highway, and each time, we are relieved to see the numbered markers. I look for dunes to photograph and yell directions to Bets, who does her best to follow my muffled shouts. Finally, we stop on a ridge. I carefully set the four-by-five up on the tripod before running back to the RZR to hand Betsy my helmet. It is impossible to focus with the alien-like armor, as I need to look through my loupe at the scene projected on the ground glass.

By mid-morning, the sun is blazing. I think of Charis lying on the warm sand.

An hour later, when the sun was climbing higher and the fine, soft sand was pleasantly warm, I thought it was time for a sunbath. I called to Edward, who was working on a higher ridge and across a small valley from me, to alert me if someone approached, then I stretched out on the side of a bank where my footsteps coming and going had created a narrow shelf. When I next looked around, the camera had moved to the near side of the ridge and was aiming down at me.

After Edward made a few back views I decided to try diving down a steeper part of the sand bank. It was a giddy experience, like going slow-motion over a waterfall, and after a trial run or two to get the hang of it, I could fling myself down with abandon. By this time I had the bank pockmarked with footsteps and gouges. Edward used these indentations to his advantage in the nudes he made—they created dark accents in the monochromatic sand—and when the call came to "Hold it!" I used them to keep me from sliding farther down the slope.[62]

In Edward's images, Charis is unshaven, a scar visible on her abdomen. Her arm and leg hairs are bleached from the almost daily sunbathing that she and Edward did on their deck back home in Santa Monica Canyon. Most importantly, we see her face. Charis is seen as a sexual woman, a troubled sleeper, a lost soul rolling about as if in a strange dream, falling and sinking in a sea of sand. We can see the contrast between how comfortable the sun's warmth is on her body and how uncomfortable it is for her to hold a pose, with controlled concentration, on an incline. Perhaps this camera-to-subject distance came about by circumstance rather than choice, as Edward stood on a high dune across from Charis, letting the landscape dictate his composition. Or perhaps Edward was already thinking about the landscape photographs he would make for *California and the West* if he received the Guggenheim fellowship. Or perhaps during this first year of living with Charis, he was still so newly in love that he was interested in revealing her particularities as a person by allowing for more space around her in the frame. By now he had woken up more times than he could count to find her sleeping beside him. Whatever the reason, Charis is presented as herself here, as an independent being. The Dunites might say that Edward's images of Charis capture the freedom and wonder of the place and its inhabitants. For them, being nude and surrounded by miles of sand would have been the most natural thing in the world.

Time passes quickly in this mysterious place. We sprint from dune to dune, flying nose-first into valleys before picking up enough speed to soar over swells of sand. We move from deep shadows to glaring vistas. As Bets and I race to return our RZR on time, Moy Mell once again comes into view. It won't be until later, back in Chicago, emerging from the darkroom, that I fully see the magic of the dunes and understand why Edward was drawn to making photographs there. He had told Charis, "You won't believe it. Everything is black-and-white!"[63] To her dismay, she saw only beige sand and blue skies, not at all the scene that Edward saw in his mind. Over time, Charis learned how to visualize a scene like Edward, in black and white and gray, and I was learning too.

After a long day of shooting, Charis and Edward returned to the cabin in Moy Mell where they were staying. They took turns showering by tipping sun-warmed water from a pail on the roof. After watching a sunset that painted the dunes in pastels, they ate a simple supper of cheese, crackers, and apples before heading to bed. In the morning, when Charis and Edward went on a walk, they encountered an old cabin disappearing in the sand.

A couple was methodically sweeping the last of the sand out the door toward the nearest hummock, which was two feet away and already higher than the window. Like most of the men here, the husband had a beard and wore only shorts and sandals. His wife wore a loose shirt over shorts and her hair pulled back in a clasp. A baby in its diaper was asleep in a rope cradle hung across the corner of the single room. At the rate the sand was moving, they told us, they could count on two more weeks at most before it would be too dangerous to stay in the cabin. They seemed to take their coming eviction calmly, although they hadn't found a place to settle.

I tried to picture myself with a small baby, no future home in sight, and the sound of sand pouring in the door all night—you couldn't close it for fear of being trapped. My imagination wasn't up to it, but the effort at least made me appreciate what comfort I had at home. On the drive back to Rustic Road we discussed the pros and cons of the dune dwellers' back-to-nature existence. Of course it wouldn't do for Edward—a photographer needed a darkroom, lights, running water, etc.[64]

In Charis's memoir, she doesn't mention whether or not she wanted to have children with Edward, or whether they ever talked about it. Stories such as this, as well as a photograph that Edward made of a child's grave in northern California, make me wonder.

In time, sand overwhelmed most of the cabins, except for one that was moved to town in 1946. It was moved once again, in 2010, to the Oceano Train Depot, which is now home to the local historical society. The cabin sits in a parking lot surrounded by asphalt and weeds, but it's still here.

Highway 1 is known for its dramatic beauty. Betsy and I pull over every few minutes, but our excitement is intermingled with fear: road signs warn of landslides and falling rock, and fence-like orange mesh outlines the most susceptible areas, an attempt at containment we know is effective for only nominal seismic movements. We catch glimpses of the Pacific as we crawl up the coast, its cobalt surface interrupted by feather-backed waves, a brackish mist infusing the air. I sit with Gina Weston's directions for Wildcat Hill on my lap as we wind around twisting curves. With anticipation, we turn onto their private drive. Emerging from a tunnel created by the arms of an old cypress tree that reach across the road, we find a garden, complete with a robust lemon tree, rows of vegetables and herbs, and a bird coop that is home to white doves.

I get out of the car and feel exhilarated to be standing in front of Gina and Kim Weston's home, which once belonged to Charis and Edward. Here is where Charis wrote the text for *California and the West*, *The Cats of Wildcat Hill*, and dozens of articles with Edward for *Camera Craft* magazine. Here they experienced the joys of being a newly married couple and the pain of the death of Charis's father. Charis's childhood home, located next door, was where Edward made the photograph of Charis floating nude in the sun, in the backyard pool. And Wildcat Hill was where they returned in late December of 1941 after traveling for *Leaves of Grass*. The trip foreshadowed the turmoil of their relationship in years to come—a complicated web of misunderstandings that grew from Charis's attraction to another man while on the road for *Leaves of Grass*, her need to be supported as a serious writer, and Edward's as-of-yet undiagnosed Parkinson's disease, which led to bouts of depression.

The house and surrounding property look as they do in the pictures I've seen. Here is the victory garden Charis nurtured during the war years, now with varieties of roses, fruits, and vegetables that Gina and Kim have introduced. And there on the facade of the main house, next to where an American flag blows in the wind, is Edward's darkroom window. An image taken by Beaumont Newhall in 1940 shows Edward leaning out of this window smiling proudly for the camera, his hair whipped by the ocean breeze. It had always been a dream of Edward's to live in a place where he could be inspired by nature and make work. Many artists, including Ansel Adams, were envious of Charis and Edward's life together on Wildcat Hill. In the closing remarks of a letter, Ansel writes, "What really impressed me almost more than anything about you two is the wonderful mental and physical health you have. Swell kind of living. Swell kind of work."[65]

After spending the majority of 1937 and 1938 on the road, accumulating hundreds of negatives and countless pages of written notes, it came time for Charis and Edward to work on editing the text and printing the photographs for the publication of *California and the West*. After considering their options, they decided to settle down in Carmel, where they had first met. Charis secured a parcel of property from her father. The home that Charis grew up in, Ocean Home, was in foreclosure, but H. L. agreed to sign a deed of transfer for 1.8 acres across a ravine from the main house. He warned them that the bank already possessed Ocean Home and that the transfer might be declined, but the bank eventually agreed to sell Charis and Edward the land for a thousand dollars. Edward's son, Neil, built the house for $1,200, including $275 for his labor. After decades of worrying about how to make ends meet, Edward finally had a home of his own, a solitary and simple place that would allow him time to focus on his work.

Over the years, some additions were made, a bedroom on the main house, and then a separate studio and darkroom for Kim. Kim Weston followed in the footsteps of his grandfather (Edward), father (Cole), and uncle (Brett) in carrying on the Weston tradition of working as a photographer by trade. A wood sign hangs proudly above the studio and includes the newest member of the family to carry on the Weston tradition, Kim's son, Zach:

FOUR GENERATION GALLERY
Edward—Cole—Kim—Zach WESTON

Bets and I walk up the gravel path to find Kim's studio door open and Gina sitting at the computer. A black-and-tan striped cat sleeps in the chair next to her. The studio walls are covered with Kim's photographs of nudes, some taken on the Wildcat Hill property, others taken in more exotic locations. A large worktable sits in the center of the room, and a daybed beneath a window overlooks the vine-covered ravine. Gina takes off her reading glasses to greet us. She is in her late fifties, with baby blue eyes. The dimples in her cheeks accentuate her smile, which she seems to have flashed often, a confirmation of which were the uplifted wrinkles around her eyes. Betsy walks over to the cat, who opens her sleepy lids and purrs.

"This is Charis, and somewhere roaming around outside is Eddie," says Gina. The humor in naming the cats after Charis and Edward strikes me—Charis and Edward completed their collaboration, *The Cats of Wildcat Hill*, which pairs Edward's four-by-five photographs of their cats, often named after close friends, with Charis's recollection of their feline adventures and mishaps. As Betsy sits with Charis on her lap, Gina tells us where to eat downtown, where her favorite places to walk along the coast are, and when we should time our visit to the state preserve at Point Lobos in order to avoid all the tourists. She mentions that Point Lobos may become a national park, and that if that happens it will mean droves of tourists traveling down from Monterey in buses. She is worried about their favorite walking paths being overtaken.

Gina walks with us to Bodie Room, which was Charis's writing studio, but is now rented out to overnight guests under the name Bodie House. Bodie House was originally a garage, but Neil built a second garage and converted this one into a studio for Charis. She named it Bodie Room after the brand name on its tiny wood stove, and the rusted *Bodie* nameplate now hangs on the outside of the guesthouse. Gina asks us to take off our shoes when walking around because the hardwood floors are new and explains how the gas heater works, promising that Carmel will be cold in the mornings. She also tells us that a photoshoot will be taking place the next day, and that we shouldn't be alarmed to see photographers working with a couple of nude models. She has one last request, that we won't let Eddie inside at night.

Tangerine-colored curtains fill the bedroom with an amber glow from the afternoon sun. Inside the closets, we find archival photography boxes, a stack of contemporary paperbacks, and a selection of movies: childhood classics, a few action flicks, and two VHS tapes about Edward's career. Throughout the house, wooden handles are attached to the walls; the placement is thoughtful, every couple of feet at just the right height—knowing that Edward died of Parkinson's disease, I immediately think of him using them to move about the house.

Betsy reclines on the couch underneath a row of windows eating the remaining strawberries from a green plastic bin resting on her belly. A writing desk sits beside the couch. My mind flashes to Charis typing on her Royal Signet, a cigarette burning in an ashtray as she works. Piles of notes are strewn about the place, their corners lifting slightly from the ocean breeze. She looks up to greet us with her warm blue eyes.

When Charis and Edward moved into their new home on Wildcat Hill in 1938, they entered a productive and supportive period of their lives as companions, collaborators, and dedicated artists. Edward was awarded a year-long extension of the Guggenheim fellowship, and he used that time to print the hundreds of negatives taken on their trip across the West. Charis describes their first years together at Wildcat Hill as "pleasantly domestic."[66] Edward spent his days in the darkroom while Charis wrote in Bodie Room. They took

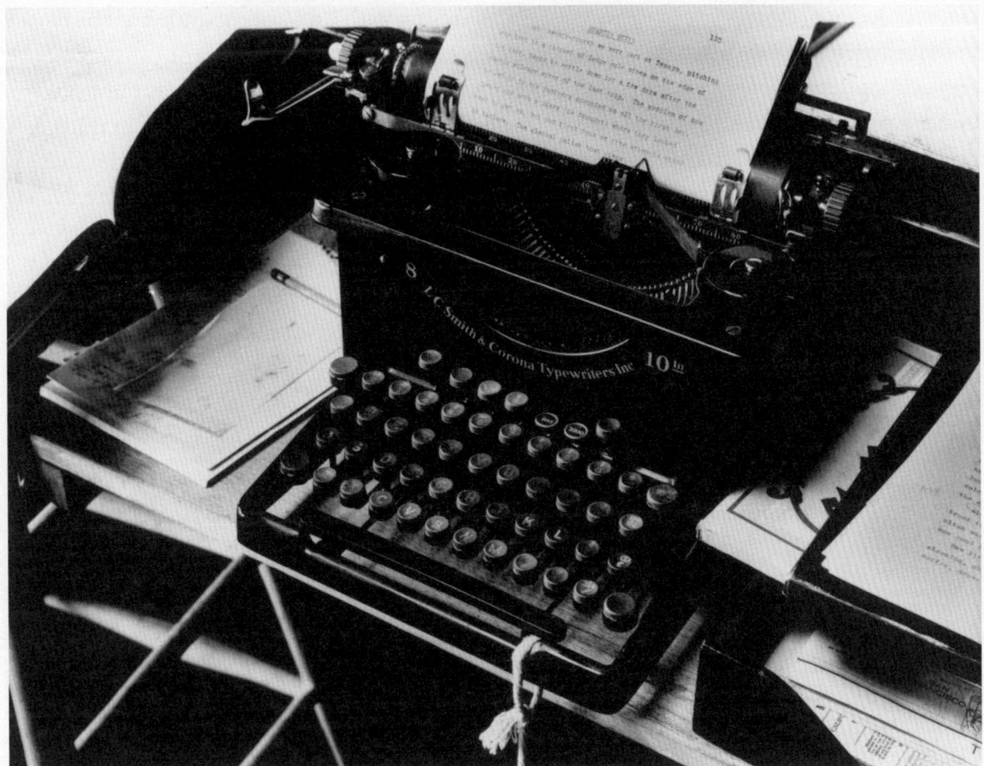

frequent breaks to swim or picnic at Point Lobos, and were known to throw the occasional party on weekends, when they would move things out of the way to make room for a dance floor. They also spent a lot of time tending to the growing cat population at Wildcat Hill.

In 1939, Edward began printing a set of five hundred images from the Guggenheim travels to be housed in the Huntington Library in San Marino, California. Later that year, he and Charis got married in Elk, California: the ceremony was quiet and modest, just Charis and Edward and a judge. They exchanged gold bands purchased from a pawn shop. People in Carmel liked to talk, and so when asked if the news of their marriage was true, Charis would "tell people she encountered on the south side of Ocean Avenue 'Yes,' and on the north side 'No.' "[67]

When Betsy and I got married in 2009, same-sex marriage wasn't yet legal in Illinois. We had a ceremony with friends and family in Chicago then made our way to Provincetown, Massachusetts, where marriage was legal. I was nervous about getting married again, but standing next to Betsy in a quiet public park, with only an officiant as our witness, I felt overwhelmed by our love when the officiant proclaimed, "And by the power vested in me by the state of Massachusetts, I pronounce you legally married." Returning to Chicago, Betsy and I, too, entered a partnership centered around a mutual respect for each other's needs as artists.

In 1940, Charis's serious writing collaboration with Edward expanded as she began to write articles as a ghostwriter for *Camera Craft*, a well-known photography magazine. Sometimes the work was published with both of their names, sometimes it was published under a pen name, F. H. Halliday, that allowed Charis to write about their lives in third person, but more often than not, the writing was attributed to Edward. The articles that Charis ghostwrote for *Camera Craft*, sharing Edward's insights about photography, include "What Is a Purist?," "Photographing California," "Light vs. Lightning," "What Is Photographic Beauty?" and "Thirty Years of Portraiture." An excerpt from "What Is Photographic Beauty?" reads:

> *Guided by the photographer's selective understanding, the penetrating power of the camera-eye can be used to produce a heightened sense of reality—a kind of super realism that reveals the vital essences of things. But it is not enough for the photographer to see and recognize this super realism. It is whether or not he is successful in transferring that vision to his finished print that determines the presence or absence of photographic beauty in his work. In this connection we must examine the third unique property of the medium—the ability to present an unbroken sequence of subtle gradations.*[68]

Another segment, from "Thirty Years of Portraiture," argues:

> *Portraiture will always be an art of discovery. No matter how much you learn from experience there is always more to be learned. The human face you want to record is not a stone or a stump; besides the changing daylight upon it, it has a changing light of its own. It is a living thing, in constant transition, now concealing, now revealing the person behind it. To translate all this to film and paper is an absorbing and exciting task that can never dull as long as you continue to approach it with an open mind.*[69]

When *California and the West* was published in 1940, it was a huge success. The price was affordable at $3.75, and Charis's writing interested a wider audience. The royalty checks they received afforded them time for their creative work. Within two years, the book was in its second printing. Combing through Charis's archives at the Center for Creative Photography, I found clippings that she had saved touting the success of the book. There was a "Best Sellers of the Week" list from January 19, 1941, listing *California and the West* as number seven on the nonfiction list. Reviews of the book in daily newspapers often praised Charis as a writer.

> *Nor must Mrs. Weston's text be neglected. She has an observant eye and a knack for putting down the details of such a trip as this must have been with humor and shrewdness. Best of all, perhaps, she doesn't try to "write"— at any rate, not with a capital "W." Here's the story; here's the way it was;*

*that's her guiding principle. And she conducts the tour expertly and with a
great deal of charm.*
—*San Francisco Chronicle,* December 11, 1940[70]

*The Westons spent two years and a Guggenheim fellowship of two thousand
dollars making the photographs that went into "California and the West."
Edward was the master photographer and coffee-maker, Charis the
chauffeur, shopper for canned goods, and the narrator of one of the most
delightful diary-stories we've read in many a moon. The picture of her in the
book bears a marked resemblance to Amelia Earhart, but her literary style is
peculiarly her own. It is as fresh and brisk as some of the breezes the picture-
making Westons encountered in their jaunt about the Far West. This book
has 126 pages of story and contains 96 photographs for which superlatives are
not superlative enough. They're unbelievably perfect and the narrative is the
perfect companion for them. The book is one every photographer will consider
a must have, that everyone who loves beauty, who likes to travel, who wants to
know about the West will want.*
—the *Observer,* Raleigh, N.C., December 8, 1940[71]

I walk around Wildcat Hill with my camera mounted on a tripod. The roses at the
edge of the garden beckon to me. I lift one—its pale-pink petals browning at the edges—
and inhale its fading fragrance. At the victory garden, the doves coo in their cages. Charis
started the garden because of food rationing during the war. As she tells it, "My mother had
grown an amazing array of flowers at Ocean Home. Now I set out to grow all the vegetables
I could coax out of the earth on the remaining corner of my childhood terrain. Edward
helped till a level area below the house, and I did everything it said to do in the *Sunset
Vegetable Garden Book.*"[72]

I pass Edward's darkroom window and walk around back. I dig my feet into the
steep hillside to keep from sliding and climb to the top of Wildcat Hill. I can see Bodie
House, the main house, Kim's studio, and the garden nestled among the cypress trees,
the Pacific in the distance. If I listen hard enough, I can hear the crooning of the doves and
the faint sound of cars passing below on Highway 1. To my right, a wall of Monterey pines
partially blocks the view of Ocean Home next door. A thick carpet of vines and miniature
orange nasturtiums cover the ravine between Wildcat Hill and Ocean Home, and
underbrush and towering pines make it difficult to see. A fence blocks the view of the
backyard where Charis's swimming pool had once been.

I turn my gaze back to the view below. In 1942, Edward made a picture entitled
Wildcat Hill in which Charis sits on the roof of Bodie Room reading a book, a sweet feline
curled by her side. The roof, the ladder, Charis, and the cat are all bathed in light. The rest
of the scene—the chopped wood in the foreground, the silhouette of cypress trees, the
underbrush and ground—is in shadow. This idyllic scene holds a hint of loneliness, as if

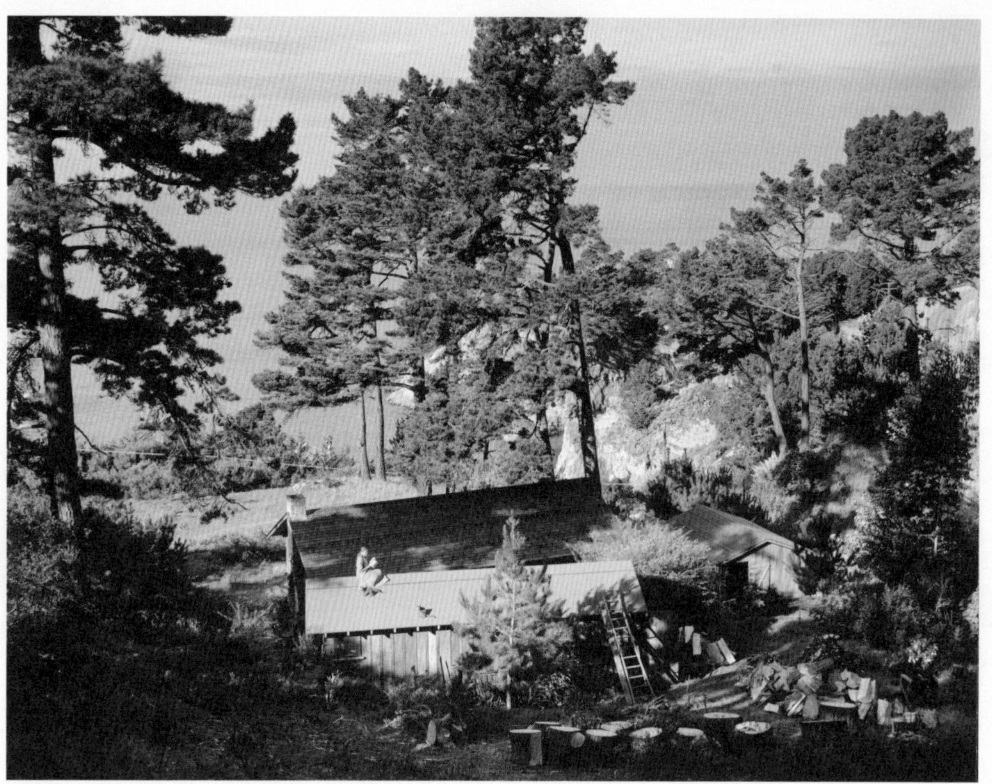

the photograph knows something that Edward doesn't, that he is growing more distant from his subject. Photographs tend to reveal something about photographers that they may not be aware of themselves. Aspects of photographers' lives can materialize in their images before they even have words for what is happening in their relationships.

I walk down the hill to the side of Bodie House where Charis posed for *My Little Grey Home in the West*, titled after a popular song of the same name by D. Eardley-Wilmot (a pen name used by May Eardley-Wilmot). By this time, Charis and Edward had been together nine years. The lyrics to the song tell one story, while the image Edward made tells another. Charis holds an apple in her left hand and a sign that was once propped in Edward's old studio window, in her right. The bottom of the sign rests on her thigh, creating a makeshift fig leaf. In her memoir, Charis provides a rare interpretation:

> *A picture can be viewed in many ways. Over the years I have taken umbrage at some people's insistence on reading symbolism into Edward's work; however, even I can see potential to be mined in* My Little Grey Home in the West. *Its title came from a popular sentimental song Edward remembered from years before, and at first glance the picture may seem a lighthearted spoof.*

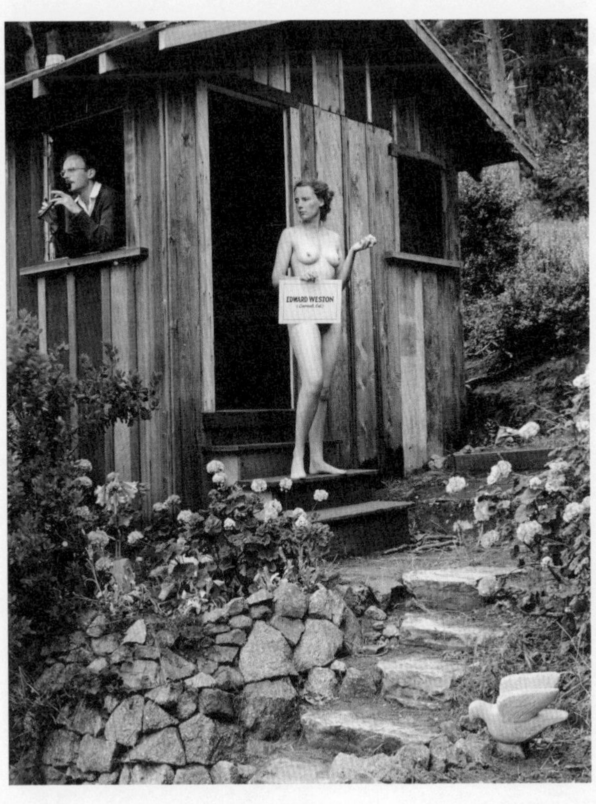

Edward Weston
*My Little Grey Home
in the West,* 1943

*But let me practice what I have inveighed against. I stand naked
on the steps of Bodie Room like Eve about to be banished from Eden, with the
incriminating half-eaten apple in one hand and in the other a sign saying
EDWARD WESTON (CARMEL, CA), held as a fig leaf to cover my shame.
My brother plays the recorder out of the side window, an uninterested
accompanist, while I stand in the middle of a mosaic of my years with Edward:
our pre-dawn trysts engraved on the sign from his Carmel studio; the weathered
boards of Bodie Room standing as well for our "palatial shack" and all of
the promise of starting our own home together at the end of the Guggenheim
travels—Bodie Room, which later became my refuge from Edward's
displeasure; Edmondson's beautiful stone dove signifying both the sadness and
delight of our Whitman odyssey; and finally the rock walls of the war years
carefully constructed to shore up, but ultimately serving to separate.*[73]

Gina graciously allows me to make photographs in the main house. Designed with
Edward's needs as an artist in mind, the 20-by-28-foot room functioned as a studio and

living space, complete with a darkroom and kitchen at one end and a fireplace at the other. A skylight provided extra brightness when Edward showed his photographic prints to visitors. When Charis and Edward lived here, the furnishings consisted of a brown velour couch, a bed covered with a Navajo rug that sat close to the fireplace, a model stand, a large kitchen table that also served as a work table, and Edward's writing desk. Charis shares that, "Mornings at Wildcat Hill began with the sound of pine chips snapping in the fireplace and the grrag-grrag-grrag of the coffee grinder. When I turn over to open my eyes, I see Edward sitting at his desk, finishing his second cup of coffee and dealing with the last item on his spindle—a bill, a query, or a letter from a friend."[74] No matter where he lived, it was at this writing desk that Edward wrote letters to friends and entries in his *Daybooks*.

Looking at the writing desk with its built-in bookshelf, I notice a humorous note in Edward's cursive proclaiming, "I do not lend books to friends. I do not want to lose my books, nor my friends." Edward's eight-by-ten camera sits on a tripod with its legs extended near the desk. I am jealous of its wide-angle lenses, which collapse space in a way that neither of my cameras' lenses can. This allowed Edward to easily photograph Charis in tight spaces and also gave the monumental feel to his close-ups of driftwood and other natural forms. On the mantel above the fireplace are four of Edward's photographs in white frames, including his most famous bell pepper and one of Tina Modotti reciting poetry. Gina jokes about how fun it was to live in a museum, but I suspected I'd find living amidst Edward's legacy rather tiresome.

Near the dining area, a door leads to Edward's modest darkroom. Inside, things are set up to evoke Edward's spirit, as best as objects can. The simplicity and order of the darkroom feels calming. Everything looks as he had left it. Developing trays sit next to dark bottles labeled "developer," "stop," and "fixer" in a simple sink. Dodging and burning tools made from black cardboard and coat hangers with curlicue ends are neatly arranged next to a timer and pencil. Edward never used an enlarger, just a contact printing frame, where he laid each eight-by-ten negative on a sheet of gelatin-silver paper before exposing it with light from the single frosted bulb that hung from the ceiling on a cord.

Photographs of Edward posing proudly with his cameras are hung on the pine walls of the darkroom. I am delighted to see a drawing that Charis mentions in her memoir— "Zohmah, a good friend of theirs, had made the drawing not long after we were settled, showing the inside of the house from rafter's eye view, with fold-up walls, that could be viewed from any orientation."[75] Zohmah was also the friend who had said upon seeing Charis's Lake Ediza portrait, "You don't do anything and come across twice as sexy."[76] That image had been printed in this room. I am suddenly overwhelmed. Edward's photographs, with their lush blacks and luminous whites, were printed on this simple contact printing frame, with the light from this one bulb, as the breeze from the Pacific swept up the hillside and tapped gently on the darkroom window.

To my surprise, in the contact printing frame sits the original *Springtime* negative taken by Edward in 1943, six years after he made the Lake Ediza portrait and two years before Charis would leave the relationship. Charis's body is warmed by sunlight filtering through the window screen. Outside, two worn and curled shoes are propped on a pipe underneath the window ledge. The heads of three daisies rest diagonally on the slanted roof

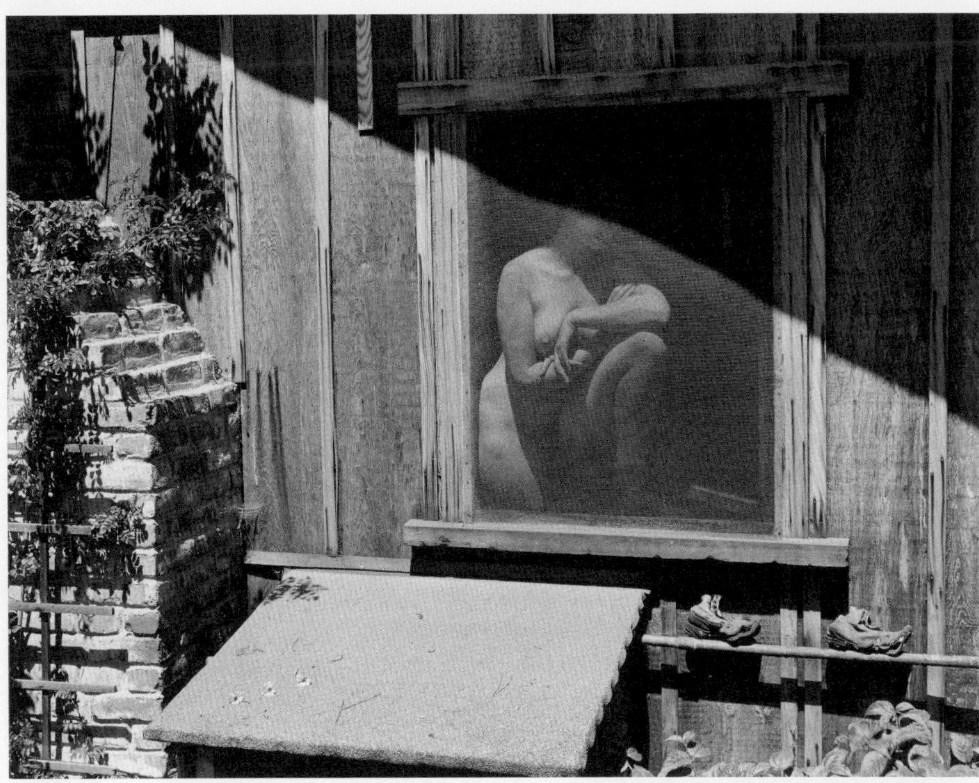

that covers the woodpile. Although the picture is called *Springtime*, it is full of symbolism that signals separation and strain. Edward is outside, regarding Charis through a screen in the window; the shoes are worn, the flowers cut. I wonder whether Edward had made the photograph with a specific metaphor in mind, or whether he understood something deeper about their strained relationship by looking at his own images over time.

Finding the negative for *Springtime* in Edward's darkroom on Wildcat Hill is a completely immersive experience; the image itself is alive, with traces of its past, clues for the discovering, in the present moment. Just outside of this darkroom, I can be in the same space in which the negative was made. Charis and Edward's presence is everywhere in the house: light pours in through the windows and skylight, the desk ready for its writer, the firewood stacked on the grate and ready to be lit. I can look from Edward's view where he made *Springtime*—standing outside the living room window—as well as from Charis's view from the window inside.

Back in Bodie House, we crawl into bed. I lay my head on Betsy's chest as we watch a VHS documentary about Edward called *Nudes and Peppers* released in 2004. A short cameo features Charis in her late eighties, talking about her life with Edward. Here is Charis in color, blue eyes, translucent pale peach skin. Her shirt, skirt, and sweater are all blue, slightly darker shades than her eyes. There are no color images of Charis when she was young. We can't know the tone of her skin, the exact color of her eyes and hair. In my mind, she's black and white through the decades, until she turns to color in her later years. Charis in her eighties reminds me of my grandmother, slightly plump with full hips and loose arm skin, her playful grin and bright engaging eyes inviting you to be near. Charis holds up a photograph Edward made of her on the roof of their house in Santa Monica Canyon. She smiles proudly at the camera as she talks. Her enthusiasm radiates from the screen.

Rarely have I been able to photograph Betsy as I see her in my mind. Perhaps it is the difference between the camera's lens and the eye's lens, as I focus on parts of her only visible at the close proximity I often keep. I notice these intimate details—the barely visible white hairs on her upper lip, the length of her eyelashes, the constellation of freckles that only surface in the summer—as she talks in her way or sits as she does or walks with her gait. The picture of her in my mind somehow doesn't translate, doesn't represent her, when her image is fixed as a photograph. Most of our time together is spent about two feet apart. We both talk softly, she is even quieter than me, and we scoot close, especially in loud places. Bets can look drastically different depending on how she is feeling, what she is thinking, what time of year it is. In the summer, her naturally pale skin is golden, her arm hairs light, her hair a brighter shade. In the winter, Bets can appear drained of warmth, especially when she is feeling blue.

Only when subjects are photographed over long periods of time can we get closer to their essence, and even then, we are still on the perimeter, left to make sense of our interpretations of them. Who the subject is changes over time, as the relationship between the photographer and sitter changes. In the beginning, a love interest is a fiction, a fantasy. We imagine who the person may become in relation to us. We daydream. Only after the relationship is established, over years and shared experiences, does it settle into a rhythm, a pattern that is easily recognized. Honoré de Balzac famously said, "Marriage must incessantly contend with a monster that devours everything: familiarity."[77] Desires, fantasies, and fictions fade with time. The heat of a glance, the electricity of a touch, become distant memories. Over the years this familiarity can grow to be comfortable, easy, and warm. The camera allows us to see a scene for what it has become: the process, the slow accumulation, of a person taking a photograph of another person. They carry the shared history of their relationship with them; it is in their bodies, their gestures, the space between them. It is in the room.

I look at Betsy as she poses on the couch in the late morning light. She is handsome, her hair swept to the side. Her arms, curled in a diagonal zigzag, emphasize her angular features. I wonder if the melancholy she was experiencing a few days earlier will rise to the surface, only to be found when we get the film back. When I first started making portraits of Betsy, I was interested in exploring my feelings about our relationship—our experiences as a couple, my attraction to her androgyny—and to questioning, through my photographs, societal expectations about gender and beauty and the roles that we perform within these constructs. My reasons for photographing Betsy are one thing, but if this work is a reflection of our lives together, I know that my own understanding of this image, like those Edward made of Charis, will change as both of our own lives evolve over time.

I am so close to arriving at the origin of the postcard image that first captivated me years ago that my skin tingles with the alertness of want. It is to be a quick visit. Gina and Kim Weston's neighbor, who owned Ocean Home, isn't thrilled about me being there. Walking through the front door, I catch a glimpse of the house where Charis grew up. The view of the Pacific Ocean from the front windows is stunning, but somehow the entire place feels too dark and cold. The air, suppressed. The current owner has decorated the home with a mix of East-meets-West, over-the-top Victorian florals and minimal Japanese prints. On the wall leading into the kitchen is a photograph of a well-dressed man standing outside of Ocean Home, taken in the early 1900s. I ask the owner, who is holding one of his yippy dogs, about the picture. He says it is a photograph of one of the first owners, he didn't know who, but liked the man's swagger. I look closer. This was indeed a photograph of Charis's father, H. L. Wilson, standing proudly before his new home. I tell him that although H. L. was not well known now, he was once regarded as an important writer. His novels were serialized in the newspaper and many of them had been adapted as movies or for the stage. I show him the photograph of Charis floating in the pool. He doesn't seem the slightest bit interested and makes a fuss about having to keep the dogs inside. The dogs bark from behind the glass door as I work in the backyard.

> *In terms of natural setting, though, Ocean Home was an ideal place in which to grow up. Our large and airy house faced a wide sweep of the Pacific.... The grounds, which Helen [Charis's mother] designed, included an eight-foot-deep diving pool, where we learned to swim and where, for a time, she raised trout—fat, shadowy fish that darted about in its depths. There were also rising terraced gardens culminating in a rock fountain which had a lion's head that occasionally sprouted water. Frogs in the swimming pool made a great echoing chorus at night, but now and again dead silence would fall and I'd lie in my bed, heart-still, wondering what they had heard.*[78]

While securing my camera on the tripod, I look up the hill for the rhododendron where Charis and her brother buried their father's ashes, but I don't see it. I stand still, looking at the grass that was two shades of green, the lighter shade evidence of where the pool had once been. A beautiful oak tree stands tall to the east, its shadows reaching across the yard, and before I press the shutter, I look up at its branches, swaying gracefully, lightly in the coastal breeze.

We drive a short distance to Point Lobos State Natural Reserve. Betsy and I arrive early enough to park near Whaler's Cove, where two scuba divers are standing in half-zipped wetsuits that hang from their waists like peeled second skins, the impressions from their masks still imprinted on their cheeks. Bets and I walk along the rim of Whaler's Cove to Granite Point. Sticky monkey flowers, seaside daisies, and blooming bluff lettuce provide a constellation of bright color at our feet in stark contrast to the grey fog rolling in over Carmel Bay.

Carefully, I make photographs of the surf, wild and fierce, as it comes crashing in around us. The force of the energy pounding at the cliffs is intense. It seems that at any moment the precipice we are on could be grabbed up and swept away by the surf. On the other side of the bay, at the mouth of the Carmel River, is the place where a teenage Charis had been standing when a dissolving bank plunged her into the roil of the channel and rushed her out to sea—she had almost drowned.

We walk on to China Cove, which unlike Granite Point, is protected from the force of the sea. Here, young Charis often gathered kelp, tying strands to her ankles so she could float without drifting away. She would sway back and forth, in harmony with the ocean's movements. Charis mentions in *Through Another Lens* that she "loved to swim to a series of 'caves'—some of which had long since lost their roofs—that connected this beach and the

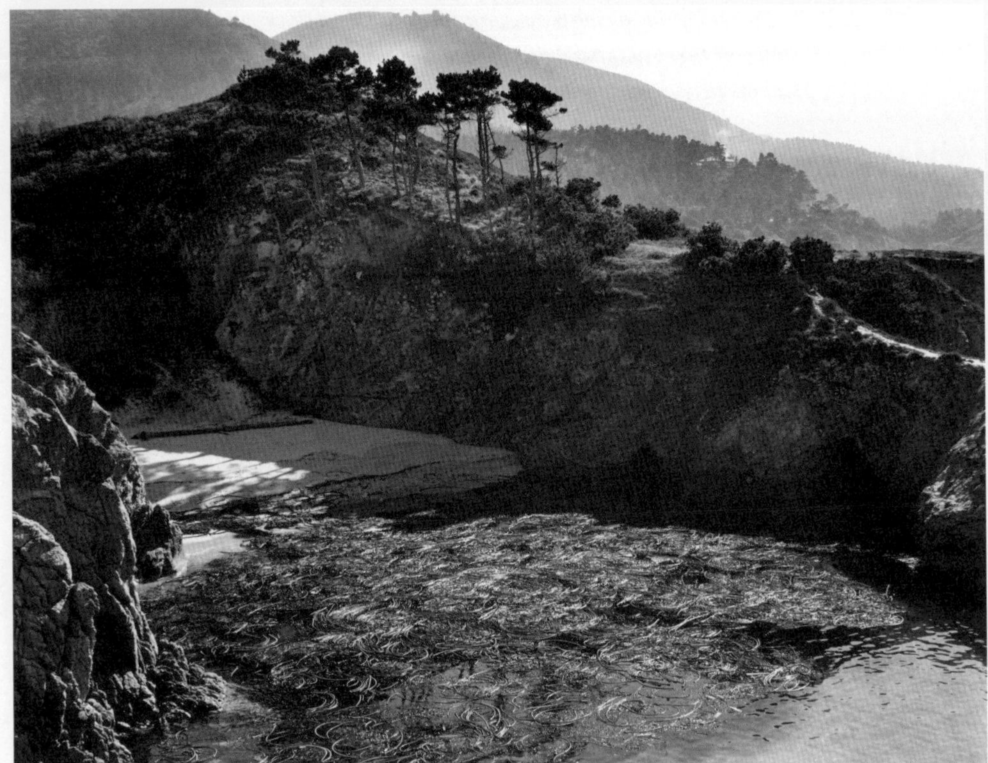

next one over. Starfish, urchins, anemones, crabs, limpets, periwinkles, and other colorful sea life spread over the bottom and sides of these rocky grottoes."[79] I steady myself as I focus the image of the cove. As the waves undulate below, I think about Charis and Edward's relationship, and how Point Lobos and Carmel both symbolize the pleasure of their love's beginning and the pain of their relationship's end.

When they moved to Wildcat Hill in 1938, Point Lobos soon became one of Edward's favorite places to make work.

> *Edward began by saying he was all through with it. (He'd been saying that ever since he left Carmel in 1935.) Hadn't he photographed there for six years, done every twisted cypress on the cliffs and every eroded rock on the beaches? True enough, but that had been a period of close-ups: details of rocks, fragments of trees. At first we just went to swim and look at the scenery and walk; but Edward took his camera along in case he might see a cloud or something. He made a few negatives; we went oftener; he made more. Soon we were going out once a week and Edward was making more negatives than ever, most of them quite different from his earlier seeing of the same material. He did tide pools, landscapes, groves of cypress, seaweed and kelp*

199

in the water, breaking waves, and long views of the rugged shoreline. In the summer there was fog drifting over the rocky inlets; in the fall there were big storms to churn the foam up on the dark rocks.[80]

When Point Lobos was officially closed to the public from 1942 to 1944, Edward was unable to make photographs here. The war years were particularly stressful. Charis shares in her memoir that, "Although none of Edward's sons served on the front lines, they all were involved in the war effort."[81] This part of the coast was being used by the US Army and Air Force to conduct military operations. The US Army Coast Artillery Corps set up anti-aircraft gun emplacements, and both Charis and Edward volunteered for the Aircraft Warning Service, a plane-spotting program led by the army for civilians. The observation station at Yankee Point was close to Wildcat Hill; Charis worked the midnight to 3:00 a.m. shift, and Edward, from 3:00 to 6:00 a.m. I wonder what their exchanges were like late in the night, in those few moments between shifts. During this time, Charis also volunteered at one of the Monterey canneries. Later, she took a job delivering mail, arriving at work at 5:00 a.m. and finishing her seven-mile route by 2:00 p.m. In hindsight, she realized that all of this extra work was a way to avoid time at home with Edward.

> *Edward had begun to sit silently for long periods, and sometimes wouldn't respond even when I spoke to him. As long as we were working on a project together, all was fine, but when we were between articles or other jobs and no visitors were there, he often reverted to silence. His heel would start tapping the floor in what sounded like repressed irritation, until it drove me out of the house—up to Bodie Room or into the garden.*
>
> *It is clear to me now that he was suffering from depression, but in those days we didn't know what that meant; no one considered it a serious medical matter. I feared Edward's moodiness was a reaction to my presence and thought the wisest thing to do was give him some breathing space.*[82]

When friends visited for picnics at Point Lobos or to stay overnight with them at Wildcat Hill, Charis and Edward were able to keep up appearances. For a time, no one suspected that anything was amiss between them. And they found periods of relief from the strains in their relationship as they worked together on *The Cats of Wildcat Hill*. Even so, the last paragraph, reads:

> *Jasmine knows there is something wrong with this picture. It is someone's job to be out on guard duty, patrolling the grounds. The night has really just begun and there will be menaces of many kinds to deal with before it is over. Jasmine is not tempted by stroking hands and soothing words, now that he knows he has work to do. He shrugs off petting impatiently and, without a backward look for the comfort and security of the fireside, walks out through the cat door into the night.*[83]

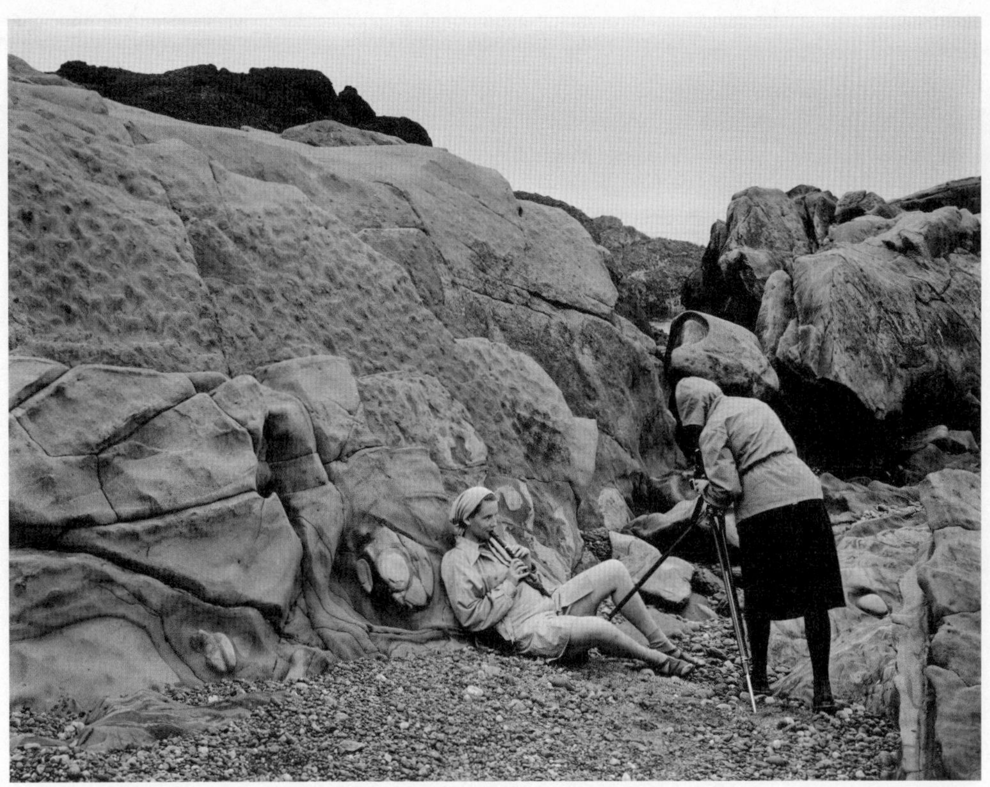

I can't help but wonder if this was a reflection of Charis and Edward's relationship—the two of them passing like ships in the night as they took turns on the night watch. When left alone together, without a project to take their minds off things, the tension between them was palpable.

> There were no scenes—no battles, vituperation, accusations, tears, or periods of short-lived truce. Rather, a portcullis had dropped between us and I could find no way through. In some ways this was worse than if we had fought, because everything was left to the imagination, and mine assigned me all of the blame. I became ever more fixed on the idea that my behavior, and finally just my presence, accounted for the disintegration of our shared lives.[84]

Though Charis and Edward did not yet know about his illness, which is often accompanied by severe depression, they understood that their relationship was suffering. As Charis reflects in her memoir, "Still, I suspect the outcome would have been the same. It was what was happening between the two of us that drove events, and a doctor's diagnosis of the cause of Edward's difficulties would have been unlikely to change the behavior that made our life together impossible."[85]

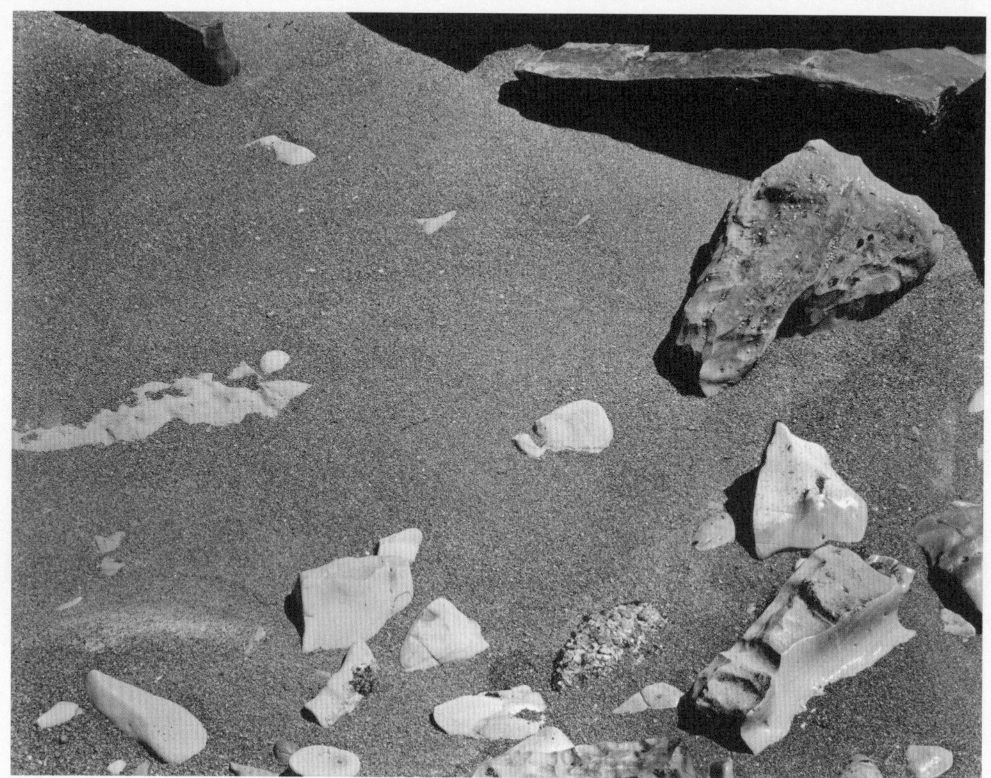

When Point Lobos reopened after World War II, the reserve became Edward's primary subject, as it remained in the last years that he made photographs. In the cypress trees, Edward found subjects that could speak to time and erosion. These trees, grasping the continent's deteriorating western edge, and everything at Point Lobos, are shaped by the forces of wind and waves. Photographer Minor White compared these photographs to Beethoven's last quartets.

Shortly before Charis left Edward in 1945, they agreed to spend the day with Imogen Cunningham at Point Lobos. Edward made a picture of Imogen as she photographed Charis playing a recorder. Imogen wears a light windbreaker with the hood pulled over her head as she looks down into the lens of her waist-level camera. One of her tripod's legs rests between Charis's parted legs. Charis, her muse, looks up into Imogen's lens as she plays. Edward watches from afar. In his photograph, the subjects do not meet his gaze; they are in a world of their own and do not acknowledge his presence.

Imogen's image of Charis was made within seconds of Edward's photograph of them. The tension in Charis's hands suggests that she is about to lift the recorder to play. And yet, she has taken a moment to pause. The slight furrow of her brow suggests that her thoughts are elsewhere. Imogen has not asked Charis to meet our gaze; instead, she photographs Charis alone with her thoughts, perhaps without her knowing the shutter is being clicked. I see a profound sadness in this image, perhaps because I am aware of the discord between Charis and Edward. I know that it won't be long before their relationship dissolves.

Imogen took two more photographs that day—one of Edward and Charis together and one of Edward on his own. In the image of the two of them, Charis nestles in close to Edward, yet there is an awkwardness between them, as if they were asked to scoot closer to one another but are resistant to do so. Her hand stays curled in a loose fist beside her waist, rather than on his knee. Edward stares at a point in the distance to the left of the frame, while Charis drops her gaze lower right, looking toward the ground. It's almost as if these are two separate portraits that have been composited together.

In Imogen's image of Edward on his own, he is leaning against the rocks, perhaps to counter the beginnings of instability from his yet-to-be-diagnosed illness. He is looking slightly higher than the camera's lens, presumably directly at Imogen. Edward's confidence is present in his stance, hand on hip, yet the expression on his face is one of preoccupation. I wonder if being such close and longtime friends with Imogen allowed him to let his guard down. In the image she captures an unspoken vulnerability, a fragility that complicates the manliness of his body language.

Edward was diagnosed with Parkinson's a few months after Charis left him. As the disease progressed, he relied on the support of his sons. Cole and his wife, Helen, moved to Wildcat Hill; they stayed in the main house, while Edward spent most of his time in Bodie Room. He photographed around Wildcat Hill and Point Lobos, working with determination.

In 1948, Edward made his last photograph. At Point Lobos, scattered rocks, like shards of bone, touch the edges of the frame. Unlike his earlier works that feature a single piece of driftwood or monumentalize a nautilus shell, these fragments of rock are dispersed; they emerge from, and sink back down into, the sand. Alan Trachtenberg discusses this image in an essay on the work of Edward's final years.

> *It is tempting to see in* [Rocks and Pebbles] *a recognition of the breaking asunder of physical powers, the encroaching darkness of an unhappy death, the shattering of vision. But to make an allegory of it fails to answer all the questions provoked by this difficult picture. Lacking a commanding center, the picture consists of intervals: stone and sand, light and dark, open and closed shapes. Its figures are exactingly concrete, its structure mysteriously abstract. We hear a melody more than we see a distinct form. The image tends to lend evidence to Charis Wilson's observation about Weston, that he "liked to find the coded messages, the surfaces behind the surfaces, the depths below depths, that gave ambiguous accounts of the nature of things." We are not accustomed to thinking of Weston as an artist either of ambiguity or of coded messages, of meanings of any sort. Crystalline exactness of perception, with an absolutely certain sense of what is being pictured, marks his major work—the tightly framed portraits, shells, nudes, sand dunes, mushrooms, roots, and undulating horizon lines. In* [Rocks and Pebbles] *everything*

enclosed in the frame seems in ambiguous relation to everything else. Without a center the picture exposes the camera's willfulness in drawing a four-sided boundary around this particular scene. The scene appears less scene than event, an event of seeing, a construction of perception itself. Is the construction a translation of an inner state, a feeling, a mood? [Rocks and Pebbles] *seems as close to an "equivalent"—to use Stieglitz's term—as one can find in Weston's work.*[86]

Edward died at Wildcat Hill in the early morning of January 1, 1958. His sons scattered his ashes in a cove at Point Lobos that they privately called Weston Beach. In 1979, the name became official when the US Board on Geographic Names accepted Ansel Adams's proposal to dedicate the beach in his friend's honor. Weston Beach has eroded considerably in the decades since Charis and Edward were last there, but sea life thrives in the tide pools and in the cracks and crevices of the rocks that remain. Betsy and I delicately move across slippery rocks covered with kelp and patchworks of bright green moss and watch hundreds of purple shore crabs navigate the water flowing in and out of the pools, their claws clicking rhythmically in a staccato symphony.

At the Big Sur Campground, our cabin has a double bed with a floral quilt, an overhead light, and outlets to charge our phones. A roof made of translucent corrugated fiberglass provides a dreamy view of the redwoods swaying above us, sunlight filtering through. The warm smell of cedar is intoxicating. This kind of luxury is not something Charis and Edward often experienced on the road; they mostly slept in sleeping bags under open skies. When it rained, Charis preferred to sleep deep down in her sleeping bag under a tarp, while Edward did his best to keep from freezing inside the car. When it was cold, they wore pajamas under their clothes and multiple pairs of socks. They camped on cliffs when thick morning fog blanketed the landscape below; on creek banks, where they battled the wind, retrieving blankets blown into gullies; near cave openings, where thousands of bats emerged at dusk. On the north coast, they camped on beds of pine needles beneath towering redwoods. As Charis writes in *California and the West*, "redwoods—impossible to photograph perhaps, but generous with their leafy, aromatic shade—couches of piled-up needles in which your sleeping bag sinks two feet. Admittedly the camp-ground is too full of squalling babies and blaring radios, but after a while the noise abates and you lie on the softest of mattresses looking up at the giant pillars of redwood trunks that all seem to lean in over your head."[87]

We decide to take the rest of the day off. The remainder of the afternoon is spent on the front porch drinking beer, smoking cigarettes, and writing in our sketchbooks. I change into shorts and prop my legs on the front porch railing. The bruise on my shin from the week before is now a lump of light lavender and lemon. Other campers play cards or relax in their customized camping chairs, drinking and chatting. Teenage girls ride their bikes around the campground loop. Their chitchat marks time with each lap. In the distance, we can hear the laughter of children as they float in inner tubes down the Big Sur River, which right now is really more of a stream because of the drought. Bets uses the skills she learned from summers spent at Girl Scout camp to make a fire and whittle sticks for roasting hot dogs and marshmallows. A good-looking guy traveling solo pulls up at the site next to us; he sets up his tent before climbing back on his motorcycle and leaving in a whirl. The sun begins to set, campfires crackle and pop.

The next morning as I walk around the campsite, rays of light reach down through the redwoods, more visible in the smoke rising from early morning fires. The smell of bacon fills the air. I see a couple in their twenties molded together in a hammock suspended between two redwoods. At another site, a teenage girl sits on top of an RV reading a book as her mother, who wears bright red boxing gloves, spars with a man below. The adults are in the shadows of the trees, but the girl is bathed in an ethereal light.

Back on the front porch drinking coffee and making a list of possible shoots for the day, I try not to stare at the attractive guy at the next campsite as he carefully packs up his things. I wonder what he is doing traveling on his own. By the look of his gear, which is pared down to the essentials, it appears that this is a fine-tuned routine. When I see him carefully fold up an Art Institute of Chicago bag and place it in one of the bike's side compartments, I become even more curious. Maybe he is a neighbor of ours in Illinois. I respect the invisible line between our campsites and resist asking questions as he finishes packing. I watch out of the corner of my eye as he brushes his teeth using water from a nearby spigot.

After my dad died, I often found myself thinking about men. I'm not sure if this was because I was grieving, or because Bets and I had been talking about whether or not to have kids. Maybe I was being pulled toward the bodies that could give us children, a last-ditch effort on my hormones' part to fertilize one of those few remaining eggs. Once, a stranger was standing in line in front of me at the grocery store. He wasn't someone who I would normally be attracted to, with preppy clothes and a sports-team vibe. I couldn't see his face, but his back looked so comfortable that I wanted to lay my head between his shoulder blades. Another time, during an artist lecture, a man I knew, but not well, sat beside me. I had an intense urge to rest my head on his shoulder, to fall into him. I could smell him, sandalwood and clean sweat.

Sometimes I walk a thin line—fantasies on one side, reality on the other. This line is something I have learned from experience not to tread on too much. I have always been attracted to both women and men. I've often told Bets that I could get a crush on a rock, and she just smiles and says that she thinks my fantasy life is healthy.

Bets sleeps as I unload and reload film holders using the foot of the bed as a work surface. Her head is covered by the quilt for warmth, her body, a modest mountain range. Hills and valleys rise and fall with each inhale and exhale.

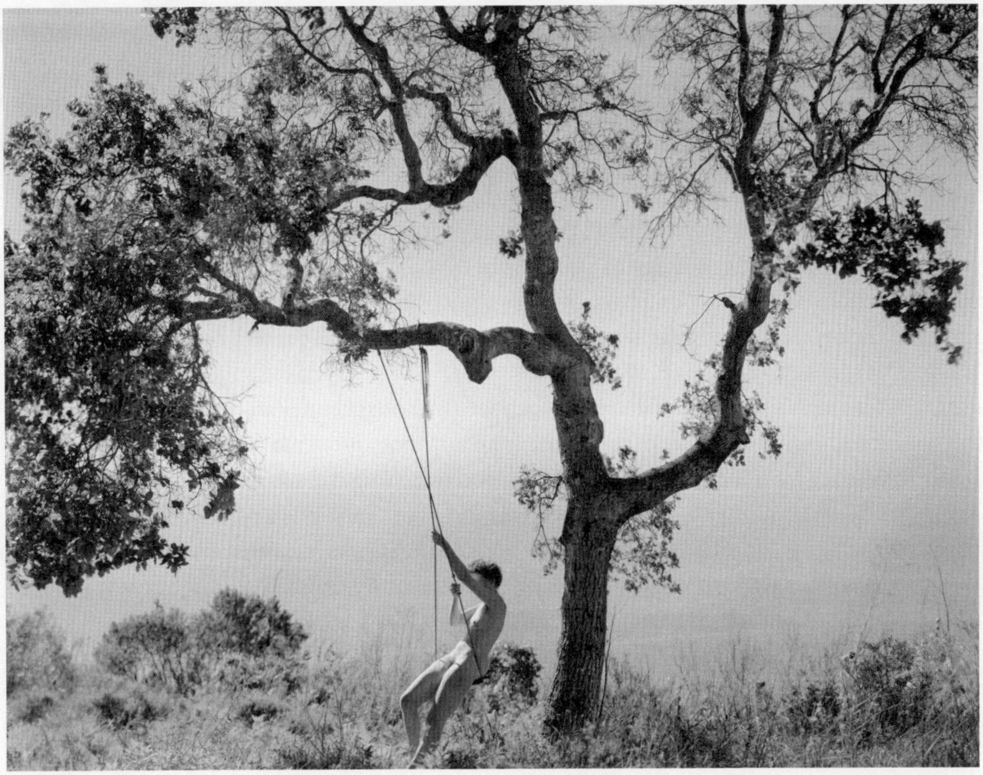

We are scheduled to meet a man named Scott at the Big Sur Bakery at 11:30 who will show us around the house where a friend of Charis and Edward's, Doug Short, used to live. Doug was the lawyer who helped Charis secure the parcel of land for their home on Wildcat Hill, as well as drafted the divorce agreement after Charis and Edward separated, and it was at Doug Short's home where Edward made one of his last pictures of Charis in 1945, *Winter Idyll*.

Searching for "Doug Short Edward Weston Winter Idyll" on the internet, I was ecstatic to find a site with pictures of the home, including one with an image of a tree with a swing that looked like the tree and swing in *Winter Idyll*. Through more research, I found out that the house was available as a vacation rental for six hundred dollars a night. We couldn't afford to stay there, so I contacted the property manager and explained that I was doing a project about Edward Weston who had been good friends with Doug Short. I included an image of *Winter Idyll* in my email, and to my amazement, the property manager agreed to let us make photographs for a few hours before the next guests arrived.

We follow Scott's truck to a driveway with a gate, where he enters a code. The gate slowly opens, and we creep along a narrow dirt road past private drives that lead to luxurious homes, each poised precariously on rugged bluffs that face the sea. We pass a few workers who are removing debris from the road before winding around a last curve to arrive at the home where Doug Short once lived.

I show Scott the photograph, and the three of us walk over to a tree that has the same shape as the tree in the photograph with a swing made from a single piece of wood and two pieces of rope. The tree in Edward's photograph is smaller, younger, and has fewer leaves because the image was made in January. What puzzles me is that the tree in *Winter Idyll* appears to stand at the edge of a cliff. As in that picture, a heavy fog hides the sea below, but there is more ground and several young oaks between the tree we are looking at now and the drop off. Perhaps Edward's use of his eight-by-ten camera created a dramatic collapse of space.

Through sliding glass doors, we can see the housekeeper stacking empty beer bottles into a box. On the side of the house is an outdoor shower and generous clawfoot bathtub where I imagine Betsy and I soaking and watching the sunset, could we afford to stay here. We walk along the property's edge, and Scott shows us a path that leads to a private beach nine hundred feet below. He adds that the hike is strenuous but well worth it. As he makes his way back to his truck, he tells us that we can stay as long as we want. He reaches into the cab and hands us two plums.

By the time Edward photographed Charis in *Winter Idyll*, they must have known that their relationship was coming to an end. Edward stood so far from Charis that he would have needed to shout to direct her. In the first nudes Edward made in his studio in Carmel, he and Charis were close enough for a whisper, close enough to feel the heat and energy between their bodies. That dramatic intimacy and intensity was transformed by the comfortable companionship they built as collaborators. Charis came to be depicted in her entirety, if no further than an arm's length away; in Edward's final images, Charis is still desirable but out of reach. In *Winter Idyll*, she leans back in the swing, her arms lifted as she holds the ropes, the left one hiding her face. She is suspended in a pause between her life with Edward and the life that now stretched out before her.

Everything is a haze as we enter the desert and head back east. Dust devils swirl in the distance. The temperature climbs. A thirteen-member motorcycle gang passes us one by one, their Harleys outfitted for a long haul, the last bike with a side car full of gear. We go by a hand-painted sign that reads "Freedom Is Not Free, Thank Your Veterans," followed a few miles up the road by a sign with changeable letters that declares "Laura Loves Kate." Bets and I give each other a high five, and I motion for her to give me a smooch, even though I am at the wheel. We listen to Timber Timbre and settle into the drive. Bets pulls her knees to her chest, which always amazes me. How can someone so tall make themselves so small?

———————————

With the desert spread wide before us, I think about the photographs I have made on the road. I was beginning to understand that the landscape photographs I was making, some from Edward's view, some on paths of our own, were less about re-photography and more about photography's relationship to capturing a moment in time. It is about how the record created was, on one hand, a memento; and, on the other, a document that carries with it a shifting understanding based on who sees it, where they see it, and through what personal and cultural filters they bring to it. My images are documents of a pilgrimage taken after the tremendous loss of my father; of the shared grief we feel for Betsy's brother. Making them and traveling together is a way to cope with loss by being on the road. This pilgrimage for Charis has become its own type of pilgrimage to a meaningful place; a place connected to someone important in one's life. Charis was important to me. She helped me to become aware of my potential to better understand Edward, a Modernist "master," against whom I had instinctually lashed out because I had learned about him through the filter of all the cultural and artistic biases of our times. Through Charis, he had become more empathetic, more complex as an individual and an artist. Her story introduces me to the Edward I would most like to meet. In an essay by Robert Adams entitled "The Achievement of Edward Weston: The Biography I'd Like to Read," Adams shared his disdain for a biography written about Weston by Ben Maddow and his hopes for a future rewriting.

> *If, then, we are led eventually by a full-scale biography to combine what we might learn from Weston's pictures about, among other things, the three truisms—that he was a prodigious lover, that he was apolitical, and that his final landscapes are especially significant—might we not see more clearly the nature of Weston's achievement? As remarkable as was his creation of the pictures—and perhaps to some degree through that—he appears to have become, after many failed attempts, another person, growing away from his earlier egoism and its disappointments toward a more generous view of other people and of the world as a whole.*[88]

As for the portraits I was making with Betsy, I was beginning to see how they related to images I had made of her over the years—they hold love, desire, longing, grief, and tenderness. They are the evidence of my struggle with the power a photographer brings to a subject they love deeply. They reflect Betsy's willingness to be seen, to be understood through her moods, and they show a glimpse of our life together as women.

Pouring days and months, years of research into someone you'll never meet, is a curious endeavor. The affinity I feel for Charis is in keeping with my fascination with photographer-sitter relationships, and my pleasure felt in the presence of strong, independent women. I have come to deeply relate to the experiences she shares in her memoir—the endless possibilities associated with being on the road for the sake of a project; grief she experienced over losing her father, and the confusions of marrying someone at a young age. Most poignantly, I understand the difficult process of eventually leaving someone you love. This more than anything, I related to: Charis's telling of her marriage's dissolution. The love she must have still had for Edward, years later, to write a sensitive and compelling story of their lives—I find this overwhelming.

Charis and Edward drove through the Mojave on their travels for both *California and the West* and *Leaves of Grass*. As our path converges with theirs along these roads, these veins that line the land, I think about how much Charis and Edward's lives had changed between their first trip across this desert to their last one. When they set out on their first Guggenheim trip in April 1937, they crossed this stretch of land on their way to Death Valley and were exhilarated. A new chapter was beginning for them both. The openness of the land that stretched for miles before them mirrored the openness of their future. Their life together was still on the horizon. As they took to the road for *Leaves of Grass* four years later, Charis had a premonition. "A feeling of anguish swept through me, a pang of desolation, a sense of onrushing personal disaster. I felt sure that things would never be the same again, that our future was being reshaped by whatever lay ahead."

I knew what lay ahead for Charis from my own experiences. I knew how hard it was to try to make a marriage work before finally letting go. I was twenty-two when I got married the first time. Within months as a married couple, I found myself in the depths of a crush on another man. When my husband and I moved to another city, I convinced myself that things would work out. The next two years were hard for us. We both felt confined by the expectations of married life. We worked long hours at jobs that didn't make us happy; neither of us were following our passions. I silently started to have doubts about our marriage, and more specifically, about marriage in general. I once again felt the pull of attraction—this time to a woman. I didn't want to get a divorce, and although I loved my husband, I started to feel like I was living a lie.

Bets rests her bare feet on the dash as she quickly makes drawings of motorcycle parts, with a felt-tipped pen in her sketchbook, for a sculpture she is thinking about making. After miles of mesmerizing terrain, we come across a strange scene: hundreds of old shoes strewn across the ground. We are going eighty miles an hour. I wonder if I'm beginning to hallucinate. "Let's turn around," I say to Bets. I am sure if we had not retraced our steps that the lost picture would have haunted me, and I would have wondered if what I had seen ever existed at all.

This is a scene for Edward. Shoes found in the landscape were one of the many sub-categories he obsessively photographed while on the road. There are shoes of all styles and sizes tangled up in brush, shoes with their laces twisting around dead tree branches. The rubber of my own tennis shoes is softening, like taffy, in the unrelenting heat. A pair of combat boots sits underneath the overpass, in the middle of the wash, waiting for a monsoon to take them away.

We climb in elevation until we reach Flagstaff, where we unroll the windows for a blast of the cool air. Crossing into New Mexico, we follow county roads through Thoreau, Seven Lakes, White Horse, Pueblo, Cuba, La Jara, Regina, Coyote, and Youngsville until we arrive in Abiquiu. As we unload the car in the moonlight, I catch a glimpse of Betsy, her body held in its soft, cool glow. She often says that she is new to this world, here for the first time, learning new things. I see her through the eyes of my old soul. She looks beautiful and alien and unfamiliar. And I love her.

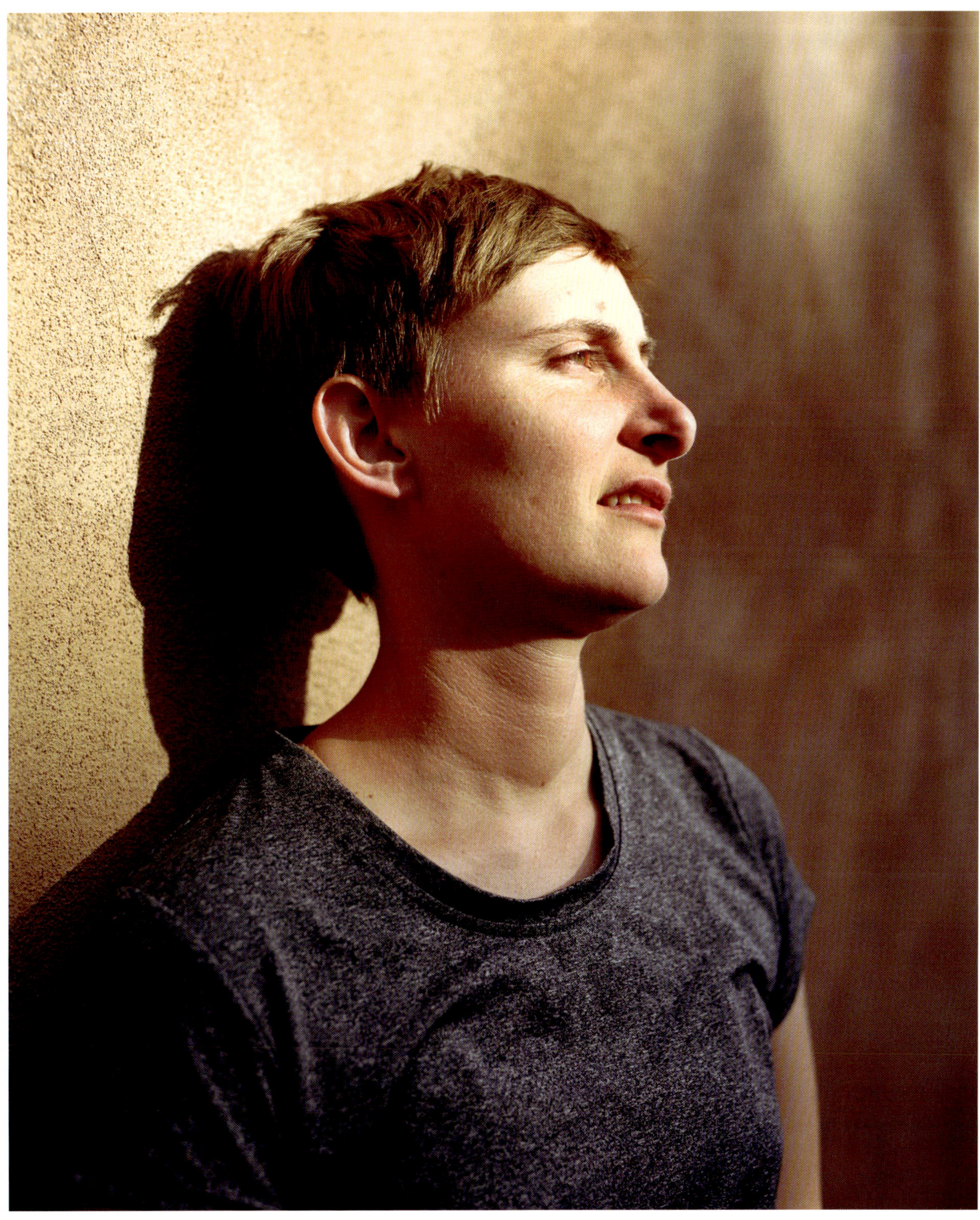

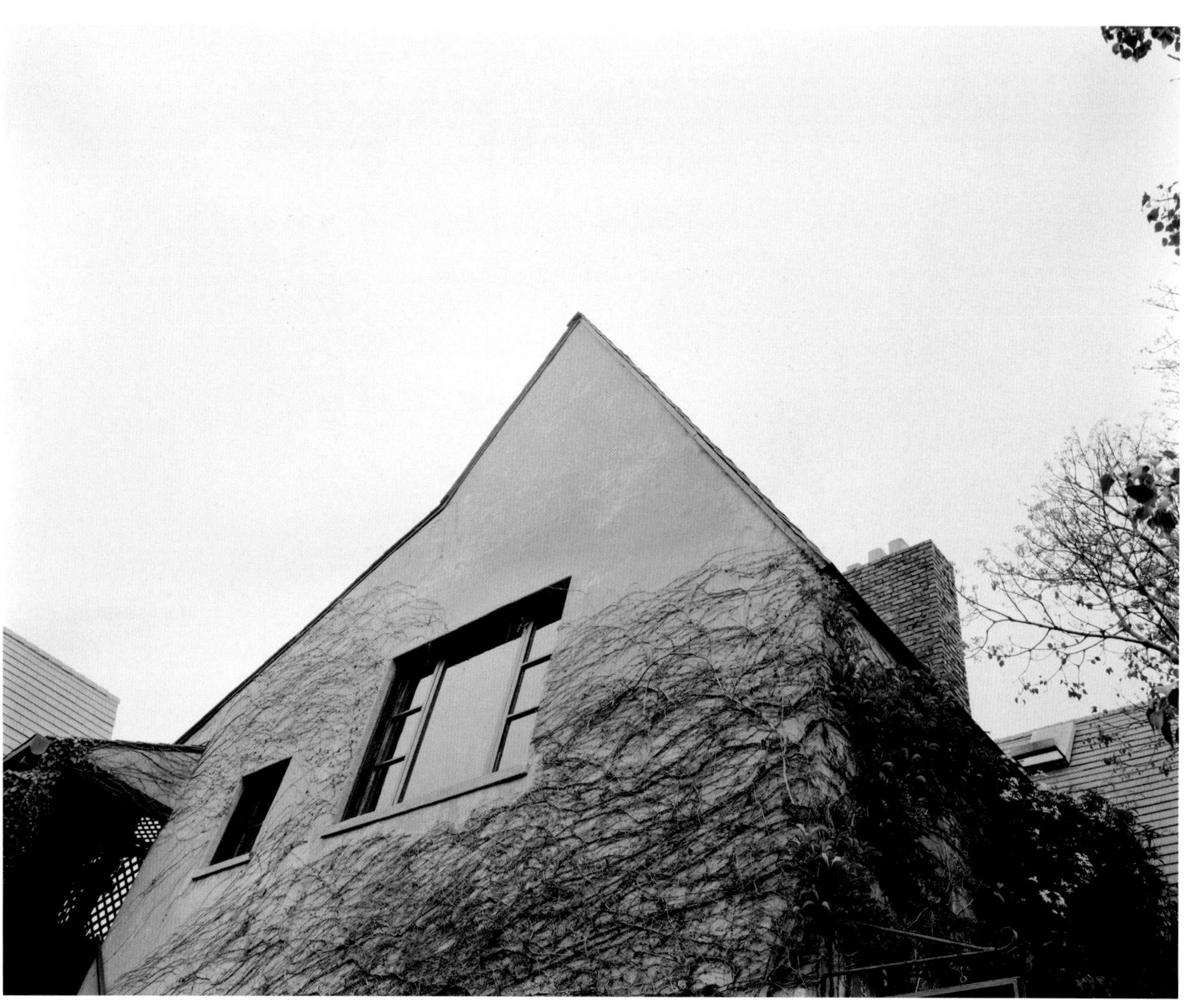

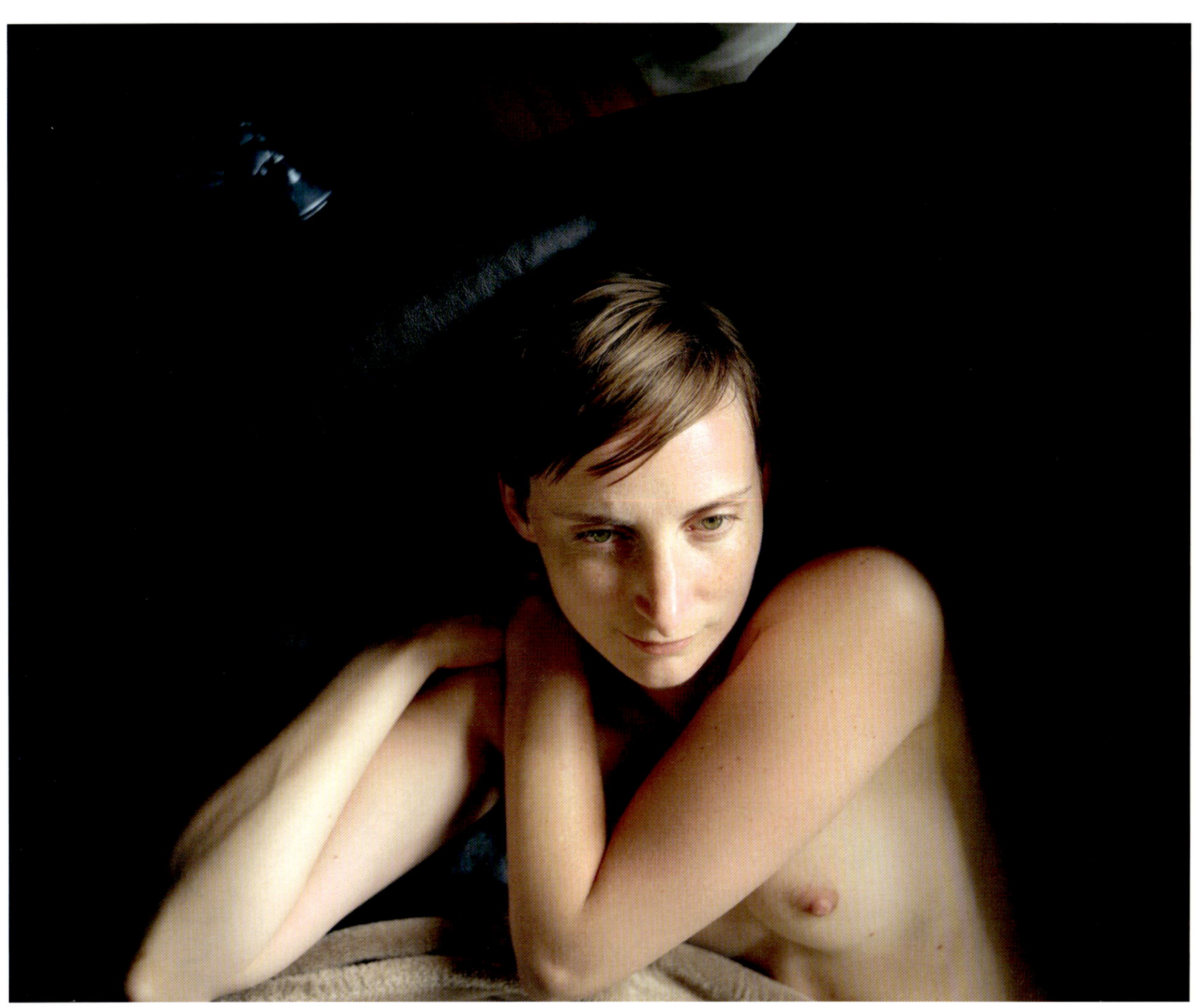

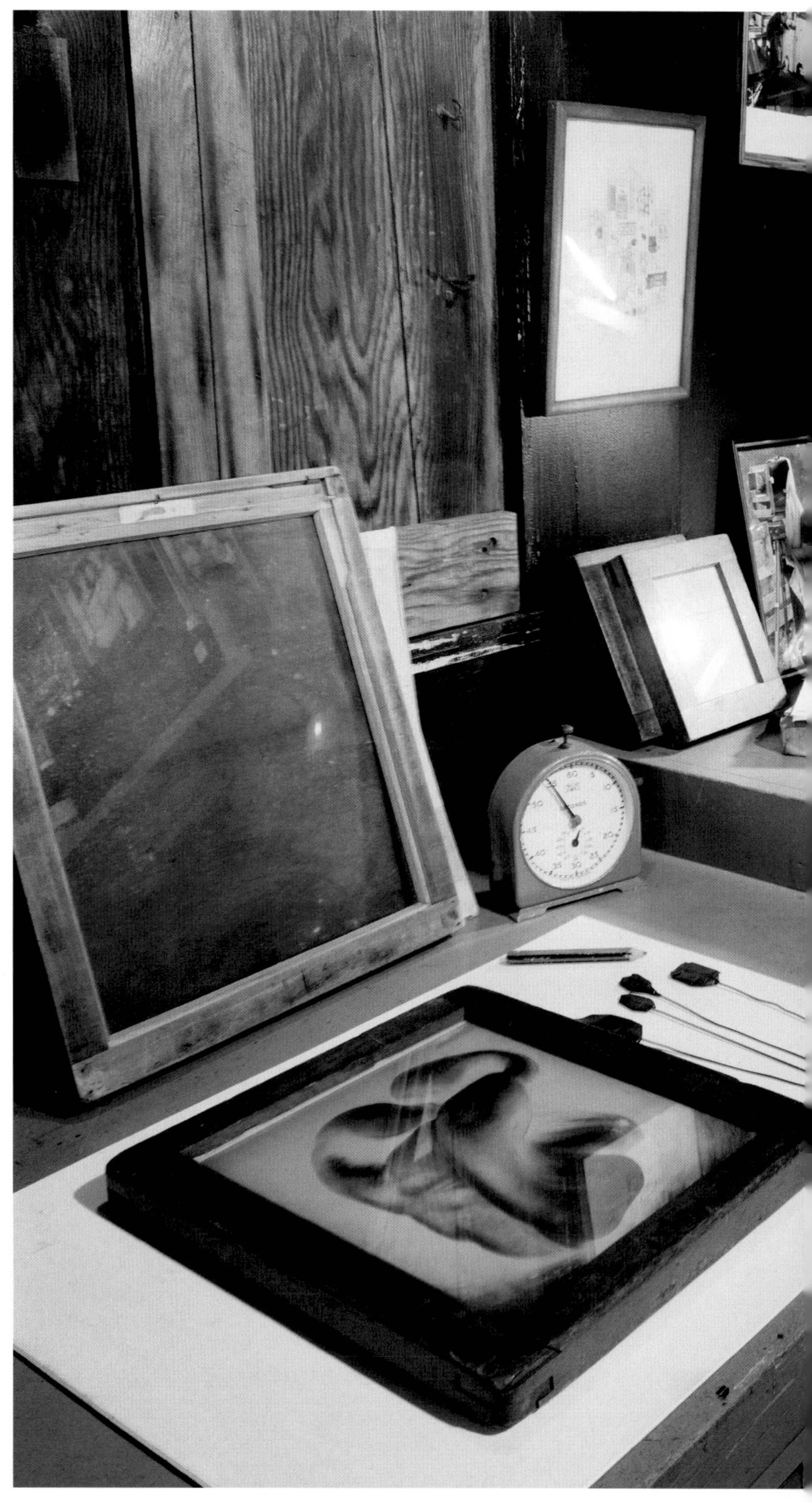

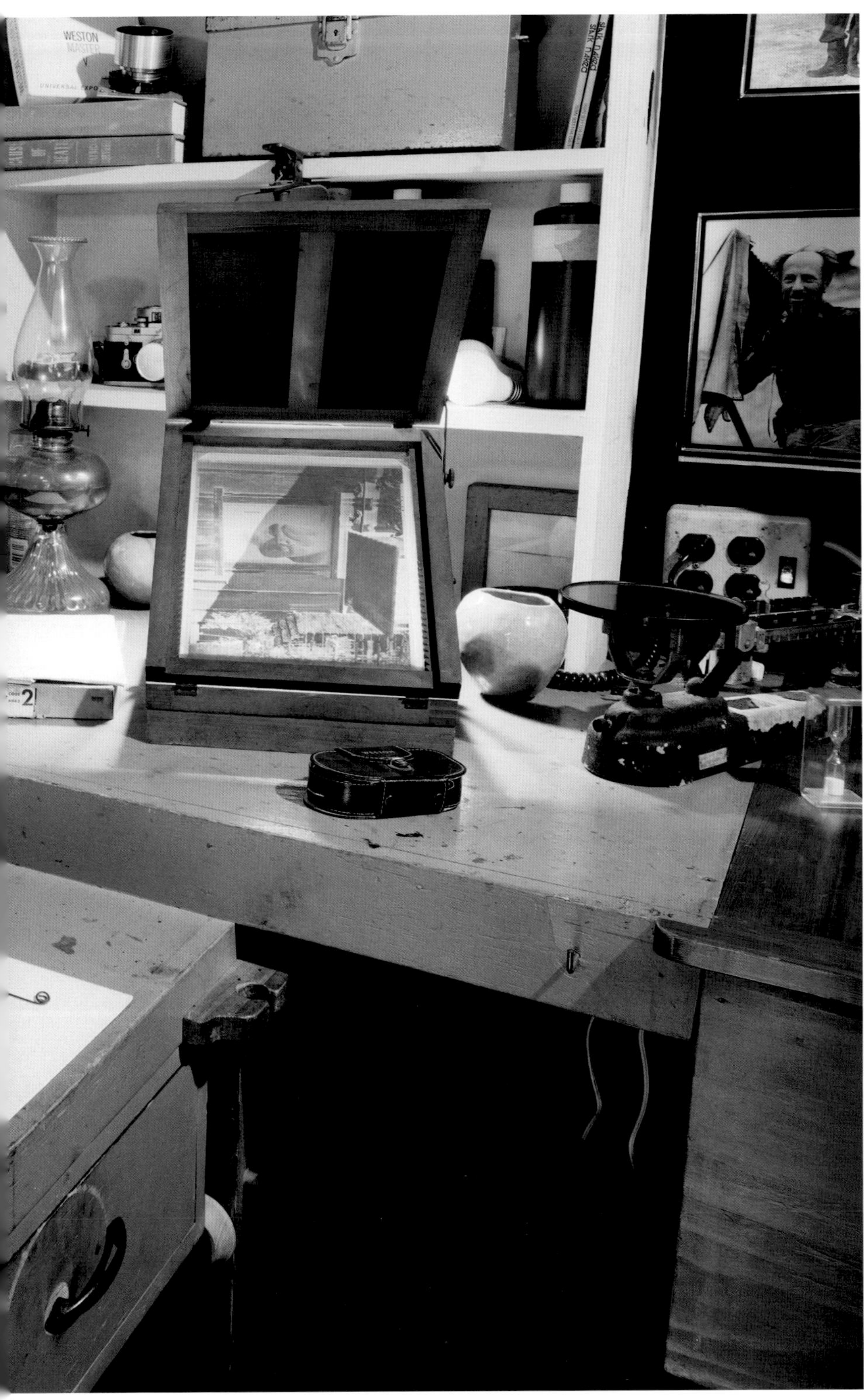

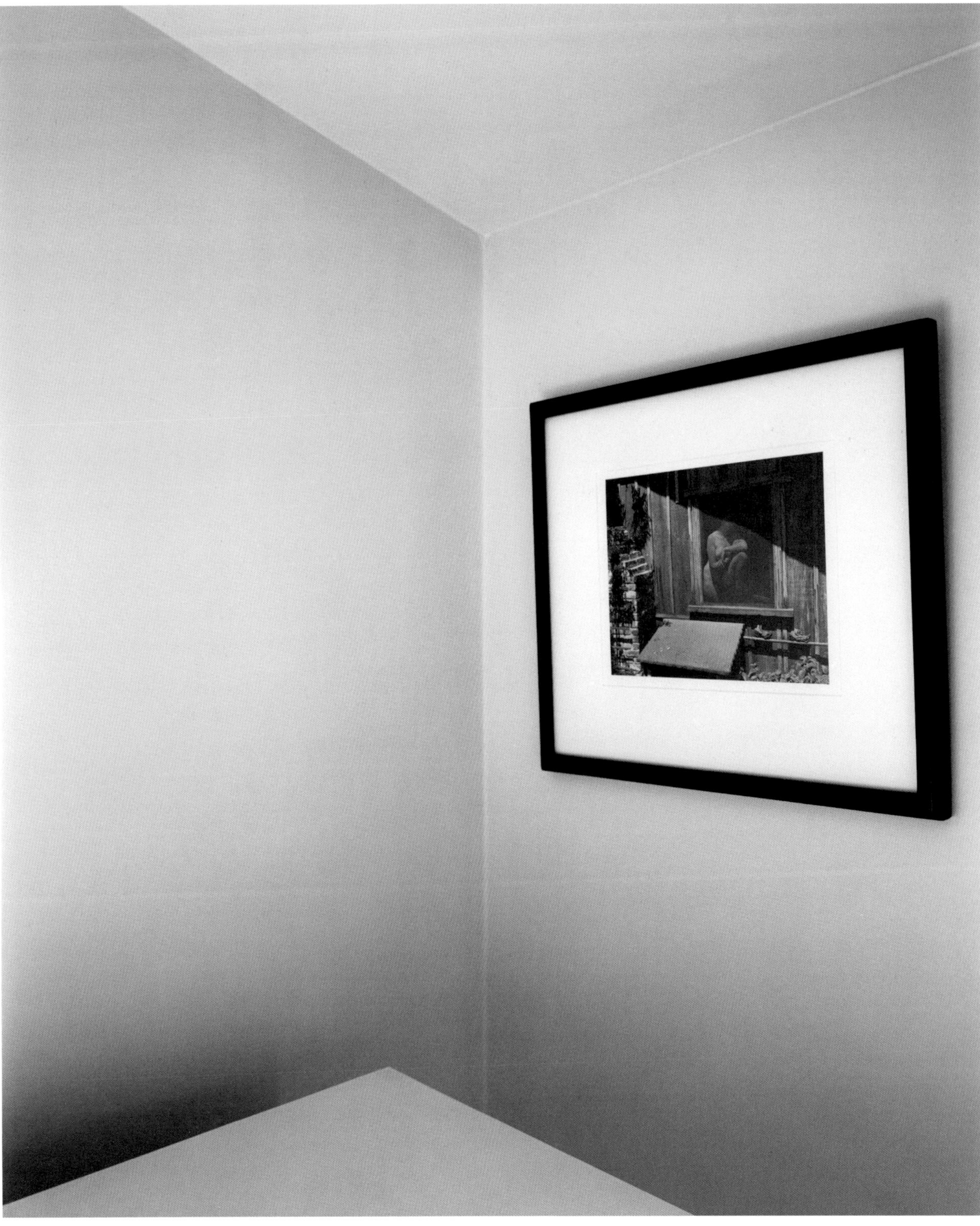

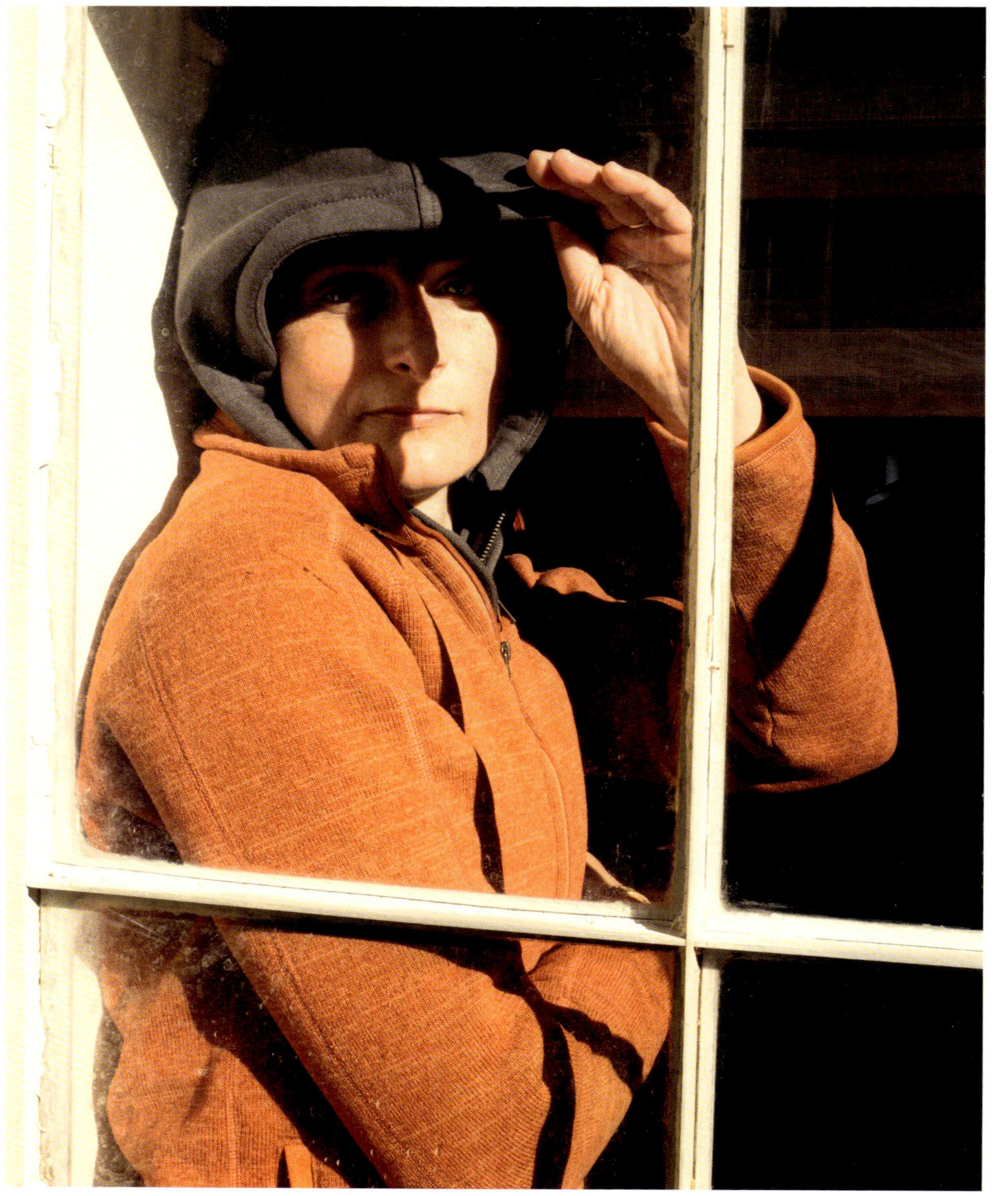

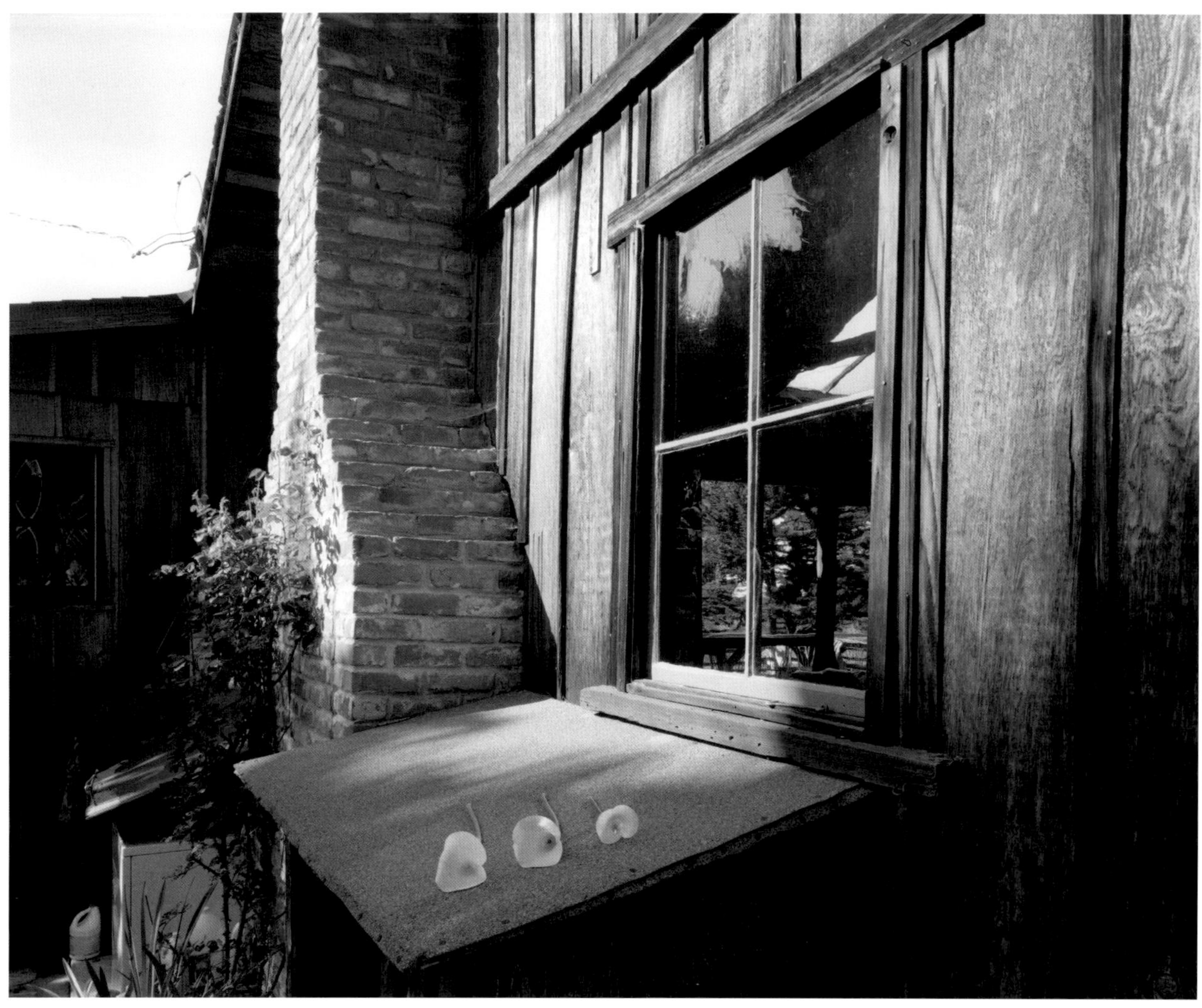

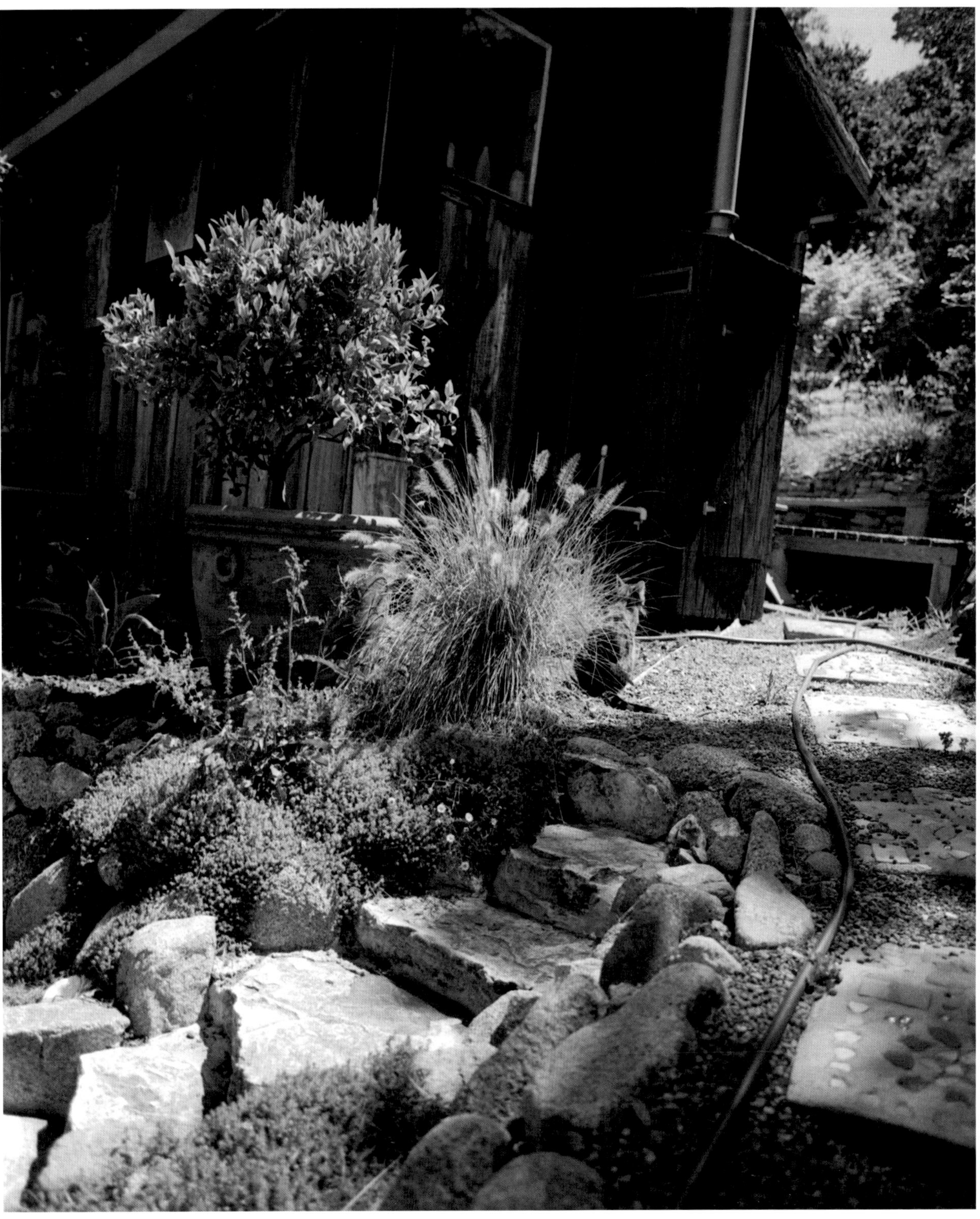

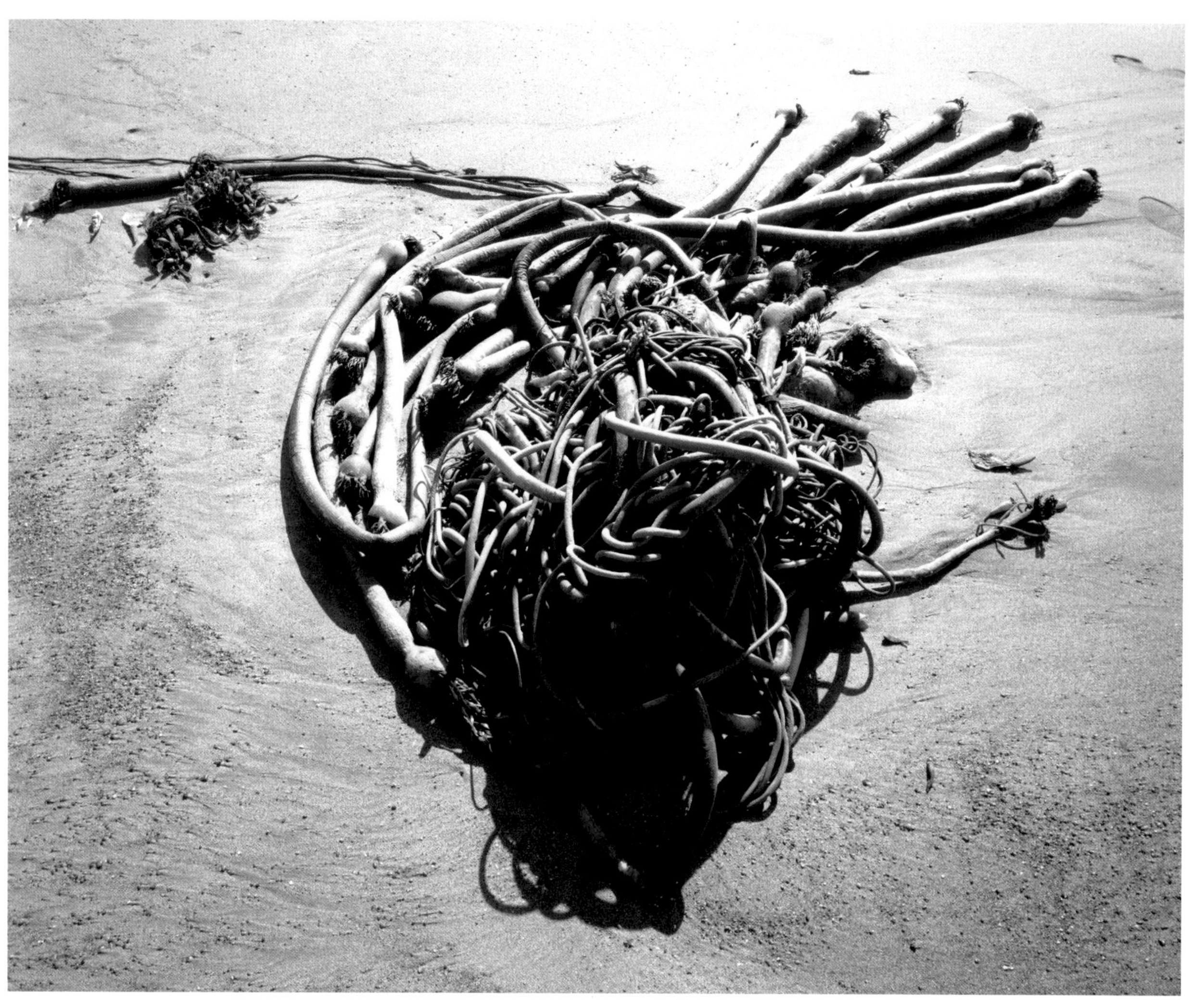

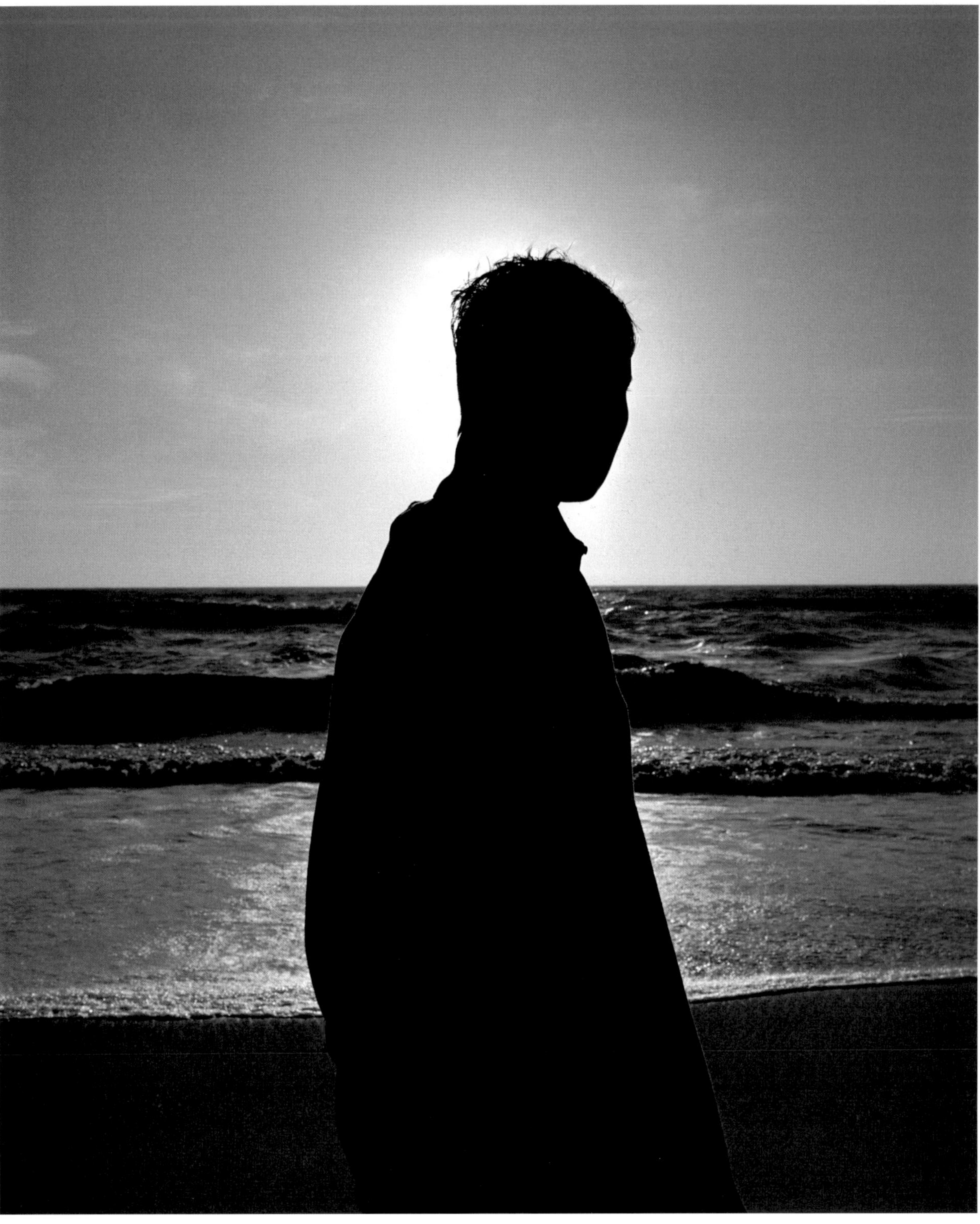

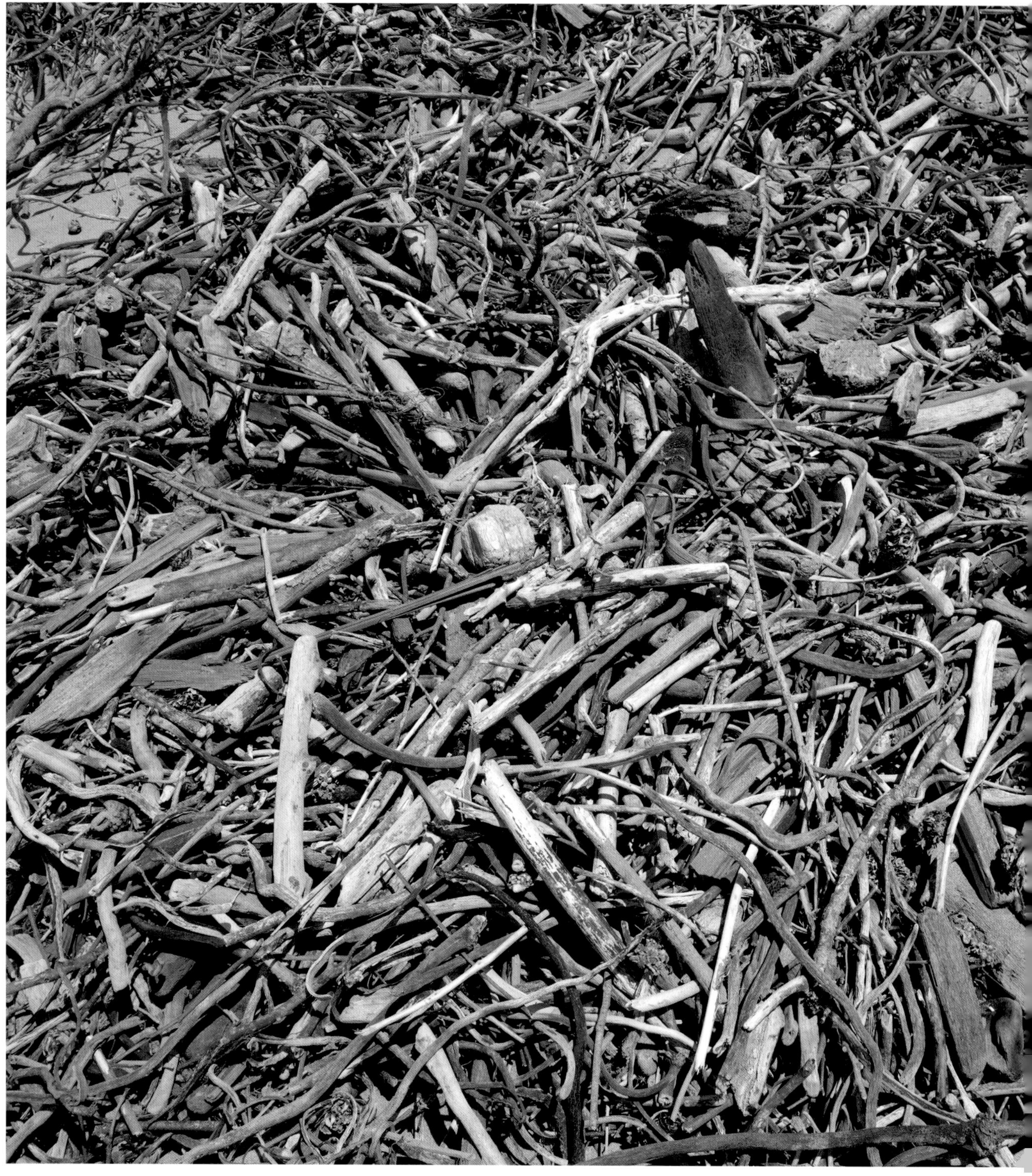

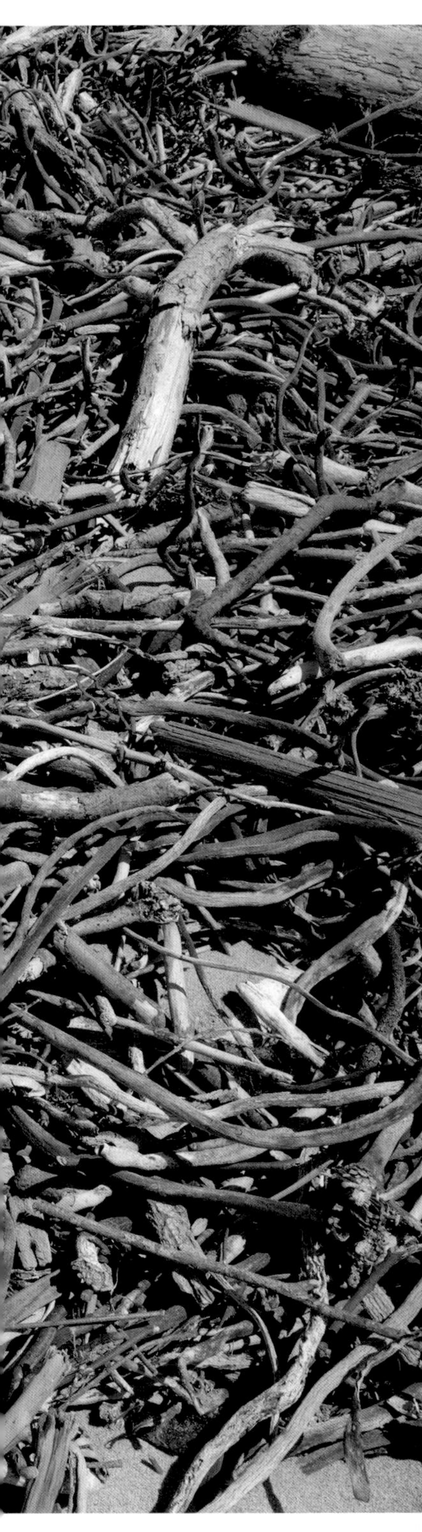

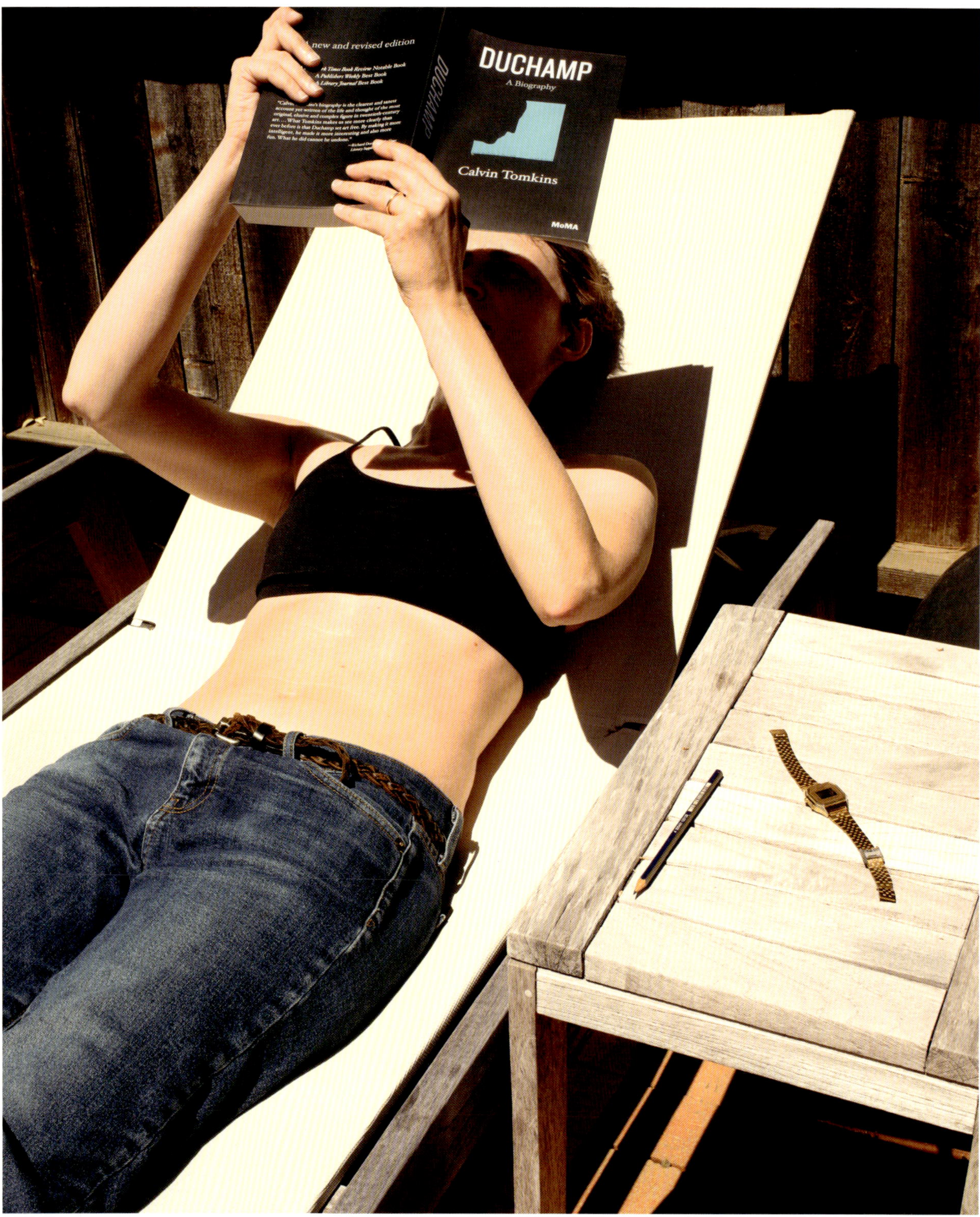
new and revised edition
DUCHAMP
A Biography
Calvin Tomkins
MoMA

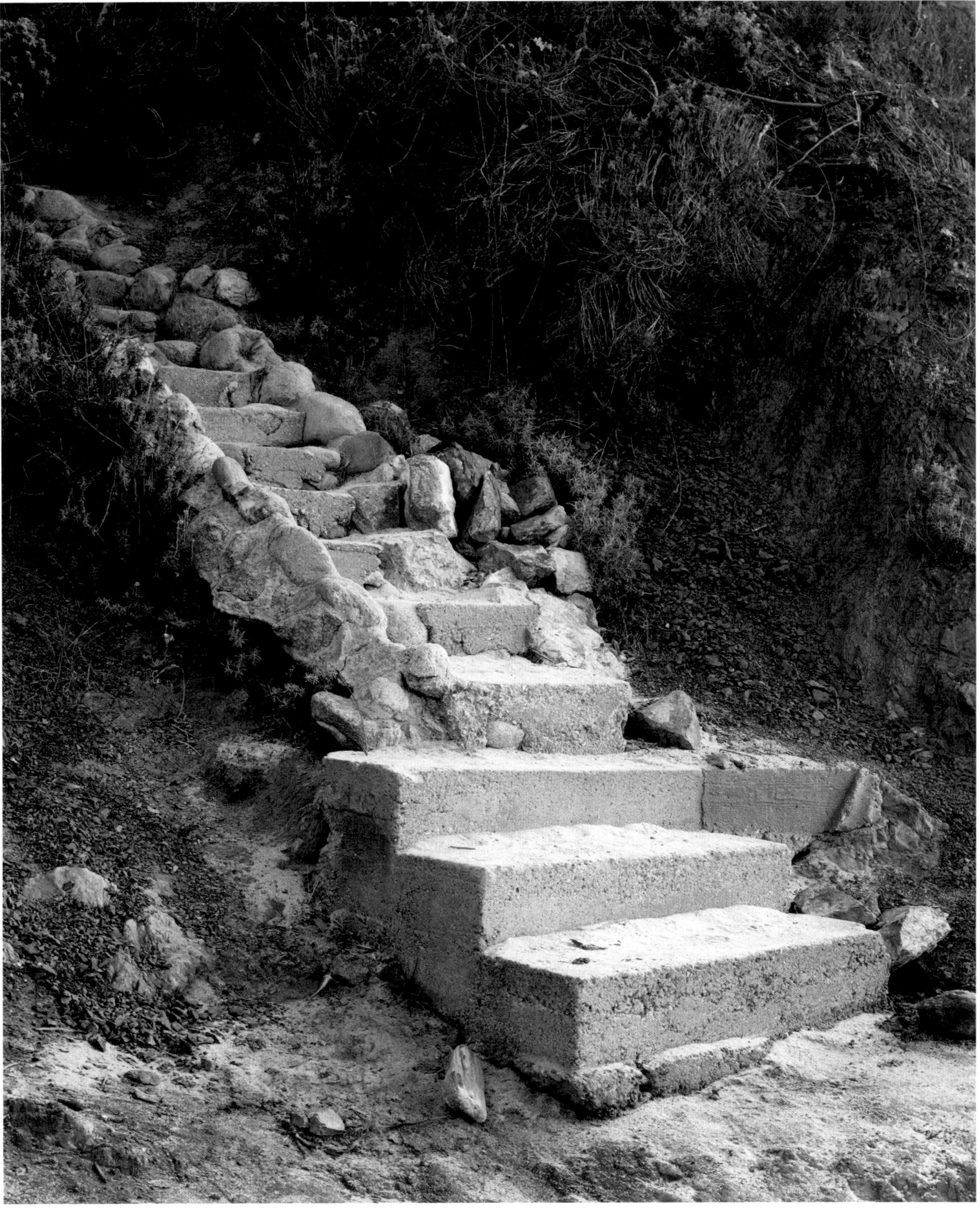

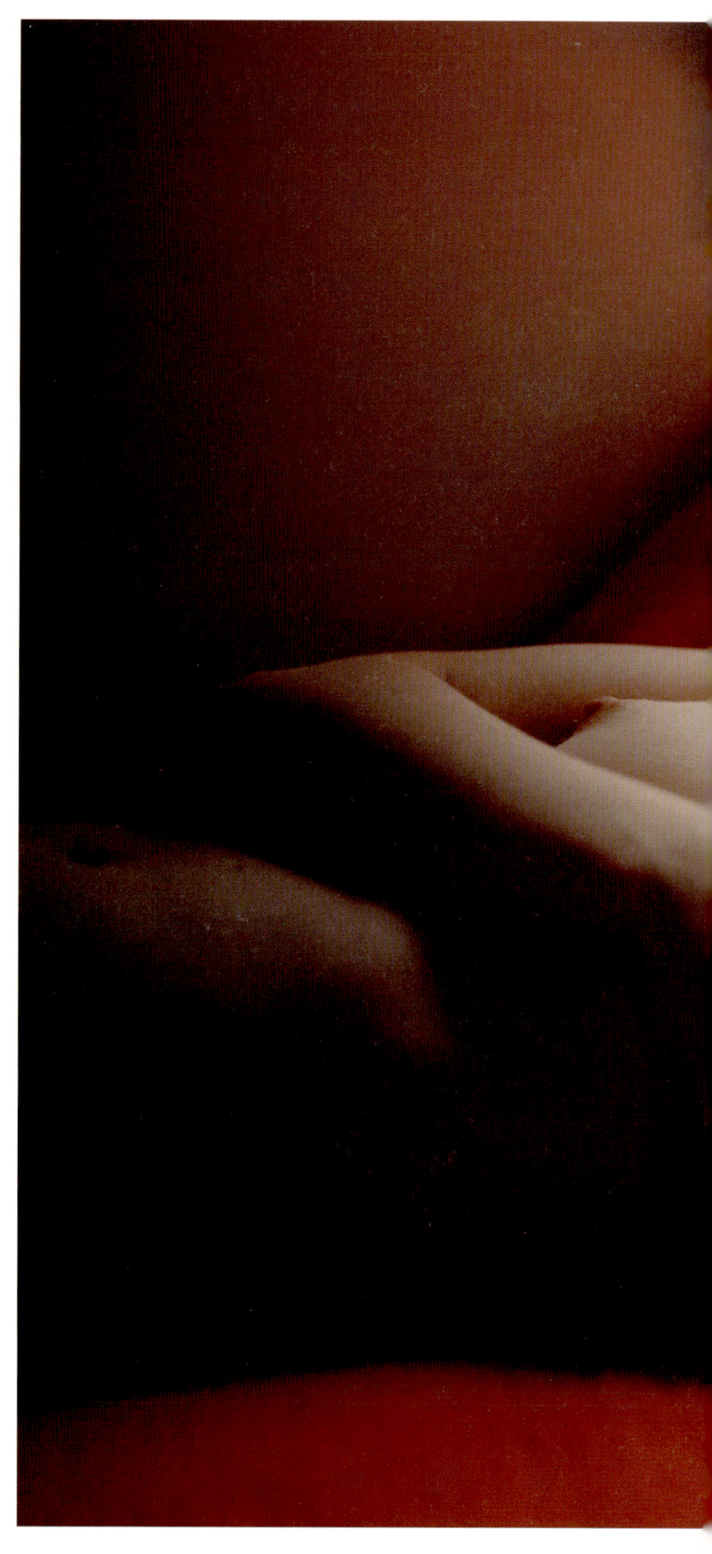

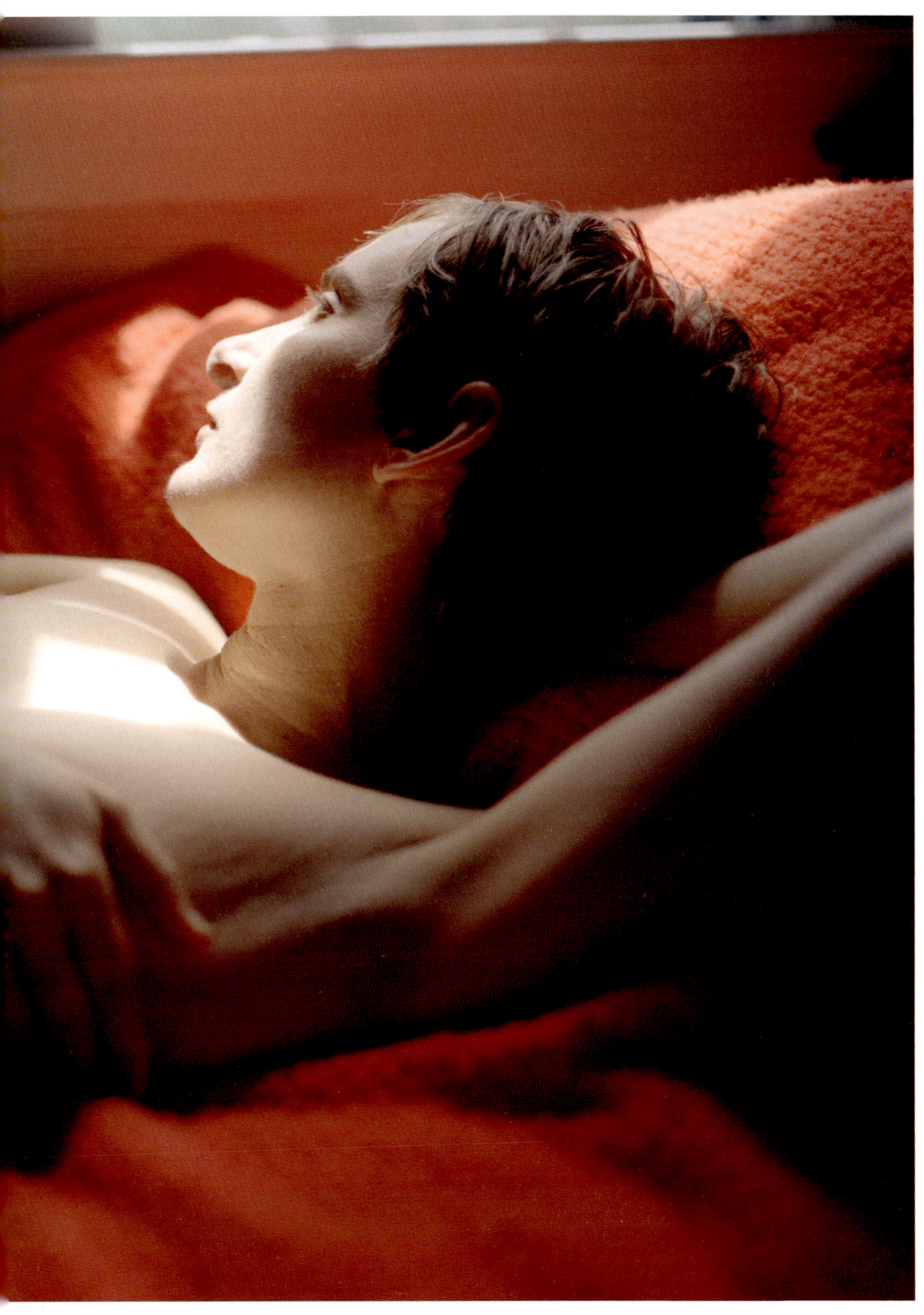

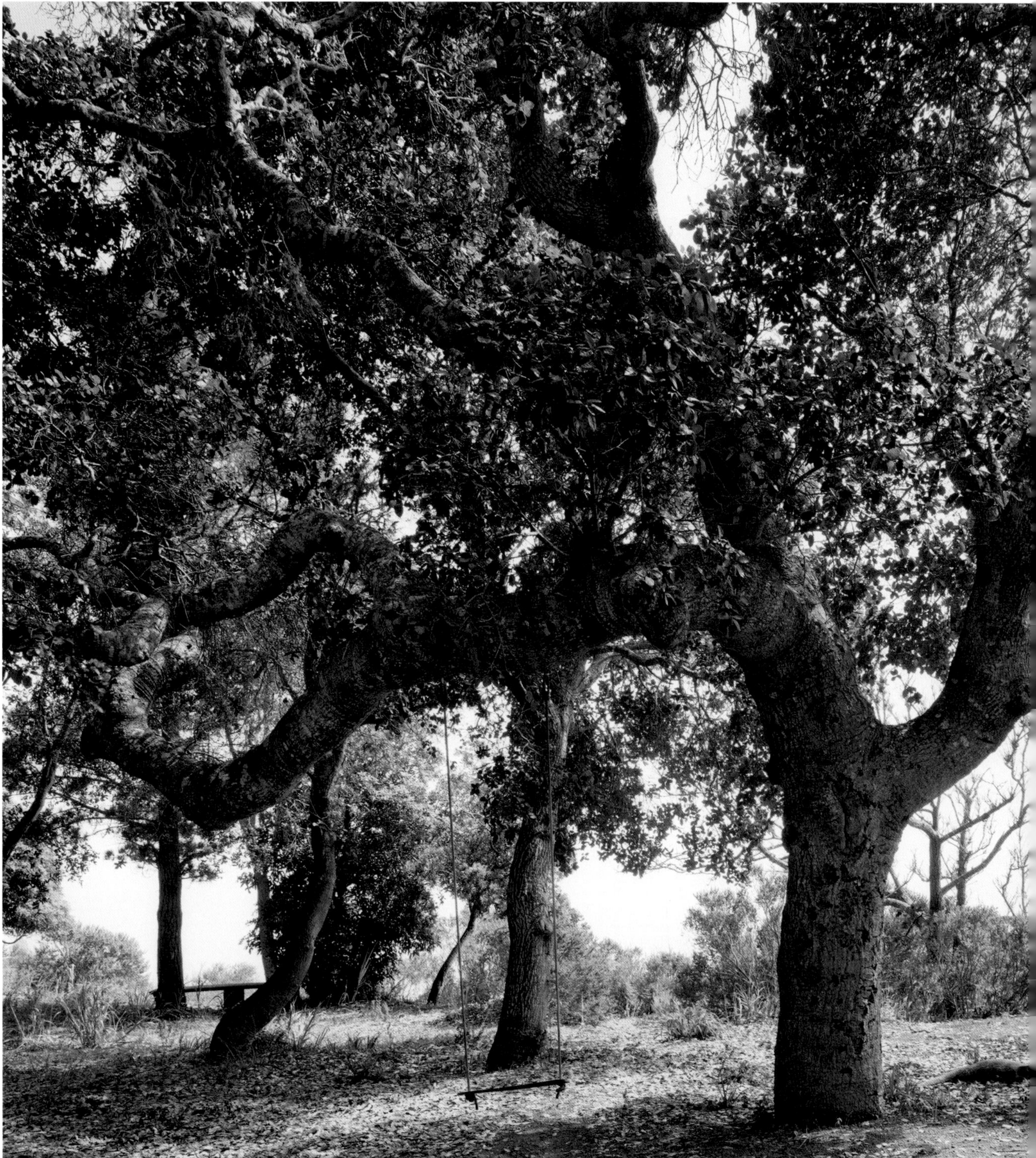

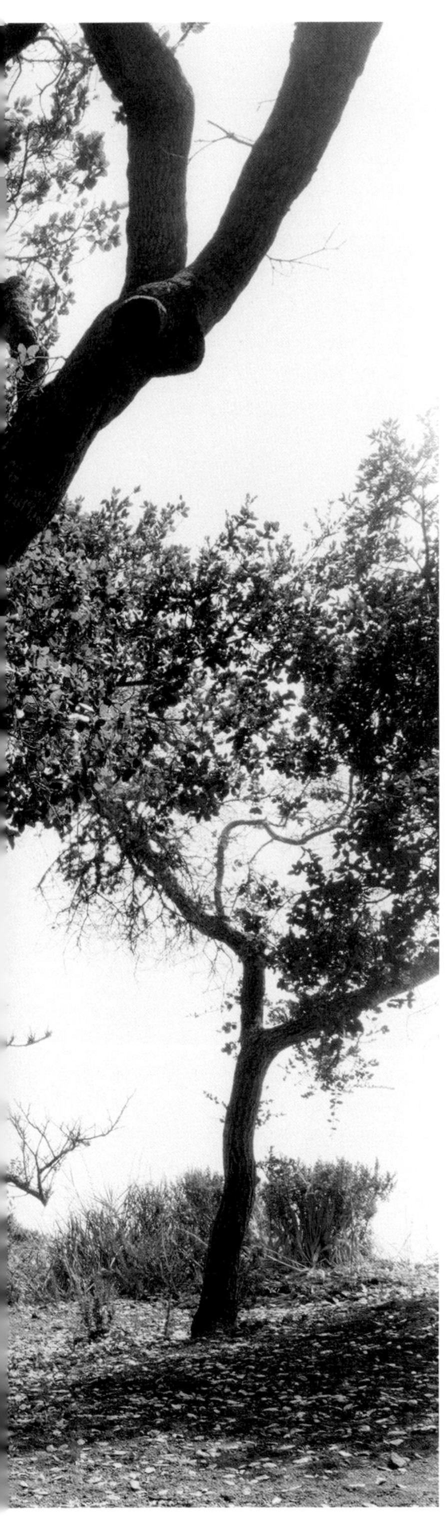

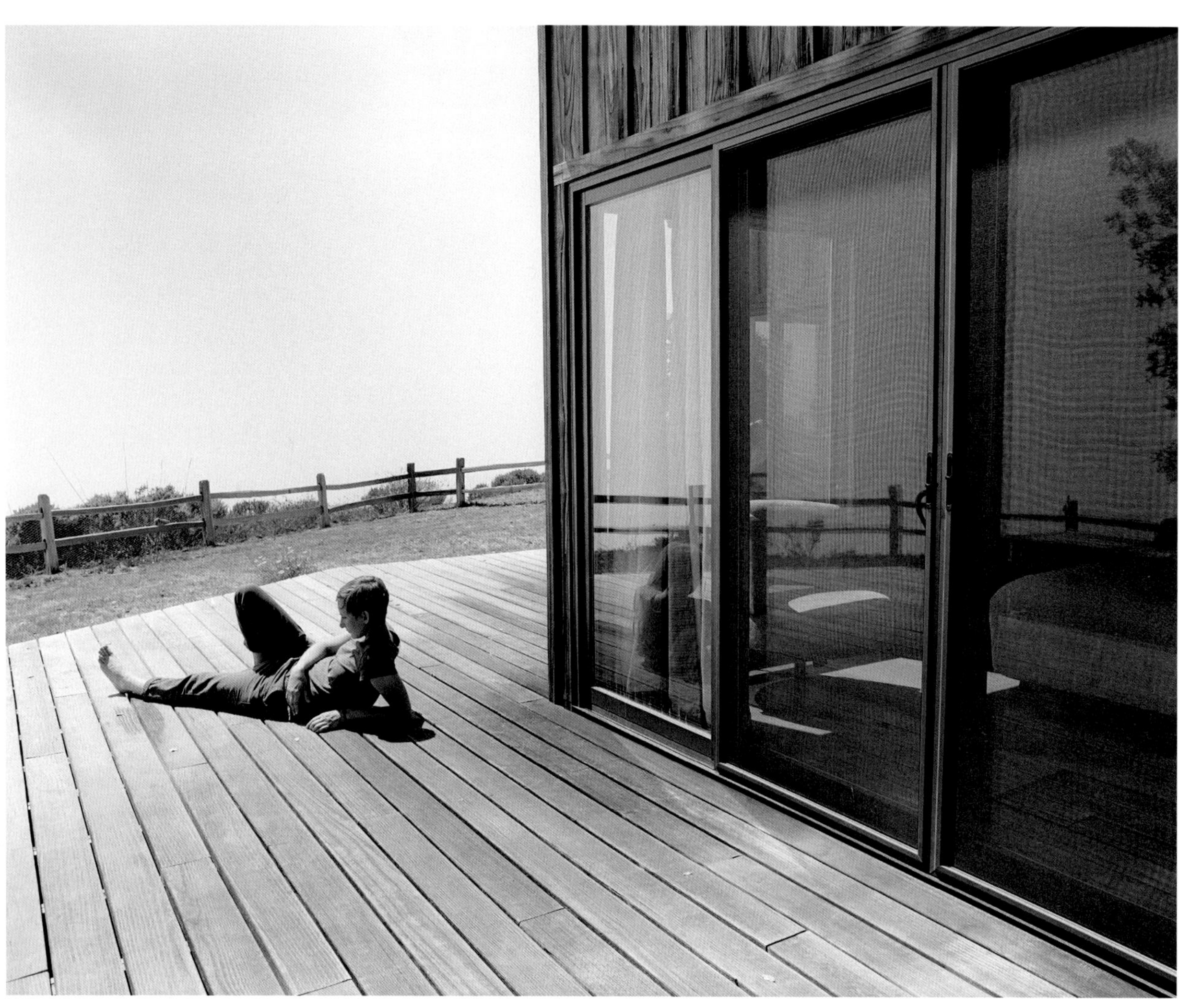

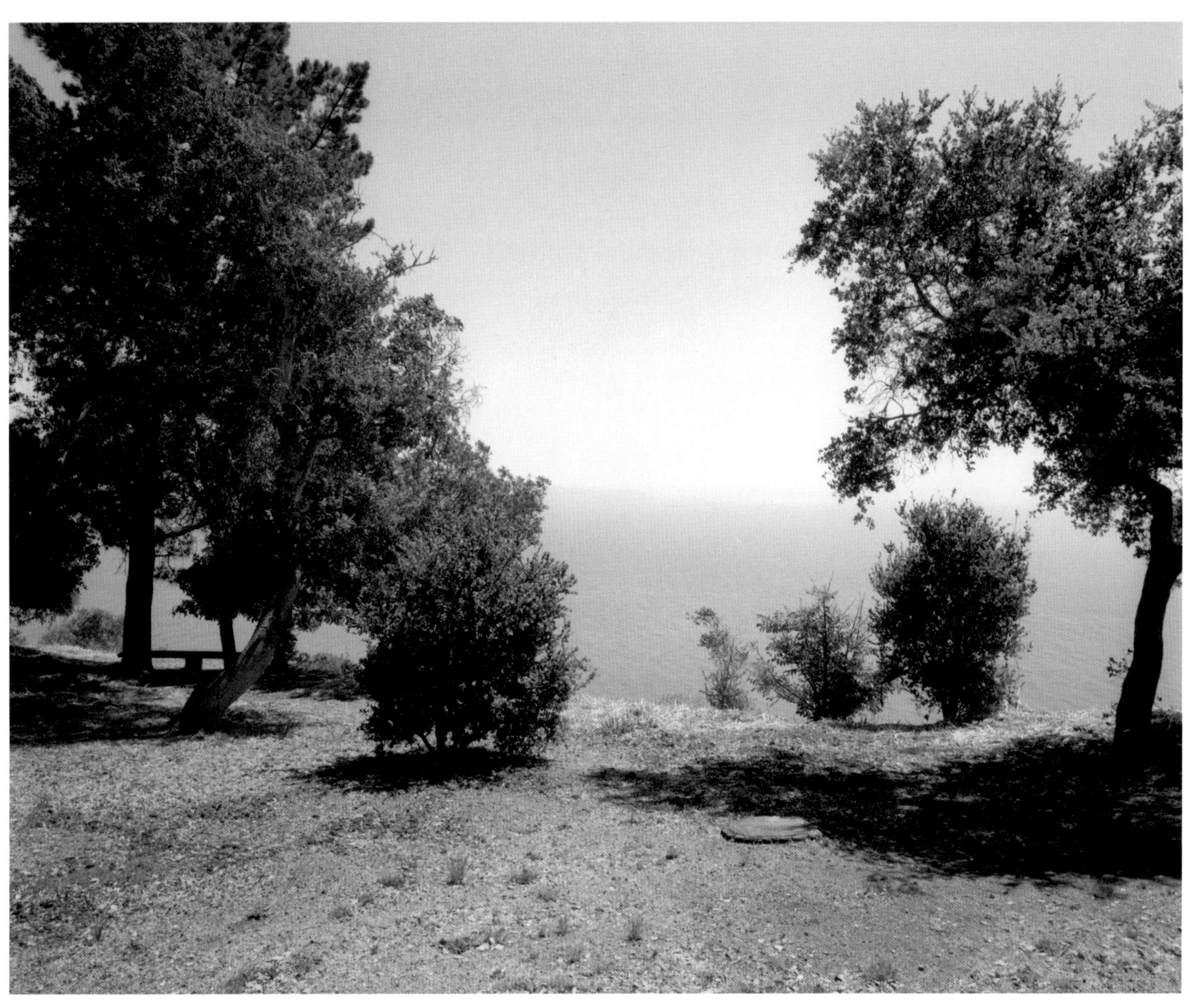

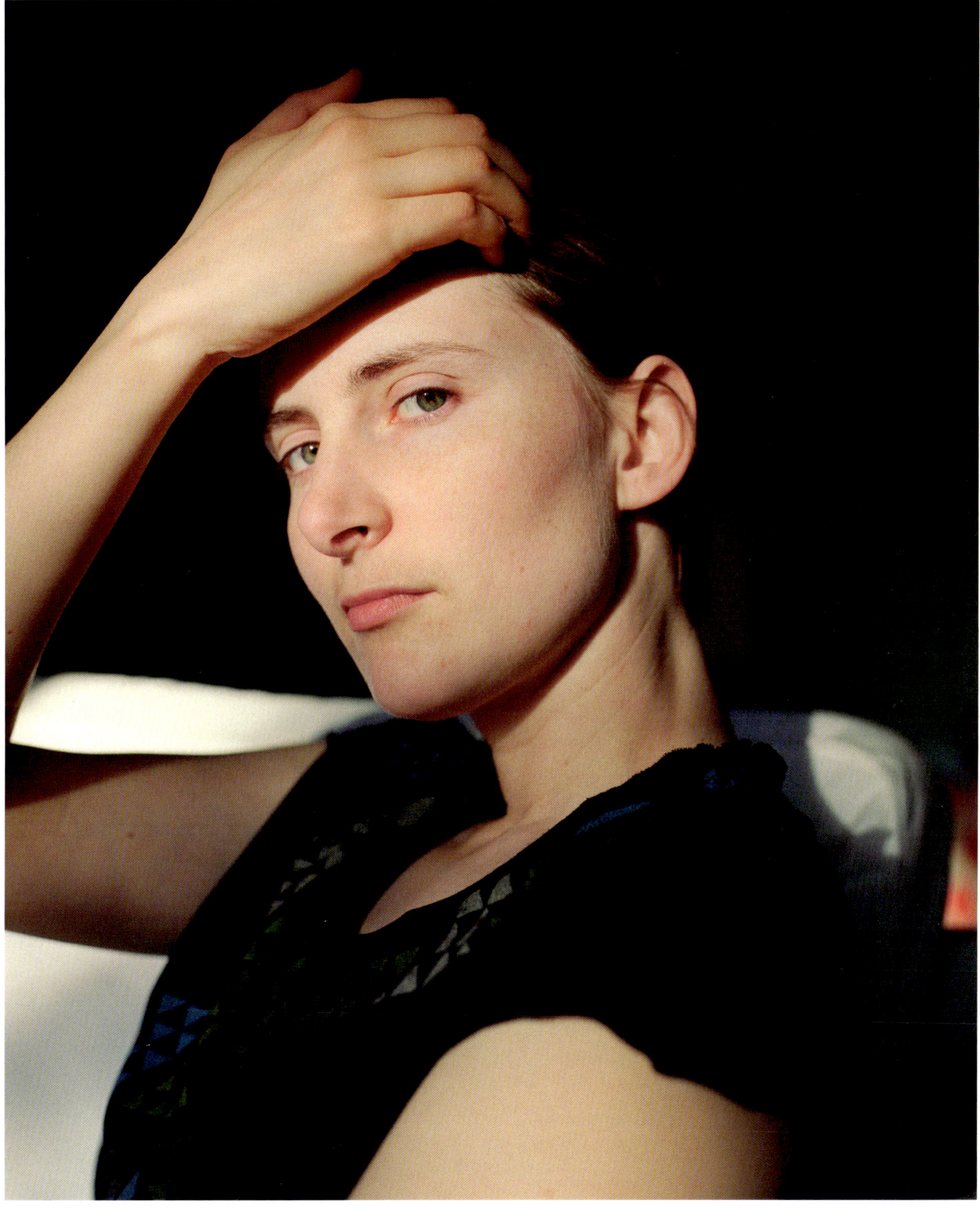

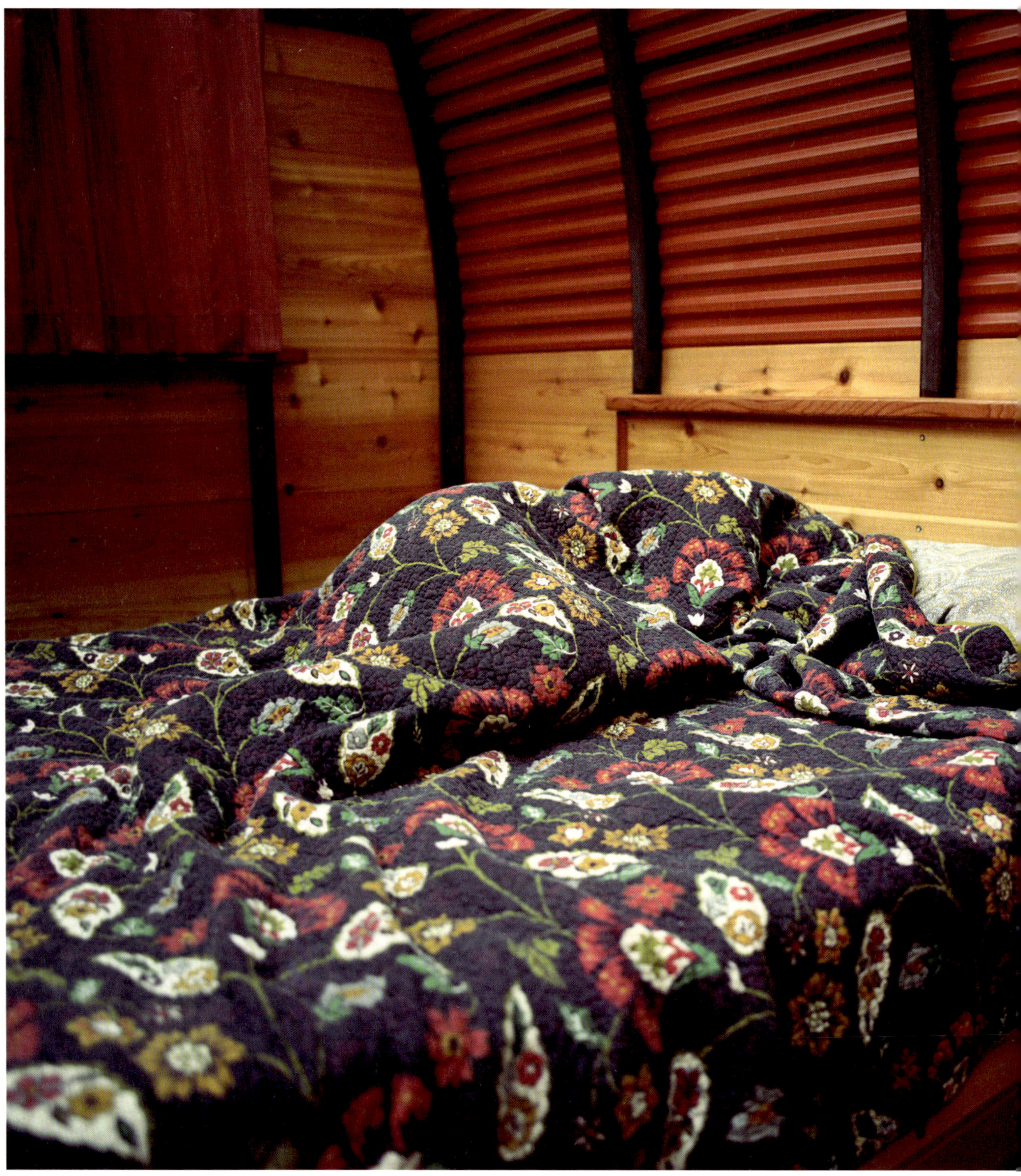

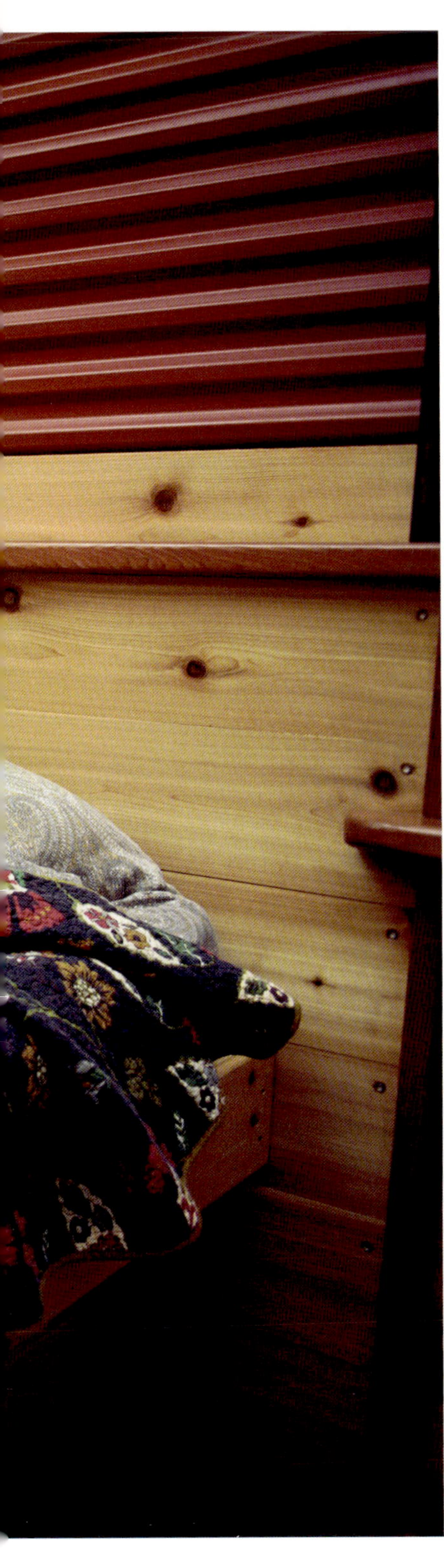

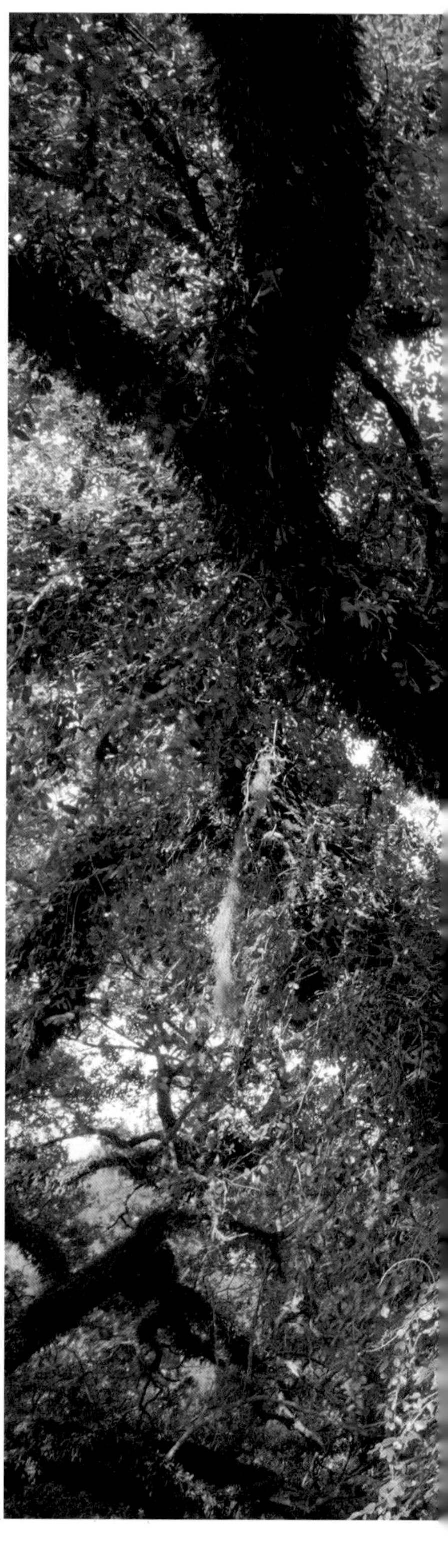

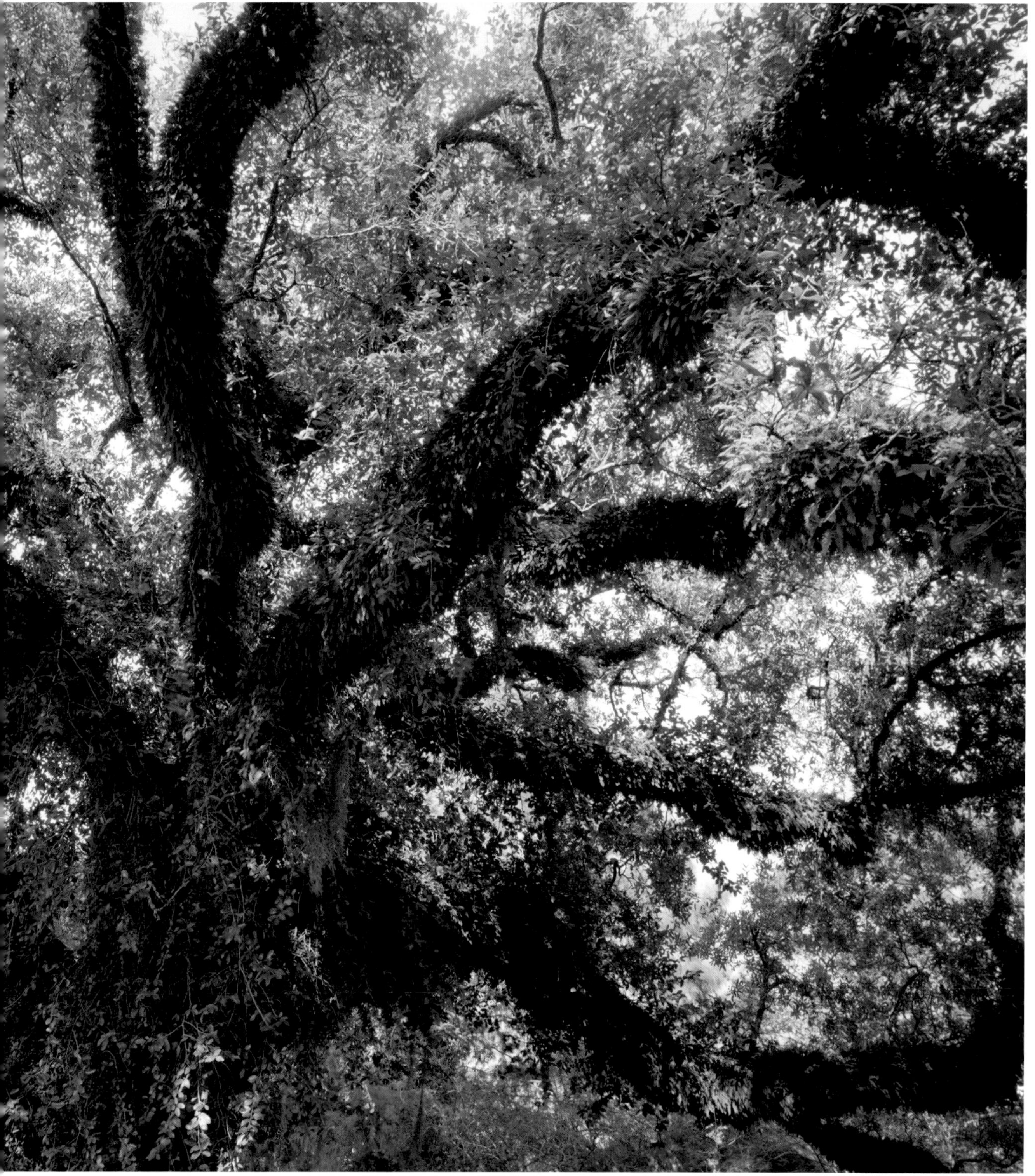

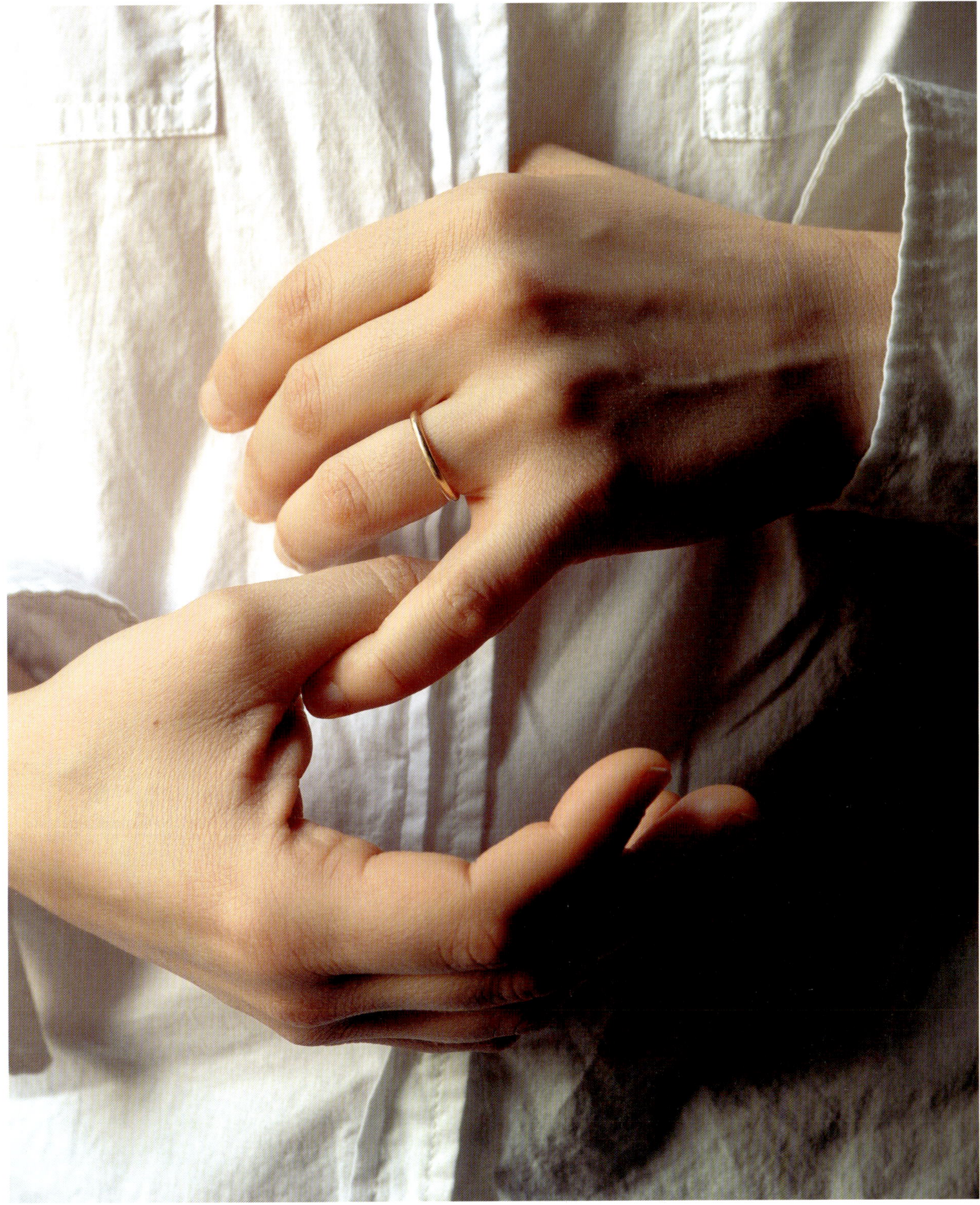

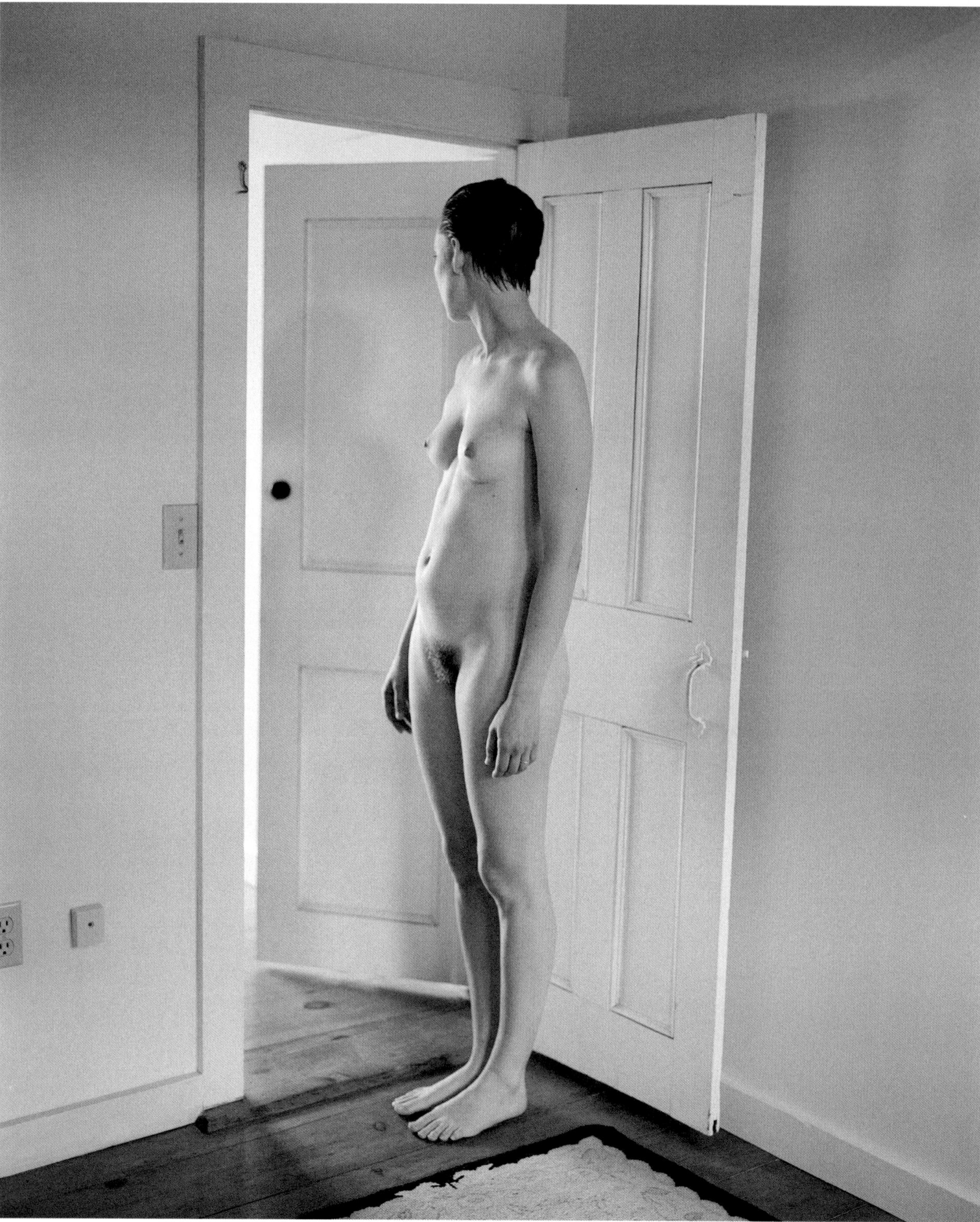

We continue to climb in elevation through the Carson National Forest. The pine trees blur as if painted by Gerhard Richter. The shades of green and brown move fast, and my eyes do their best to focus on something, anything. We pass through the southernmost range of the Rocky Mountains until we reach the open grasslands of the Great Plains. Cattle ranches and farms spot the landscape. Somewhere along the way, on a service road next to the highway, we see half a dozen people trying to get a bull into the back of a trailer. They hold ropes with long leads and keep their distance, as the bull stands his ground and stomps and red dust rises all around them.

This part of I-40 overlaps with historic Route 66, which many towns boast about. At some point, we take our bras off through the armholes of our t-shirts. "Let the littles be free!" I exclaim. At a traffic light, we stop behind a car with a red bandana fastened over a tail light with red duct tape. As we cross the border into Texas, we are greeted by a sign announcing "Drive Friendly, the Texas Way," which is mostly true. Though Bets and I could probably never live here unless we moved to one of the more liberal areas, like Denton, Austin, or Houston. There's so much about being here that makes me nostalgic: big skies, scrubby mesquites and mistletoe, storms rolling across the western plains, the perfume of rain hitting dirt, Tejano music blaring from the cabs of doublewide pickup trucks, the heat rising from asphalt on summer nights.

Charis and Edward spent time in Texas for *Leaves of Grass*. When they arrived in Sweetwater, Edward jumped out of the car to photograph telephone poles after what felt like an eternity of nothing to look at but the ever-horizontal line of the west Texas plains against the sky.

We listen to old country songs as we drive through Clyde, Baird, Cisco, Eastland. Bets texts with the cat sitter and friends back in Chicago. She is flying home tomorrow. Although she has settled into the trip and grown to enjoy it, I can tell that she is ready to get back. She will have some good studio time on her own before I return. I'm continuing on to spend a few days with my mom, as I have regularly since my dad died. On my way back to Chicago, I will stop in St. Martinville, Louisiana, to make one more picture for Charis.

At the airport the next morning, Bets and I press our foreheads together for a few seconds. Her nerves are on edge, as they always are at the airport. She is wearing the most feminine-looking clothes she brought with her, a pink pinstriped button-down shirt and navy chino-style shorts. She looks over the puzzle of our belongings in the hatch and pulls out her suitcase. We both laugh as the electric typewriter jiggles, threatening to break free. I give her a quick squeeze and breathe in the smell of her. I watch as she moves down the sidewalk, handsome and beautiful, through the double doors and out of sight.

The garage smells of old tools, oil, and fertilizer. I am glad that it still feels like Dad might be here. Inside, the house has settled in almost imperceptible ways, though it looks the same. Mom was always the one who did the decorating, keeping up with the seasons by trading miniature ghosts and goblins for winter trees and wooden Santas. Dad's one contribution was his prized catch, a nine-pound largemouth bass, its tail preserved in a flick, the scales airbrushed to enhance its rainbow color. Mounted on a plaque, his trophy takes the prominent place on the mantel. Mom's hand-sewn quilts are carefully displayed on quilt racks. But the house feels different. Mom's jazz station on the radio has replaced the monotone drone of Dad's golf tournaments on the TV. And in their room, Mom has hung a photograph of Dad near his side of the bed.

The photograph was probably taken the last year he was a football coach at the high school; it's an 11-by-14-inch enlargement that I had made the day before Dad's funeral at a one-hour photo service. When I took it to a local framer, I remember thinking that Dad had become this photograph, as if his being had been sucked into this one image and that from here on out, we'd have this representation instead of him. Photographer and writer Arthur Ollman was right when he said, "It is only after time has acquainted us with death that we realize how embalming a photograph can be."[90] At my father's funeral, we all looked at this photograph, his stand in, where it rested on an easel near a giant spray of flowers. This is the photograph we used for the obituary. And it is this picture I see Mom reaching toward a few days later when I check on her in the morning; her arms are stretched across his side of the bed, empty, until I crawl in beside her.

After three years, it still seems like he could come home after a day of golf, smelling of sunlight and dirt, chipper from the time he'd spent with his friends playing the game he loved. At any moment, he could enter the kitchen, doing an impromptu dance with a mischievous smile on his face, happy to see us. After all this time, Mom and I still can't open the family photo albums or look at those amusing self-portraits Dad took on family vacations.

The day before I leave for St. Martinville, Mom and I go for a walk after dinner. It is a Monday so we can walk the golf course. A hawk circles overhead. Dad seems to be in everything now—he's in the hawks that circle above us, the scent of cedar, the lake waves lapping against the dock. He seems closest in the places he knew deeply, like Texas and Oklahoma, but anywhere I pay attention to nature, he is there. He's in creeks and mesquites and wide-open plains. He's in the smell of dirt and rain. He can only come so close, but he knows everything about me, everything about us, everything about everything. He knows about my tattoos and bad habits and misplaced attractions and deep love for Bets. He knows that it takes me a few seconds to realize I can't call him, and that I want to call him all the time.

The next morning, I catch the glint of my gold earrings on the nightstand, and as I look around at the objects in my old room, I am aware more than ever of the impermanence of the stories we tell, the things we leave behind.

As they traveled for *Leaves of Grass*, Charis and Edward had a rare disagreement at an auto court in Lafayette. They made a habit of discussing the day's route while drinking coffee and packing. Charis suggested that they stop to see the Evangeline Oak, located two miles off the main road, in St. Martinville. She was enthralled by Longfellow's poem *Evangeline*—the tale of Evangeline's search for her lost love, Gabriel, from whom she was separated when the British invaded Canada and forced the expulsion of the Acadian people. As Evangeline makes her way across the United States, she searches for Gabriel to no avail. Local lore has it that the oak tree where Evangeline waited for him was on the banks of Bayou Teche.

Edward was irritated by having so little to photograph in Texas, not to mention the days spent in Port Arthur waiting for a new shipment of film. He was eager to push forward to New Orleans. Charis, on the other hand, was agitated by their quick pace. On the *Leaves of Grass* trip Charis and Edward kept a tighter schedule than they had in their previous tours. The itinerary was grueling; the long stretches between stops became tedious. Edward made more than seven hundred 8-by-10-inch negatives in six months. His photographs would be accompanied by Walt Whitman's text this time. Charis, who had hoped to take notes for a project of her own, felt that there was not enough time to interview residents at length or to get a real feel for the places along the way.

They spent hours in the car, with Charis at the wheel, watching everything pass in a blur. Because Charis was driving, she often found sites for Edward to photograph. By this time, she was able to see places as Edward did, knowing what he might be interested in based on how the scene would translate on film.

> *I was about to remind Edward of times I'd convinced him to go see something and my hunches had panned out, when the look on his face stopped me dead. His eyes blazed with an anger I had witnessed before but never felt turned against me. All he said was "It's my grant," but the effect was devastating. Suddenly the picture maker had come unstuck from the man I knew, loved, and trusted. He stood there glaring at me with hostile eyes in which I could read myself as a drag, a stumbling block, and— worst of all—a stranger.*
>
> *Edward and I had disagreed at times about numerous things, but our differences had been adjusted and absorbed in the constant latitude we allowed each other. This time was different and I had no defense against it. I surrendered instantly. The whole exchange lasted no more than three minutes and I wouldn't understand until years later how great a chasm had opened between us. At the time I told myself it wasn't that important, there was a lot more Whitman trip ahead, and if I missed out on the Evangeline Oak, I would find other riches to mine.*[91]

When I was thinking about the photograph I would make for Charis, I found pictures of the Evangeline Oak photographed at different times of the year. Postcards from the 1930s depicted this magnificent tree on the banks of Bayou Teche. I also learned about the Old Castillo Bed & Breakfast, where I could even stay in the Evangeline Room, complete with a view of the oak from the inn's second-floor balcony. I booked the room and planned to arrive in the late afternoon, photographing the tree upon my arrival and again as the sun set. I intended to take more images the next morning, before heading up through Louisiana and Mississippi on my way back to Chicago. It felt important that I make this trip and take this picture for Charis on my own. Traveling without Bets, I thought Charis's presence would be more pronounced and allow me to stay focused on the task at hand, the picture she might have wanted were she here with me. This was something I could do for her.

A wall of dark gray looms in the distance as cars coming from the east drive with their headlights on. A dangerous storm I am not prepared for is ahead. In Lake Charles, whitecaps form on the Calcasieu River. Birds fly against the wind, working hard to move but appearing motionless, like one of Eadweard Muybridge's animal locomotion photographs, frozen in motion. The winds howl. I-10 is closed from Jennings to Lafayette due to severe flooding. With ominous clouds on my left and a ditch of overflowing water on my right, I follow the detour.

Near St. Martinville, the air smells rotten, yet somehow sweet, as fields surrender their crops to the water's rush. I stop at a bridge to look at the rising Bayou Teche. The swirling currents on its surface trace movements from below, churning the mud, logs, and loot it carries with it.

After hours of treacherous travel, I stand as close as I can to the Evangeline Oak, the tips of my boots touching the receding water line as it inches its way back into Bayou Teche. On any other day, I would have been able to walk along the brick footpath to a gazebo and a bust of Henry Wadsworth Longfellow made of plaster and proudly perched on top of a three-foot-tall pedestal. A photograph for a postcard would have had the tree in the foreground, the gazebo beyond, overlooking the river. On this turbulent day, the gazebo's front rail is broken and hanging, its gabled top slightly askew. The pedestal that Longfellow rests on is completely submerged, so he looks like an unnamed white man standing shoulder deep in the river, lifting his head to take a breath, perhaps before going under completely.

The Evangeline Oak is not a beauty but a wild beast, its energy held back only by its thick bark. I had imagined lying under this tree, photographing the branches overhead as Charis might have seen them if she were to lay on the grass. But to do that today would mean to sink in unsettled waters.

<hr>

A fan swivels back and forth on the innkeeper's desk lifting the edges of papers with its oscillations. It is muggy inside and smells faintly of mold and mothballs. The innkeeper greets me. "The Evangeline Room you reserved has some water damage," she says. "You'll be stayin' in the Longfellow Room instead. It's a larger room, but I won't charge you extra."

The Longfellow Room is identified by an engraved gold plaque outside the door. The room is the size of a studio apartment. I put my gear on the floor and sit down to read a brochure from the nightstand that gives a short history of the inn. When steamboats carried goods up and down the river, the inn was a common stop for merchants and customers. When railroads became more popular than steamboats, the inn was purchased by the Sisters of Mercy who operated a convent school there for ninety years. The guest rooms had been the nuns' living quarters. Gold light filtered through stained glass above curio cabinets housing dishes, goblets, glasses, bibles, figurines, and other knickknacks. The room notably lacks Longfellow's presence; there are no paintings or books or other memorabilia to tell his story.

I stare at my reflection, broken into many parts by a group of mirrors on the wall of the sitting area. My right eye is in one mirror, my left thigh, another. I move around trying to arrange as many of my body parts in the mirrors as I can before retiring on the settee to read a copy of a book called *Le Petit Paris*. The book, which was written in the early 1900s, describes the area around St. Martinville to French speculators and exhorts them to come and buy land that was "there for the taking." There is no mention of the Native Americans who had been massacred, or of the surviving men, women, and children who were sent to reservations. Only photographs of prominent white businessmen are reproduced in the pages of *Le Petit Paris*—European white men interested in sugarcane, cotton, and crayfish. I think about the enslaved Black men and women who had attempted to escape their farms and plantations by following the river north through thick kudzu forests.

———————————

A little after 8:00 a.m., I am back on Market Street, where an older Black man, wearing a fedora hat, is sweeping the curbs and gutters. A young teenager with a pick in his well-groomed afro stops to look at the river and the oak for a few minutes before moving on. The water has subsided a fair amount in the night. Candy wrappers, plastic grocery bags, leaves, and twigs litter the ground, but there is a sense of calm in the air that had not been there the day before. It still isn't possible to walk around the tree without wading, but I can get a little closer.

I pull my black t-shirt over my head and stretch it to cover the bellows of the four-by-five. I extend the legs of the tripod so that the photograph will be made from my (and Charis's) height, five feet, eight inches. Charis had witnessed Ansel and Edward's debates about how their heights—Ansel stood six feet, two inches, to Edward's five-four— impacted their image making, the respective choices they were forced to make to allow for better photographs.

The Evangeline Oak takes form on the ground glass. It is a while before I like the composition. I finally emerge from beneath my shroud to find three young monks standing beside me. I feel as if I have time traveled. All three of them wear brown robes with a simple belt fastened around their waists. I have the sense that they have been standing there for a while, patiently watching me.

"There isn't going to be a procession down the river as originally planned," the oldest young monk tells me. "We hoped that the river would be safe enough, but now the Assumption of the Virgin Mary will be taken to each stop along the river by car." He speaks as if I too were waiting for the procession. I quickly pick up a film holder, and the monk, reading my gesture, says in an even-toned voice, "We aren't rushing you. You can take your time, but soon many others will be joining us."

I take a few more exposures from where I'm standing and then move to make a couple more exposures of the branches, the sunlight outlining the Spanish moss.

Nothing about photographing the Evangeline Oak is as I'd imagined. Things were uprooted and unsettled, as was perhaps fitting. Charis had felt a rush of uncertainty about her and Edward's relationship; the hours I'd spent to reach the tree in the heavy rains and flooding had been both chaotic and emotional. I had thought that I could do this alone, in the present moment, for her, to make something right in the past. But I could not intervene with what was and what had been. The fissure that had opened between them on that day in Lafayette in 1941 only grew wider as they drove east.

As I drive north, I think about the ways that Edward and Charis both contributed to the growing fault lines in their relationship, about what unfolded as they continued their travels for *Leaves of Grass*. They stayed with friends, as was their habit, and at one of their stops, Charis fell in love with one of their hosts, someone they both knew.

> *In New England rain dogged us almost everywhere, making this the most disappointing segment of our trip for photographic quarry. If bad weather had been the only problem, we could have kept each other's spirits up, but we were in the grip of something far more disturbing. I had fallen in love with another man.*
>
> *Married, middle-aged, a father, successful in his profession, he had been our host along the way. He was mature, had a sharp intellect, and seemed to have read everything. He and I stayed up late talking while Edward kept to his usual early bedtime, and I found it irresistible when he said that after he graduated from college, he "had to go to bed for a year just to catch up on reading."[92]*

Charis and her love interest talked about literature and poetry: "There seemed no limits to his horizons, in thinking, reading, or feeling and I basked in his obvious

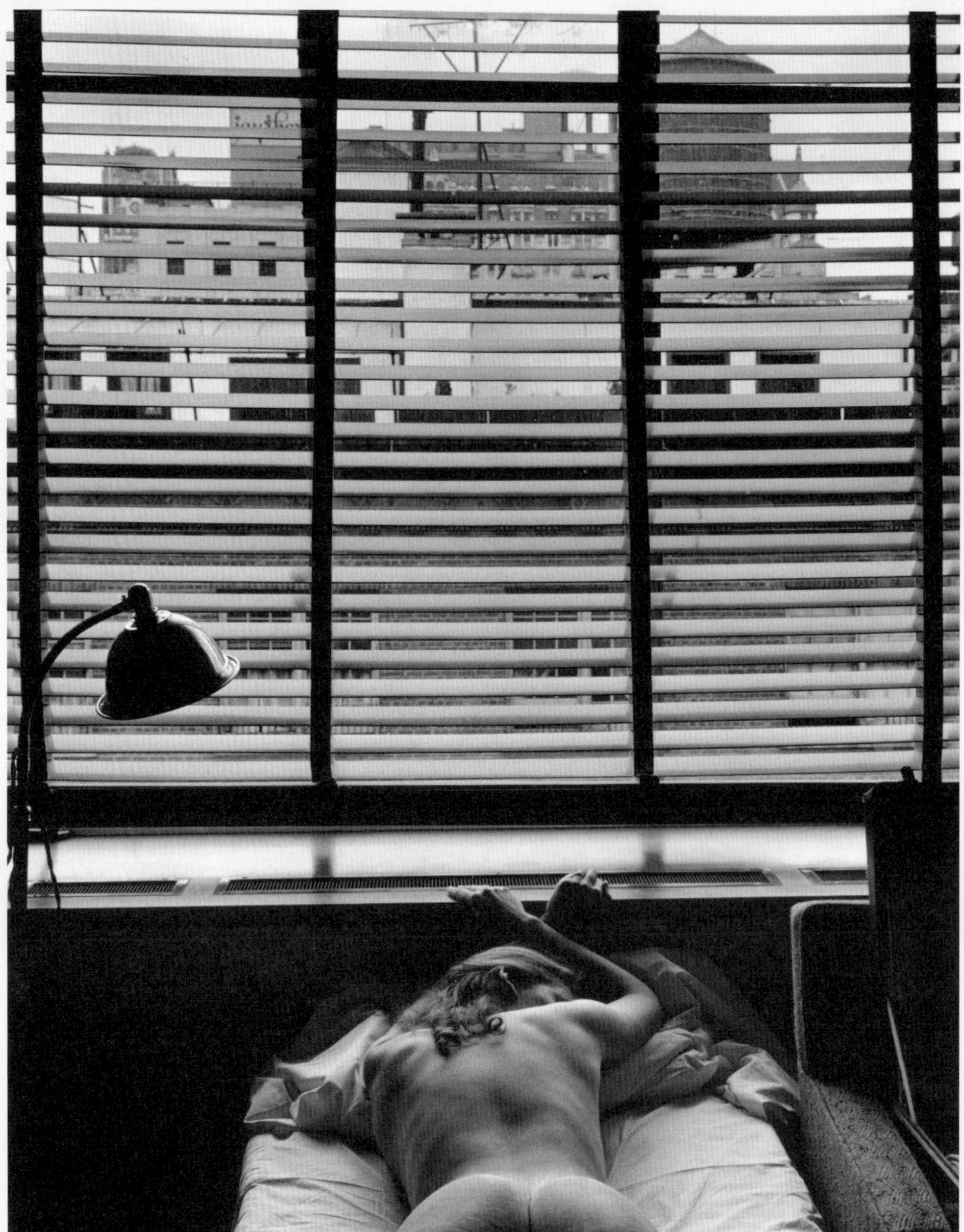

admiration of me as a person and an author."[93] Before the night was over, they made plans to meet for dinner in New York a few weeks later, when their paths would cross again for separate reasons.

Charis was honest with Edward about her feelings, and in the weeks before they arrived in New York, the wounds and anxieties they each carried grew deeper. As the days passed on the road, Edward found it harder to make photographs, while Charis was beginning to realize that her attraction to this man was perhaps mere fantasy. He was someone whom she desired but he was unattainable. She began to have second thoughts about meeting up with him once they reached New York.

When they arrived in the city, Edward broke from photographing landscapes for the book and turned his camera toward Charis. He made a photograph of her at David McAlpin's apartment, where they were staying. She is nude, face down on a bed with her head turned to one side. The camera is at the foot of the bed, capturing her body as it fills the bottom third of the frame, the rise of her backside just above the picture's bottom edge. Daylight illuminates Charis's fingers, shoulders, ribs, and the small of her back. A single lamp hovers above her. Could it have been meant as a symbol? Edward's desire to interrogate Charis's inner feelings?

> *I've never liked the nudes he did of me on the bed with the venetian blinds behind, maybe because things were so awry between us. I knew by now that I could not go ahead with an affair, but neither could I bear the thought of cutting things off. My friend was in New York and came to see us in the evening, to look at prints and to take me to dinner. Edward liked many of the same things in him that I did, and the two got along well despite the undercurrents.*[94]

That night Charis had dinner with her love interest. She wore a new outfit and carried a purse that she had bought earlier that day. They sat close together on the same side of a booth; the attraction they felt toward one another was intense. In the end, Charis told this man she could not be with him. She was committed to Edward. Afterward, she returned to find Edward waiting in the apartment. And although Charis decided to stay with him, he was deeply hurt. In her memoir she reflects, "I was sick with regret for what I had lost and consumed with guilt for what I might have done. Despite my turning away from this [new] relationship, Edward and I both bore emotional scars that never completely healed."[95]

On the East Coast, it rained day after day, and on the few days that it was not raining, Edward found it hard to make pictures anyway. Many critics and historians in looking at the photographs Edward made for *Leaves of Grass*, describe them as funereal or distant. In his essay "The Final Years," Alan Trachtenberg writes:

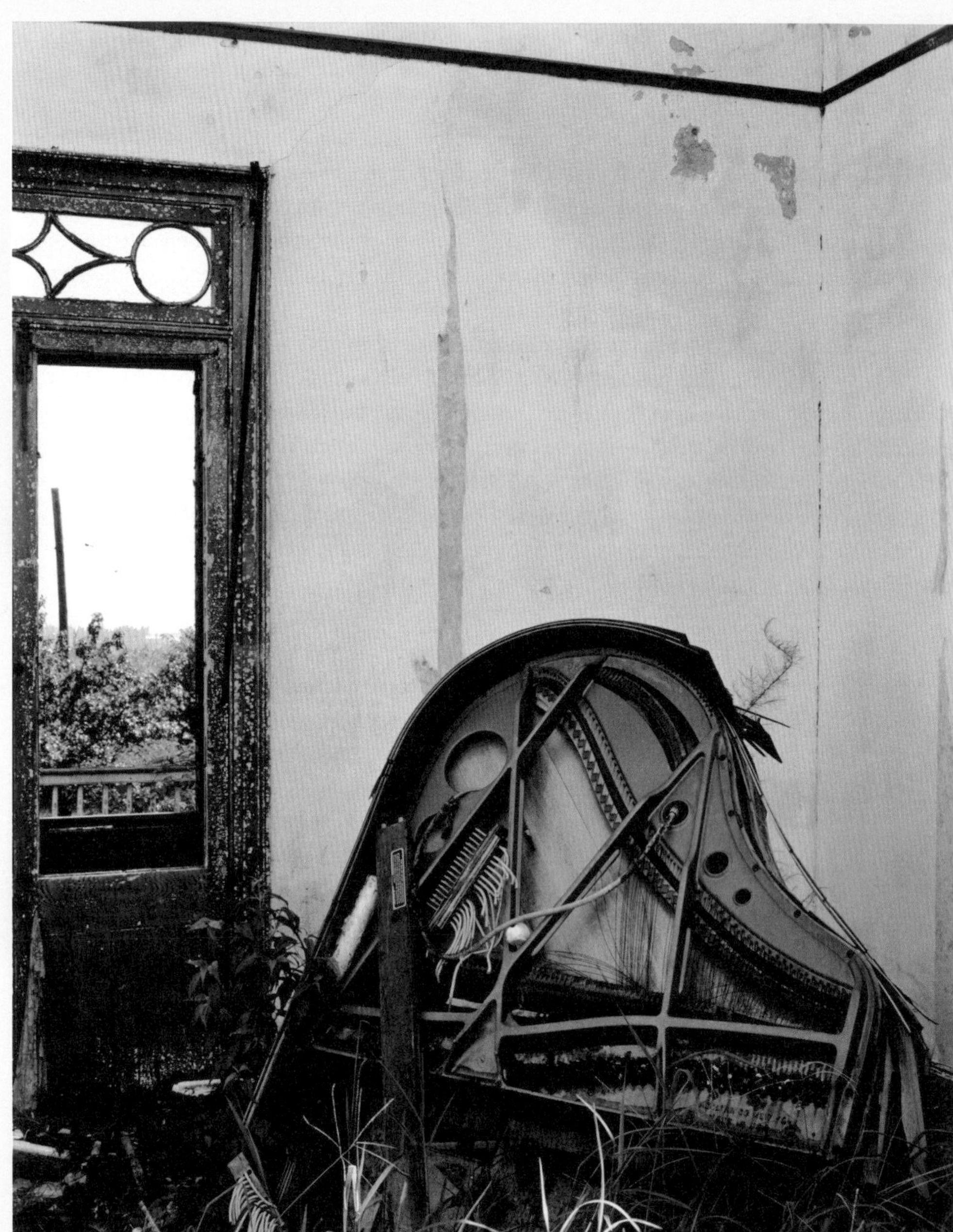

A sense of age and aging hangs over the pictures made in 1941–42. The decrepitude and deterioration of Louisiana plantations and graveyards strike a chord with abandoned houses and distant views over rooftops in Eastern and Midwestern cities. Old places, old things, old faces settle into an impression of inertness. Moreover, the pictures seem to hold the viewer at a distance, as if vistas are needed for contemplating the visible facts of the American scene. Weston's earlier work had struck a note of passionate lyricism; now, contemplation seems the dominant mode. Landscapes heavy with clouds seem brooding. Houses seem empty and still. And the handful of portraits (eight of forty-nine published images) suggest a human presence that is lost, distant, remote, in some instances sullenly withdrawn. In one case the face is hidden, in another it grudgingly reveals itself from beneath the shadow of a hat. There are no smiles, no laughter, no gestures of exuberance….

We can only speculate, but might he not have come to feel that the way of seeing in his strongest earlier pictures was not appropriate to the making of the Whitmanlike vision of the country as a whole? The differences lie in the nuances, subtleties of tone, slight shifts of compositional emphasis: elusive differences but distinct enough to notice. Did Weston have less heart for this project than earlier ones? Or is it a different kind of heart, an attentiveness to the possibilities within himself for commanding a larger, more cultural vision than his earlier purism and intensely personal formalism had allowed? Whatever the cause, the pictures project solitude, distance, withdrawal, as much in the receding distances of the many long urban views as in the self-enclosure of the few portraits. Weston seems disconnected from "his America," or perhaps, disconnectedness is what defines the America he discovered.[96]

Charis left Edward in November 1945. She was twenty-nine; he was fifty-eight. Feeling the need for a new start, and knowing it would be too difficult for her, as well as for Edward, Charis decided that when she left Wildcat Hill, she would also leave behind the many friends whom she loved dearly. She first moved to Los Angeles, and there, became active in the progressive movement. She had begun work on a book called *Gold Rush Country* about the "neglected coastal region north of San Francisco"[97] and decided to drive up to Eureka to investigate a lumber strike. While doing research, she met Noel Harris, a twenty-seven-year-old trade unionist, and they fell in love.

Charis and Noel got married in Reno, Nevada, on December 13, 1946, the day after Charis's divorce from Edward was final and eleven months after she had left Wildcat Hill, which she sold to Edward for ten thousand dollars on a payment plan of sixty dollars a month without interest. Every month, with his check, Edward sent Charis a letter. His shaky handwriting and the considered brevity of the letters revealed the progression of his Parkinson's disease. And still, each letter was signed *My love, Love,* or *Love always, Edward.*

Charis and Noel had two children, Rachel and Anita. In the years that followed, Charis devoted her time to raising the girls. She worked on *Gold Rush Country* for several years, but after multiple extensions, the publisher, Duell, Sloan & Pearce, who had also published *California and the West*, decided to drop the project.

Charis kept in touch with Edward, giving him updates on her daughters and brought them with her for a visit to Wildcat Hill in 1955.

> *Except for the addition of a small bedroom facing the ocean, I found everything as before—the old split bamboo wastebasket on one side of the door, the cat door on the other, the chair by the fire, H. L.'s print on the wall, the writing table, the Mexican chest—all was the same, except for Edward, who was locked in a body that had become a prison. His eloquent eyes peered out through eye holes in the mask that Parkinson's had made of his face and seemed to say, "Isn't this a mess—but we can't do anything about it."*[98]

As I cross the border into Mississippi, I leave the floods behind; it is raining here, too, but steady and slow. For a good part of the drive, ominous clouds hover overhead, their intense grays complimenting the vibrant green grasses of the fields that spread out around me. Large white flowers line the sides of the road, heavy, hunched over, from the weight of the rain.

I call Bets who says she is sore from working out. She has also been reading a lot to prepare for one of the courses she would be teaching in the fall. We ping-pong titles for her upcoming exhibition. "Should the show's title be spelled *Let's Be Honest* or *Lesbi Honest*?" she asks, before landing on *Let's Be Honest*.

I use the rearview mirror to put on bright red lipstick. A friend of ours had given us two matching Chanel red lipsticks as a wedding gift, I'm sure as a reference to lipstick lesbians. I couldn't bring myself to wear the shade much in public but love to wear it on road trips, with no other makeup, my oily hair pulled in a high ponytail so that I can rest my head on the seat cushion. I feel sexy in my disheveled clothes, bold in my anonymity as I pump gas, an actress in some B movie.

The rain is more insistent, hard and heavy, when I finally arrive at the hotel in Tunica. I trade my lightweight tennis shoes for cowboy boots in the car in hopes that my feet will stay dry as I run across the parking lot. But by the time I make it inside, I have one dry foot; the other is wet from a hole that has worn through the boot's sole.

The farther I get from St. Martinville, the more surreal the whole experience seems—
the flood, the dead animals on the road, the detritus along the river, the drowning
Longfellow at the Evangeline Oak. The lone tree standing in a scene of tragedy rather than
triumph. Arno Rafael Minkkinen, a photographer whom I admire, once told me that going
on a photographic pilgrimage is always nice, because you start to feel like the people you
are following are right there, in the car with you. I imagine Charis sitting next to me. Not
young Charis, feet on the dash, smoking a pipe, but Charis in her eighties, after she has
completed *Through Another Lens*. Her smile is as vibrant as ever at the excitement of being
on the road. Older Charis is a wiseass, and a flirt. She has a sparkle in her eyes, a fire. She
can hold her own.

As we drive together, I ask her about the man she almost had an affair with, the
man she met up with in New York City—I've scoured the memoir and pored over her
correspondence at the Center for Creative Photography looking for clues about who he
might be. Though Charis was careful never to mention him by name, I have my theories
and feel certain that the answer is hidden somewhere in plain sight, in her book or in her
materials in the archive.

Whomever Charis had been in love with, this secret was hers to keep. Knowing
his identity would have provided yet another filter through which to look at Edward's

photographs. But looking through misguided filters was something that Charis fought hard against—after all, it was the interpretations of Edward and his work that left Charis feeling so unsettled and angry in the decades after his death.

As we drive along, with me behind the wheel, I ask Charis if it had been hard to write her memoir. A lot had happened in the forty years since Edward died: In 1967, one of her daughters, Anita, was brutally murdered at a campsite in Scotland when she was nineteen years old; that same year her relationship with Noel dissolved, and I imagine that grief overwhelmed Charis completely. She struggled to make ends meet at times, teaching writing classes intermittently. She was in her late seventies when she applied for funding for her book; she even applied for a Guggenheim but did not receive it. It was only through the generosity of Wendy Madar, a writer and childhood friend of Charis's daughter Rachel, that she was finally able to complete *Through Another Lens: My Years with Edward Weston*.

Wendy and Charis, with extra help from Rachel, sifted through Charis's notes and wrote and revised drafts until finally, when she was eighty-three, the book was published. On the cover of the book's jacket is a portrait of Charis and Edward, their faces freckled from the summer sun. Charis's hair is in braids, and Edward's dome is bald, his side hairs a bit wild. Edward stands taller than Charis; she leans into his chest. The request had been of the photographer taking the picture—who insisted that Edward stand and Charis sit, so that she would appear to be shorter than him. We are set up to believe a fiction in which we are compliant. But as we turn to the dedication page, we read:

> *For my daughters—*
> *Anita Kathryn Harris—*
> *who never completed her story*
>   *and*
> *Rachel Fern Harris—*
> *who graces the world with hers*
> *and for Wendy Lee Madar—*
> *who allowed me to finish my own*[99]

From the beginning, we understand that this is Charis's story, and that it is important to share because it's for women—women striving to find their place in a man's world. Women who want to feel free in their body, their sexuality. Women who have been left out of histories, in part because they did not write about their work or the work of others.

Along our last stretch of road, I share stories with Charis about the amazing women I know. I tell her about my life with Bets. I tell her about Barbara Kasten, a dear friend of mine, with her grace and style, and how not a day goes by that she doesn't go to her studio—how she is still making work well into her eighties. And I tell her about other artists and writers I know who have sacrificed a great deal to make their work. Women who define their lives on their own terms, not by what society expects of them.

I thank Charis for writing her memoir and tell her that I wish I could say that what she set out to do had worked, that all the time and effort she put into telling her side of the story had paid off. That the years of collecting memories—making notes on napkins, the

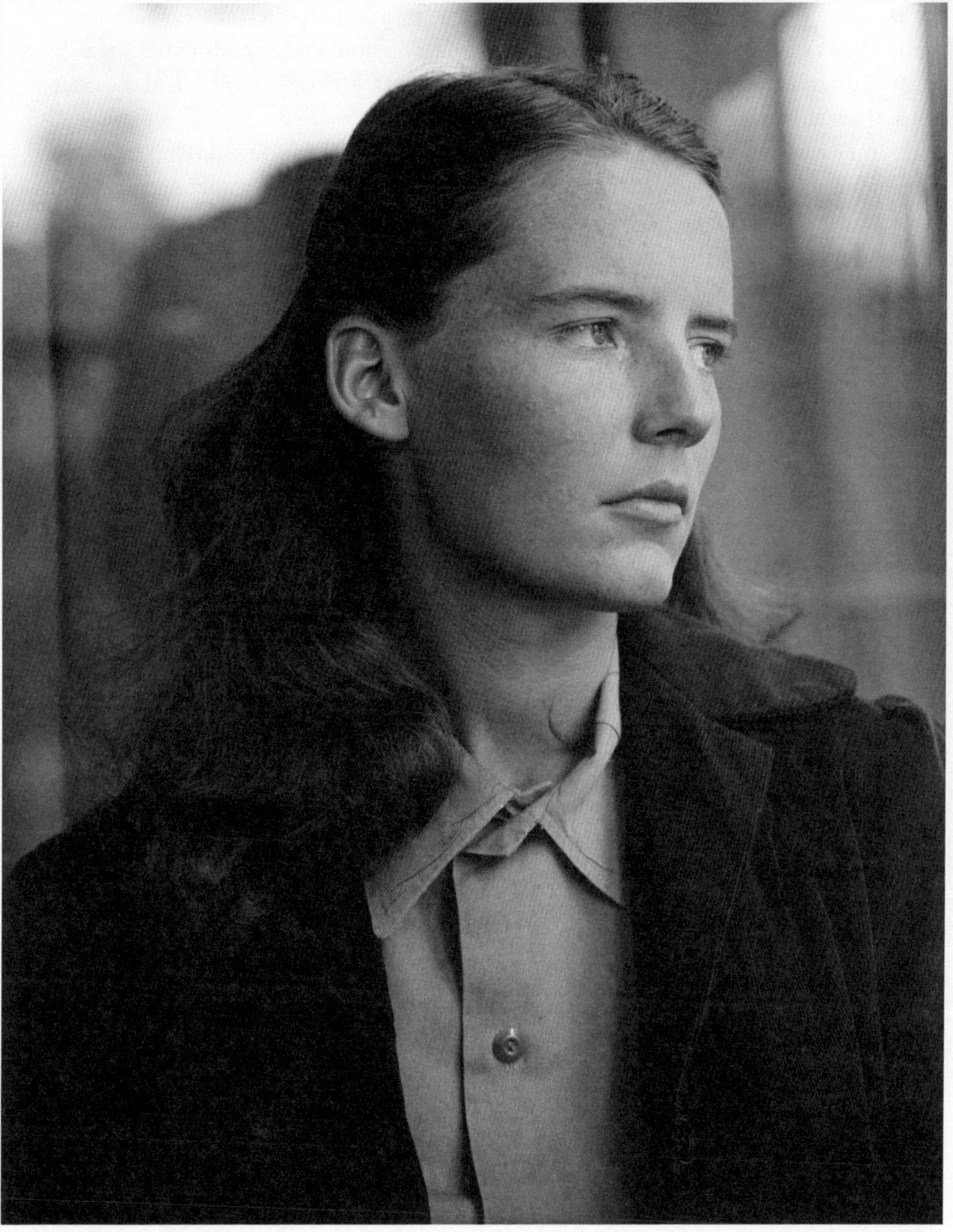

Edward Weston
Charis Wilson, 1941

edges of receipts, the backs of envelopes, triggered by a certain smell, taste, sound, or sight—had succeeded in complicating people's impressions and appraisals of Edward and ensured that she was remembered for her achievements, artistic integrity, and the craft and heart of her work.

Her words *had* worked to change my understanding of Edward. They had helped me to see him as a deeply complex and interesting human being, as someone who rebelled against social conventions, who had intimate relationships and friendships with both men and women. She had also given me a whole new appreciation of his work; he had been freed from the limited art historical interpretations I had inherited or been taught.

Ultimately, making pictures for Charis was not something that I could do for her. Instead, what I learned was a new way of seeing, through a context that she carefully outlined, a frame of reference that allowed her to have power, freedom, and confidence in her body and sexuality and as an artist. Charis wrote *Through Another Lens* not only out of love and concern for Edward and his legacy but also to disavow the narrow perspectives that had reduced her story to being "one of his nudes," a participant in one of his "philanderous affairs," or simply "his muse." These are delimiting terms of possession that fail to capture what an active partner Charis was to Edward. It is through Charis that I choose to see Edward and the pictures they made together. Someone once told me that no one is gone until their last story is told, and I'm glad that Charis shared her story.

Charis's writing enticed me to experience the places she had gone, to see them through her eyes and my own. I leaned against the same cool rocks and rested in the shade of the same trees that she had. My hands, like hers, touched the calm surface of Lake Tenaya. Charis was with me, waiting to be found—her body still resting on boulders and tree trunks and her shape still visible on the sand.

To see Edward's exquisitely printed photographs in the viewing room at the Center for Creative Photography comes with requirements. I stand a few feet away as I carefully examine each image and wear a sweater to stay warm in the temperature-controlled room. I use my cell phone for taking notes. In examining the original gelatin-silver photographs instead of the reproductions I had devoured in source after source, I find a new admiration for Edward's work. The details in the shadows, information that turns to solid black in most reproductions, are exquisite. A thrill rises up inside me. I can see a depth in his work that I never thought was there, a beauty that I had once interpreted as sterility. I am aware of the goosebumps on my arms, and the watchful eye of the archivist as I bend closer to each object, surrounded by the lulling sound of the air conditioner's hum and the institutional beige and gray of the furniture and carpet.

In a temperature-controlled vault, a facsimile of Charis's original travelogue, each section tied with ivory thread, fills four reams of paper and sits in an archival box. The room smells of old paper and time. Fluorescent lights buzz above rows of shelves housing the collections of people Charis knew: Edward Weston, Ansel Adams, Willard Van Dyke, and Sonya Noskowiak. Some of the items Edward photographed when making *Valentine* for Charis in 1935 are there. The originals of their marriage certificate and divorce papers, as well as the deed for the property on Wildcat Hill, rest in a carefully labeled folder. Audio tapes that Charis recorded on the road in her seventies and eighties are there. Her soothing voice shares the excitement of her long-ago adventures with Edward for *California and the West* and documents the ways in which landscapes had visibly changed, or stayed the same. In another box sits Edward's wedding ring, a plain gold band, from his marriage to Charis. All of these things, so carefully kept, cataloged, and labeled, were waiting for me, and there they will remain, waiting for someone else to find them.

My hard drives and negatives, carefully organized and stored in boxes with metal hinges, are unlikely to find their way into an archive like this one. My family photographs will yellow and fade, crack and peel at the edges; perhaps they'll be found in an antique mall someday, or perhaps they won't be found at all. The hundreds of images I have made of Betsy will be edited, some of them making their way to the walls of museums, some of them into books. Each selection creating a story, a glimpse of understanding who Betsy is and who I am, to be interpreted through the lens of our ever-changing culture and experiences that continually shift and evolve through time.

Two days after leaving St. Martinville, I cross the border into the Land of Lincoln. I am almost home. Concrete walls replace trees, highway lanes multiply, and CTA trains whiz by on tracks that run parallel to I-94. As Chicago's skyline comes into view, it begins to rain. From where I sit in the bumper-to-bumper traffic, I can see sailboats in marina stalls. I look beyond them to the horizon, to where Lake Michigan meets the sky.

*In a world as myriad as ours, the gaze is
a singular act: to look at something is to fill
your whole life with it, if only briefly.*

—Ocean Vuong

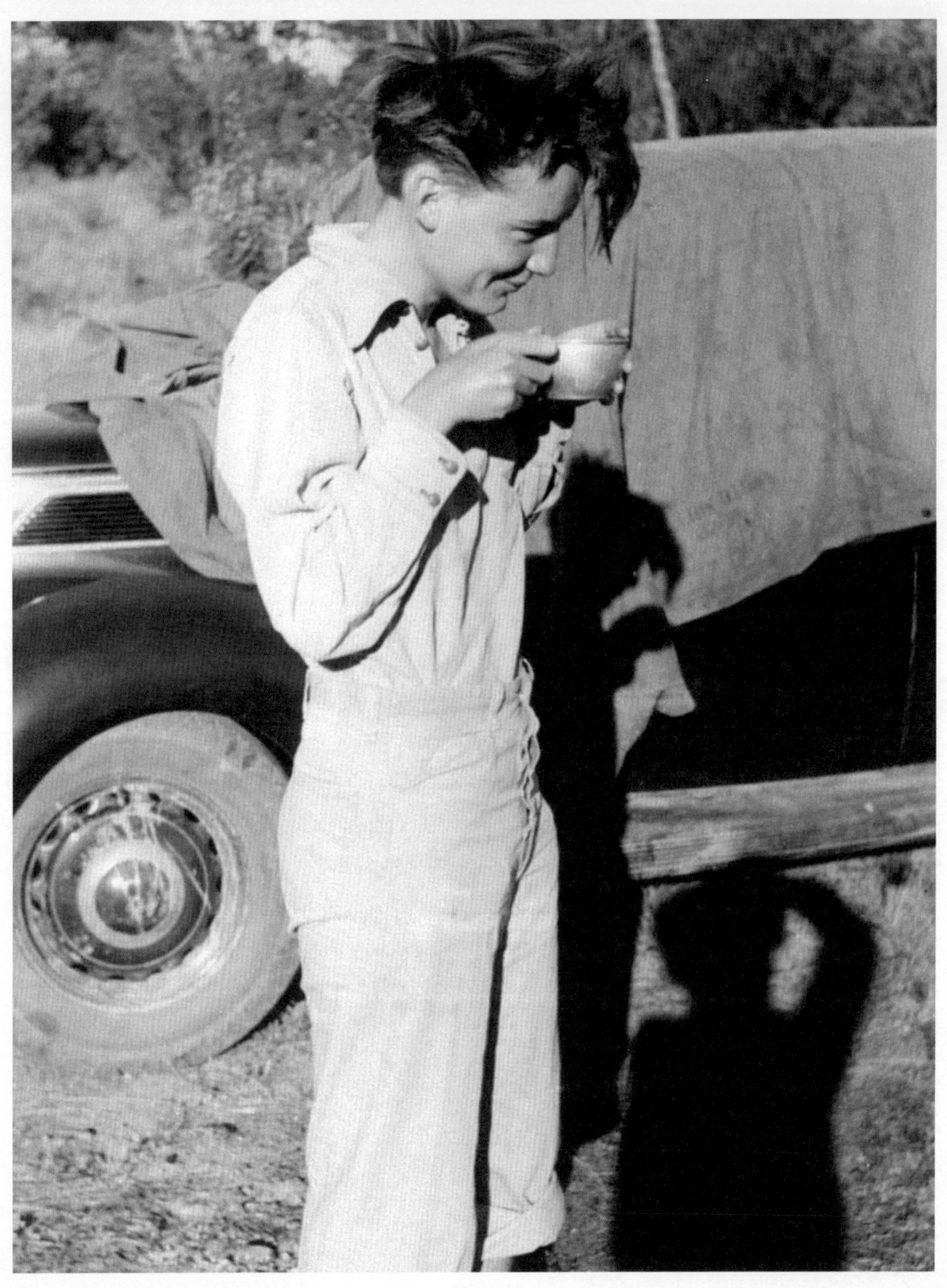

Willard Van Dyke
*Charis with a Cup
of Coffee, Smith River
Camp*, 1937

AFTERWORD
BETSY ODOM

Kelli often refers to a photograph of me that she's never successfully taken, a certain way that I sit on the couch or on the floor, leaning back on my elbows with my knees open toward her: me in my most natural state. As a pose, it never made sense in *Pictures for Charis*—it is not especially visually interesting or sensitive—my body settles into space like a pile of clothes lying in a corner. But I think Kel is attracted to my unselfconsciousness, my repose. Only she knows what I really look like. Although she has taken hundreds of photographs of me, in intimate moments she would often say something like, "I wish I could photograph you the way I see you." I chose to participate in *Pictures for Charis* because I appreciate its connection to queerness, the parallels between creative relationships past and present, the layers of hope and sadness, and the connections to Kel's past work, with which I had fallen in love in my early twenties, before I even met her, when we were both living in Texas. As an artist and a spouse, my investment in the portraits was and is complex, but I recognized that Kel's impulse to make portraits of me was an expression of love, as was my willingness to be portrayed.

The fantasy of sharing and photographing a truly unselfconscious moment is a particular elephant in the room of the model/sitter relationship. How does one perform unselfconsciousness? That there are so many portraits of people asleep is no surprise. I am aware of being photographed, and I am aware that on some level the photographer does not want me to be self-aware, so the relationship I have with a photographer is already one of conflict. In practice, Kel and I achieve, if not unselfconsciousness, a sort of agreed-upon state of lesser-awareness; I lowered my guard and relied on the trust that came from our years together and her vision of me. There are a few pictures that I'm uncomfortable with her showing, not because they are explicit, but because I feel too vulnerable. But generally, it feels good to see the images she has made.

Although the "unselfconsciousness" in our model/sitter relationship makes for images that feel "trustworthy," I tend to be more interested in the other, more mercurial, examinations of relationships that portraits enable. I have been photographed by other women/trans photographers—Eileen Mueller, Jess T. Dugan, Terry Evans—and I am introducing performance into my own sculpture practice. Interestingly, my relationship to each of these photographers manifests so clearly in the images: in Terry's, one of mutual admiration; in Eileen's, queer brotherhood; in Jess's, tentative trust. What happens in Kelli's images feels totally different. The portraits Kel makes describe our relationship in a way, especially the older ones, but they also reach moments of abstraction. When modeling for other photographers I can't help but think about the viewer. With Kel, I consciously surrender control over how I think the viewer will receive me (in so much as that is possible). I am giving something to her directly, so there's a distinct intensity in the work. With other photographers and in my own work, I model with a goal in mind, but in *Pictures for Charis*, I leave that to Kel.

People ask me how Kelli photographing me is a departure from what Weston did—as if the nature of lesbian desire is somehow impossible to translate through the imposing masculinity of the lens. Is Kelli invoking a female gaze? Is there even such a thing as a female gaze? For the most part, I find these kinds of questions uninteresting; they seem to fall into the modernist folly of divorcing an image from its context. The portraits and landscapes in *Pictures for Charis* are not iconic but rather serve as indexes to a complex mesh of individual desires. When Kel photographs me, she is asking us to explore where we fit into the gendered dynamics of looking, where her sexuality and my androgyny provide expressions of emotion and desire. Recontextualizing Weston's images in this way is on one hand radical—Kel's project liberates Charis with a long overdue recognition of her place in Weston's work. But does examining portraits of Charis, the portraits of me, through a queer lens, also grant permission to enjoy them non-reflexively—can this form of looking and seeing escape dominant power structures? Or do we inevitably fall back into the "male gaze?" Exhausting. It's no coincidence that my favorite portraits in *Pictures for Charis* confront the viewers' gaze with a mix of empathy and non-ado.

I find value in the idea of "queering" something; in this case, queering the tradition of photographing your wife. "Queering" has worked basically the same way for the last thirty years and is part of the foundation of my own practice as a sculptor. The formula can be quite simple: splice together images of, or sentiments about, your favorite gays and queer icons, insert them into predominant narratives, and see what happens. Obviously, to make identity into something actionable, wieldable almost, suggests a kind of ownership and agency that always needs examination. Still, whenever I leave the city, I remember that queer visibility remains important. In the book, Kel writes a little about my experiences as an androgynous person in public spaces, the pain of that. I think now that these portraits of me celebrate the qualities that people are so scared of—Kel's photographs offer me an alternative to that experience. Perhaps they can do the same for others like me.

Kel sometimes refers to me as a "reluctant model." It is true that I am not like Charis, gleefully rolling in the dunes without prompting. I kept the performance in front of the camera to a minimum; I was only looking to connect with Kelli during the process. Perhaps the most truthful aspect of this work is that this is just the sort of thing married artists do for each other. If I ever needed to make a mold of someone's body part, I'd ask Kel. In that sense, the images also document an overlap in our creative practices. I never feel objectified in these images—the bits of context or aspects of personhood dissolve feelings of blankness, and instead, prompt further questions about gender, aging, and performance of the self, all sensibilities that emerge in my own work in different ways.

The next step of this project involves me coming to terms with my image and story being in a book, displayed on museum walls, and reproduced and collected. I don't really know how I'll look back on this moment. I believe strongly in *Pictures for Charis* and collaborated in its very personal creation. Yet, I am a very private person. *California and the West* was a creative outlet for Charis, who used it to express herself as a writer as well as a model. *Pictures for Charis* deepened my connection with Kel and provided me with a journey to a different life and time. I suspect that my lesbian modesty will loosen up over time, as I do feel proud of the ways Kel is presenting me. For now, I feel awkward and proud, bashful and eager, about the project. The thought of looking at someone look at a picture of me is anxiety provoking, but who doesn't enjoy being admired from time to time? With *Pictures for Charis*, Kel has asked me to show myself to the world through her eyes. I trust her vision.

LETTER TO RACHEL. NEGATIVE.
THE ART OF SEEING.

In Weston's 1939 photograph, your mother
Floats on her back in a key-hole shaped
Pool. For a long time it reminded me
Of Millais' Ophelia, drowned among the lilies
And waterweeds, a bouquet of flowers
Clutched in her hands, her dress billowing
Folds of grief the lost glimpse in sleep.
But Charis is nude—her long, slender body
Floats in a peace nothing could disturb.
Not even death. Which isn't the reason
I keep coming back to it. But to glimpse
How of art a moment might be suspended,
And how Weston must have loved her
To catch that pose. How I love
To look, catching in her grace
The likeness, the subtle, haunting trace
Of you.

— from Signatures *by Joseph Stroud,*
a close friend to Charis[100]

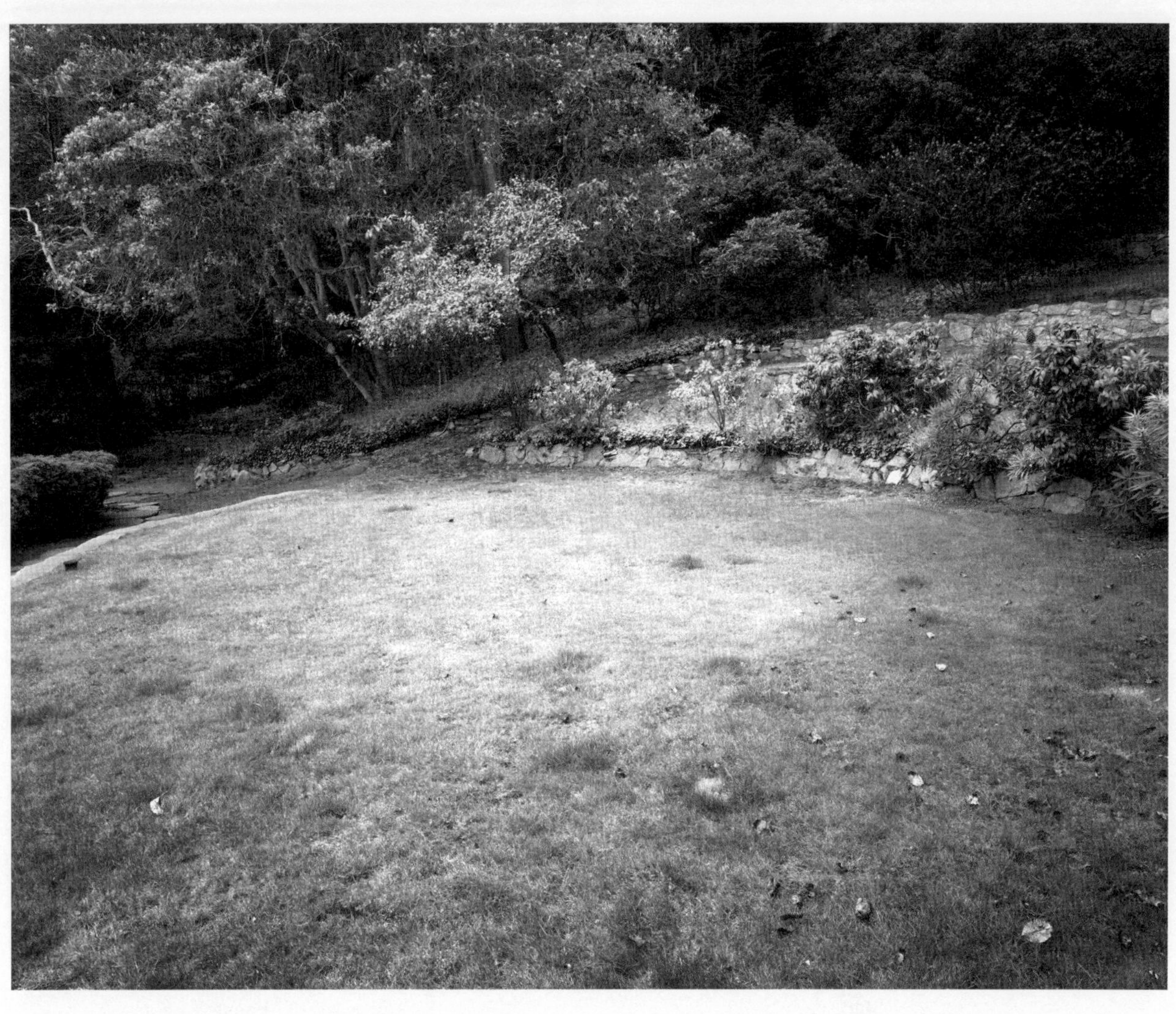

Kelli Connell
*Ocean Home Backyard
(Floating Nude)*, 2016

ENDNOTES AND CREDITS

1. Charis Wilson collection, 1877-2011. AG200. Center for Creative Photography. University of Arizona, Tucson.
2. Ibid.
3. Charis Wilson and Wendy Madar, *Through Another Lens: My Years with Edward Weston* (New York: Farrar, Straus and Giroux, 1998), x.
4. Charis Wilson Weston and Edward Weston, *California and the West* (New York: Duell, Sloan and Pearce, 1940), 18–19.
5. Ibid., 18.
6. Wilson and Madar, *Through Another Lens*, 95.
7. Wilson Weston and Weston, *California and the West*, 116.
8. Ibid., 19.
9. Ibid., 20.
10. Ibid., 115.
11. Ibid., 21.
12. Ibid., 21.
13. Ibid., 26.
14. Wilson and Madar, *Through Another Lens*, 138–39.
15. Ibid., 138.
16. Edward Weston, *The Daybooks of Edward Weston, II. California*, ed. Nancy Newhall (New York: Aperture: 1973), 79.
17. Wilson and Madar, *Through Another Lens*, 127.
18. Ibid.
19. Ibid., 128.
20. Ibid., 129.
21. Wilson Weston and Weston, *California and the West*, 49.
22. Ibid., 28.
23. Wilson and Madar, *Through Another Lens*, 122.
24. Ibid., 168–69.
25. Ibid., 118.
26. Ibid., 143.
27. Ibid., 315.
28. Wilson Weston and Weston, *California and the West*, 161–62.
29. Wilson and Madar, *Through Another Lens*, 146.
30. Wilson Weston and Weston, *California and the West*, 62.
31. Ibid.
32. Ibid., 78.
33. Ibid.
34. John Muir, *The Yosemite* (New York: Century Company, 1912), 232–33.
35. Wilson Weston and Weston, *California and the West*, 77.
36. Wilson and Madar, *Through Another Lens*, 154.
37. Ibid., 153.
38. Deborah Bright, "Of Mother Nature and Marlboro Men: An Inquiry into the Cultural Meanings of Landscape Photography," in *Illuminations: Women Writing on Photography from the 1850s to the Present*, eds. Liz Herron and Val Williams (Durham, NC: Duke University Press, 1996), 336.
39. Wilson and Madar, *Through Another Lens*, 3–4.
40. Ibid., 6.
41. Ibid., 8–9.
42. Edward Weston, *Edward Weston: Nudes*, remembrance by Charis Wilson (New York: Aperture, 1977), 6.
43. Wilson and Madar, *Through Another Lens*, 12.
44. Ibid.
45. Charis Wilson collection, 1877-2011. AG200. Center for Creative Photography. University of Arizona, Tucson.
46. Wilson in Weston, *Nudes*, 6.
47. Ibid., 8.
48. Wilson and Madar, *Through Another Lens*, 20.
49. Ibid., 13.
50. Ibid., 32–33.
51. Weston, *The Daybooks. Vol. II, California*, 283.
52. Charis Wilson collection, 1877-2011. AG200. Center for Creative Photography. University of Arizona, Tucson.
53. Wilson and Madar, *Through Another Lens*, 60.
54. Ibid., 61.
55. Ibid., 66.
56. Ibid.
57. Ibid., 99.
58. Ibid., 88.
59. Ibid., 98.
60. Ibid., 107.
61. Ibid., 110–111.
62. Ibid., 111.
63. Ibid., 108.
64. Ibid., 113.
65. Charis Wilson collection, 1877-2011. AG200. Center for Creative Photography. University of Arizona, Tucson.

66. Wilson and Madar, *Through Another Lens*, 215.
67. Ibid., 208.
68. Edward Weston (with Charis Wilson Weston), "What Is Photographic Beauty?" *American Photography*, 46 (1939), 254.
69. Edward Weston (with Charis Wilson Weston), "35 Years of Portraiture," *Camera Craft*, September 1939, 460.
70. *San Francisco Chronicle*, December 11, 1940. Clipping from Charis Wilson collection, 1877-2011.AG200. Center for Creative Photography. University of Arizona, Tucson.
71. *Observer*, Raleigh, NC, December 8, 1940. Clipping from Charis Wilson collection, 1877-2011.AG200. Center for Creative Photography. University of Arizona, Tucson.
72. Wilson and Madar, *Through Another Lens*, 314.
73. Ibid., 343.
74. Ibid., 216.
75. Ibid., 189.
76. Wilson Weston and Weston, *California and the West*, 144.
77. Honoré de Balzac. *The Physiology of Marriage, Complete*. Project Gutenberg. Retrieved June 22, 2023, from https://www.gutenberg.org/files/16205/16205-h/16205-h.htm
78. Wilson and Madar, *Through Another Lens*, 22.
79. Ibid., 218.
80. Wilson Weston and Weston, *California and the West*, 119–20.
81. Wilson and Madar, *Through Another Lens*, 333.
82. Ibid., 336–37.
83. Charis Wilson and Edward Weston, *The Cats of Wildcat Hill* (New York: Duell, Sloan and Pearce, 1947), 90.
84. Wilson and Madar, *Through Another Lens*, 344.
85. Ibid., 345.
86. Alan Trachtenberg, "The Final Years" in *Edward Weston: Forms of Passion*, ed. Gilles Mora (New York: Harry N. Abrams, 1995), 288.
87. Wilson Weston and Weston, *California and the West*, 70.
88. Robert Adams, "The Achievement of Edward Weston: The Biography I'd Like to Read," in *Edward Weston: 100 Centennial Essays in Honor of Edward Weston*, eds. Peter C. Bunnell and David Featherstone (Carmel, CA: Friends of Photography, 1986), 34.
89. Wilson and Madar, *Through Another Lens*, 234–35.
90. Arthur Ollman, *The Model Wife* (Boston, New York, London: Bulfinch Press/Little, Brown and Company, 1999), 32.
91. Wilson and Madar, *Through Another Lens*, 255.
92. Ibid., 280.
93. Ibid., 281.
94. Ibid., 290.
95. Ibid.
96. Trachtenberg, "The Final Years," 93.
97. Wilson and Madar, *Through Another Lens*, 345.
98. Ibid., 359.
99. Ibid., dedication page.
100. Joseph Stroud, *Signatures* (New York: Boa Editions, 1982), 55.

Thank you to Rowland Saifi for reading early versions of this book. Your generosity, encouragement, and invaluable mentorship helped this project find its form. For reading drafts of this manuscript, for your honest comments and insight, thanks to Aimée Beaubien, Chas Bowie, Whitney Bradshaw, Paul D'Amato, Odette England, Terry Evans, Sonora Jha, Aryn Kyle, Lesley Martin, Judy Natal, Melissa Pinney, Colleen Plumb, Kristen Wilcox, and Krista Wortendyke. A deep bow to Hannah Beresford and Rebecca Senf who read many drafts; your edits and spot-on suggestions were profoundly helpful.

Deep gratitude to editor, Alexa Dilworth, for your enthusiasm for this project, and for understanding it so thoroughly with great care. Thanks also to Catherine Taylor for your attentive eye on the final manuscript.

The superb team at Aperture deserves many thanks. Lesley Martin, your keen vision and guidance has been invaluable; thank you for supporting this project, from its earliest stages to completion. Tremendous gratitude to Emily CM Anderson, for your elegant, dynamic, and astute design. Thank you to Noa Lin, Iesha Coppin-Forde, Susan Ciccotti, Andrea Chlad, and Minjee Cho for your efforts in bringing this book to life, and to everyone at Aperture for their support.

Thank you to curators Gregory Harris (High Museum of Art), Rebecca Senf

(Center for Creative Photography), and Barbara Tannenbaum (Cleveland Museum of Art), for your steadfast belief in this work.

Generous support for this book was provided by the Center for Creative Photography, Tucson; the Cleveland Museum of Art; High Museum of Art, Atlanta; Museum of Contemporary Photography at Columbia College Chicago; Max McCauslin and John Smith; and the Peter Salomon Endowment for the Advancement of Women Photographers; Joe Williams and Tede Fleming; Julie and Will Hobert; and Suzette Bross.

This project was generously supported by fellowships and grants from the John Simon Guggenheim Memorial Foundation, Illinois Arts Council, Chicago Department of Cultural Affairs and Special Events, Society for Photographic Education, and Columbia College Chicago.

Portions of this project were completed at LATITUDE Chicago, MacDowell, Peaked Hill Trust, and PLAYA; these residencies offered the invaluable gift of time to focus on work.

For their patience, warmth, and expertise during research visits at the Laura Volkerding Study Center at the Center for Creative Photography, thank you to Leslie Squyres, Emily Una Weirich, Emilie Hardman, and all of the staff. Profound gratitude to Rachel Fern Harris, for her permission to use materials from the Charis Wilson Archive and for her generous support of and belief in her mother's work.

Sincere appreciation to Gina and Kim Weston for opening your home on Wildcat Hill and for being most-excellent hosts. Thank you to Tim Allen for letting us stay and work at the Coastal Ranch property in Big Sur and to Thaïsa Way for gifting us time to work at your home in Truro.

A huge thanks to Mark Klett and Byron Wolfe for helping us find the juniper trees Edward Weston photographed in Yosemite.

Thank you to the Center for Creative Photography, the Ansel Adams Publishing Rights Trust, and Paul M. Hertzmann, Inc. for the generous loan of images reproduced in this book.

Thank you to Kiba Jacobson, for your friendship, inspiration, and collaboration. Sincere gratitude to Jaime Connell for the love and time we shared together.

And most of all, thank you to Betsy Odom, for countless hours of traveling, photographing, reading numerous drafts, and listening to me talk about photography for hours on end. You have given me your love and steadfast support, in equal measure.

BIOGRAPHIES

Kelli Connell (born in Oklahoma City, 1974) is an artist whose work investigates sexuality, gender, identity and photographer/sitter relationships. Her work has been published as part of *MP3: Midwest Photographers Project* (Aperture, 2006) and her monograph, *Kelli Connell: Double Life*, was published in 2011 by DECODE Books. Her work is in the collections of the Metropolitan Museum of Art, New York; Los Angeles County Museum of Art; J Paul Getty Museum; Philadelphia Museum of Art; Museum of Fine Arts, Houston; Columbus Museum of Art; Milwaukee Art Museum; High Museum of Art; Dallas Museum of Art; and Museum of Contemporary Photography, among others. Connell has received fellowships from the John Simon Guggenheim Memorial Foundation, MacDowell, Illinois Arts Council, and Center for Creative Photography, Tucson. She has been an Artist-in-Residence at PLAYA, Peaked Hill Trust, LATITUDE, Light Work, Visual Studies Workshop, and Ox-Bow. Connell lives in Chicago, where she teaches at Columbia College Chicago.

Betsy Odom is an artist, curator, and educator based in Chicago. She received her MFA from Yale University School of Art and a BFA from the San Francisco Art Institute. Her work has been exhibited internationally including at the ThreeWalls Gallery and DePaul Art Museum, Chicago; San Francisco Museum of Art; Amel Bourorina Gallery, Berlin; and Barry Whistler Gallery, Dallas, among other venues. Odom has been the recipient of several fellowships including an Illinois Arts Council Artists Grant, a Chances Dances Critical Fierceness prize, and two grants from the Chicago Department of Cultural Affairs.

KELLI CONNELL: PICTURES FOR CHARIS

Photographs and text by Kelli Connell
With an afterword by Betsy Odom

Cover image—*Doorway II*, 2015

Project Editor— Lesley A. Martin
Designer— Emily CM Anderson
Production Director— Minjee Cho
Production Manager— Andrea Chlad
Separations— Thomas Bollier
Editorial Assistant— Noa Lin
Senior Text Editor— Susan Ciccotti
Text Editor— Alexa Dilworth
Proofreaders— Isla Ng, Catherine Taylor
Work Scholar— Iesha E. Coppin-Forde

Additional staff of the Aperture book program includes: Sarah Meister, Executive Director; Emily Patten, Managing Editor; Caroline Foulke, Assistant to Managing Editor; Karina Eckmeier, Designer and Project Manager; Kellie McLaughlin, Chief Sales and Marketing Officer; Richard Gregg, Sales Director

Special thanks—
Kelli Connell: Pictures for Charis was made possible, in part, with generous support from the Center for Creative Photography at the University of Arizona, Tucson; the Cleveland Museum of Art; and the High Museum of Art, Atlanta. Additional thanks to Julie and Will Hobert; Joe Williams and Tede Fleming; Suzette Bross; Max McCauslin and John Smith; and the Peter Salomon Endowment for the Advancement of Women Photographers for their support.

The publication of *Kelli Connell: Pictures for Charis* coincides with an exhibition of the same name coorganized by and on view at:

Center for Creative Photography, University of Arizona, Tucson, February–August 2024

High Museum of Art, Atlanta, September 2024–January 2025

The Cleveland Museum of Art, January–May 2025

Copublished by Aperture and the Center for Creative Photography

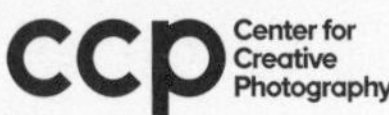

Center for Creative Photography
1030 N. Olive Road
Tucson, AZ 85719
ccp.arizona.edu

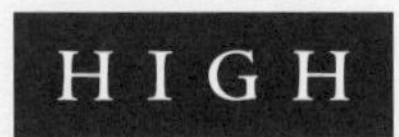

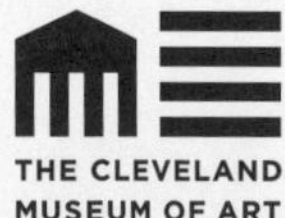

FIRST EDITION, 2024
PRINTED BY PRISTONE IN SINGAPORE
10 9 8 7 6 5 4 3 2 1

LIBRARY OF CONGRESS CONTROL NUMBER: 2023916409
ISBN 978-1-59711-559-9

aperture

548 West 28th Street, 4th Floor
New York, NY 10001
aperture.org

Aperture is a nonprofit publisher dedicated to creating insight, community, and understanding through photography.

To order Aperture books, or inquire about gift or group orders, contact: orders@aperture.org

For information about Aperture trade distribution worldwide, visit: aperture.org/distribution